INTERESTS, INSTITUTIONS, AND INFORMATION

INTERESTS, INSTITUTIONS, AND INFORMATION

DOMESTIC POLITICS AND

INTERNATIONAL RELATIONS

Helen V. Milner

PRINCETON UNIVERSITY PRESS   PRINCETON, NEW JERSEY

Copyright © 1997 by Princeton University Press
Published by Princeton University Press, 41 William Street,
Princeton, New Jersey 08540
In the United Kingdom: Princeton University Press,
Chichester, West Sussex
All Rights Reserved

Library of Congress Cataloging-in-Publication Data

Milner, Helen V., 1958–
Interests, institutions, and information : domestic politics and
international relations / Helen V. Milner.
p.   cm.
Includes bibliographical references and index.
ISBN 0-691-01177-X (cl : alk. paper). — ISBN 0-691-01176-1 (pb :
alk. paper)
1. International relations.   2. National state.   3. World
politics—1989–   4. Information policy.   I. Title.
JX1391.M524   1997
327— dc21   96-30099

This book has been composed in Caledonia

Princeton University Press books are printed
on acid-free paper and meet the guidelines
for permanence and durability of the Committee
on Production Guidelines for Book Longevity
of the Council on Library Resources

http://pup.princeton.edu

Printed in the United States of America

10   9   8   7   6   5   4   3   2   1

10   9   8   7   6   5   4   3   2
(Pbk.)

To David _____

FOR MAKING IT POSSIBLE AND BETTER

Contents

Tables and Figures ——————————

Table

Figures

Acknowledgments _____

THIS BOOK was seven years in the making and thus I have incurred many debts. The Social Science Research Council provided me with two years of leave which were devoted to researching this project. Columbia University also provided me with leave time, research support, and an intellectually stimulating environment. I thank them both gratefully.

Most of my debts are to the individuals who helped me through this process. Robert Jervis, Robert Keohane, Jerry Cohen, David Lake, David Baldwin, and Ron Rogowski all read earlier versions of the manuscript and gave me very helpful comments. I greatly appreciate the time they spent carefully and constructively helping me improve the manuscript. Peter Rosendorff's contribution was also very important. Chapter 3 and the appendix are work we did together, an earlier version of which appeared in *Economics and Politics* (July 1996). Peter and I spent many hours batting around ideas that would eventually become those chapters.

Bob Putnam, Harold Jacobson, and Peter Evans included me in their project on two-level games; chapter 6 here draws on my chapter in their volume, *Double-Edged Diplomacy*. Geoffrey Underhill and William Coleman also invited me to be part of their research group at the European Consortium on Political Research (ECPR) conference in Madrid in 1994, which produced a special issue of the *Journal of European Public Policy* (vol. 2, no. 3 [1995]) in which an early version of chapter 8 appeared. The editors at *World Politics* accepted my review article on cooperation (1992) but hoped I would give them a theory of the domestic influences on cooperation as well. I hope this book serves that purpose.

My colleagues at Columbia have been a great help. David Epstein, Sharyn O'Halloran, and Chuck Cameron answered endless questions about game theory and recent work in American politics. Alessandra Casella and Dani Rodrik provided similar support in the field of international economics. Doug Chalmers, Steve Solnick, and Peter Johnson answered many queries about politics in their countries of study. Last but not least, the "IR gang"—Jack Snyder, Dick Betts, Dave Baldwin, Greg Gause, Ed Mansfield, Hendrik Spruyt, Arvid Laukaskas, and most especially Bob Jervis—provided constant intellectual stimulation and made me realize how difficult it would be to convince anyone of my ideas. I also want to thank the graduate students I worked with who never let an idea go by unchallenged. Finally, I would like to thank the anonymous reviewers as well as Malcolm Litchfield at Princeton University Press, all of whom helped me greatly.

I owe a huge debt to my husband, David. He not only spent a great deal of time commenting on the manuscript but also kept us fed. Every summer when I hunkered down to write, he made sure the rest of the world stayed away. Without his support and advice, this book would not exist.

INTERESTS, INSTITUTIONS, AND INFORMATION

One

Introduction

HOW CAN WE understand the relations between countries? Has the peace process in the Middle East, for example, been driven by changes in the balance of power among the countries or have domestic politics played a significant role? Has domestic politics played as important a role in U.S.-Japanese relations as have changes in power resources between the two countries? Most dramatically, can changes in the relations between the United States and the former Soviet Union in the last decade be explained by external factors or must one examine internal changes, especially in the former Soviet Union, to appreciate the end of the cold war? If domestic politics played a role in these and other cases, what role did it play and what internal factors were most important?

This book argues that domestic politics and international relations are inextricably interrelated. A country's international position exerts an important impact on its internal politics and economics. Conversely, its domestic situation shapes its behavior in foreign relations. Some scholars—usually Realists—believe that ignoring domestic politics by treating states as unitary actors is useful for understanding international relations (Waltz 1979). Such an approach, I contend, is misleading. Both scholars and policy makers will overlook key elements explaining a country's behavior if they fail to consider its domestic situation. Relaxing the unitary state assumption generates new, fruitful observations about international politics. Bringing domestic politics back into international relations theory is the purpose of this book.

In the 1960s and 1970s theories of international relations that focused on domestic factors abounded. Various Marxist, bureaucratic politics, and psychological approaches tried to explain state actions in foreign policy as a result of internal variables (e.g., Kolko 1968; Allison 1971; Rosenau 1966, 1969; Snyder, Bruck, and Sapin 1962). Domestic variables, however, were largely driven out of international relations theory in the 1980s with the rise of structural Realism. Only toward the end of the decade, with the development of the "Democratic Peace" and two-level games approaches, has domestic politics begun to reappear in international relations theory (Doyle 1986; Russett 1993; Putnam 1988). Reviving domestic explanations of foreign policy and making them as theoretical and parsimonious as Realist analysis have become important ambitions, which this book seeks to forward.

If the internal characteristics of nations have important, systematic effects on their behavior, assuming these characteristics away leads to a fundamental misunderstanding of the causes of their behavior. One will assume that the country's behavior was caused by international influences when it was actually motivated by domestic ones. Waltz (1979) claims that failure to examine international structural factors first leads to misattribution of the causes of states' behavior. This failure, he claims, leads to the infinite proliferation of variables as explanatory factors. But this methodological argument is mistaken. If there are systematic domestic effects that operate among states, then failure to examine them also leads to the infinite proliferation of variables. For example, if democracy makes states less likely to fight one another, then failure to identify a domestic variable like democracy will lead the analyst to attribute the pacific nature of certain states to many other causes. Since no other variable is likely to group all the democracies together, one will tend to develop specific explanations for each case, thus producing a proliferation of explanatory variables. It is not the level of analysis—domestic or international—that matters but whether the effects of a variable are systematic and cross-national (Przeworski and Teune 1970).

Although many scholars have recognized the interdependence of domestic and international politics, few have developed explicit theories of this interaction. The goal of this book is to provide such a theory. The emphasis here is on developing a parsimonious, abstract model of the interaction between domestic and international politics. Recently, the notion of "two-level games" has gained prominence (Putnam 1988). Although promising as a framework for analysis, this approach does not constitute a theory with testable hypotheses, as even its proponents admit (Evans, Jacobson, and Putnam 1993).

The main idea behind such games is, however, fundamental: political leaders are constantly playing in the domestic and international arenas simultaneously. They are trying to achieve their various goals using these two arenas, and they face different—and sometimes contradictory—pressures and constraints from each. Their behavior can only be understood when both internal and external factors are considered. Putnam describes two-level games as follows: "At the national level, domestic groups pursue their interests by pressuring the government to adopt favorable policies, and politicians seek power by constructing coalitions among those groups. At the international level, national governments seek to maximize their own ability to satisfy domestic pressures, while minimizing the adverse consequences of foreign developments. Neither of the two games can be ignored by central decision makers" (1988:434). Nor can they be ignored by analysts studying domestic or international politics.

This new metaphor prompts a change in the designation of the actors. No longer are states the actors; rather, central decision makers, legislatures, and domestic groups become the agents. The state as agent is a casualty of the elimination of the unitary actor assumption. Moreover, a new element of politics has been injected into the picture: "Unlike state-centric theories, the two-level approach recognizes the inevitability of domestic conflict about what the 'national interest' requires" (Putnam 1988:460). The definition of the "national interest" becomes a central variable in this approach.

The two-level game approach has thus added a vital new "level of analysis" to international relations. But it has remained underdeveloped theoretically. A number of recent articles have proposed more rigorous, formal treatment of such games; however, the impact on international relations per se is often unclear (Mayer 1992; Iida 1993a, 1993b; Alt and Eichengreen 1989; Tsebelis 1990; Lohmann 1993; Pahre 1994; Downs and Rocke 1995; Mo 1991, 1994, 1995). A goal of this book is to advance the theoretical conceptualization of such games and to develop testable hypotheses about their impact. The method chosen to do so is rational choice theory.

Rational choice theory has three advantages: it pushes one to specify explicitly the assumptions of the model used, to derive one's conclusions logically, and to examine systematically the effects of changes in any variable used in the analysis. The explicitness of the argument and the incontrovertibility of the logic make this approach appealing. The results are intersubjectively transmissible and repeatable. Rational choice analysis, however, also has important limitations (e.g., Elster 1979, 1986; Tversky and Kahneman 1986; ISQ 1985). Some of these actually work to undermine its advantages. First, the models are driven by the assumptions used; often changes in these alter the results obtained, sometimes significantly. Second, unless one is familiar with the approach, it can be mystifying rather than illuminating. The assumptions become buried in the analysis, and the mathematics obscures the logic. Instead of being intersubjectively transmissible, rational choice models become the exclusive domain of a small clique of like-thinkers.

These and other problems make rational choice modeling a tricky form of analysis to employ. In order to illuminate rather than obscure, I attempt to avoid or at least mitigate these problems by leaving the formalization of the model to an appendix and using ordinary language to explain the assumptions and results. The model is also applied to a number of case studies, which should help to elucidate the logic behind them as well as examine the validity of the hypotheses. Obviously if one rejects the basic assumption that agents are, at times and to some extent at least, rational—that is, they pursue goals and try to achieve them in the most efficient manner—then even these attempts to deal with the potential problems of the rational choice approach will be of little avail.

The Empirical Puzzle

The interaction of domestic and international politics is the central focus of this book. The particular empirical puzzle, however, is why nations cooperate with one another. More specifically, I ask when and under what terms are countries able to coordinate their policies in an issue area. Addressing this question raises its opposite, that is, when and why are countries unable to cooperate. For instance, throughout much of the post-World War II period the advanced industrial Western nations were able to cooperate on international trade issues; in monetary affairs, cooperation has waxed and waned over the same period; and in the area of fiscal policy, coordination has been virtually nonexistent during this time. What accounts for these variations? Why does the extent of cooperation vary both across issue areas and over time?

Another question needs to be asked. Why are certain countries better able to cooperate at certain times? For example, Britain has been a leading proponent of military cooperation among the advanced Western nations in the postwar period, whereas France has been a less cooperative partner in this domain. Britain, on the other hand, has found it difficult to embrace economic cooperation involving the West European countries, whereas France has often been a leader in this area. These variations across countries, as well as over time and among issue areas within the same country, suggest that neither the national nor the international level of analysis is sufficient to explain the patterns of cooperation that we observe in world politics. What factors are responsible for such variations?

These issues merit attention not only because cooperation among nations is often assumed to be desirable socially but also because it is anomalous theoretically.[1] Questions about international cooperation are salient, and their answers are not obvious because of the dominant theoretical baseline used to explain international politics. In the United States at least, Realism has attained a preeminent place in theories of international relations. A "Realist approach"—if a single approach can be identified among the many "Realists"—has trouble explaining cooperation (Morgenthau 1948; Carr 1946; Wolfers 1962; Waltz 1979; Walt 1987; Mearsheimer 1990; Krasner 1991; Grieco 1990). Cooperation appears as an element of the power balancing process necessary for nations to survive. States must balance against one another to survive in the anarchic realm of world politics, and cooperation is one external manifestation of this balancing behavior. Coordinating policies with another country allows one to balance against the threat or power of a third country. This balancing is likely to be short-lived and not very well institutionalized since one's allies always remain potential enemies. Moreover, in the absence of an external threat requiring collaboration for defense, cooperation seems inexplicable for Realists. Thus although Realist analysis provides some leverage on the question of why nations ally with others, it provides little guidance as to why a nation would cooperate on particular issues (and not others) and only at certain times. In addition, long-term,

---

[1] Cooperation need not necessarily improve one's welfare. As many economists suspect, cooperation may just be collusion, a way of fixing prices to increase one's profits.

institutionalized cooperation among nations seems particularly anomalous. Realist explanations of international cooperation are discussed below, in the section "Alternative Explanations: Realism and Neoliberal Institutionalism"; here the point is simply to note that Realist approaches in general have trouble accounting for patterns of international cooperation. They often appear as empirical anomalies for Realists.

What Is Cooperation?

The central empirical issue is to explain the likelihood and terms of cooperation among nations. But what do we mean by cooperation? Defining cooperation is important for two reasons. First, explicating the defining characteristics of cooperation allows one to use the concept to determine whether cooperation occurred in each of the case studies. In effect, one can code the dependent variable. Second, exploring the phenomenon of cooperation gives one a sense of its pervasiveness. It delimits the activities that count as cooperation and thus allows one to gauge its frequency, which in turn suggests the importance of explaining it.

One of the notable features of the recent literature on international cooperation is the acceptance of a common definition of the phenomenon (e.g., Keohane 1984; Oye 1986; Grieco 1990; Haas 1990; Putnam and Bayne 1987; Milner 1992). Following Keohane, these scholars have defined cooperation as occurring when "actors adjust their behavior to the actual or anticipated preferences of others, through a process of policy coordination" (Keohane 1984:51–52). Policy coordination in turn implies that each state's policies have been adjusted so that their negative consequences for the other states are reduced.

This conception of cooperation, which is similar to that used by social psychologists and sociologists (Deutsch 1949; Parsons 1951; Homans 1961; Blau 1964; Marwell and Schmitt 1975), has two important elements to it. First, it assumes that an actor's behavior is directed toward some goal(s). It need not be the same end for all the actors involved, but it does imply goal-oriented behavior on their part. Second, the definition implies that actors receive gains or rewards from cooperation. The gains acquired by each need not be the same in magnitude or kind, but there are gains for each. Each actor helps the others to realize their goals by adjusting its policies in the anticipation of its own reward.

Cooperation can thus be conceived as a process of exchange. Both involve the pursuit of "want-satisfaction" through behavior that is contingent on the expected response of another (Blau 1964:6; Heath 1976:2). Cooperation among nations is a specific type of exchange. It involves the adjustment of one state's policies in return for, or anticipation of, the adjustment of other states' policies so that both end up better off. Exchange here refers to the mutual accommodation of nations' *policies* rather than to the economists' focus on goods and services. This conception of cooperation as exchange underlies much of the literature on international relations.

One function of a definition is to enable us to classify different acts as being an instance of the concept at hand. Having a widely accepted, clear definition of international cooperation means that the discipline should be able to agree on which acts count as cooperation and which do not. This latter element—what is not cooperation—is also important. Cooperation is usually opposed to either competition or conflict, both of which imply goal-seeking behavior that strives to reduce the gains available to others or to impede their want-satisfaction. But other alternatives to cooperation exist. Unilateral behavior in which actors do not take account of their effects on others as well as inactivity may also serve as alternatives to cooperation. Although perhaps not attempting to lower the gains of others, these forms of behavior can be considered uncooperative if they do not reduce the negative consequences of each parties' policies for the others. What counts as cooperation thus depends on the presence of two elements: *goal-directed* behavior that seeks to create *mutual gains* through policy adjustment.

Cooperation can take a number of forms (Young 1989:87–96).[2] It can be *tacit*; that is, mutual policy accommodation can occur without communication or explicit agreement. It can evolve out of the tacit bargaining of the actors, emerging as their expectations converge. Policy coordination may also be explicitly *negotiated*. As a result of explicit bargaining nations agree to adjust their policies mutually. This type of cooperation is easier to identify than is the tacit form, since in the latter the counterfactual is more difficult to establish. In either type political leaders decide to adopt a different policy than they otherwise would have. In the negotiated case leaders often make more explicit what they would do if no agreement were reached and thus that they are changing their policy. My focus is on negotiated cooperation; the model and cases studied involve international negotiations to achieve mutual policy adjustment. There is no apparent reason, however, why the conclusions reached about negotiated cooperation should not apply to its tacit forms.

The relationship between *policy coordination* and *cooperation* is also important. Analysts often differ over what they mean by these terms as well as over the relationship between them. Policy coordination, I argue, is a form of international cooperation; cooperation and coordination refer to the same basic phenomenon. Coordination implies mutual policy adjustment among

---

[2] Young and others (Martin 1992) also view "coercive cooperation" as an additional form. As defined here, cooperation includes even coercive forms, as long as both players mutually gain from policy adjustment. The actor being coerced gains from having the threat (promise) associated with changing his behavior avoided (implemented).

countries intended to reduce the negative (or enhance the positive) effects of one country's policy choices on the others. Crucially, this means that in the absence of "coordination," countries' policies would have been different (Putnam and Bayne 1987:2; Webb 1991:311–12). A compelling case for making a distinction between cooperation and coordination does not seem to exist. Many authors use the two interchangeably (Feldstein 1988), as is done here.

Within this broad definition, policy coordination or cooperation may encompass a wide variety of activities, all with the goal of mutual policy adjustment. Putnam and Bayne, for example, discuss four different types of coordination (1988:260). Mutual enlightenment involves the exchange of information about countries' policy intentions, so that their policy choices are affected; mutual reinforcement entails obtaining international support for one's policies, usually so they can be implemented in the face of domestic opposition; mutual adjustment means reshaping policies so they conflict less; and mutual concession implies a "package deal," where policy makers condition their choices on the behavior of other states.

Fischer (1988:35–38) presents a more systematic analysis of the different types of cooperative policies. Four different levels of policy coordination are distinguished, each representing greater levels of political commitment: the exchange of information to facilitate tacit policy coordination, the negotiation of specific policy "deals" on a one-time basis, the establishment of a set of rules guiding policy choice, and the surrender of national policy instruments often to form a larger policy community. Within this scheme, the last level—for example, a monetary union with a single currency and central bank, or in trade a customs union that entails a single market, or in the security area a pooling of national military units into a single international one—represents the most extreme form of international cooperation.

All these different mechanisms for achieving mutual policy adjustment are considered forms of cooperation and as such are the focus of explanatory attention (the dependent variable). This review is intended to suggest the breadth of activities that count as cooperation, and hence the importance of the phenomenon. My argument does not attempt to explain why some forms are chosen rather than others, but it does suggest that the forms chosen depend much on domestic politics.

Domestic Politics and International Relations

My central argument is that cooperation among nations is affected less by fears of other countries' relative gains or cheating than it is by the *domestic distributional consequences* of cooperative endeavors. Cooperative agreements create winners and losers domestically; therefore they generate supporters and opponents. The internal struggle between these groups shapes the possibility and nature of international cooperative agreements. International negotiations to realize cooperation often fail because of domestic politics, and such negotiations are often initiated because of domestic politics. All aspects of cooperation are affected by domestic considerations because cooperation is a continuation of domestic political struggles by other means.

Existing theories of international cooperation neglect this influence of domestic politics because they treat the state as a unitary actor; my goal is to remedy this neglect. International factors matter for cooperation. But what is needed is a *theory* of domestic influences, especially one that takes into account their interaction with international factors. This book attempts to develop a systematic and parsimonious model of the domestic influences on international politics. It begins from the premise that the state is not a unitary actor.

The assumption that the state is unitary is highly consequential. It has been taken to mean that all states are the same; as Waltz (1979) says, they are functionally "like units." They all perform the same tasks and, when facing similar external conditions, make similar choices. But although states may perform many of the same tasks, they do not perform exactly the same ones and they do not make decisions about these tasks similarly. Differences among states in their internal preferences and political institutions have important effects on international politics. The central problem for theory building is to develop a parsimonious way to categorize the differences among states that are relevant to international politics.

The unitary actor assumption is often taken to mean that domestic politics is organized hierarchically, with a single actor at the top making the final decisions; that is, power, or decision making, flows along a vertical hierarchy—from top to bottom—and the group or individual at the top is the unit making the decisions. Anarchy, at the other end of the continuum, implies an absence of hierarchy or a situation where each actor has a veto and thus makes its own policy choices. Anarchy literally means no ruler, whereas the etymology of hierarchy comes from the Latin term for the high priest as ruler. Each stands on the opposite ends of a continuum displaying the possible distributions of power among actors.

Realists, for example, assume that international politics is anarchic and domestic politics is hierarchic. As Waltz (1979:88) says in discussing the ordering principles of systems: "The parts of domestic political systems stand in relations of super- and subordination. Some are entitled to command; others are required to obey. Domestic systems are centralized and hierarchic. The parts of international-political systems stand in relations of coordination. Formally, each is the equal of all the others. None is entitled to command; none is required to obey. International systems are decentralized and anarchic." In this book I challenge this premise about the principles ordering domestic politics, showing how relaxing the assumption that domestic politics is hierarchical affects international politics. Elsewhere I and others have talked about the consequences of relaxing the presumption that international politics is always pure anarchy (Milner 1991; Ruggie 1983; Keohane 1984). Both assumptions can be altered, but only the domestic one is changed here.

Most politics—both domestic and international—however, lie in between these two poles in an area I call *polyarchy*[3], a structure more complex than either anarchy or hierarchy in which relations are shaped more like a network. No single group sits at the top; power or authority over decision making is shared, often unequally. Relations among groups in polyarchy entail reciprocal influence and/or the parceling out of distinct powers among groups.

My central claim is that states are *not* unitary actors; that is, they are not strictly hierarchical but are polyarchic, composed of actors with varying preferences who share power over decision making. The struggle for political power domestically is critical for them. The survival of the state is an important value for decision makers, but most decisions do not directly concern the state's survival. Once one leaves the world of unitary actors and pure hierarchy, the behavior of states changes. Having, say, two players internally make a decision results in a different outcome than if just one does, assuming their preferences differ. The search for internal compromise becomes crucial in polyarchy. International politics and foreign policy become part of the domestic struggle for power and the search for internal compromise.

Domestic politics, then, varies along a continuum from hierarchy to anarchy, with polyarchy in between. Three factors are decisive in defining a state's placement on this continuum: the policy *preferences* of domestic actors, the *institutions* for power sharing among them, and the distribution of *information* among them. The distribution of power and information among domestic groups and the divergence among their preferences define the extent of polyarchy. First, polyarchy assumes that actors' preferences differ. If all important domestic actors have the same preferences, then even if they share power the situation will resemble a unitary actor one. With the same preferences, no matter which domestic actors hold power the same policies will be chosen. Therefore the extent to which preferences differ is an important variable. Second, decision making must be shared. If one actor controls all decision making, one is back to the unitary actor model where hierarchy prevails. Third, if one group controls all relevant information about an issue, then again one moves back toward a more hierarchic structure. Thus interests, institutions, and information are key variables.

[3] Robert Dahl coined this term to refer to the degree of democracy present in a country (1984:75–93). Here the term is used differently; it refers to the power-sharing arrangements among domestic groups.

Generally three sets of actors inhabit domestic politics. An executive (e.g., the president, prime minister, or dictator) and a legislature compose the two main political groups; the executive includes the bureaucracy or the various departments and ministries of government. The third set of actors is composed of societal interest groups. If the preferences of these three sets of actors differ regarding an issue and they share control over decision making about that issue, then domestic politics cannot be treated as if it involved a unitary actor. Instead of pure hierarchy, now polyarchy reigns. On the other hand, if these actors have the same preferences, then a single "national interest" may exist and the unitary actor assumption is tenable. This scenario seems most likely in extreme situations; when a house is engulfed by fire, to use Wolfers's metaphor (1962:13–16), or a country is being invaded by another, the inhabitants' preferences are more likely to coincide. Similarly, if the actors have different preferences but only one actor controls decision making, then hierarchy holds and the unitary actor assumption is appropriate. Indeed, the more control over policy choices one actor alone, say, the executive, possesses—that is, the less he or she has to share decision-making power with others—the more the situation resembles that of a unitary actor or a strict hierarchy.

Domestic politics is rarely a pure hierarchy with a unitary decision maker, even in nondemocratic systems. The support of the professional military, the landed oligarchy, big business, and/or a political party is usually necessary for even dictators to remain in power and implement their policies. These groups, then, can often exercise veto power over the executive's proposals and in other ways, such as setting the agenda, may share power with the executive. Even such autocratic leaders as Hitler and Stalin depended on the support of internal groups to retain their positions and make policy. As one study of Stalin notes, "Most revisionist accounts of the 'Cold War' . . . portray the Soviet leaders both as monolithic and essentially passive. . . . The Soviet decision-making process, however, was contingent as much upon developments in [internal] factional struggles within the Soviet Empire, as upon 'objective' Soviet interests abroad. . . . Thus, as in so many other instances, Soviet 'policy' . . . largely seems to have been a function of the ebb and flow of [domestic] factional conflict" (Ra'anan 1983:8). Or, as a student of Kremlinology observed about Stalin's dictatorship, "Stalin's Russia was a giant struggle under the carpet . . . You knew something was going on here and every once in awhile you would see a corpse or a limb sticking out. You never knew why" (*New York Times*, July 18, 1996, sec. A, p. 3).

Evidence suggests that even Adolph Hitler faced a polyarchic situation. As a recent review of historiography on his regime notes, "Modern historical research has demolished the old concept of Hitler marching at the head of a tightly organized, unified column, whose members all subscribed to exactly the same ideals" (Hiden and Farquharson 1989:75). Scholars in the field describe his regime as "polycratic," involving rivalry among at least four centers of power.

Similarly, Franco's regime in Spain is often seen as being dependent on the support of various domestic groups:

> While we can be certain that whatever institutional changes were adopted were initiated by Generalissimo Franco himself or had his active support, . . . the heterogenous nature of the Nationalist coalition [supporting him] ruled out certain courses of action which might otherwise have been possible: no single group was in a sufficiently powerful position to become dominant within the new Spanish state. Most importantly, instead of developing into a totalitarian single-party state . . . the Franquist regime evolved into an authoritarian no-party system, within which "limited pluralism" flourished. (Gunther 1980:6)

States controlled by leaders like Hitler, Stalin, and Franco are not pluralist democracies, but history shows that even within such allegedly unitary, hierarchical states dictators were unable to dictate: domestic groups with varying preferences competed for influence over policy and the dictators depended on them to various extents in making policy. Although these states are classified toward the hierarchical end of the continuum, even they show signs of polyarchy internally.

Democratic systems are even more likely to be polyarchic. Like nondemocratic states, they vary in their principles of internal organization, some being more anarchic and others more hierarchical. In most cases at least two sets of actors vie for control over decision making. Usually both the legislature and the executive influence policy making. Or sometimes two or more political parties may be in competition, the governing party or coalition and its opposition. In corporatist systems, three actors are important: the executive ("the state"), organized labor, and organized capital. These actors share control over the key elements of policy making: setting the agenda, devising policy proposals, and amending, ratifying, and implementing policies. Domestic actors may either share control over these elements of the decision-making process or possess distinct powers.

Domestic political institutions determine how such control is distributed among the actors. For example, constitutions often assign certain powers to the executive and others to the legislature. In many democracies the legislature acts as a body of representation; rarely does it have the power to initiate policy proposals but almost always it has the capacity to ratify or reject the executive's proposals. This in effect gives the legislature an ex post veto over the executive. The executive is most often able to formulate proposals and set the agenda but must have these initiatives ratified by the legislature. Although this may seem a particularly American view of politics given its presidential system, in most other democracies the executive depends on the confidence of his or her majority in parliament. As scholars of Britain and

Canada have emphasized, "Parliament looms large in the deliberations of the executive, exercising its influence largely through the law of anticipated reactions but also through more overt expressions" (Jones 1991:126; Campbell 1983:12–13). In effect, the legislature and the executive share power over decision making, each holding different roles in the process. Most democratic systems are a variant on this theme. In the United States and the Federal Republic of Germany, for example, the judiciary is a third actor who shares authority with the legislature and executive.

The key to understanding policy making is to realize how the game between the domestic actors is played. This game depends on three variables: the differences among the players' policy preferences, the distribution of information domestically, and the nature of domestic political institutions. The greater the divergences among their preferences, the more equally information is possessed, and the more institutions disperse power over policy, the more polyarchic is the domestic situation. In the extreme, if each player can veto a policy choice, then one approaches a situation of anarchy. Tsebelis (1995), for instance, focuses on domestic actors as "veto players," showing that the difficulties of policy making grow as the number of such players increases, their preferences diverge, and their internal coherence declines. Actors' interests, information, and political institutions are the three key variables here, as the next three sections detail. These three variables determine the extent of polyarchy domestically and thus the nature of the domestic game that shapes international cooperation.

The implications of polyarchy for international politics are central. As the rest of this book argues, polyarchy changes the way international politics is played. Rather than the struggle for state survival taking priority, the struggle for internal power and compromise dominates foreign policy making. The executive does not always prevail, as theories based on the unitary actor assumption, like Realism and statism, maintain (Waltz 1979; Krasner 1978). Since executives share decision-making power with other internal groups, policy choices will differ from a situation of executive dominance. Policy choices—whether for domestic or foreign policy—are the result of a strategic game among the internal actors. In general, external conflict and cooperation reflect the struggles and consensus erected out of domestic politics.

The Interests of Actors

This book attempts to make a contribution to comparative politics as well as to international relations. It argues that international relations scholars need to take comparative politics into consideration, and it joins several debates in the comparative politics literature. First, it explores the relationship between actors' interests and political institutions. It examines how interests and institutions interact to determine policy choices. Second, it discusses the relative importance of societal and political actors in shaping policy. It thus enters the debate over state-society relations. Third, it engages in the debate about the relative merits of presidential versus parliamentary systems of government. It asks whether the presidential-parliamentary distinction can help explain states' ability to cooperate internationally.

A major theme here is the relationship between actors' interests and political institutions.[4] Although it seems commonsensical to note that both interests and institutions exert an important influence on political outcomes, scholars have often neglected one of these variables and privileged the other (e.g., Rogowski 1989; Hall 1986; Frieden 1990; Haggard 1990). Much of the "new institutionalism," for example, has focused on institutions to explain political outcomes while disregarding actors' interests (e.g., March and Olson 1989). Rational choice models have also tended to focus on institutions. After the work by Arrow (1963), McKelvey (1976), and Plott (1967) which demonstrated that under majority rule almost no configuration of actors' preferences could yield a stable equilibrium, scholars such as Shepsle (1979) began investigating the properties of institutions that could yield political equilibria. Structure-induced equilibria became a dominant theme, and institutions took pride of place over preferences.

But a central issue for comparative politics is the relationship between institutions and actors' preferences. As Riker (1980:432) has argued:

> Social scientists are now, and probably have always been, of divided opinion about the degree to which institutions as well as personal tastes affect the content of social decisions. It is clear that the [preferences] of at least some members of society do ineradicably influence these decisions. . . . On the other hand, we cannot leave out the force of institutions. The people whose [preferences] are influential live in a world of conventions about both language and values themselves. These conventions are in turn condensed into institutions, which are simply rules about behavior, especially about making decisions . . . Ambiguity arises, however, when we attempt to assess the relative significance of these two kinds of forces. Very probably, both are necessary and neither is alone a sufficient condition for

[4] Interests and preferences need to be defined and differentiated. As chapter 2 elaborates, actors' interests represent their fundamental goals, which change little. The interests of economic actors involve maximizing income, whereas those of political actors largely concern maximizing the chances of retaining political office. On any issue, these generic interests do not distinguish among political actors or economic ones. What differentiates them is their policy preferences, which derive from their interests. Preferences refer to the specific policy choice that actors believe will maximize either their income or chances of reelection on a particular issue. Although all political actors may share the same interest, their policy preferences will vary according to their political situation, for example, their party affiliation, constituency characteristics, and so on. The same is true for economic actors. Interests are the stable foundation on which actors' preferences over policy shift as their situation and the policy area vary. Preferences are a variable; interests are not.

outcomes. If so, a full statement of social causation must include both of them. . . .
One fundamental and unresolved problem of social science is . . . to learn to take
both [preferences] and institutions into account.

I examine preferences and institutions since polyarchy has implications
for both. Part of the puzzle is to explain how they interact to produce international cooperation. Chapter 2 sets out to examine interests and the policy
preferences derived from them and, along with chapter 3, explores their
impact on cooperation; chapter 4 introduces variations in institutions to examine their effects. In this spirit the book advances hypotheses about the
influence of both preferences and institutions on international cooperation.
This introduction lays out the main themes in the discussion of interests and
institutions that follows.

Domestic politics matters because the state is not a unitary actor.
Groups within it have *different policy preferences* because they are differentially affected by government policies. Any change in policies, as might
occur because of international cooperation, has domestic distributional
and electoral consequences. These domestic consequences are the "stuff"
of politics. First, they mean that some societal actors oppose and others
favor cooperation. These groups will pressure the government to cooperate or not; they will promise to increase, or threaten to withdraw, their
electoral support. In turn, political actors will favor or oppose cooperative
policies depending on their relationship to these societal actors. There is
unlikely to be a unified view of the "national interest" and of the effect of
cooperation upon it. Second, policy choices have electoral ramifications.
When choosing policies, a country's political leaders will not only be buf-
feted by the pressures of groups with conflicting interests but also will
have to consider the electoral consequences of these choices. Policies that
promote the economy will be favored by political actors since they will
enhance their likelihood of retaining office. Hence cooperative policies
that improve aspects of an economy will gain favor; those that hurt the
economy by increasing unemployment or inflation will be opposed. Political leaders' policy preferences vis-à-vis international cooperation will be
shaped by these two forces.

Political and social actors' preferences over policy are a key variable in
this book. The differences in policy preferences among actors who share
power over policy making exert a powerful influence on how domestic politics affects international cooperation. The *structure of domestic preferences*
is a compact way of discussing these preferences. This structure refers to the
relative positions of the preferences of important domestic actors on the
issue at hand. The three main sets of internal actors here are the political
executive (the president or prime minister), the legislature, and interest

groups.[5] The preferences of each group are arrayed along a unidimensional scale. Where each lies relative to the others and to the foreign country partially determines the nature of the domestic game. Which actors are most dovish (i.e., closest in preferences to the foreign country) and which are most hawkish, as well as how far apart their preferences are, are important matters for the domestic game, as chapter 3 shows. Also crucial is the fact that the structure of domestic preferences differs by *issue area*. On different issues the actors will have different preferences, and hence the structure of these preferences may vary. No single national structure of preferences exists; rather, this structure will change with the issue area. If preferences are similarly structured in two different countries, one should expect their domestic games to be similar, ceteris paribus. The structure of domestic preferences is a central independent variable explaining cooperation.

Chapter 3 develops two hypotheses that show the effect of the structure of domestic preferences on international cooperation. The dependent variable has two parts: I am interested in both the *probability* of international cooperation and the *terms* of any cooperative deal that is possible. The structure of domestic preferences affects both these aspects. First, when the most dovish domestic actor holds greater internal decision-making power, cooperation is most likely. When the more hawkish actor is most powerful in domestic politics, the chances for cooperation decline but, when possible, its terms become more favorable to the hawk. Second, not only does the relative position of the actors matter, so does the distance between their preferences. When the executive and the legislature have policy preferences that are far apart, government is more divided and cooperation is less likely. Moreover, the terms of any cooperative deal possible also change as these divisions in government rise. The structure of domestic actors' preferences matters greatly for international cooperation, as I will show.

This argument about the role of preferences has two important differences from standard arguments about their role (Milner 1988; Rogowski 1989; Frieden 1990, 1991). First, in many earlier arguments only the preferences of societal actors were examined; political actors' preferences were not considered independent of societal ones. Here the preferences of both societal and political actors influence policy choices. Second, preferences do not translate directly into policy as in standard arguments. Instead policy is determined by the strategic interaction among the actors' preferences, given the institutional context. The role of political actors and the strategic interaction between them and societal actors becomes central to the domestic game of international cooperation.

---

[5] An arbitrary game-theory convention has been adopted to use the feminine pronoun for the executive, the male pronoun for the median legislator, and the plural for the interest groups. This convention helps to distinguish among the actors without having to repeat their names constantly.

Domestic Political Institutions

Institutions are prominent features of politics. Douglass North defines them as "the rules of the game in a society or, more formally, the humanely devised constraints that shape human interaction" (1990:3). Similarly, March and Olson (1989:18) claim that "political institutions define the framework within which politics takes place." Although agreeing with this broad definition, Jack Knight imposes another important condition to narrow down the scope of institutions: "First, an institution is a set of rules that structure social interactions in particular ways. Second, for a set of rules to be an institution, knowledge of these rules must be shared by the members of the relevant community or society" (1992:2–3). The importance of these similar definitions is that they view institutions as socially accepted constraints or rules that shape human interactions; in contrast, all these authors distinguish institutions from organizations, which are agents rather than structures.

Political institutions shape the process by which preferences are aggregated domestically. Within a country every groups' preferences do not have the same impact on politics. Some groups' preferences are weighed more heavily in any decision process and, as Schattschneider (1960) reminds us, part of the reason is the institutional structure. Institutions create a mobilization of bias in favor of certain actors.

The political institutions in which I am interested are those that determine how policy is chosen; they refer broadly to the legislative process. These determine which actors share what powers over the policy-making process; they define in part the extent of polyarchy domestically. In the policy-making process four elements are key powers for domestic players: the ability to initiate and set the agenda, to amend any proposed policy, to ratify or veto policy, and to propose public referendums. Control over these powers gives an actor influence in the policy-making process; it means his preferences are more likely to be reflected in the ultimate policy choice. Variations in which actors control these legislative powers occur not only across political systems but also within each system over time and across issues. For instance, Italy's parliament has greater ability to initiate legislation than does Britain's; however, the ability of Italy's parliament to initiate legislation differs depending on the issue under consideration (Norton 1990a; Cotta 1994).

In chapter 3 I assume a certain distribution of these legislative powers. The executive is able to set the agenda and parliament can only ratify, never amend. The executive also has no control over referendums or vetoes. Interest groups directly influence political actors' preferences and serve as information providers, but otherwise they are not directly involved in the decision-making process. The results presented in chapter 3 depend to some extent on this institutional arrangement. In chapter 4 I vary the institutional context to show what happens when the distribution of these legislative powers varies. The general conclusion is that institutions matter but that preferences are primordial since they circumscribe the degree to which institutions can produce variance in the outcomes.

Two hypotheses about the effect of institutions on international cooperation are developed in chapter 4. First, the probability and terms of cooperation depend on the distribution of legislative powers. When these powers are concentrated in the executive, the probability of cooperation will depend on how close her preferences are to those of the foreign country; moreover, the terms of any agreement will more closely reflect her preferences. However, when these powers are dispersed among the domestic actors, the probability of cooperation changes and so does its terms. When legislative powers move from the executive to the legislature, the terms of any cooperative agreement will become more favorable to the legislature. Second, changes in these institutions after a cooperative agreement has been negotiated at the international level will spell trouble. Domestic actors will be more likely to veto the agreement if domestic institutions change during the negotiation process. Hence opponents of cooperation will try to change these institutions. If they are successful, the probability of international cooperation will decline. Chapter 4 argues that these hypotheses hold regardless of whether the system is presidential or parliamentary. The differences between presidential and parliamentary systems are less important for the relationship between the executive and the legislature than is the distribution of legislative powers, which varies greatly within both presidential and parliamentary systems.

These hypotheses provide *specific* links between institutions and outcomes. Certain institutions privilege particular actors, and hence policy choices reflect their preferences more. These arguments about institutions are more substantive and narrow in their claims than are more well-known arguments about the role of institutions (e.g., Hall 1986; Haggard 1990; Sikkink 1991). Moreover, these arguments explicitly link institutions and preferences. They demonstrate how the structure of preferences delimits the effects of institutional variation, and they investigate how institutions privilege particular actors' preferences. They do not address explicitly the issue of how institutions shape preferences (Dowding and King 1995:2–9). They also endogenize institutions, as chapter 4 discusses. If institutions affect policy outcomes, then actors will have preferences over institutions as they do over policies (Knight 1992). Although by definition institutions are harder to change than preferences, they can become part of the domestic game. Whoever controls institutional choices will be very powerful.

The Distribution of Information

In addition to interests and institutions, the role of information domestically is important. When all actors do not possess complete information about an issue—that is, when some possess private information unknown to others— this creates inefficiencies and political advantages. Studies in international political economy have neglected the role of information. In contrast, studies in both economics and international security have dealt extensively with the problem of incomplete information and the signaling games it creates (e.g., Schelling 1960; Tirole 1989; Jervis 1970, 1976; Powell 1990; Downs and Rocke 1995; Iida 1993a, 1993b; Fearon 1995). In general, this literature has suggested that the uncertainty created by incomplete or asymmetric information leads to outcomes that prevent optimal levels of exchange or that foster conflict. In other words, incomplete information leads to inefficient outcomes.

> Until recently, however, little attention was given to the causes of costly delays and failures to agree [in negotiations]; indeed, these inefficiencies were seen by some authors as due to irrational or misguided behaviors, or simple mistakes . . . An alternative hypothesis is that . . . bargaining is substantially a process of communication necessitated by initial differences in information known to the parties separately. . . . From an ex ante perspective, therefore, the costly process of bargaining can be an efficient way of establishing a common informational basis for an agreement. In extreme cases, moreover, informational asymmetries may preclude agreement. (Keenan and Wilson 1993:46)

Or, as one study about the effects of incomplete information on economic cooperation concludes, "Uncertainty, though making coordination more desirable, probably makes it more difficult to achieve and to sustain" (Ghosh and Masson 1994:240).

Similarly, in security studies uncertainty has been linked to conflict. As Fearon (1995:409) argues in explaining war, "Under broad conditions the fact that fighting is costly and risky implies that there should exist negotiated agreements that rationally led states in dispute would prefer to war . . . [E]ssentially two mechanisms, or causal logics, explain why rationally led states are sometimes unable to locate or agree on such a bargain: (1) the combination of private information about resolve or capability and . . . (2) states' inability . . . to commit to uphold a deal." These findings suggest that if incomplete information exists in international political economy issues it should have negative effects, reducing cooperation and fomenting conflict.

Many studies in international relations, however, have dealt with incomplete or asymmetric information *among* states (e.g., Jervis 1970, 1976; Fearon 1995); that is, state A is assumed not to know something about state B, and/or vice versa. The problem of domestic uncertainty has been less studied. Incomplete or asymmetric information problems at the domestic level can take a number of forms, but they all involve at least one actor lacking important information about an issue. Downs and Rocke (1995) give several examples. One is where the executive must choose international trade agreements not knowing what her domestic interest groups will accept. Iida (1993a) addresses another kind of uncertainty in two-level games where the executive does not know with certainty what international agreements the median voter will accept. Iida's conclusions, which mirror those of the economists and security studies, show that uncertainty is necessary for failure of agreement, thus creating inefficient outcomes.

Information problems are also important in the two-level game here. In general, incomplete information has two effects. Not only does it create inefficient outcomes, it also confers political advantage. Chapter 3 explores two-level bargaining first with complete information on the part of all the actors. It then introduces a particular type of domestic uncertainty; the legislature does not fully know what agreement the executive has negotiated with the foreign country, but the legislature must decide whether to ratify the agreement. The analysis shows two effects of uncertainty on cooperative agreements. First, uncertainty makes for inefficiency since it means mutually beneficial agreements are sometimes rejected by the legislature. Second, this asymmetric information has political benefits (costs). It allows some actors to reach outcomes closer to their preferences than otherwise. In our case the executive with private information benefits at the expense of the legislature. The distribution of information domestically is thus an important issue; it creates inefficiencies as well as political advantages.

In most cases political executives (prime ministers, presidents, or dictators) are seen as possessing informational advantages over other domestic actors. In foreign affairs particularly the executive branch, including the bureaucracy (ministries), may well possess much private information about foreign countries, international negotiations, and foreign policy choices. The electorate and legislators are likely to know less about foreign affairs. Interest groups, on the other hand, may be as well informed on issues of interest as are executives. In general, asymmetries of information domestically work in favor of the executive. The executive's dominance over the foreign policy process is likely to be a function of how great her private information in this area is. Hence, as pointed out above, the extent of polyarchy depends in part on the distribution of information domestically. Where executives have much more information about foreign affairs than do other domestic actors, ceteris paribus, the unitary actor model becomes more relevant. An important caveat, however, is that this result largely depends on the political institutions in place. As indicated above, where other domestic actors lacking information hold a role in policy making, they will more often veto policy choices when such uncertainty exists. Thus certain institutional configurations, combined with uncertainty domestically, make rejection of the executive's policies more likely and undermine her dominance. The effects of incomplete information depend on both institutions and preferences, as chapter 3 shows.

How common is incomplete information, especially domestically? In the eyes of some, incomplete information seems to be a constant affecting all transactions (e.g., Jervis 1970, 1976). Although incomplete information may be common, it may have less impact than one would expect. Over time actors may have incentives to find ways to gain enough information to act as if they were perfectly informed. This book assumes that asymmetric information may exist, but it argues that actors can—and have incentives to—devise strategies to overcome this problem. In the model here, the legislature, lacking information about the international agreement negotiated, depends on the signals of knowledgeable interest groups. Although they have their own preferences, these interest groups provide important information to the legislature about the nature of the agreement. They help inform the legislature at low cost, and thus they make cooperation more likely. The inefficiencies and political advantages associated with incomplete information are thus reduced or eliminated through this mechanism. This unexpected result shows that incomplete information need not always create inefficiencies.

In addition to the hypotheses generated about interests and institutions, the book also examines two hypotheses about the role of information, which are developed in chapter 3. First, the comparison of two-level games with complete and incomplete information shows that incomplete information generates greater failure to cooperate. Where asymmetries of information exist domestically, international agreements are less likely. Uninformed domestic actors will reject certain international agreements that they would not reject if fully informed. Moreover, the executive, if she possesses an informational advantage, will be more likely to achieve agreements that reflect her preferences. Information is power; hence more uncertainty means less cooperation, and it advantages the actor who has private information.

Second, under certain circumstances, incomplete information may not be harmful to international agreements. When the less informed group, the legislature, can depend on the signals of informed interest groups, cooperation will be more likely and successful agreements will be closer to the legislature's preferences. In this case the endorsement of at least one interest group is a necessary condition for the agreement to be accepted. Thus when asymmetries of information are mitigated by the presence of an informed signaler who endorses the proposed international agreement, cooperation becomes more likely (even than in the complete information case) and its terms change so that the more informed party loses its advantage. Information is power; hence actors lacking it will seek ways to overcome this political disadvantage. In doing so, they may well overcome the inefficiencies associated with incomplete information.

Three features distinguish the way the information issue is treated in this study from many other studies. First, the distribution of information domestically is treated as a variable. It can range from all actors possessing full information to one possessing private information, with an intermediate stage where the less informed depend on signals from others. Each of these distributions affects the probability and terms of international cooperation. Interestingly the intermediate stage is the most favorable for cooperation. Not only is the distribution of information treated as a variable but it is endogenous to the game. When uninformed, the legislature can choose to depend on informed interest groups to offset the executive's advantage. Among the various distributions of information, this one brings the legislature to its optimal position for influencing the agreement. If acquiring full information is costly (which is likely but not part of the model), then this strategy will also be most efficient.

Second, the "solution" to the information problem of legislatures is to depend on informed interest groups. This attributes a relatively novel role to interest groups. Rather than being just pressure groups who seek to influence the policy choices that political actors make, interest groups act as information providers to political actors. They do not do this gratuitously but to influence policy. In doing so, however, they have unintended effects: they provide information to the legislature, making cooperation more likely, and change the terms of cooperative agreements.

Third, the effect of the distribution of information depends on the structure of preferences and the political institutions. Information, institutions, and interests are all important. Although I disentangle their effects here by the use of the ceteris paribus assumption, they are in reality tightly interrelated. Neglect of either of the three is likely to bias one's analysis. Hence domestic interests, institutions, and information are the central independent variables in this study of international cooperation.

Alternative Explanations: Realism and Neoliberal Institutionalism

The most prominent theories of cooperation today tend to treat the state as a unitary actor, and this distinguishes them most clearly from the theory advanced here. These arguments are presented to show their contrasting hypotheses; they are not systematically tested in this book. Heuristically, it is important to understand the different predictions that each makes and to contrast their arguments explicitly with the domestic politics one. What do existing theories of international cooperation predict about the probability and terms of a cooperative agreement? This section answers that question.

One variant of Realism, Hegemonic Stability Theory (HST), asserts that a concentration of power resources in a single state will lead to stability and openness in the international economy. Such stability and openness often depend on cooperation, which in turn is more likely when capabilities are concentrated in one state. The desire and ability of states to create an open trading system has been attributed to the existence of a hegemonic power (Kindleberger 1973; Krasner 1976; Lake 1988; Gowa 1993). The hegemon is necessary because it has both an interest in free trade and a stable trading system and the means to police others' behavior (Krasner 1976). For macroeconomic cooperation, the theory has been used to explain the creation of international monetary systems. In particular, the classical gold standard, the Bretton Woods system, and the European Monetary System (EMS) have been attributed to the existence of a hegemonic state within the system (Gilpin 1987; Cohen 1993; more doubtful is Eichengreen 1989).

Controversy has arisen, however, over many aspects of HST (Lake 1993; Strange 1987). In particular, the role of the hegemon has been seen in two different lights (Snidal 1985). One stresses the hegemon's power and its ability to coerce other states into playing by the hegemon's rules. The hegemon coerces other states into "cooperative" behavior that benefits it. In the benign version, the hegemon is necessary to resolve fears of exploitation and cheating by others. It acts to ensure that everyone plays by the system's rules, which in turn makes all the states better off. The literature is split, then, between a coercive view of the hegemon and a more benign one, each implying different motivations for the hegemon and the weaker states.

The predictions of HST about cooperation are therefore ambiguous. Its basic point is that the distribution of power resources in the international system will determine the probability of international cooperation. When power resources are concentrated in one state, the chances for cooperation will rise. This suggests, for example, that the Bretton Woods Monetary Agreement and the North American Free Trade Agreement (NAFTA) were the result of the United States' overwhelming power, and that European Monetary Union (EMU) is a function of the hegemony of Germany in Europe (e.g., Garrett 1993). The theory is more ambivalent about what the terms of the agreement should look like; that is, who should reap the greater benefits? In general, it assumes that this question involves only the comparison of gains at the national level; domestic distributional considerations should not matter. Depending on the version used, the hegemon should either benefit the most or the other states should since the hegemon must pay the costs for enforcing the agreement.

The other version of Realist theory focuses on the potential for balancing and the relative gains involved in any international agreement. The central claim is that countries will try to cooperate when they can balance external threats by doing so but will agree to cooperate only if the net gains they receive from it are evenly distributed (Grieco 1990). Even if cooperation allows countries to balance against a larger threat and provides gains for all concerned, it will not be undertaken if one party gains more than the others. Here relative gains, not absolute ones, are the source of state action.

This argument about balancing and the distribution of gains suggests several hypotheses. First, the motivation for states to join should be the presence of an external threat. For instance, the Bretton Woods agreement, European integration, or more recently NAFTA should be related to efforts by the states involved to balance against a greater external threat. Second, cooperation should be realizable only if the agreement provides a relatively balanced distribution of gains. The terms of the agreement should involve each country receiving an "equitable" share of the gains. This argument does not indicate a priori what "balanced" means.

In contrast to Realism, some have explained international cooperation as a result of transnational institutions and ideas. Scholars have focused on international "regimes" and transnational communities of like-minded experts—so-called epistemic communities—to explain cooperation (Krasner 1983; Keohane 1984; Haas 1990, 1992). Although these arguments differ, they share a number of commonalities, not the least important of which is their opposition to Realism. Regimes, it is contended, facilitate cooperation through the functions they perform for states: they allow the decentralized enforcement of agreements, improve each side's information about the behavior of others, and lower transaction costs. Regimes thus reduce states' uncertainty and mitigate their fears that others will defect, thus inducing cooperation.

One would thus expect the highest probability for cooperation in new areas among countries already involved in regimes (Keohane 1993). For example, monetary cooperation in Europe might be attributed to the prior existence of the European Community (EC), since it provides a framework for negotiation and allows bargains to be struck across issue areas. One would anticipate that countries already coordinating policies in regimes would be most likely to find new cooperative agreements. The regime should also play a key role by addressing concerns over cheating; the terms of the agreement should reflect this concern. How regimes affect the specific terms of the agreement is more uncertain. If preexisting regimes embody certain norms, rules, and principles, one might expect that these would guide the agreement. This is where regime arguments seem to link with those focused on ideas.

Arguments about the role of ideas have focused on transnational "epistemic communities," which are "networks of professionals with recognized expertise and competence in a particular domain and an authoritative claim to policy-relevant knowledge within that domain or issue-area" (Haas 1990; 1992). Because of their shared sets of normative and causal beliefs and common policy practices, such communities can induce cooperation (Haas 1990:55; 1992:3). In environments of high uncertainty policy makers are likely to rely on such communities for their advice. Epistemic communities frame the issues for collective debate, provide novel solutions, and create new perceptions of national interests. These claims echo arguments by economists about the need for policy consensus. For instance, Cooper (1989:181) claims that "international consensus about practical knowledge, along with shared objectives, is a necessary condition for close international cooperation" (see also Frankel 1988; Frankel and Rocket 1988).

The epistemic communities argument suggests two hypotheses. First, international cooperation should be more likely when epistemic communities exist. For example, the existence of a transnational group of Americans, Canadians, and Mexicans believing in free trade should make an agreement like NAFTA more likely. Second, these groups should set the terms of the agreement; their ideas and particular solutions should become focal points for resolving key issues.

These four existing arguments generate different hypotheses about the probability and terms of international cooperation than does the model here. The empirical cases presented do not provide a rigorous test of these hypotheses; the way they were chosen prevents that. The cases are primarily intended to see if they lend support to my hypotheses. These alternative hypotheses, however, are examined in the cases in order to bring out the role of systemic factors.

The Plan of the Book

This book is divided into two main parts. Part 1, including chapters 2 through 4, contains the theoretical arguments. Chapter 2 explores how the preferences of the actors in the model are determined. It differentiates interests from policy preferences, showing how the latter derive from the former. This chapter examines the preferences of both national political leaders and societal groups and in so doing lays the basis for the discussion of the central independent variable, the structure of domestic preferences. Chapter 3 presents a systematic and parsimonious two-level model to show how domestic politics affects international cooperation. The model avoids treating the state as a unitary actor, but it maintains the assumption of international anarchy. It examines how the structure of domestic preferences and the distribution of information domestically shape international negotiations. It explores what happens to cooperation in the presence of two features of polyarchy: divided government and asymmetric information. This chapter provides the theoretical core for the book.

Chapter 4 examines the effect of political institutions on the probability and terms of international cooperation. It argues that the way powers over policy making are allocated among domestic actors makes a difference for international cooperation. Different allocations, and hence different political institutions, change the probability of cooperation and its terms. The ability to alter these institutional arrangements is also important; it is a powerful capability. Changes in these institutions during international negotiations affect the likelihood of agreement as well.

Part 2, including chapters 5 through 8, comprises the case studies, which examine democratic countries and their attempts to cooperate. Although the argument made here could also apply to nondemocratic nations, the analysis captures most easily the nature of politics in democratic ones. In each empirical chapter, two different cases are compared. Each set of cases belongs to the same time period, and all but the last chapter involve the same countries. In chapter 5, the U.S. and British negotiations over monetary cooperation at Bretton Woods and over trade policy in the case of the International Trade Organization (ITO) are examined. Chapter 6 explores the negotiations between the United States and Britain over cooperation in civil aviation and oil policy. Chapter 7 compares the attempt by France and Germany to create the European Coal and Steel Community (ECSC) with their proposal for a European Defense Community (EDC). Finally, chapter 8 looks at two recent cases: the United States, Mexico, and Canada during negotiations over the North American Free Trade Agreement (NAFTA) and the European negotiations over monetary union in the Maastricht Treaty.

Each chapter seeks to explain the probability of international cooperation and its terms. First, why was an agreement concluded in one case and not another? Second, whose ex ante preferences were most closely accepted in the agreement; that is, who had most influence over the terms of the agreement? Three independent variables are examined: the structure of domestic preferences, the distribution of information internally, and the institutional arrangements for making policy. Do the hypotheses developed about these three factors in chapters 2 through 4 explain the differences in outcomes in the eight cases?

The first three sets of cases involve a successful and a failed instance of international cooperation. This comparison was chosen in order to analyze what accounts for the variation in the dependent variable. Because each pair involves the same countries at (roughly) the same time, it holds the international context constant. This points to a problem for theories that focus on international variables. If the international system is relatively constant in each case and the international position of the countries is the same, how do we explain failure to achieve cooperation in one case and success in the other? Each case in the pair involves a different issue area and at least two countries; hence it allows for the possibility of variation in the structure of domestic preferences, the distribution of information, and/or the institutional process. Thus the method of pairing provides variation in the outcomes and asks whether this is related to variation in the independent variables here—that is, the structure of domestic preferences, the distribution of information, and the domestic institutional context—while holding constant aspects of the international situation.

The last set of cases in chapter 8 differs from the others. NAFTA and the Maastricht Treaty were both successfully concluded and occurred in a different international environment than the first three sets of cases. The end of the cold war and the bipolar division of the world, as well as the decline of U.S. economic hegemony, contrast strongly with the system in the late 1940s and early 1950s. Do the domestic variables that are important in the first three sets of cases still play a role even though the international environment has changed? Given that both agreements were successfully negotiated and ratified, can the domestic variables identified by the model account for this? While not allowing variation on the dependent variable, this chapter examines the effects of variation in the character of the international system on the domestic environment. Comparison of these cases with the earlier ones is also telling. The cases in chapters 5 through 8 span more than five decades (1940–93), which allows interesting comparisons over time. Have changes in the international system affected the way domestic politics influences international cooperation? The methodology of this chapter, then, is distinct from that used in the earlier case study chapters.

The cases combine those involving European integration and those between European countries and other developed nations. Of the eight cases, three focus on cooperation among the EU countries. Unlike many studies, no claim—implicit or explicit—is made here that European cooperation is different in nature than that among other states (Haas 1968; Moravcsik 1991; 1993). No separate theory of European cooperation is considered necessary. European integration can be understood with general theories of international cooperation.

The model suggests that it is rational for political leaders to *not* initiate cooperation at times. One source of bias in studies of cooperation is that only cases where cooperation was attempted at all are studied. But in some issue areas cooperation has never or only rarely been essayed. For instance, after World War II the developed countries raised the issue of cooperation in shipping and ship building, but nothing ever came of this. Fiscal policy is another area where coordination has rarely if ever been attempted. Leaving these cases out of one's "sample" is a source of bias, as students of deterrence have observed (Achen and Snidal 1989). In an effort to correct this, I have added a discussion of Britain in the cases on European cooperation. Why did the United Kingdom not participate in the ECSC or the EDC, and why has it had such a difficult time with the EMU? The "nonissue" of British involvement in early EC cooperation is an intriguing problem that attempts to overcome the case selection bias.

The book concludes by evaluating the strengths and weaknesses of the model in light of the case studies. Its contributions to international relations and comparative politics are also discussed. It explores the general conditions under which international cooperation is most likely. Finally, it examines the implications of polyarchy for the theory and practice of international relations. What does polyarchy mean for the extent of cooperation or conflict internationally?

Part One

THE THEORY

Two

Actors' Interests, Policy Preferences, and the Demand for International Cooperation

WHEN domestic actors share power over decision making and their policy preferences differ, treating the state as a unitary actor risks distorting our understanding of international relations. Instead polyarchy reigns, affecting how states act in international politics. This chapter lays the basis for my primary claim: the structure of domestic preferences holds a key to understanding international cooperation. Domestic actors' preferences are primordial. This chapter sets forth the interests of three key groups of domestic actors: the executive (the prime minister or president), the legislature, and interest groups. It then derives their policy preferences from these basic interests. The central question addressed is why these groups would ever be interested in cooperating. The main concern is to show when these three sets of actors will have policy preferences that favor international cooperation and when important differences in their preferences will arise.

The *policy* preferences of actors in domestic politics derive from their basic interests. Actors are assumed to have certain fundamental interests, captured by their utility functions, which they attempt to maximize. For political actors, this means maximizing their ability to retain office; for social actors, maximizing their net income. For both, their most preferred policy—or their "ideal point"—is that policy choice in the issue area that maximizes their basic interests—that is, retaining political office or maximizing income. This chapter seeks to model how these actors' policy preferences are shaped and to suggest the conditions under which various structures of domestic preferences are more likely. In particular, I am concerned with the case of divided government, where the preferences of the executive and the legislature diverge. As I will show in chapter 3, structures of preferences involving divided government have important consequences for international cooperation. This chapter shows the conditions under which (more) divided government is likely.

The Agents: Executives, Legislatures, and Interest Groups

Two sets of policy preferences are of importance: those of political actors, such as the executive and the legislature, and those of societal actors, such as interest groups. Each of these three groups is assumed to be unitary and rational. These assumptions are significant, and here I explain what they mean for each set of actors.

The executive refers to the executive branch of government or the cabinet either led by the prime minister in parliamentary systems or the president in presidential ones, as well as the departments supporting the cabinet in both systems. Obviously, to claim that the executive branch is unitary is to make a simplifying assumption. Politics within the executive branch may be as complex and consequential as politics between it and the other branches (King 1976). For heuristic purposes, however, the executive is considered to act as if she were a unitary entity. This can be justified in three ways. First, since the prime minister or president is *primes inter pares* among the cabinet, all decisions must have her backing to go forth. Therefore the prime minister or president is the actor referred to by the executive. Second, one could argue that on each policy issue the cabinet minister in charge of that issue is the most important (or only) decision maker, and hence the minister is the unitary actor meant by the executive (Laver and Shepsle 1995). In contrast, by the executive one might refer to the median cabinet member; that is, the minister who casts the deciding vote for a policy represents the executive. Whichever way one proceeds—and I use the first formulation—the consequence is to make the executive branch a unitary actor.

The executive is also treated as being rational. The executive wants to maximize her utility, which is assumed above all to depend on reelection. Reelection is not the only goal attributed to political actors; some have argued that political actors desire to implement their party program most of all (e.g., de Swaan 1973). In reality, some combination of these two motives is probably most accurate. Here, however, I make the simplifying assumption that staying in office is the main goal of executives. As Snyder and Diesing note, "Any politician who wishes to participate in public action is thus faced with the imperative of maintaining or increasing his power, authority or influence. As Sam Rayburn observed, 'To be a statesman you have to get elected'" (1977:354).

This assumption of an "office-seeking" motivation has a long tradition (Downs 1957). Practically, what this assumption means is that the policy preferences of executives need not follow their party platforms nor their campaign promises. Instead, executives can pick and choose among policies to best serve their immediate electoral interests. Moreover, it means that electoral considerations motivate policy choices. "Economic policy is chosen by political agents and political agents seek to win office through elections. An adequate theory of economic policy formation, therefore, will take account of the electoral incentives facing political decision-makers" (Austen-Smith 1991:73).

In order to maximize their chances of reelection, executives have to worry about two factors: the overall economy and the preferences of interest groups that support them (e.g., Grossman and Helpman 1994, 1995). Executives first must ensure that the general performance of the economy is good. A declining economy may lead voters to support those out of power in the hope that they can improve the situation. As the leading, recent survey of the relationship between economics and elections in Western democracies shows, voters use retrospective economic evaluations of their national situation both to punish and reward incumbents (Lewis-Beck 1990). This "performance constraint" forces executives to be concerned not just with policies that please their particular constituents but also with those that serve the general economy. It may also create a trade-off with the second element in executives' utility function: their support for special interests.

Although ultimately voters elect political leaders (directly or indirectly), special interests can be an enormous help to leaders. They can produce contributions, votes, campaign organization, media attention, and so on, all of which may make the difference between a winning and a losing campaign. Leaders need the support of interest groups, and to gain it they must promote (retard) the policies that help (hurt) these groups. "Politicians seek office through elections; to run campaigns they need resources; to acquire such resources, they include redistributional policies in their platforms . . .; these [policies] induce the favored interest groups to provide such resources to support the relevant candidate" (Austen-Smith 1991:73). Hence executives will be concerned with maximizing their chances of reelection, which depend on both the state of the economy and the support of key interest groups. Executives will thus try to choose policies that optimize both the state of the national economy and the interests of their interest group supporters. Policies entailed by international cooperation will only be chosen if they fit this criteria.

The second actor is the legislature. Again it is assumed to be unitary and rational. Neither of these assumptions is unproblematic. The title of an article by Kenneth Shepsle (1992) summarizes the problems of the unitary actor assumption: "Congress Is a 'They,' Not an 'It': Legislative Intent as Oxymoron." As with the executive, legislatures have important internal politics that affect how they operate and what policies they adopt (e.g., Fenno 1973; Krehbiel 1992). Moreover, bicameralism explicitly undercuts the assumption of legislative unity. Nevertheless it seems useful to abstract from these considerations. What we want to know is whether the legislature will vote in favor of an international agreement proposed by the executive. Hence the focus is on the median legislator. The member of the legislature who casts the deciding vote on the international agreement becomes the actor who represents the "unitary" legislature. His preferences are what we mean by the legislature's preferences.

Like the executive, legislators are assumed to be rational. They seek to maximize their utility, which derives from maintaining their office. As political actors, both the legislature and the executive are assumed to have similar interests, although they may prefer different policies to maximize these interests. Hence legislators want reelection, which depends on the state of the economy and the support of their interest group constituents. Policies that enhance the economy and bring gains to their interest group supporters will be their preferred ones. These, however, may or may not be the same policies that the executive prefers.

Why, if the legislature and executive share common interests, might their policy preferences differ? Executives and legislators represent different constituencies. Both the type and importance of special interests in their constituencies may differ. In presidential systems, where the two are elected in separate elections this point is fairly obvious. Executives must worry about a national constituency, whereas legislators are concerned with their local district. Depending on the electoral laws, their district may represent a small or large part of the nation. Moreover, in multimember districts legislators may represent only part of their district, further narrowing their constituency and differentiating it from the executive's. As Olson (1993) and others (e.g., Lohmann and O'Halloran 1994) have noted, politicians with more encompassing jurisdictions are more concerned with overall national outcomes and thus have different preferences than those with more narrowly defined jurisdictions.

In parliamentary systems differences in preferences between the executive and the legislature seem less likely. The executive is usually chosen by the legislature; thus the election for legislators may be considered the same as that for the prime minister. Nevertheless each legislator is concerned primarily with his district whereas the prime minister must be concerned with all the districts, especially the median one. As Shugart and Carey (1992:3–4) observe:

> A major dilemma in democratic regimes concerns a divergence between what representative assemblies do best and what executives must do if democracy itself is to function well. Assemblies. . . are intended to be representative of the population. A typical democratic assembly is elected for the purpose of giving voice to the interests of localities or to the diversity of ideological or other partisan divisions in the polity or society. That is, assemblies are ordinarily expected to be parochial in nature. Executives, on the other hand, are charged with acting to address policy questions that affect the broader interests of the nation, as well as to articulate national goals.

The national focus of the executive and the more local concerns of legislators help explain why, although they may have the same interests, legislators and executives may have distinct policy preferences.

The third set of actors are interest groups. Each group is assumed to be unitary and rational. Politics within an interest group is important, as the literature on collective action suggests (Olson 1965). But I assume that each interest group behaves as a unit, reflecting the median member's preferences. Moreover, as discussed in detail later, each interest group is rational; it tries to maximize its members' income—for example, wages, profits, and so on. This assumption needs less justification than the others since it is fairly standard. Hence an interest group prefers policies that maximize its income, and it will support (oppose) policies entailed by international cooperation that promote (detract from) this interest.

In the model the policy preferences of these three domestic groups and of the foreign country are used to define the "structure of preferences." This structure relates the relative policy preferences of these groups along a single dimension. It assumes, that is, that the actors have preferences for a policy that can be arrayed along a line; they desire more or less of the policy. Their preferences are reducible to a single dimension. This assumption is a substantial but frequently employed one (McKelvey 1979; Schofield 1983; Enelow and Hinich 1990; Romer and Rosenthal 1978, 1979; Ferejohn and Shipan 1990; Laver and Hunt 1992). Empirically, this assumption does have some support as well (Poole and Rosenthal 1991). Thus one can label the preferences of each group as more or less hawkish or dovish, given their relationship to those of the foreign country. Actors whose preferences are closer to those of the foreign country are termed dovish; actors farther away are considered hawkish. The terms *hawk* and *dove* are used to simplify categorization of the actors' preferences; they are not intended as normative or pejorative terms. Rather than saying they are to the left or right of another actor, one can say a group's policy preferences are more hawkish or dovish than another's. The structure of preferences, then, varies according to the relative positions of the actors' preferences.

The Executive's Preferences versus the Legislature's: Divided Government

This section discusses why policy preferences might vary among political leaders, particularly between the executive and the legislature. As noted above, political actors have the same basic interest—retaining political office—but may have different policy preferences. A divergence between the policy preferences of the executive and the median legislator creates divided government. The more divergent these preferences are, the more divided government is.

Here divided government is a continuous variable. Most often it is used as a dichotomous one—either the party in control of the executive is the same as the majority in the legislature or it is not. This dichotomous usage is not always helpful since intraparty differences can matter. If the majority legislative party also controls the executive but lacks party discipline and/or is internally divided, then even so-called unified government may appear divided. In addition, though, the use of divided government as a continuous variable allows one to appreciate how both parliamentary and presidential systems may be divided and to understand how degrees of internal division matter. As chapter 3 shows, divided government—and the degree of division—matter for international cooperation. Here I address when the executive's ideal policy choice will differ from that of the median legislator and what factors will drive them further apart.

Divided government is a term usually reserved for presidential systems. In this context it occurs when the president's party is not the one in control of the majority in the legislature. In these systems two agents are elected— usually in separate elections—to represent the public: the executive and the legislature. The potential for conflict between these two is elevated when they have different policy preferences. Used dichotomously, this term implies that the preferences of the executive and the legislature differ (e.g., O'Halloran 1994; Lohmann and O'Halloran 1994); party affiliation is employed as a proxy for preferences. As a continuous variable, this term describes how much these preferences differ. It also captures the divergences in preferences that may occur even when the same party controls both but party discipline is low and/or the two agents have divergent preferences because of their different constituencies. In two-party presidential systems, like that in the United States, divided government may be sporadic; however, in multiparty presidential systems, like many in Latin America, legislative majorities depend on coalitions of parties, thus making divided government fairly constant.

Divided government is also an obvious possibility in "semi-presidential" political systems. In these systems a blend of presidential and parliamentary procedures is employed (Lijphart 1984; Shugart and Carey 1992; Baylis 1996). Semi-presidential systems—like the Fifth Republic in France and the current systems in Finland, Russia, and some countries in Eastern Europe—combine a popularly elected president with a cabinet run by a prime minister and dependent on the legislature's confidence, thus creating two agents to represent the electorate. When the legislative majority comes from the same party as does the president, these systems work much like unified presidential ones. When the executive comes from a different party than the one that controls the legislative majority, divided government emerges in which the conflict between prime minister and president can be intense.

Parliamentary systems are not usually associated with divided government; they should be, however. Fiorina (1992:112–25) notes the strong similarity between divided presidential systems and coalition governments in parliamentary systems:

Most of the world's governments are *not* unified ... Rather, governments controlled jointly by coalitions of two or more parties are, of course, the norm in
European democracies, and in democracies generally. ... The analogy between
divided government and coalition government is worth exploring ... [I]n both
cases each party needs the acquiescence of others in order to govern. In both
European coalition governments and American divided governments, one party
cannot govern alone. ... Most generally, the analogy between divided government and coalition government suggests that much of our theoretical treatment of
two-party and multi-party politics exaggerates the differences. (112–13)

Divided government in this broad sense is also the norm among all types
of democracies. As Alesina and Rosenthal claim:

Long periods of divided government are hardly an American monopoly. On the
contrary, in parliamentary democracies cases of unified government are rare.
Laver and Shepsle (1990) appropriately define a government to be unified whenever a single party both forms the political executive and commands a majority in
the legislature. In the period of 1945–82 fewer than 15% of the governments of
parliamentary democracies satisfied this definition. All other governments were
not unified: at least two parties were needed to participate either in the government or in the parliamentary majority supporting the government. Therefore, if
one views coalition government as an example of division of power, divided government is the norm rather than the exception. ... [D]ivided government in
America and coalition government in Europe have much more in common than it
would first appear. (1995:243)

Parliamentary systems may be just as susceptible to divided government
as presidential ones. As Laver and Shepsle (1991:251–52) note:

Since most European parliamentary democracies use proportional electoral systems, and since it is very rare indeed for any European party to win over 50% of
all votes cast, most Western European legislatures have no single party controlling a majority of the seats. This means that the legislative investiture and confidence votes that allow Western European political executives to gain and retain
office are based on multi-party coalitions. It is not uncommon for the coalition of
parties that make up the executive to differ in politically salient ways from the
coalition of parties that supports the executive in the legislature. ... [C]ontempo-
rary experience suggests that divided government is common both in the U.S.
separation-of-powers system and in Continental European coalition systems. It
is Great Britain and some of the Commonwealth countries that are exceptional in
this respect.

In a humorous passage Laver and Shepsle (1991:262) spell out the differences for the relationship between the executive and the legislature under

divided government in the United States and in parliamentary contexts:

> In short, a situation of divided government in the U.S. can turn the executive into a neutered duck, while constitutionally denying the legislature the right to shoot that duck. European legislatures, in contrast, have the constitutional right to shoot any duck they like, neutered or otherwise, if the fancy takes them. What we have seen, however, is that the fancy may not take them—that there may well be circumstances in which the legislature lacks the political will to shoot even the most irredeemably neutered duck, given their low collective opinion of whatever else is on offer.

Divided government is constitutionally enforced in the United States; it is strategically chosen in the parliamentary systems.

Divided government would seem to have different ramifications for presidential and parliamentary systems. In parliamentary systems, the fates of the executive and the legislature are linked. If the legislature does not support the prime minister, the government may fall and new elections follow. Legislators thus have to calculate the costs of new elections when deciding to vote against the prime minister. In presidential systems a vote against the executive does not usually lead to new legislative elections. Hence it would seem that legislators in parliamentary systems would be less likely to vote against the government, implying that even when divided government occurred the executive might not worry about its legislature's approval of its policies. Huber (1996:279), for example, shows that the ability of prime ministers to call votes of confidence allows them to exert "substantial influence over final policy outcomes, even when these procedures are not invoked." However, the prime minister is still constrained to propose a policy that the legislative majority favors over the status quo; the legislature in effect retains ratification powers.

Two factors mitigate the power of the executive in parliamentary systems. First, the prime minister will for the same reasons be highly motivated not to propose an agreement that fails to satisfy the legislature. The costs to the prime minister of legislative rejection may be very high; this is unlike a president who can survive legislative rejection and hence has less reason to anticipate and accommodate her legislative majority. Second, in parliamentary systems not all votes are votes of confidence, leading to new elections if they fail. In some cases, like Germany, only constructive votes of confidence are allowed, meaning that an old government cannot be turned out until a new government is at hand. In others, legislators can choose which votes are no-confidence or censure ones. For these two reasons I expect divided government to have fairly similar consequences in both systems.

Divided government, then, may characterize both presidential and parliamentary systems, especially multiparty ones where coalitions predominate. In the latter, divided government implies divisions not only between the legislature and the executive but also within the cabinet itself. Furthermore, bicameral legislatures make the probability of divided government even more likely. In systems where there are two chambers, there is a greater chance that one chamber will be controlled by parties not in the government. Even if the chamber controlled by the opposition is less important than the other, this can still represent a situation of divided government. In the early 1990s, for instance, control of the British House of Lords by the Labor Party and of the German Bundesrat by the SPD rendered government more divided in both countries.

Unified government is most likely in two-party systems. But even in these cases unified control depends on another factor: party discipline. Party discipline seeks to ensure that members of the governing party in the legislature vote for the policies proposed by their party in the government. When in opposition, party discipline requires that they do not vote for the government's proposed policies. The threat of party discipline raises the costs of not voting the party line. Since the executive is often the head of her party, party discipline compels members of the legislature in the executive's party to vote for her proposed policies by threatening various penalties if they do not. Even if large numbers of constituents or important interest groups press their legislators to oppose the policy, if party discipline is strong the executive will receive her party's votes. Under such conditions, legislators will pay a large cost should they decide to vote against their party on the executive's proposed policy. Among political systems, the mechanisms of party discipline vary, although candidate selection and campaign funding are two important means. On the other hand, the legislator may have to pay electoral costs for maintaining party discipline. If the preferences of constituents or important interest groups differ from those of the party on an issue, the legislator is forced to choose between the two. Following the party line may prove costly to the legislator at the next election, in terms of votes, endorsements, or campaign funds. The legislator must balance these costs to maximize his utility and electoral chances.

The degree of party discipline varies within a political system as well as among them. Different parties in a country may exhibit different levels of discipline. For instance, many scholars attribute greater party discipline to conservative, right-wing parties than to left-wing ones, although some, including Duverger (1959), have maintained the opposite. But party discipline also varies over time within the same party. At certain points a party may exercise more control over its members than at others. The nature of the issue at hand (how contentious it is, for example) clearly matters, as does the degree of government popularity. The British Conservative Party is a good example. In the early 1980s it was the model of a highly disciplined party; by the early 1990s it was so riven by factions that it depended on other parties for support on crucial votes and had trouble supporting its own prime minister.

In countries with high levels of party discipline the executive and the legislators of the same party will have the same preferences. In two-party systems when discipline is strong and one party controls both the executive and the legislature, the ideal policy choice of the median legislator will be identical to that of the executive. Indeed, in two-party parliamentary systems divided government is likely only when party discipline in the majority breaks down. As Crossman (1972:31) says, "The British Cabinet's concern today is not for its majority over the opposition, because that is almost automatic, but for its majority inside its own party. The key to power is *inside* the party. It is not in Parliament as such, it is in the party. And the opposition the Government fears is not that of the Opposition on the front bench opposite. . . . The only doubt the Prime Minister has is about his own supporters." Lack of party discipline in two-party systems—whether presidential or parliamentary—can seriously impair unified government.

The likelihood and extent of divided government are thus dependent not only on the preferences of the actors but also on the political institutions in place. Institutions cannot be neatly separated from the structure of domestic preferences. Constitutional systems, the number of political parties, and party discipline all affect the degree of divided government. In presidential systems where the legislature and executive are elected in separate elections, in multiparty parliamentary governments, and in two-party parliamentary systems when party discipline is lacking, the median legislator's preferences will often diverge from those of the executive. Divided government will be a possibility. The executive will have to be concerned about her majority in the legislature when undertaking international cooperation.

The Policy Preferences of Political Actors

When will political actors—executives or legislators—be interested in coordinating policies with another country? Why would they ever prefer multilateral over unilateral policy making? In this section I relate political actors' preferences for cooperation to their reelection prospects. In particular, I show how under certain conditions international cooperation can improve the overall state of the economy, thereby increasing their probability of remaining in office. As noted above, political actors also care about the preferences of interest groups; this element of the politicians' utility function is examined later in this chapter within a general discussion of the conditions under which interest groups prefer cooperative policies.

If the political actors making this choice are politicians who must be (re)elected to office, then their reasons for seeking cooperation with other nations can be related to electoral concerns. If politicians want above all else to remain in office and their reelection depends in part on economic conditions, then politicians will worry about the state of the economy. They will be concerned with the prospects for economic growth, employment, and inflation. This is a fairly standard set of assumptions, but it says nothing about why coordinated, multilateral policy making should be preferred. Indeed, as many economists note, taking care of the economy will begin at home.

Domestic, unilateral policy choices have much more effect on a country's economy than do international cooperative ones. Economists have shown that the gains from cooperation are small (Oudiz and Sachs 1984; Kenen 1987). Although acknowledging the primacy of domestic policy tools for influencing the national economy, international cooperative efforts are sometimes chosen and the reasons require explanation. My argument is not that cooperative policy should replace unilateral, domestic policy. A policy involving cooperation with other countries need not be the most economically efficient one; a unilateral domestic policy could be more efficient but less electorally beneficial to political leaders.

The central reason why rational policy makers might choose coordinated policy making depends on two factors: the degree of a nation's economic openness and the type of externalities that countries' policies generate. Openness refers to the extent of integration between a country's economy and the world economy. In trade, openness can be measured by the ratio of exports and imports to GNP. In monetary markets, capital mobility is a measure of openness. The growth of economic openness for a state means that other countries' policies have greater reverberations on that country's economy. As Cooper (1986:299) notes, "Increased openness in terms of goods or securities generally weakens the effectiveness of traditional instruments of macroeconomic policy on national output . . . [B]y the same token its impact on income in the rest of the world is increased. Thus, with increased interdependence, policy actions in one country become larger 'disturbances' in the other country." Greater openness also means that a country's prices of goods and capital are increasingly constrained to the world level. Only by coordinated action with many countries can these effects of openness be overcome.

Openness is associated with greater impact for other countries' policies on the home country. When through its choice of policies a foreign country generates costs or benefits for another country that are not included in the foreign country's calculation of the optimality of the policy, we can speak of externalities.[1] Two conditions are necessary for an externality to be present: (1) actor A's utility function includes variables whose values are chosen by

[1] Externalities are "present when the actions of one agent directly affect the environment of another agent [and] the effect is not transmitted through prices" (Papandreou 1994:5). There is a long history of ideas about externalities, beginning with Alfred Marshall and A. C. Pigou. Unfortunately many meanings have been associated with the term over the years. As a recent assessment claims, "At least one hundred years have passed since 'external economies' entered into economists' vocabulary. The concept has been used widely, but no precise and agreed-upon meaning of the term seems yet to have emerged" (Papandreou 1994:14). Externalities are related to other important concepts, such as interdependence, transaction costs, unintended consequences, and market failure; see also Mishan (1971).

actor B, who pays no attention to actor A's welfare, and (2) actor B does not receive the benefits or costs of his effect on actor A (Baumol and Oates 1975:17–18).

Externalities generate demand for cooperation. "The gains [from cooperation] are supposed to come specifically from taking into account externalities, or 'spillover' effects, that one country's policies have on other countries' economies, which the countries would have no incentive to do in the absence of coordination" (Frankel 1988:354). The externalities generated by other countries' policies tend to grow in importance as an economy is opened. As these externalities rise, ceteris paribus, so do the gains from cooperation, and hence so do the incentives for it. "Differences between countries in the expansiveness of macroeconomic policy spill over into trade balances. . . . Thus, as international trade becomes more important, countries face larger international payments imbalances as a consequence of divergent macroeconomic policy choices, and each government's interest in international policy coordination to reduce its burden of adjustment increases" (Webb 1991:316). Thus a country's level of economic growth, employment, and/or inflation may depend critically on the behavior of other states, not just on its own policies. Unilateral, domestic policies will exert the largest impact on the country, but as openness grows so too do the home effects of foreign countries' policy choices.

Openness and the presence of externalities are likely to generate demand for international cooperation among political actors. If countries' economies are tightly woven together through trade and capital flows, they may not be able to achieve their economic goals without other states' help. If rates of growth, employment, and/or inflation in one state depend on the policies chosen in other states, then politicians' reelection hopes are tied to the behavior of these foreign countries. Getting foreign countries to alter their policies to reduce (increase) the negative (positive) externalities they create for the home country may require a coordinated approach to policy making. For example, in an open world economy one country's efforts to increase growth may be unsuccessful without the cooperation of other states. The cases of the United States in the late 1970s and France in the early 1980s suggest that this is true, regardless of the exchange rate system. Unilateral attempts to promote growth proved unsuccessful; coordinated reflationary policies seemed to offer the best way for these leaders' to realize their objectives.

Cooperation is frequently desired to change the policies of other countries; either to prevent them from adopting some policy they intend to or to push them to adopt a policy that they would not otherwise adopt. If political leaders in country A with an open economy believe that country B will adopt policies that generate negative externalities for A's economy, then country A may hope to block country B from doing so. International coordination may be a way to prevent country B from unilaterally imposing negative externalities on A and thus from hurting country A's leaders' electoral chances. Country A may have to give up something in return, but this should be worth the price of binding B. Similarly, if political leaders in country A want country B to adopt a particular policy that generates positive externalities for country A, but that country B is not keen about, then international coordination may offer a way to craft a deal to get B to do so.

Leaders may also seek international cooperation to avoid domestic political problems. Policies have differential effects internally; some groups gain and some lose from a policy choice. Political leaders, as I argued above, care about both overall welfare and special interests' preferences. Powerful groups within a country may be able to prevent the adoption of policies they dislike in a unilateral setting, even when political leaders favor them. International coordination can allow political actors to overcome this opposition and adopt policies that they otherwise could not. Cooperation can bring additional gains (in the form of increased positive externalities or reduced negative ones) that accrue to other domestic groups, ones whose support in turn makes the policies desired by political actors more feasible and durable. For example, in trade negotiations offers of liberalization by foreign countries may mobilize exporters in the home country to push for reductions in domestic trade barriers, which otherwise would be opposed by protectionist domestic groups. Political leaders may desire trade liberalization because it promotes employment and growth and helps interest groups that support them, thus enhancing their reelection prospects. As one commentator notes, "Unless there is a significant group within a particular country that is leaning toward the proposed policy change anyway for purely internal reasons, it may be useless or even counterproductive to try to push a coordinated strategy" (Schultze 1988:56–57).

On the other hand, cooperation may allow leaders to bind themselves, thus "locking in" their preferred policies. If domestic groups want politicians to take actions that politicians believe would be deleterious for the economy and for reelection, they may wish to prevent themselves from being forced domestically to adopt such policies. International cooperation may be one way for political leaders to commit themselves to *not* doing something. This could apply to trade policy where national leaders may want to advantage groups desiring freer trade and avoid sectoral pressures for protectionism by forging international agreements that lock free trade policy into place. Or, in the macroeconomic area, for example, "participation in the ERM [Exchange Rate Mechanism] introduced an external discipline and thus reinforced the hand of institutions and interstate groups inside a country fighting for less inflationary policies" (Tsoukalis 1993:201). Both arguments depend on the existence of internal factions with different policy preferences; they are not understandable from a perspective that views the state as a unitary actor.

In each case political leaders must believe that the political benefits from international cooperation outweigh the costs; that is, the no cooperation outcome is seen as worse than the cooperative one. In the face of noncooperation the domestic economy would be worse off, and hence their reelection chances would be worse. This raises the issue of the costs of cooperation. As noted above, cooperation often has sizable domestic costs for political leaders, and thus their interest in it may seem puzzling. But it is only when these costs are expected to be less than the benefits that political leaders will initiate cooperative agreements.

What are the political costs of cooperation? The central costs for political leaders are two: the distributional consequences of choosing cooperative policies and the loss of unilateral control over a policy instrument. Cooperation involves a change in a country's policies; it adopts a policy that it otherwise would not choose. This change may have distributional effects internally. For example, trade agreements may require countries to reduce protection to various industries; this policy will redistribute income from these industries to others. Indeed, as studies by Hufbauer and Elliott (1994) indicate, the major redistributive effects of changes in trade policy occur at the domestic level, not across countries. Hence the distributive effects of policy changes induced by international cooperation may hurt special interests whose support is valued by political leaders, thus undermining their enthusiasm for cooperation.

Second, once committed to international cooperation, political actors are prevented from manipulating some policy variable that they otherwise could. As Wolfers (1962:27) claims, "Cooperation means sacrificing some degree of national independence with a view to coordinating, synchronizing, and rendering mutually profitable some political, military, or economic policies that cooperating nations intend to pursue." In trade policy, for example, cooperation might mean that policies like quotas are completely outlawed or that tariffs on goods are "bound" to low levels, which in principle cannot be changed without new international negotiations. In the macroeconomic area, the policy instrument lost is often exchange rate control. Monetary union, which goes even further, means the loss of one's own currency and of autonomous monetary policy. The costs of the loss of these instruments are both real and symbolic. In the future, political leaders may pay an electoral cost when they cannot improve the economy before an election by changing monetary policy or when they cannot politically appease potential supporters by raising trade barriers. The symbolic cost may entail a loss of "sovereignty" in the eyes of domestic constituents. These costs may be very high, so high that political leaders would not rationally choose cooperation.

This argument begins to lay out the microfoundations for a political approach to explaining international economic cooperation. But this approach needs more microfoundations to explain the issue areas in which leaders will choose to cooperate.

The Demand for Cooperation by Political Leaders by Issue Area

This section argues that political leaders' demand for cooperation will vary by issue area. The definition of issue areas here rests on the policy instrument involved. Policy instruments are assumed to correspond to issue areas. Although numerous policy instruments exist I examine four: trade and industrial policy (tariffs, quotas, and subsidies), T; monetary policy (money supply), M; exchange rate policy, E; and fiscal policy (public expenditures and taxes), G.

The central variables differentiating issue areas (or policy instruments) are two. The first concerns the nature (positive or negative) and *extent of externalities* that other countries' policies can impose on the home country. The traditional argument about economic openness is that as it grows externalities will rise as well, but that these may be positive (benefits) or negative (costs); that is, as an economy becomes more open, the effects of other countries' policies on it will be felt more. These effects may be both unintended side-effects and intentional influences. Logically, if the externalities experienced by the home country in a policy area become negative or more negative as its openness increases, the demand for cooperation by political leaders in the home country should rise. It follows, therefore, that if across issue areas, given a level of openness for the country, the negative externalities in one issue area (say, trade policy) are greater than in another issue area (say, monetary policy), the executive's demand for cooperation will be greater in the former area (trade policy), ceteris paribus.

The second variable is the nature and extent of benefits that the country's own unilateral use of the policy instrument can provide domestically. Let us call these the *home country benefits* of the policy instrument. The costs of cooperation include, as stated above, the losses associated with giving up unilateral use of the instrument. The net benefits of the unilateral use of a policy instrument also include the effects of foreign countries' retaliation against the home country for its unilateral use of the policy instrument. In sum, each leader's utility must be calculated by summing two factors: (1) the net home benefits she gets from using the policy instrument unilaterally (the benefits to her economy and interest groups minus the costs of retaliation, given its probability), and (2) the net external costs imposed on the home country by foreign countries when they use the policy instrument. Political actors' demand for cooperation is a function of these political costs and benefits.

A political leader is concerned with both sides of the instrument's effects: how much benefit he or she can get out of its unilateral use *and* how much does he or she have to pay when other countries unilaterally use the instrument. If the policy instrument does not have much home benefit (e.g., because it provokes costly retaliation by other countries or is domestically ineffective) and the externalities imposed by other's use of it are high, then

TABLE 2.1
The Demand for International Cooperation

	Low Externalities	High Externalities
High Home Benefits	no/least demand	some demand
Low Home Benefits	little demand	most demand

cooperation may return the highest utility to the leader (Table 2.1). If the policy instrument has significant home benefits and low externalities, then a leader's interest in cooperation will be slight. Moreover, if both the home benefits and the externalities are low, a leader's interest in cooperation will remain limited since attempting to cooperate has costs in itself and the instrument has few. A problem arises when the home benefits of a policy instrument are high and so are its externalities. Here a leader will be torn between the domestic value of the instrument and its external costs. The demand for cooperation will fall in between the case where home benefits are low and externalities are high and the case where home benefits are high and externalities are low.

A country's level of economic openness influences the home benefits it derives from a policy instrument. First, increased trade and capital openness reduce the home effectiveness of macroeconomic policy instruments (Cooper 1986:299). Second, the costs of foreign retaliation will vary with the degree of economic openness among the countries. As countries become more economically intertwined, retaliation becomes more costly but also more effective. In the extreme, countries without international economic ties will not be able to retaliate economically and cannot be retaliated against by others. The probability of retaliation, however, also depends on other aspects of the policy area; it is not a simple function of the level of economic openness.

A simple model is proposed of the effects of economic openness and the externalities it imposes on a political actor's utility in different issue areas. Cooperation means relinquishing the unilateral use of a policy instrument— of either the money supply M, fiscal policy G, trade and industrial policy T, or exchange rate policy E. For monetary cooperation this might mean a fixed exchange rate system, where E and M are no longer variable. For trade policy the level of protection may become fixed, so that T can no longer be varied. One sees immediately that one cost of cooperation is the loss of a policy variable.[2] When will this cost be outweighed by the benefits of cooperation for each policy instrument?

[2] The loss of policy tools affects the government's ability to realize its multiple objectives. If a government has two objectives and two policy tools, reaching its goals may be possible. Giving up one tool without altering objectives makes life much harder since the government now has only one tool for two targets, which, according to the Tinbergen Rule, makes achieving both targets impossible.

Political actors want to be (re)elected. Their reelection depends on the state of the economy—the rate of growth, inflation, and unemployment, in particular.[3] To understand policy makers' preferences, given this utility function, I use the modified Mundell-Fleming model (MMF). Using particular assumptions, this model shows the relationship between macroeconomic variables. The model has been much challenged since the 1970s by the rational expectations approach. But as Krugman (1993) argues, although it is ugly and ad hoc, MMF is the best macroeconomic theory available. For political science the model's relevance is more apparent. It assumes that actors operate in the short run and face various rigidities in markets. These assumptions, rather than those of the rational expectations school, appear more appropriate for the study of political economy.

Employing the model in a two-country framework, economists have been able to show the home and foreign effects of policy changes (and exogenous disturbances) (e.g., Mundell 1963, 1968; Cooper 1985, 1986; Mussa 1979; Krugman and Obstfeld 1991). Using several assumptions, one can present a model showing the home and foreign effects of policy changes in the four issue areas. Since the rate of unemployment is negatively correlated with the growth rate, the growth rate is assumed to be a proxy for politicians' employment targets. In general, leaders will maximize their utility as the actual level of growth and inflation match their desired levels. Their objectives are to achieve these desired levels of growth (employment) and inflation. Since leaders tend to be preoccupied with the next election, their interest is in the short-term state of the economy. Thus the short-run Phillips curve is used to describe the relation between these objectives; that is, in the *short term*, increases in the inflation rate when they are unexpected are associated with decreases in unemployment (or increases in the growth rate). The desired levels of these objectives will vary for different political leaders. Partisan affiliation may matter: left-wing party leaders will prefer higher growth and less unemployment and will accept higher inflation; leaders of right-wing parties will prefer less inflation and will accept less growth and more unemployment (Hibbs 1978; Alesina and Roubini 1992; Alesina and Rosenthal 1995). Policy choices may vary by party, as discussed later. But the utility function described is general to all leaders.

Thus leaders' objectives are to attain a certain rate of inflation—maybe 0—called π^*, and a certain rate of output growth, called x^*. A political leader's utility, then, is a function of the difference between the actual inflation rate, π, and the leader's preferred rate, π^*; it is also a function of the distance between the actual growth rate, x, and the leader's preferred growth rate, x^*. The leader's utility declines as either of these values diverge

---

[3] Alternatively one could assume that leaders had the same utility function but were motivated by the "national interest"; that is, they believed that achieving high growth and low inflation was optimal for the country as a whole (Lindbeck 1976).

from his or her preferred rate. The actual rate of growth depends on the natural rate plus an amount generated by unexpected inflation—that is, the short-run Phillips curve relationship. In turn inflation equals a weighted average of changes in domestic and foreign prices (p and p') or changes in domestic prices plus the real exchange rate, E (e.g., Canzoneri and Henderson 1991). *Hence any policy that affects domestic or foreign prices or the real exchange rate affects output in the short run.* Because of various rigidities in markets, however, these changes do not immediately alter the rate of inflation, at least in the short run.

Usually this model focuses on monetary policy; M is the only variable that the government is allowed to control. The approach here is broader. Assume that the government has four variables it can manipulate (Mussa 1979). Say the government controls the money supply M, fiscal policy G, trade and industrial policy T, and the nominal exchange rate E. Each of these can be related to the inflation rate, π. Even with sticky domestic prices, each of these policy instruments works through the real exchange rate to affect the growth rate and the inflation rate. Hence each may have effects at home and abroad when the economy is open.

Monetary Policy

Since monetary policy is the usual context in which the above model is used, the discussion begins there (Canzoneri and Henderson 1991; Artus 1989; Blackburn and Christensen 1989; Dornbusch 1980; Krugman and Obstfeld 1991; Persson and Tabellini 1990; Mussa 1979). In a closed economy inflation π is simply a function of the *domestic* money supply M in the short run; that is, the government's main tool to affect the inflation rate is the money supply. If one assumes an open economy, then π is also a function of the foreign government's money supply M'. This means that the home government's ability to realize its objectives depends also on the foreign country's policy behavior—its choice of M'.

In this situation the leader's utility function is such that inflation at home is a positive function of the home country's money supply and the change in that money supply and a *negative* function of the change in the foreign country's money supply (Canzoneri and Henderson 1991:14). The home leader's ability to attain her objectives depends on the behavior of the foreign country and its monetary policy choices.

In an open economy—that is, one with perfect capital mobility between it and the rest of the world so that its interest rate is constrained to the world's interest rate—with flexible exchange rates, a political leader might be tempted to use monetary policy to improve employment should she face a recession at home and upcoming elections.[4] In this case an increase in the money supply will have a powerful (short-term) effect on growth and employment at home as a result of two mechanisms. First, it will lead to a reduction in the interest rate at home which in turn will lead to a capital outflow and a depreciation of the exchange rate which will then stimulate the production of tradables; second, it will, through the initial interest rate reduction, increase output and thus increase imports, again depreciating the exchange rate as the current account goes into deficit. The exchange rate depreciation will then boost exports and lessen imports, improving the current account and promoting growth. In the short term the leader at home will be better off. In these circumstances the home benefits of monetary policy are high.

The use of monetary policy in a floating rate system under conditions of high capital mobility creates problems for the foreign country. Monetary policy under such conditions can become a zero-sum game. The home country's attempts to reach its objectives by increasing M have a negative effect on the foreign country. Exchange rate depreciation in the home country is an appreciation abroad, the effect of which is to lower the foreign country's exports and increase its imports—basically to lower its home demand and thus reduce growth and employment in the short term. Monetary policy becomes "beggar-thy-neighbor" in these circumstances. The home country's actions to help itself make it harder for the foreign country to reach its objectives. Thus the externalities of monetary policy are high when the economy is open and exchange rates are flexible. Devising a means to control the unilateral use of monetary policy might appeal to leaders in both countries.

This is true whether monetary policy is stimulative, as above, or contractionary. If the home country contracts the money supply, then its interest rate rises and an inflow of foreign capital occurs, so that the exchange rate appreciates. This reduces the current account and, along with the effect of increased interest rate, pulls down domestic output, Y. Although the initial reduction in Y reduces demand for imports from abroad, the appreciation of the exchange rate may overwhelm this, producing an increase in foreign exports and hence foreign output, Y_F. But this may also produce negative consequences for the other countries. The appreciation of the exchange rate causes higher import prices abroad and thus induces higher wage demands, which help ignite inflation abroad. Thus, in a floating exchange rate system, monetary contraction at home to reduce inflation may just export it abroad (Krugman and Obstfeld 1991:569–70).

---

[4] Although one assumes that political leaders control monetary policy, this may not always be so. In some countries independent central banks may control the money supply, and they may be less willing to do political leaders' bidding. But as Wooley (1984), Lohmann (1995), and Clarida and Gertler (1996) have shown, even the most independent of the central bankers may respond to political pressures.

When capital is fully mobile and exchange rates are fixed, monetary policy is not an independent policy tool. The central bank must defend the exchange rate using the money supply; hence any change in M leads to an offsetting change in it as well in order to maintain the exchange rate. As Mundell (1963) showed, with capital mobility and fixed rates policy makers lose autonomous control of their monetary policy.

What about the possibility of retaliation, when capital is mobile and exchange rates are flexible? The likelihood that countries will use countervailing monetary policies against one another depends on at least two factors. First, is monetary policy seen as a domestic instrument whose effects abroad are largely unintended? If a country views the other's use of monetary policy as directly attacking it, the motivation for retaliation may be high, as in situations of competitive devaluations. Second, monetary policy may be too important domestically to be used for retaliation. If retaliation is not feasible, the home benefits from autonomous monetary policy may be high but the externalities may also be high, leaving political leaders with a mild interest in cooperation. If retaliation is feasible, demand for cooperation should be high.

It is useful to contrast this case to the situation where the home economy is closed, or where capital is not mobile between the home economy and the world. With flexible exchange rates, an increase in the money supply in the home country has the same internal effects as above but now it does not have the same external effects. Because interest rates are independent in these circumstances, change in the money supply in the home country does not affect the foreign country. There is "complete macroeconomic independence" when capital is not mobile and exchange rates are flexible (Mussa 1979:166). The externalities of monetary policy are thus eliminated. Hence one would expect political leaders' demand for cooperation to be greatly reduced when the economy is closed, since monetary policy retains its important home benefits and has few externalities. The move to an open economy with capital mobility and flexible exchange rates should thus increase the demand for monetary policy cooperation. As Mussa (1979:179) notes, "Under fixed rates, capital mobility facilitates the spread of monetary disturbance [or policy change] from one economy to the whole world. Under flexible rates, however, capital mobility magnifies the effect of a monetary disturbance [or policy change] on the economy in which it originated and results in *negative* transmission to the rest of the world."

In an open economy cooperation in the monetary area could mean a variety of outcomes, ranging from the mutual adoption of target zones, adjustable pegs, fixed exchange rates, or even monetary union. The fixing of exchange rates means that monetary policy no longer has the same internal effects. Indeed, as noted above, because of the need to maintain a fixed exchange rate, leaders cannot use monetary policy for internal objectives. Any change in the money supply affects interest rates and thus exchange

rates, requiring an opposite and equal change in the money supply in order
to return the exchange rate to its fixed level. Monetary union entails an even
greater loss of monetary sovereignty, as now the national currency is eliminated and the countries no longer have purely domestic control over money
supplies (Gros and Thygesen 1992). These cooperative policies eliminate
the externalities associated with monetary policy in open economies, but
they also eliminate national control over monetary policy.

Fiscal Policy

Monetary and fiscal policy are interesting to compare. Fiscal policy refers to
government spending and taxes, G; here I assume a debt-financed increase
in government spending, not a tax-financed one. In an open economy with
perfect capital mobility and flexible exchange rates, a change in fiscal policy
has limited or no effects on employment or inflation in the short term
because of its two contradictory effects (Dornbusch 1980; Krugman and
Obstfeld 1991; Persson and Tabellini 1990; Mussa 1979; Blackburn and
Christensen 1989; Frenkel and Razin 1992). An increase in fiscal spending
produces two consequences: it increases domestic demand, which draws in
more imports and puts downward pressure (depreciation) on the exchange
rate; it also temporarily increases interest rates, leading to capital inflows
from abroad, an appreciation of the exchange rate, and a consequent reduction in domestic demand. The initial increase in domestic growth is checked
by the currency's appreciation. Hence the net effect on growth and employment in the short run is likely to be much smaller than in the closed economy case and may even be nonexistent. If the two effects exactly counterbalance each other, then fiscal policy will have no effect on domestic growth. As
Frenkel and Razin (1992:69) conclude, "Under flexible exchange rates with
zero initial debt, a debt-financed fiscal policy loses its potency to alter the
level of economic activity; its full effects are absorbed by changes in the
exchange rate (terms of trade)." Political leaders will thus see fiscal policy as
having few home benefits.

A political leader's utility function for fiscal policy is notable since it is a
positive function of both the home and foreign fiscal policy, unlike monetary
policy (Persson and Tabellini 1990; Frenkel and Razin 1992). What about
the externalities of fiscal policy? In an open economy with flexible exchange
rates, an increase in fiscal spending at home is likely to have positive externalities for the foreign country. An increase in government spending (or a
decrease in taxes) produces both a short-term increase in domestic demand
and an appreciation of the home currency, which is equivalent to a depreciation abroad. Both these effects expand foreign output as the foreign country
is able to sell more abroad. The one negative foreign effect of a fiscal stimu-

lus is to draw foreign capital into the home country, which has contractionary effects abroad. Under conditions of full capital mobility, then, the primary effects of a fiscal policy expansion at home are expansion abroad
(Frenkel and Razin 1992:77–78). (A fiscal contraction [cuts in government
spending or increased taxes] will work to slow growth abroad as it does at
home. However, it will also lead to capital outflows from the home country,
benefiting the foreign one. Depending on the foreign country's economic
situation, this could create negative externalities.) In general, in an open
economy with flexible exchange rates fiscal policy seems to have fewer negative externalities than does monetary policy, but it also has low home effect.

In an open economy with fixed exchange rates (as compared with flexible
rates), the demand for cooperation for fiscal policy might become even less
significant. Fiscal policy under such circumstances becomes highly effective
domestically; its home benefits greatly increase from a flexible rate system.
As Frenkel and Razin (1992:50) show, "The flexible exchange rate permits
almost full insulation of the foreign economy from the consequences of the
domestic tax-financed fiscal policies... Under a fixed exchange rate ... a
fiscal expansion that induces a rightward shift of the IS schedule gains full
potency in raising the level of output because the offsetting force induced by
currency appreciation is absent." A fiscal stimulus has the same effects as
above on the home country, except now, in the presence of capital inflows
and potential exchange rate appreciation, the government must intervene
with monetary policy (stimulative) to maintain the exchange rate. The increase in the money supply necessary to lower the interest rate at home
provides a second domestic stimulus. Hence fiscal policy becomes doubly
powerful. Political actors should be even less interested in cooperating
in this situation, since the home benefits of fiscal policy have become
significant.

Under a fixed exchange rate with full capital mobility, fiscal expansion at
home may also have positive effects abroad. An increase in home government spending has two effects abroad: it increases the demand for foreign
goods and increases the world rate of interest, which lowers foreign (and
home) demand. If the interest rate effect is weak and/or home government
spending falls largely on foreign goods, then fiscal expansion will be expansionary abroad as well (Frenkel and Razin 1992:63–65). Hence home fiscal
policy will tend not to generate negative externalities for foreign countries,
again reducing countries' interest in cooperation.

The likelihood of retaliation by a foreign country for a fiscal policy change
at home depends on various factors. First, the effects of fiscal policy abroad
tend to be positively correlated with those at home; stimulus at home is
likely to lead to stimulus abroad, although to a lesser extent than at home.
Thus in an open economy with flexible or fixed exchange rates, fiscal policy
does not have the beggar-thy-neighbor quality that monetary policy does.

Depending on the goals of other states, this may make retaliation less likely. Second, if fiscal policy is seen as a purely domestic instrument, retaliation may be less likely; in addition, it may be too important domestically to be employed as a retaliatory tool. Third, the difficulties of targeting fiscal policy may reduce its utility for retaliation. In most countries fiscal policy is an area where the legislature plays a major role. Unlike monetary policy, which is usually the preserve of the executive and her central bank, fiscal policy requires numerous actors to accept changes in it.

Trade and Industrial Policy

What should the demand for trade and industrial policy cooperation by political actors look like? How does an across-the-board increase in trade protection or subsidies in the home country affect home and foreign output in the short run? (Note that this section examines the effects of these instruments on national output; the next section considers the impact on societal groups and their demands. Both these elements affect political leaders' utility functions.) Trade and industrial policy are considered as a single form of policy because each has similar effects on the trade balance. Tariffs, quotas, and subsidies change the relative prices of home and foreign goods. In the short run (and absent retaliation) such measures are likely to have a beneficial effect on home growth and employment (Dornbusch 1980; Krugman and Obstfeld 1991). A tariff will raise the price of imports and shift demand to domestic goods, thus producing a short-term increase in home output.[5] A quota will limit the number of foreign goods that can enter the home country and will again shift demand to domestic goods. (One difference between these two is that tariff revenues flow to the government whereas quota rents become industry profits.) Subsidies lower the price of the home good, thus increasing foreign demand for it and/or decreasing domestic demand for the foreign country's competing goods. In effect they increase home exports and/or decrease home imports, improving the domestic economy and hurting the foreign one. A policy maker, facing recession at home close to election time, may choose trade or industrial policy, then, to boost employment in the short run. Thus the home benefits of protection and subsidization may be powerful especially in an open economy. Indeed the more open the economy is to trade, the more powerful these effects could be.

The utility of a political leader in the trade and industrial policy area, similar to that in monetary policy, is a *positive* function of the home country's trade policy and a *negative* function of the foreign country's trade policy. The

---

[5] This depends on whether the price elasticity of demand for home imports is greater than one. If it is not, then an increase in protection may lower the volume of imports but not their overall value and hence may not lead to an increase in domestic demand.

externalities of a broad protectionist or subsidization policy are thus likely to be significant. Like monetary policy in an open economy, trade and industrial policy have beggar-thy-neighbor effects. The boost in domestic demand created by the protection or subsidization leads directly to a decline in the foreign country's exports and hence to a fall in its domestic output. The rise in home employment comes at the expense of foreign employment. The foreign policy maker is thus made worse off by the home country's trade and industrial policy. The externalities in this situation are high and negative.

The probability of retaliation depends on several factors. First, is trade or industrial policy seen as targeting the foreign country's exports? (As the strategic trade literature reminds us, subsidies can have the same targeting effect against foreign exports [Krugman 1986; Brander and Spencer 1985].) When both countries perceive this and can directly see its effects, retaliation becomes more likely. Second, the harder it is to argue that trade policy is purely a domestic matter, the more likely retaliation is. Third, if retaliation enables the foreign country to neutralize completely the internal effects of trade policy in the home country, then it also will be more likely. This is most probable when the two are trading partners. If retaliation is likely, then the net home benefits (after retaliation) for trade and industrial policy may be very low. Given the high negative externalities of trade or industrial policy, the demand for cooperation in this area should be significant. The more open the economy is to trade, the greater the externalities, and hence the stronger political leaders' demand should be for trade and industrial policy cooperation. On the other hand, given the strong home benefits of these policies, only if offsetting retaliation is very likely will cooperation bring net benefits to policy makers.

Exchange Rate Policy

The exchange rate can only be considered an independent policy tool when governments employ sterilization policies; otherwise exchange rates are endogenously determined by monetary (and fiscal) policy (Dornbusch 1980; Mussa 1979; Krugman and Obstfeld 1991; Marston 1988). The following discussion assumes sterilization. In an open economy, political leaders' demand for cooperation should be high in this issue area. When capital is fully mobile and trade is important to countries, the exchange rate has crucial consequences at home and abroad. The exchange rate tells the relative prices of home and foreign goods. Therefore, any change in the exchange rate has strong mutual effects. Since domestic income is a function of the trade balance in an open economy, changes in the exchange rate can have powerful effects on output. The home effects of a depreciation (devaluation in a fixed rate system) in the short run are to raise the relative price of imports and lower those of exports. This means that for the home country the volume of imports will fall and the volume of exports will rise. Under certain conditions demand will shift to domestic goods, and the home trade balance will improve.[6] In this situation both the home trade balance and home output will improve. Hence the exchange rate devaluation can have powerful home benefits in the short run.

For exchange rate policy, the political leader's utility is a positive function of the exchange rate, meaning that depreciation of the home currency (or, equivalently, appreciation of the foreign currency) creates temporary growth through a short-term, unexpected boost to inflation. The external costs of exchange rate policy are then substantial but negative. Like monetary, trade, and industrial policy in an open economy, exchange rate policy is beggar-thy-neighbor. It improves home output and employment in the short term at the expense of foreign output and employment. A depreciation (devaluation) at home means an appreciation abroad. This raises the cost of the foreign country's exports and lowers those of its imports, thus reducing demand and hence output in the foreign country. Under certain conditions (e.g., the Marshall-Lerner one), this worsens its trade balance, thus hurting output and employment. Hence the externalities of a change in the exchange rate can be very important and negative. The more open the economy, the larger these negative externalities will be.

Although the home benefits of exchange rate policy may be high, the potential for retaliation varies. The more exchange rate policy seems targeted against foreign countries and the more direct and visible its effects abroad are, the more likely retaliation is. In addition, when it cannot be claimed a purely domestic policy, retaliation by the foreign country is likely to be swift and offsetting. Hence the net home benefits of exchange rate policy (after retaliation) may be very low. Combined with the extremely negative externalities of exchange rate policy, this implies that the demand for cooperation should be very high.

In sum, political leaders' demand for cooperation should vary by issue area. Different policy instruments have varying domestic and external effects in an open economy, thus making cooperation more or less desirable. Countries faced with high negative externalities from another country's unilateral use of a policy instrument will evince a strong interest in cooperation. But this interest will be checked by the degree to which the same policy instrument is useful at home—that is, the extent to which it can improve the economy in the short run. If the policy instrument is very useful domestically, leaders will be reluctant to give it up in a cooperative deal. The utility

---

[6] This is the Marshall-Lerner condition: the sum of the price elasticity for foreign demand for home imports and of home import demand is greater than one (Dornbusch 1980:59–62). This condition is named after two of the economists who discovered it: Alfred Marshall and Abba Lerner.

of a policy instrument internally, however, is also a function of the costs and likelihood of retaliation by foreign countries for its use. If an instrument is useful unilaterally but provokes swift and offsetting retaliation abroad, then its actual utility is limited. In such a case, if its negative externalities are important, the demand for cooperation will be strong.

There is an important political difference between fiscal policy (G), on the one hand, and monetary policy (M), trade and industrial policy (T), and exchange rate policy (E), on the other. Changes in M, T, and E that may improve the home economy can have strong, negative effects abroad. The means to achieve one's internal goals involve shifting price disadvantages onto foreign countries; they are aggressive, beggar-thy-neighbor policies. In contrast, the consequences of fiscal policy tend to be positively correlated across countries. Depending on the other country's goals, home country fiscal policy may have positive externalities abroad. However, the demand for cooperation also depends on the likelihood of retaliation. Since this probability is difficult to know a priori, it is impossible to predict the demand for cooperation for each policy area in the abstract. Nevertheless, ceteris paribus, one would expect the demand for cooperation to be less strong in fiscal policy than in the other three issue areas.

The economic relationships described above hold only in the short run. It is assumed that political actors focus on the short term, basically until the next election. They try to maximize their utility in the short run. In the medium to long run, attempts at expansionary policies in each area will induce domestic price changes that in turn may offset their short-run effects. As many monetarists argue, the more rapidly prices adjust, the less the Phillips curve relationship used here will hold. Instead the policy changes will induce price changes (inflation), which nullify any real growth or employment gains. If the effect of a policy change on the economy before the next election is what drives leaders' behavior, then such short-term relationships are most appropriate. The more long-term oriented politicians are (and the more flexible prices are), the less the above discussion will hold true.

Will the demand for cooperation vary by the political leaders' partisan affiliation? Will governments led by left-wing parties (labor and social democratic ones) have different preferences vis-à-vis cooperation than right-wing parties (Christian democratic and conservative ones)? The utility function used above is general to all political leaders. What varies in it according to the government's partisanship is the weight given to the control of inflation versus the promotion of growth and employment. One could imagine that left-wing governments would be more concerned about growth and jobs than inflation (Hibbs 1978; Alesina and Roubini 1992); this means that growth and employment are likely to be a greater priority than inflation control. Conversely, for conservative governments, inflation control would be more important than employment. Hence the form of the

utility function does not change; rather, the weight given to the two competing objectives does.

The functional relationships described above will not change no matter
which party is in power. What will affect the demand for cooperation is how
far the economy is from its leaders' objectives. The state of the economy at
the time the leader makes her calculation is vital. If the inflation rate is high
and especially much higher than desired $(\pi - \pi^* >> 0)$, then leaders from
conservative as well as left-wing governments will be concerned about its
control, although the conservatives will be more willing to take action to
control it at any given rate. If employment and/or growth is low and/or
much lower than desired $(x - x^* << 0)$, then leaders of all parties will be
concerned but left-wing governments will be more worried. Economists
make the same point by noting that the nature of the shock that an economy
faces is crucial. They assume the economy starts out a full-employment
equilibrium and then receives a shock, either from the external economy or
internally. The nature of the shock determines what policies should be chosen (e.g., Canzoneri and Henderson 1991). The actual levels of inflation and
employment make a difference to leaders' behavior, no matter what their
partisan affiliation.

A political leader's demand for cooperation will thus vary according to
several variables. First, the more open a country's economy is and the more
important externalities are, the more its leaders should have a general interest in cooperating with other countries. In addition, the more open it is, the
less effective home macroeconomic policy instruments will be and hence
the lower the costs from cooperation (Cooper 1986:299). Second, this interest in cooperation will vary by issue area. In those areas where the net home
benefits from a policy instrument are high, there will be resistance to cooperation. As a policy instrument's negative externalities grow, interest in coordinating polices will rise. The higher the probability of foreign retaliation
that offsets a policy change, the more likely countries are to seek cooperative outcomes since their home benefits decline with the likelihood of retaliation. Different issue areas thus produce varying levels of political actors'
demand for cooperation. Third, the government's partisan orientation will
affect the weight it gives different objectives. Fourth, the state of the economy at the time will matter a great deal. As it diverges further from the
desired levels of inflation and growth, political leaders will be more motivated to seek policy change; however, this may or may not involve international cooperation. Their choice depends on the issue area and its consequences for the domestic economy. In general, a leader's interest in
cooperation will vary by both issue area and the degree of the country's
economic openness. Initiation of cooperative agreements will be most likely
by political leaders of open economies facing high negative externalities
and low home benefits from a policy instrument.

The Preferences of Societal Actors (Interest Groups)

So far I have concentrated on understanding political actors' utility functions and how their policy preferences vary with their concern for the state
of the economy. Political actors' utility also depends, as noted above, on the
preferences of interest groups. The distributional consequences of policies
motivate interest groups; they seek to maximize income, and policies affect
their ability to do so.

Such societal groups play two roles in the process of international cooperation. First, they serve as pressure groups who, through their ability to contribute campaign funds and mobilize voters, directly shape the preferences
of the executive and the legislature; that is, the preferences of interest
groups often have a significant bearing on political actors' policy preferences. Second, they also play a more indirect role by acting as information
providers to political actors, especially legislators, who have their own preferences but are not completely informed about the ramifications of policies.
In this role they do not directly shape the political actors' preferences but
rather act as signalers, alerting political actors to the consequences of various policies, in this case international cooperative ones. "There is theoretical
and empirical evidence that strategic information transmission through lobbying [of] individual candidates may . . . lead to a somewhat different view
of how legislative policy is influenced" by interest groups (Austen-Smith
1991:88).

For these two reasons the likelihood and terms of international cooperative agreements depend on the preferences of the interest groups involved
in the policy area. In particular, their preferences relative to those of other
domestic political actors—that is, the structure of domestic preferences—is
of critical importance. Thus this section explores how interest groups' preferences are likely to be shaped and where they are likely to fall relative to
the executive and the legislature.

Whereas political actors' preferences for international cooperation are a
function of electoral calculations, the preferences of societal groups depend
on the *distributional* consequences of international agreements. The effect
of cooperative agreements on societal actors' incomes is the major determi-
nant of their support or opposition to such agreements. The distributional
impact of a policy change resulting from a cooperative agreement determines the preferences of interest groups. They will prefer policies that increase their income over those that decrease it, and most prefer those that
maximize their income. Hence these groups' preferences will depend on the
issue area. Monetary policy coordination, for instance, will have different
consequences than trade policy liberalization. As for political actors, then,
interest groups' preferences will vary *by issue area* and by the specific policy

changes that an international agreement proposes. Thus even though interest groups are rarely, if ever, the formal initiators of cooperative negotiations, they may critically influence cooperation. As Evans, Jacobson, and Putnam (1993:403) conclude in their survey of two-level games, "There is little doubt that agenda-setting usually reflects leaders' preferences. International initiatives in direct response to constituency pressure were surprisingly rare." Nevertheless, societal groups have much indirect influence through their role in influencing the preferences and information available to political actors.

"Distributional politics" arguments hold that the preferences and political pressures emanating from societal groups are key determinants of both foreign economic policy and international cooperation (Gourevitch 1986; Milner 1988; Rogowski 1989; Frieden 1991). Two different logics lie behind this claim: the first emphasizes the informal ratification of policies by interest groups, and the second focuses on the effects of the loss of "business confidence." First, political leaders may listen to the preferences of societal groups because they know their policies are "voted" on after the fact. Politicians desire to retain their offices and hence to be reelected. Thus they anticipate the reaction of societal groups and avoid policies that will get them into electoral trouble. Loss of campaign support can end a politician's career. As the political scandals in Japan, Italy, and France recently make clear, the relationship between business and politicians is one of tight interdependence: politicians need campaign financing, and interest groups hope to maximize income and achieve a "friendly" regulatory environment. As Ramseyer and Rosenbluth (1993:27–28) note about Japan, "The personal-vote electoral strategy [of politicians] is obviously very expensive . . . Where does the LDP [Liberal Democratic Party] get this money and how is the party able to raise so much of it? Corporate contributors are willing to bankroll the LDP because of what they get in return: policies that favor them at the expense of the median voter. Producers pay the LDP for favorable budgetary, tax and regulatory treatment. . . . The biggest gainers [from this system] appear to be the LDP Dietmembers who greatly enhance their chances of political survival."

The distribution of costs and benefits of cooperation provides a map for understanding which groups will be for cooperation and which will be against it. The domestic distribution of the costs and benefits of cooperation helps determine cooperation's feasibility. Sectoral groups' reactions to the proposed cooperative policies will be a major concern for political actors. They will anticipate these reactions—or learn about them in the process of negotiating cooperation internationally—and choose policies based on them. In this sense all policies must be "ratified" domestically, including decisions to cooperate. "International economic issues touch the pocketbooks of increasing numbers of voters, and international agreements, no matter how attractive as a matter of abstract principle, must win 'ratification'—informally, if not formally—in the arena of domestic politics" (Putnam and Bayne 1987:276). Cooperation results when it aligns with the policy preferences of key societal groups in a number of countries.

The second logic behind the influence of interest groups is associated with Lindblom (1977), who argued that political leaders will be especially attuned to business interests. Capitalists in effect hold a "privileged position" within the polity. Like Marxist analysis, this approach focuses attention on the preferences of business, ignoring other groups. Since political leaders' electoral prospects depend on the state of the economy, they must be concerned with those groups that can directly affect the economy. In capitalist economies business controls the majority of private investment and job growth, both of which are key to electoral success. Hence political leaders must avoid policies that undermine "business confidence" or, worse yet, that provoke capital flight. They need to anticipate business's reactions to their policies and pursue those that win business "support" or else risk losing their offices.

Bates and Lien (1985), following Hirschman (1970), take this argument a step further, noting that in an open economy the influence of capitalists who can leave the country becomes ever more powerful vis-à-vis the government. To prevent capital from leaving (or not entering) the country, the government must anticipate business's preferences. In this way business exercises a structural constraint on politics and perhaps an increasing one as the economy grows more open. International cooperation will be geared toward policies that receive business support. Some have suggested that this is a key explanation for both the EC's Single Market Program (Sandholtz and Zysman 1989) and its monetary coordination efforts (Frieden 1991). Like the first argument, this one also depends on anticipated reaction. Through their influence over the economy, interest groups play a major, although often opaque, role in shaping policy making and thus influencing international cooperation.

What shapes the preferences of interest groups in international cooperation? To address this question, one must first ask who these interest groups are. This is equivalent to asking which groups are important for which policies. For interest groups, international cooperation implies some kind of policy change that has distributional consequences. It helps or hurts their income. Following Bates (1981) I use a broad concept of "income." He notes that societal groups worry about three factors: their income, the cost of the products they consume, and the cost of the products they use as inputs into their production. Their net income is equivalent to subtracting the latter two from the former. Policies that produce gains in a group's income and reductions in the costs of its inputs and consumption goods should be supported by that societal group. Policies that create losses in a group's income and gains in the costs of its consumption goods and inputs should be opposed by the group.

If a group is unaffected by the policy change, it is unlikely to become involved in the issue area. Those groups whose income is most affected by a cooperative agreement should be the ones most involved. For instance, negotiations to organize the shipping industry worldwide should involve the shipping industry as a major player, since such an international agreement will have a major distributional impact on these producers. Thus the groups involved in each cooperative negotiation should be somewhat different. Trade liberalization, for example, might evoke the attention of different societal groups than would monetary policy coordination.

Scholars differ over the appropriate interest groups to examine. At the broadest level some suggest that factors of production are of central interest; others analyze certain sectors of the economy, such as industry, agriculture, labor, and finance; still others look at particular industries or firms (Milner 1988; Rogowski 1989; Frieden 1991; Magee, Brock, and Young 1989; Smith and Wanke 1993). The approach chosen here avoids this question by examining each issue area separately. The characteristics of the issue area itself should determine how the interest groups are defined. Depending on the distributional consequences of the agreement, factors of production may be a better characterization; for others, firms and industries may be most appropriate. In any international negotiation the groups who stand to gain or lose economically from the policies are the ones who will become politically involved. Those who stand to lose should block or try to alter any international agreement, whereas those who may profit from it should push for its ratification.

Although the theoretical specification of interest groups and their preferences for every issue area has not been completed, two areas have a fairly well-developed model of societal preferences: trade and exchange rate policy. In the former a voluminous literature on the "endogenous" theory of trade exists (e.g., Caves 1976; Lavergne 1983; Milner 1988; Schonhardt-Bailey 1991; McKeown 1983; Magee, Brock, and Young 1989; Trefler 1993; for a critique, see Nelson 1988). These arguments associate industries' preferences on trade policy with two factors: the structure of the industry and its degree of international ties. The latter variable is most important here. The argument is frequently made and empirically supported that industries (or firms) with international exports and multinational operations are less protectionist than similar but domestically oriented industries. The former support trade liberalization, whereas the latter seek protection. This divide between internationally oriented and domestically oriented industries may be reproduced in international negotiations over trade policy. When the issue in those negotiations is trade liberalization versus protection, these two groups should be pitted against each other.

In the exchange rate area Frieden (1991) has provided the most comprehensive and systematic discussion of the role of sectoral groups in policy making and international coordination. Using economic theory he deduces the preferences of various economic sectors along two different dimensions of the exchange rate: the flexibility of exchange rates (fixed versus floating exchange rates) and the external value of the home currency (high versus low levels of the exchange rate). Frieden's argument proposes "systematic predictions about private-sector attitudes toward the exchange rate mechanism (ERM) of the EMS. [He] expect[s] the ERM to be most favorable for, and to evince the most enthusiasm from, firms in the financial sector, major exporters, and diversified multinational corporations with major investments or customers in the EC" (1991:447–48).

Next, Frieden (1991:450) links these preferences with the decision to cooperate:

> [The] differential distributional effects of such policy coordination are relevant. . . . [T]hose whose economic activities are most sensitive to foreign financial and exchange market conditions [will] be most favorable to the sacrifice of national policy autonomy implied by policy coordination. International investors, traders and the like are apt to be well disposed, while those in the nontradables sector—whose business may be harmed by the sacrifice of autonomy with little or no corresponding benefit from coordination—are prone to be opposed. . . . How successful the various interest groups will be at obtaining their objectives will vary from case to case and from country to country.

Some disagree with Frieden's derivation of sectoral interests. Others claim that the financial sector is not in favor of fixed rates but instead prefers flexible ones because of the profits that can be made from exchange rate fluctuations (Destler and Henning 1989:132–34; Funabashi 1989:122, 126). Henning (1994:22–35) argues that bank-industry relations determine bank preferences toward the exchange rate. Others take exception to the idea that interest groups are interested in, or can even understand their preferences about, exchange rates (Giovannini 1993; McNamara 1994).

Common to the arguments about trade and exchange rate policy is the sharp divide that is drawn between the preferences of domestically oriented groups and internationally oriented ones. Groups that derive their income primarily from domestic markets are often the opponents of international cooperation. On the other hand, groups that derive much of their income from international markets (exports, multinational production or services, international finance) tend to be supporters of international cooperation. A central dividing line, then, among societal groups depends on their degree of exposure to the international economy. This suggests that once more the degree of a country's economic *openness* is a key factor. The extent of the national economy's openness reflects the magnitude of the internationally oriented sector of the economy (relative to the domestic sector). Openness matters because it shapes how policies affect societal actors' income but also because it creates externalities from other countries' policies that interest groups want to capture or avoid.

As with political actors, the preferences of societal actors will vary with the degree of exposure they have to the international economy. In general, the greater the extent of economic openness, the closer groups will be tied to the international economy and the more "dovish" their preferences will be. Economic openness should thus create both more dovish political leaders and interest groups.

These arguments about preferences provide a baseline for predicting domestic support for and opposition to international cooperation. Societal actors' preferences depend on the differential distributional effects of policies; in turn political actors' preferences depend on the effect of policies on the overall economy and on the preferences of interest groups that support them electorally. These groups' preferences then define the structure of domestic preferences.

In the past, preference-based approaches have been on firmer ground in their predictions of groups' preferences than in their predictions about *national* policy choices. This book seeks to move beyond this earlier work: it adds political actors and strategic interaction between them and societal groups. Combining political actors' preferences with those of societal groups, the model acknowledges the interdependence among these different actors in policy making. The preferences of political and societal actors form the basis of the model, but the nature of the game among these domestic actors shapes the international outcome. Understanding policy preferences is a crucial first step, but only the first one.

The Endogeneity of Preferences?

The preferences of domestic political and social actors are a function of two factors: the issue area being considered and the national economy's degree of integration into the world economy. Integration refers to both the extent of openness and the nature of externalities imposed by others' policies. However, if preferences are shaped by the extent of economic openness, then they may be endogenous. Openness obviously arises in part as the result of prior policies and cooperation. Political leaders' earlier choices to open their economy (perhaps by cooperating) could then reinforce their desire to cooperate in the future. For instance, in the 1940s when Western nations in the General Agreement on Tariffs and Trade (GATT) decided to reduce their trade barriers, their economies became more integrated with the international economy. This new openness created stronger domestic preferences for openness, which helped promote further reductions in trade barriers. Thus, as openness grows, preferences for further cooperation may also grow. The nations of Western Europe provide another example of this. The formation of the European Community in the 1950s may have been necessary in order to generate interest in monetary cooperation later. And later, only after the Single European Act opened internal European markets was the demand for monetary union sufficient to make the Maastricht Treaty a viable option.

If one looks at what underlies preferences, prior policy choices may loom large. Plenty of other, exogenous factors have promoted openness as well: declining transportation costs and time, communications improvements, and other technological innovations (Frieden and Rogowski 1996). But preferences themselves may be partially endogenous to prior policy choices and to earlier cooperative agreements.

Nevertheless, no one-to-one, positive relationship between international cooperation and openness exists. The demand of some actors for cooperation may rise as openness grows, but other factors—namely, the nature of power sharing between the executive and the legislature and the structure of domestic preferences—also shape international outcomes. Even if (more) actors are more interested in cooperation (i.e., are more "dovish"), the domestic game will not necessarily result in a cooperative agreement. As demonstrated in the next chapter, the interaction of the foreign government, the home executive, the legislature, and interest groups in their two-level bargaining game determines the likelihood and terms of international cooperation. Understanding actors' preferences is but a first step. Their strategic interaction within defined political institutions determines the likelihood and terms of international cooperation.

Three

A Model of the Two-Level Game

COAUTHORED WITH B. PETER ROSENDORFF

THIS CHAPTER presents a formal model that reveals how domestic and international factors interact to shape cooperation among nations. It contrasts the unitary actor model against the polyarchy one and also varies the level of polyarchy to see what its effects are on international negotiations. It focuses on variations in the structure of domestic preferences—including the degree of divided government—and in the distribution of information domestically. The model shows how these variables affect the domestic ratification game and, in turn, how this affects the possibility and terms of international cooperation. It examines the effect of three factors on the likelihood and terms of an international agreement: the assumption of a polyarchic state, divided government and increases in it, and an asymmetric distribution of information domestically. It holds the domestic institutional context constant; chapter 4 discusses the effects of variations in this factor.

The goal here is to specify the conditions under which and in what ways domestic politics matters for international relations. Few, if any, studies have done this. For instance, the most systematic investigation of international and domestic theories of conflict, Bueno de Mesquita and Lalman's *War and Reason* (1992), provides a powerful argument that domestic politics affects international conflict. However, domestic politics is a black box for them: "In the domestic [game], demands are presumed to be endogenous to some domestic political process, not spelled out here, which likely varies from state to state and which precedes the actions we investigate" (36). This leaves us with an incomplete understanding of exactly how and when internal affairs will impinge on external ones. They realize this and therefore advocate that the "next step in research is to link a model like the one we propose here to appropriate models of domestic political processes" (46). This chapter undertakes just that.

The model here examines the interaction among four sets of players in a two-level game: the political executive of the home country, a foreign executive, the home country's legislature, and interest groups within the home country. It focuses on two key factors: the structure of domestic preferences and the distribution of information. First, it demonstrates the effects that different structures of domestic preferences have on international cooperation. What difference, for instance, does it make that the executive or legislature is the most hawkish player internally? What effect does increasing divergence between the preferences of the legislature and the executive have? Do increasing divisions make cooperation more or less likely? How do these divisions affect the terms of an international agreement? A central result is that the structure of domestic preferences and the distribution of information internally exert critical effects on the possibility and terms of cooperation. These features of domestic politics cannot be ignored when examining the possibility and likely terms of any international agreement.

The results here also contradict well-established beliefs about the role of these two factors. A proposition common in the literature is that divisions among the domestic actors may influence the terms of international agreements. Counterintuitively, some analysts have suggested that internal divisions in a country may create international bargaining advantages for that country; we call this the "Schelling conjecture" (Schelling 1960:28–29; Putnam 1988:440–41; Mo 1995). If a negotiator faces a situation at home where a group is strongly opposed to certain concessions, then he or she may be able to avoid making concessions in this area and thus secure a "better" agreement internationally. For instance, if farmers are rioting in the streets against reduced agricultural trade barriers that the government is considering in international negotiations, other countries may be convinced that pushing for such trade barrier reductions is a losing cause. Or, as Putnam notes, "The difficulties of winning congressional ratification are often exploited by American negotiators" (1988:440).

Little research has been done on the conditions under which the Schelling conjecture holds. The most prominent recent study concludes by drawing attention to the key factors involved while never delving into how they matter: "Domestic differences can work either to a nation's advantage or disadvantage in international negotiation. The net effect depends on the configuration of domestic factional interests, their power in internal negotiations, and on the nature of the external bargain—in particular, whether the bargain is largely about dividing a relatively fixed pie or about finding ways to bake a bigger pie" (Mayer 1992:804). The model here shows the conditions under which divided government affects the probability of agreement and when it improves the divided side's bargaining power.

Second, the model examines the effects of different distributions of information among the domestic actors. Rather than assuming that information is perfectly distributed to all actors, some are assumed to lack complete information. It is commonly argued that uncertainty—that is, incomplete information—is inimical to international cooperation. Whether on the international level (Keohane 1984; Bueno de Mesquita and Lalman 1992) or on the domestic level (Iida 1993a), lack of full information is believed to hinder cooperation. Incomplete information—and the misperceptions it allows—is the central source of conflict in the view of much scholarship in international relations and political economy. As Stein (1990:58) notes in discussing misperception that is often the result of incomplete information: "It is universally suggested that the result of misperception is conflict that would have been otherwise avoidable. Although international conflicts are often attributed to misperception, international cooperation never is." If all the actors knew each other's preferences and capabilities, then concerns over credibility, cheating, and so on, would be moot and conflict unlikely (Fearon 1995).

Contrary to this common belief, the model here shows that under certain conditions incomplete information is not harmful to cooperation. This chapter examines the role of asymmetries of information at the *domestic level*. Domestic informational problems have received little attention in international relations but, given the conclusions of the most recent and thorough empirical work on two-level games, they should be a central focus. Evans, Jacobson, and Putnam note the relative importance of incomplete information *domestically* rather than internationally:

> Our initial expectation was that the quality of available information would deteriorate sharply across national boundaries . . . Our mistake . . . was in overestimating the informational consequences of national boundaries. [Leaders'] estimates of what was ratifiable in their own domestic polities were often wrong . . . Estimates of the other side's domestic politics were often mistaken as well, but not dramatically more often than estimates of one's own polity. . . . Local misreadings of domestic politics are as likely to be responsible for failed agreements as cross-border ignorance. (1993:408–9, 411–12)

Incomplete information at the domestic level may be as important as that at the international level.

By focusing on the domestic distribution of information, the model shows that under certain conditions incomplete information need not always be a cause of inefficiency and political advantage. This argument follows the line of thinking developed in the study of American politics, which shows that incompletely informed legislators can both make "good" decisions and constrain the executive (McCubbins and Schwartz 1984; Gilligan and Krehbiel 1987; Austen-Smith and Wright 1992). The results here challenge the common wisdom about the effects of asymmetric information and lead to a new interpretation of the role of interest groups in domestic and international politics.

This chapter presents a two-level game in which the international and the domestic bargaining games are interdependent. The results of the model reflect the reciprocal influence of the two levels; the outcomes depend on *both* the international and domestic games. The two levels are modeled differently to reflect their particular characteristics. First, using a spatial model, we present a simple international bargaining game that conforms to Realist assumptions about international politics. The international game adopted does not have a well-defined institutional structure; politics on that level are assumed to be anarchic, and international negotiations are generally conducted without a constitutionally mandated sequence of moves. In contrast, the domestic ratification game incorporates a highly structured model of politics; it is a polyarchic system with a specific power-sharing arrangement among two or more sets of actors.

Initially we examine bargaining between two unitary states. Then, in steps, an increasingly complex domestic game is added. As a first step we introduce a legislature—a second actor—into the domestic environment, thus eliminating the assumption that the state is unitary. The effect of increasing polyarchy in the form of divided government is examined as well. Next we introduce asymmetric information. The legislature, lacking certain information, faces a fully informed executive. Then we bring in a third set of actors—interest groups; they provide information to the legislature, thus relieving the asymmetry of information the executive possesses. Thus an increasingly complex domestic game is added to the international one. The results in the polyarchic cases are contrasted with the pure international game between unitary states in order to address the question of *how and when domestic politics affects international negotiations.*

The results of the formal model provide the logic behind the central hypotheses advanced in this book. First, the structure of domestic preferences conditions the impact of domestic politics on international relations. A hawkish legislature makes cooperation less likely and makes agreements more favorable to the legislature when they are possible. Divided government also makes cooperation less plausible and makes any agreement reached more likely to reflect the legislature's preferences. Second, the distribution of information domestically has a vital impact on international cooperation. Under certain conditions—that is, in the presence of endorsers—asymmetric information can increase the likelihood of cooperation. In this case the endorsement of at least one interest group is necessary for successful cooperation. Agreements are also more likely to favor the legislature. Thus this chapter lays the logical groundwork for the propositions advanced in chapter 1 and examined in the case studies.

The Two-Level Game

The Players and Their Preferences

This game has four sets of players: the foreign country (F), specified here as a unitary actor, and three sets of domestic players in the home country. Internally we have the executive (the president, prime minister, or proposer), P; the legislature (the chooser), C; and domestic interest groups (called endorsers in the asymmetric information case), E. In the model all the players are utility maximizers. Each attempts to obtain a policy as close as possible to its most preferred point, that is, its "ideal point." The policy space here is represented as a single dimension. For example, if one were discussing trade negotiations, the policy choice would be a single issue such as the percentage reduction in trade barriers that all countries would accept. Using a single policy dimension is a simplification widely employed (e.g., Romer and Rosenthal 1978, 1979; Banks 1990, 1993; Ferejohn and Shipan 1990; for a multidimensional two-level game, see Milner and Rosendorff 1997).

Political actors' ideal points will reflect the policy that perfectly balances the many preferences of their constituents so that their chances of reelection are maximized. A player's utility decreases linearly and symmetrically as the implemented policy deviates from the ideal. The foreign country is a unitary actor—either a dictator or elected by majority rule—and its ideal policy is that preferred by the median voter in the foreign country, as in Mayer (1984). Similarly, the legislature and the executive seek to maximize their likelihood of reelection, and this is achieved by maintaining the overall economy at a satisfactory level and by servicing their respective constituencies while in office. Hence their optimal policies may differ. Legislators court the money and votes of both producer and consumer groups present in their constituencies, and thus will identify a policy that balances these interests and maximizes its electoral returns. Since most legislatures operate by majority rule, the preferred policy of the median member of the legislature becomes that of the entire house. The executive behaves similarly but has a more dispersed, national constituency (Lohmann and O'Halloran 1994). Call these preferred policies p, f, and c for players P, F, and C, respectively. In this chapter we vary the actors' preferences to examine the effect changes in these preferences have on international cooperation; hence our results are general to any specification of preferences.

The International Level: The Nash Bargaining Solution

To model the international game, we use the Nash Bargaining Solution (NBS). We assume only two players are involved: the foreign government, F, and the home country's executive, P. This is equivalent to assuming that we have two unitary states. The use of a two-player game here does not significantly alter our results and seems reasonable since de facto many international negotiations take place bilaterally. Even in multilateral forums, bargaining is usually conducted by the two key players negotiating first and then the other states signing on to this agreement. This, for instance, is how GATT operated through the principal supplier norm. The principal producers and buyers of a good negotiated the trade barrier reductions, and then other countries accepted this agreement. Many multilateral negotiations are thus a series of bilateral negotiations that are later "multilateralized" by the states with less at stake in each issue.

We use the Nash Bargaining Solution to solve this game because it is a simple and well-accepted bargaining model that captures the primary features of the international system. The NBS provides a method for finding a "reasonable" solution to a bargaining problem in an environment without strict rules for negotiation. The solution is reasonable in that the outcome is nondictatorial (neither bargainer can enforce his or her will without the consent of the other); it is symmetric (if the bargainers are identical, we would insist the outcome be one of identical shares); and it is Pareto optimal. Intuitively the NBS will be struck by rational players if and only if it gives each a utility at least as large as the players could guarantee themselves in the absence of an agreement and if there is no other agreement that both would prefer (Nash 1950; Binmore 1992:180–91).

Two aspects of this game make the NBS valuable for representing international negotiations. International bargaining often takes place without a well-developed institutional framework; there is a lack of authoritative norms or rules, for instance, about which player goes first, who gets to make the last offer, and so on. The NBS provides a reasonable solution in such circumstances. The bargaining mechanism is kept unspecified in order to capture the anarchy of international politics where rules and institutions are less well developed than domestically. As the results show, a common outcome of this game is no cooperation, which accords well with Realist predictions about the difficulties of cooperation under anarchy. The imposition of negotiating rules and institutions would provide more structure for the international political arena and would probably make the no-cooperation outcome less likely than in the NBS case. This, too, reflects the debate in international relations theory, where non-Realists, who believe the international system is better institutionalized, tend to see cooperation as more likely (Keohane 1984, 1989).

The NBS is appealing as a solution concept for another reason; its outcomes are intuitively satisfying. The Nash Bargaining Solution implies that the players split the difference when their bargaining powers are equal. This not only accords with our intuition and with Realist thought but also has experimental support (Crawford 1990). When bargaining powers are not equal, the more powerful player obtains more. For these reasons the NBS seems to be a good model to use to represent international politics.[1] It is less useful for the domestic side, however.

[1] The main alternative to the NBS—the Rubinstein alternating-offer game (Rubinstein 1982) which converges to the NBS when offers are made fast enough—has several drawbacks, most notably the excessive structure it places on the international game. It imposes an infinite-horizon, alternating-offer structure on negotiations over a pie that shrinks over time. Its results

The Domestic Level: The Agenda-Setter Model

To capture the essence of domestic politics, the model under discussion employs a version of the agenda-setter, take-it-or-leave-it (TILI) bargaining game (Romer and Rosenthal 1978, 1979; Rosenthal 1989; Banks 1990, 1991, 1993). The game here is modified since there are two agenda setters: the home country's executive, P, and the foreign country, F. In most countries the executive and the legislature share decision-making powers. The executive branch has the power to initiate policies vis-à-vis other countries; the executive can set the agenda in foreign affairs to a considerable extent. To negotiate agreements with foreign countries and to implement foreign policies, however, the executive often needs a vote of confidence from the legislative branch.

A broad notion of ratification is employed here. In some circumstances political leaders in the executive branch—whether the prime minister, president, chancellor, or premier—are required by the national constitution to have an international agreement approved by their legislature. Hence the executive leadership must negotiate an agreement that is acceptable to a majority of the legislature, and that majority can be a simple plurality or some supramajority (e.g., two-thirds or three-fifths). In Denmark, for instance, parliament must give simple majority approval to international agreements that do not transfer powers abroad; however, a five-sixths majority is necessary when these agreements do transfer powers beyond the state (Gjørtler 1993:357). In the United States, for example, any treaty negotiated by a president must be approved by two-thirds of the U.S. Senate. In cases of formal ratification the executive will be concerned about obtaining legislative approval, which will affect how she negotiates. Bringing home an unratifiable agreement is likely to be costly both domestically and internationally. The executive will thus need to anticipate the reaction of the legislature to any proposal it accepts internationally and make sure that it is acceptable domestically.

Ratification can also be less formal. If a political leader needs to change a domestic law, norm, or practice because of the cooperative agreement, then even if a formal vote on the agreement is not required, the domestic change itself becomes a vote on the agreement. This is also the case if the agreement requires any budgetary changes. In Great Britain, for example, this is standard practice. Britain's Parliament is not required to vote on any international agreement that the prime minister negotiates, but any legal or budgetary change that the agreement entails must be approved. Because most

---

show that the first-mover advantage is significant; however, in international politics there is no established rule for determining the sequence of moves. The players' discount rates also play an important role.

agreements do involve alterations in either existing laws or national budgets, parliament in effect exercises a right of ratification over international agreements. As Jones notes, in the United Kingdom "the government's very existence depends on retaining the confidence of the [House of] Commons, . . . especially the back-benchers" (1991:125). But, as Campbell states:

> Both the government and opposition parties must expect back-bench revolts that force withdrawal from key policy positions or, worse, embarrassing defeats in votes. For example, on May 19, 1980, Margaret Thatcher's government withdrew retroactive application of sanctions against Iran when Conservative whips found that as many as 100 of their back-benchers were prepared to vote against the government on the provision. When U.S. officials wondered out loud what type of British government could fail to deliver on a key international agreement, Lord Carrington, then the foreign secretary, directed a mini-course on British politics to Secretary of State Edmund Muskie: any British government relies on Parliament for its support. (1983:12–13)

In addition, if the executive needs the assistance or acquiescence of a domestic group to implement the international agreement, then it must obtain this group's approval of the agreement and "ratification" becomes necessary. For instance, if the cooperation of the steel industry is needed for an international agreement regulating steel production, then only if the agreement is acceptable to the industry will it be implemented. This situation is especially likely in nondemocratic countries where such groups as the military, big business, or labor organizations can exercise a veto over international agreements.

Finally, in many political systems, if the leadership negotiates an agreement that could hurt large or important segments of the country, domestic complaints about it will induce the legislature to call for some more formal or stringent form of ratification. This may be a consequence of party competition. An agreement that is contentious domestically will often induce the political parties outside the governmental majority to use it as an electoral weapon. These opposition parties will then call for a ratification vote, largely to gain competitive advantage in upcoming elections. Majority parties may also seek such a ratification vote in order to avoid or assign blame for such an agreement. For instance, during ratification of the Maastricht Treaty in Germany, as opinion polls showed that public concern over the treaty was rising, the opposition Social Democrats were able to force the government to put the treaty to a two-thirds vote in parliament rather than a simple majority vote, thus forcing the government to win the support of both the Länder in the Bundesrat and Social Democrats in the Bundestag. Generally the more domestically contentious the agreement is, the more likely the government will be faced with a more formal or stringent vote of ratification. Domestic ratification will shape political leaders' behavior in the international negotiations. *Anticipated reaction* will be at work.

This domestic ratification game is a central element of the model. The executive and the legislature share power in that the legislature must ratify the international agreement that the executive submits. The executive and the foreign country know this in advance and realize that any proposed agreement must survive this domestic test before it can be implemented. The legislature does not have the power to amend the proposed agreement; any attempt to do so constitutes its rejection and necessitates renewed negotiations with the other countries. Hence the executive proposes anticipating the reaction of the legislature, which in turn disposes. The next chapter examines the effect of changing this institutional structure.

The amount of information the actors possess also matters. Initially all the actors are assumed to have complete information; later this assumption is relaxed in order to contrast cases of complete and incomplete information. Asymmetric information is introduced: the median legislator is assumed not to be fully informed about the foreign country's most preferred outcomes and thus is uncertain about the exact contents of the proposed agreement. Under asymmetric information the model introduces an additional feature—the presence of domestic "endorsers." Because of the median legislator's lack of information, domestic groups with more complete knowledge of the proposed policy serve as information providers. Thus the effects of asymmetric information in the presence and absence of endorsers is considered.

Sequence of Moves

The sequence of moves in this game reflects the interaction of the international and domestic games. In period 1 the home executive P negotiates with the foreign executive F over a policy choice—say, the percentage of reduction in trade barriers—and an agreement, which we call agreement a, is reached. In period 2 the legislature C then ratifies or rejects the proposed agreement. If the agreement is rejected by the legislature, the status quo q becomes the outcome, meaning no cooperation is the result. That ends the game in the complete information environment.

The appendix of this book and Milner and Rosendorff (1996) contain a full specification of the model used and the proofs. This chapter presents the results using simple graphs that map the possible equilibrium outcomes onto the status quo points. There are three key issues:

1. How does the assumption of a polyarchic state affect international cooperation? When we assume that domestic groups share decision-making powers, how does this affect the prospects for cooperation?

2. How does increasingly divided government affect the possibility and terms of international cooperation?

3. How does the distribution of information domestically affect cooperation?

The Outcomes

International Negotiations without Domestic Politics

Figure 3.1 shows the results of a two-player international game without any domestic politics, where P is the executive (the president or prime minister) negotiating in the home country and F is the foreign country. The international game here assumes complete and perfectly symmetric information. The ideal points of P and F (p and f, respectively) are common knowledge, as is the position of the status quo, q. Each state is a unitary, rational actor. We assume P and F have no domestic political considerations that are not factored into their ideal points. The horizontal axis depicts all the possible values of the status quo, q. The vertical axis represents a continuum of policy outcomes on a single issue. It captures both the actors' ideal points and the outcomes of the negotiations (a). The darker line represents the equilibrium policy choices given the value of the status quo, as shown along the horizontal axis.

What are the equilibria of the NBS in this simple model? Note in Figure 3.1 that when $f < q < p$, the status quo is always the outcome. No agreement is the result because a mutually profitable bargain is not possible. When q takes any other value, mutually profitable bargains can be made. This may mean, however, that in the bargain one player ends up better off than the other; there may be asymmetric gains, but a rational player will accept this as long as it is better for him than remaining at the status quo.

Figure 3.1 shows that when the status quo is not between p and f, agreement is possible. It also demonstrates that the cooperative outcome will always lie between the two actors' ideal points, and exactly where within this area is determined by the location of q. If $q > p > f$, then p is the outcome; conversely, when $q < f < p$, then f is the equilibrium. The player with the ideal point closest to the status quo exerts greater influence. This is a fairly standard outcome in bargaining analysis. The actor with the best alternative to the agreement has greater leverage (Raiffa 1982). The status quo here should be thought of as the reversion level, or the outcome when negotiations fail: it need not be the status quo ante. Moreover, power in this game arises from the ability to set the reversion level. If one player can establish what happens in the event of no agreement, that player can exercise much control over the terms of the agreement.

As the difference between the countries (p and f) grows, two implications follow. First, the area of no agreement grows ($f < q < p$) so that cooperation becomes less likely. Second, the constraint exercised by the status quo grows. As the difference between the actors ($p - f$) increases, the actors are forced to accept more extreme outcomes. When $q < p << f$, then F will accept P's ideal point, which is now much farther away. These results coincide with conventional wisdom.

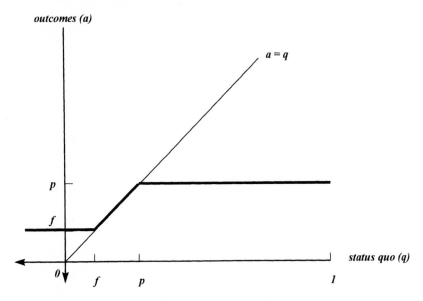

Figure 3.1 The International Game: No Domestic Politics

What is surprising about these results is that no cooperation is frequently the outcome in the *complete* information setting. Incomplete or asymmetric information is not necessary for the failure of cooperation among nations. Unlike many other studies, these results show that the difficulties of cooperation are not the fault of incomplete information; even with complete information, international cooperation may not be possible. Unitary actors are also not a guarantee of cooperation.

Domestic Politics and Complete, Symmetric Information

Now compare the unitary actor case discussed above with Figure 3.2 where we introduce domestic politics in its simplest form. We assume a polyarchic state by adding a ratification game. We introduce a parliament, labeled C, that must "ratify" any agreement negotiated internationally. The parliament takes some kind of vote—on a new law, budget allocation, or constitutional amendment—that allows it to accept or reject the executive's proposal. C is portrayed as a unitary actor, representing the median voter in the parliament; therefore C's vote decides the outcome of the ratification contest. The legislature must either accept the proposal negotiated by P and F or reject it and return to the status quo. It does not have amendment powers. We maintain the assumption of full and symmetric information in this section: P, C, and F all know one another's preferences and the nature of the proposed agreement. The parliament, which must approve the agreement by a major-

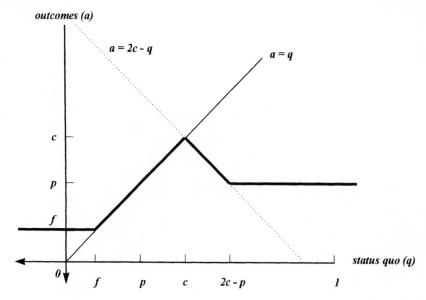

Figure 3.2 Domestic Politics and Complete Information, $p < c$

ity vote, knows the preferences of P and F and the nature of the agreement. P and F likewise know that the agreement they negotiate must be ratified by C, and they know exactly what terms C will accept.

Legislators seek to maximize their electoral prospects, and thus their preferences are dependent on a weighted sum of the preferences of their constituents—both voters generally and interest groups. The preferences of interest groups thus help shape the median legislator's ideal point. If the legislature accepts an agreement far removed from its interest groups' preferences, it must pay for this in lost electoral support, campaign funds, votes, and so on. Conversely, if the legislature adopts a policy that sends the economy into recession, it may lose the support of voters in general. For example, legislators should favor a trade policy that balances the preferences of import-competing firms and their labor unions, on the one hand, and of consumers and export businesses represented in their constituencies, on the other.

Figure 3.2 shows the outcome of the ratification game when the executive's preferences are closer to those of the foreign country than are the legislature's ($f < p < c$). The legislature is a "hawk" because its ideal point differs most from the foreign executive's. In Figure 3.2 the vertical axis represents the players' ideal points and the proposed agreement; the horizontal axis represents the position of the status quo. The darker line shows the equilibrium agreement reached along the vertical axis, given the position of the status quo along the horizontal one. It demonstrates when cooperation is possible and whose preferences are more closely adhered to by any agree-

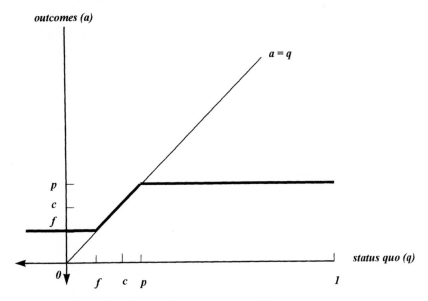

outcomes (a)

$a = q$

p

c

f

status quo (q)

0 f c p 1

Figure 3.3 Domestic Politics and Complete Information, $p > c$

ment when the structure of preferences is such that the legislature is extremely nationalist or hawkish. Figure 3.3 shows the outcomes when the structure of preferences is altered and now the executive is most hawkish ($f < c < p$). The structure of domestic preferences affects the ratification game and hence the cooperative outcomes.

When the executive is the most hawkish, as in Figure 3.3, domestic politics has *no* effect on the international negotiations. This is evident since the equilibrium outcomes in Figures 3.1 and 3.3 are exactly the same. In the domestic game when $f < c < p$, the legislature cannot exercise any constraint on the executive. This is true even when the status quo is closest to the legislature. The executive's autonomy is maximized when she is a hawk. For example, when the status quo is in between f and c, no agreement must be the outcome, for neither C nor P will move to F's side of the status quo, and vice versa. When the status quo is between P and C ($f < c < q < p$), the legislature is still without influence since P will never accept any proposal less than the status quo. This is exactly the opposite conclusion reached by Evans, Jacobson, and Putnam (1993:399) in their final assessment. They imply that the executive will pay a high domestic price for her intransigence. But it is unclear why this should be the case. How can the legislature or interest groups punish the executive or credibly threaten to do so? In addition, if they admit that the executive is the agenda setter, how can these groups force the executive to initiate cooperative negotiations against her will when she is a hawk? Being too dovish erodes one's influence.

When preferences domestically are structured differently $(f < p < c)$, domestic politics plays a significant role. The similarities between Figures 3.1 and 3.2 show the conditions under which international politics continues to dominate. Remember that Figure 3.2 is drawn for the case of $p < c$. When $q < f$, the equilibrium is always f.[2] When $q > (2c - p)$, then p is the equilibrium. Hence, if the status quo (or no agreement point) takes an extreme value (far from P or F), there are few constraints on the international negotiators. The legislature C is again unable to influence the negotiations. In addition, if q lies between p and f, the status quo is the outcome, as in the international game. In these circumstances the domestic political game has little effect.

Under what conditions does domestic politics matter? Consider now what happens when the status quo is between p and c. If P and F negotiate to the point p, C will reject such an agreement and implement the status quo since q is closer to c than p is. Hence for P and F to extract a ratification, they must offer q or better. The best ratifiable agreement, then, is q which is offered and accepted. So no cooperation is the outcome when the status quo is between p and c. P and F are unable to cooperate to realize the joint gains available under the international game.

Now consider what happens when the status quo is close to c (i.e., $f < p < c < q$) but not too extreme (i.e., $c < q < [2c - q]$). For every $q > c$ there is a point $(2c - q)$ to the left of c that C finds indifferent to q; that is, the utility for C associated with the status quo is equal to the utility obtained at $2c - q$. Since C is indifferent between q and $2c - q$, we allow C to accept an offer of $2c - q$ if it is made. Now P and F both prefer $2c - q$ to q when $q > c$. So P and F offer $2c - q$, a point that C will accept. In this region, then, domestic politics exercises a substantial constraint on the international negotiations. The negotiators will have to offer a cooperative agreement that is ratifiable, but it is one that they do not like as much.

Comparison of the international game and the domestic politics game shows what happens when polyarchy is introduced in its most basic form. When the legislature and executive share decision-making power in a ratification game, there are three key findings. First, *international agreement is less likely when domestic politics is involved*. With domestic politics, there is a range $(p < q < c)$ where the status quo is the outcome although mutual gains for the international negotiators simultaneously exist and remain unexploited. The range where q is the outcome expands when the legislature and executive share decision-making power. Hence the presence of polyarchy makes international cooperation *less* likely than in the international game. It is not just anarchy but also domestic politics that makes cooperation

---

[2] This is because F is not assumed to have any domestic politics. Once we relax this assumption, then the area $(q < f)$ is affected by domestic pressures. Generally domestic politics has no influence only when the status quo lies between p and f or is extreme.

difficult. This result suggests that even Realists underestimate the difficulties of international cooperation.

Second, in the range $c < q < (2c - p)$, the preferences of the parliament, C, have an impact on the nature of the international agreement. In this interval C's indifference point $(2c - q)$ becomes the equilibrium rather than the point p as in the case with no domestic politics. P and F find it necessary to compromise for there is no escaping the constraint exercised by the parliament under these conditions; they must agree to an outcome that they would not otherwise choose. They would prefer the outcome in Figure 3.1 where the NBS is P's ideal point. But in this range C can make a credible threat to opt for the status quo instead of the proposal preferred by P and F. *Domestic power sharing changes the terms of the agreement*; the terms will reflect C's preferences more closely. Power to define the outcome of an international negotiation thus depends not only on states' balance of capabilities but also on their domestic politics.

Third, *as the status quo moves further and further from c, the legislature's influence over the negotiations weakens*. When $q > (2c - p)$, C loses all influence over the outcome; the international negotiators will no longer feel constrained by the legislature, and they will return to their unconstrained NBS. C's threat to choose the status quo instead of the proposal that P and F preferred becomes incredible at this point. This underlines the importance of the status quo, or the reversion point. As in the international negotiations, the actor closest to the status quo has greater leverage but only up to a certain point. When the status quo becomes extreme but is still closest to the legislature, the executive gains influence largely because of her agenda-setting powers. At some point the executive's ideal agreement becomes more appealing for the legislature than the no-cooperation point. These results hold in the particular power-sharing game we examine here, that is, the ratification game. But in general the greater the legislature's capacity to initiate or amend any agreement negotiated, the more influence it will have no matter where the reversion point is, as the next chapter will show. If the legislature can set the reversion point, then its influence will be maximized.

Divided Government and Complete, Symmetric Information

What happens to international cooperation when divisions among the domestic actors rise, ceteris paribus? In particular, do growing differences between the executive's and the legislature's preferences matter? Divided government refers to a situation where the political party controlling the executive is not the same as that in control of the legislature. This occurs when the executive's and the median legislator's ideal points are far apart; the further apart, the more divided the government. In other words it is a function of how much the prime minister's or the president's preferences differ from those of the median legislator who will make the deciding vote in the ratification contest. Depending on the ratification process, this may be the legislator whose vote represents a simple majority or a supramajority.

As chapter 2 argued, divided government is possible in both presidential and parliamentary systems. It is most likely in multiparty systems—whether presidential or parliamentary—and in two-party systems when party discipline is a problem. Divided government is a common condition for multiparty systems; as Laver and Shepsle (1991:254) point out, among parliamentary systems, single-party majority governments have been a small minority among the advanced industrial countries since 1945, less than 15 percent. Most governments in these countries (87 percent) have been multiparty coalitions where the divisions are either internal to the government or between the government and legislature or both. Budge and Keman (1990:209) show that among twenty advanced industrial democracies only five have never had coalition governments during the period from 1946 to 1985: the United Kingdom, the three ex-Commonwealth countries (Australia, New Zealand, and Canada), and the United States. Since the United States has faced divided government, in the postwar years only four democracies have had long periods of unified government. Divided government, then, is a problem for more than just presidential systems; it is liable to occur in multiparty parliamentary systems as well, which account for most of the long-standing democracies in the West.

A fourth conclusion is that divided government has negative consequences for international cooperation. *The more divided the government, the less likely cooperation becomes.* To see the effects of divided government, once again look at Figure 3.2.[3] As p and c diverge, two consequences emerge. First, the area of no cooperation increases; because the range of $p < q < c$ increases, cooperation thus becomes less likely. Second, the legislature will exercise a greater constraint on the international negotiations. The region where the legislature's indifference point dominates ($c < q < [2c - p]$) will expand. *Hence, as domestic divisions grow, international agreement will become less likely, and where it does occur, the terms of the agreement will more likely reflect the parliament's preferences.*

In general, comparison of the unitary actor international game with the two-level game shows that the addition of domestic politics in the form of a ratification game makes international agreements more difficult to conclude and may change their terms. International explanations of cooperation— whether Realist or Neoliberal Institutionalist—may substantially overesti-

ture of domestic preferences is such that the executive is the most hawkish,
$< c < p$), a rise in divided government means less cooperation but only
diverging.

tic politics leads to an overly optimistic view of countries' ability to make agreements. Moreover, the terms of any agreement reflect more than just the balance of power between the countries; domestic politics also shapes these terms.

These results hold in the presence of domestic politics in both countries. When both F and P have to worry about their respective parliaments, international agreement becomes even more unlikely, as the area where the status quo dominates grows; the area between the median legislator in the foreign country and the foreign executive ($c_F < q < f$) becomes one of no cooperation. Similarly the parliament in F, C_F, may now exercise a constraint on the nature of the agreement. When $q < c_F$, then the parliament's indifference point ($2c_F - q$) constrains the two negotiators. The nature of the agreement here also increasingly diverges from that most preferred by P and F when they are not constrained by domestic politics. As one might expect, when both sides are concerned with their domestic politics the constraints on the negotiators are multiplied.

Finally, in cases where all the parties have complete information, the legislature will never reject an agreement, no matter what the structure of preferences or the degree of polyarchy. With full information, either the executive will know beforehand that no mutually profitable agreement can be reached or will anticipate the legislature's preferences correctly. Hence negotiations either never occur or are successful. Because ratification sometimes fails, it seems reasonable to modify the model to be able to account for these otherwise anomalous cases.

Domestic Politics with Asymmetric Information

The results so far have assumed that all the actors know each other's ideal points, the nature of the proposed agreement, and the reversion point q. Although this is a useful baseline, in a polyarchy, asymmetric information is likely to exist. The addition of incomplete information makes ratification failure possible. Some actors will not be fully informed; others will have private information. The less-informed group must worry about being exploited and hence will often reject agreements that have been concluded by the better-informed partner. Asymmetric information may create inefficiencies as well as political advantages.

Here we assume that the legislature C is not fully informed about the nature of the agreement that P and F have negotiated. C does not know F's preferences with certainty, but P and F are fully informed; they have private knowledge about the nature of the agreement, which is reasonable since they negotiated it without C. This need not mean that no legislators were involved in the international negotiations. Some legislators may have full information about the agreement and may have participated in its negotiation. The median legislator, however, is not a policy expert. In most democracies parliaments have few resources; legislative committees and staffs, when they exist, are small and weak. Legislators depend heavily on interest groups and political parties for cues on how to vote (Lijphart 1984; Peters 1991).

This assumption implies an asymmetry of information domestically. Members of parliament are constrained in the amount of time and effort they can allocate to each parliamentary decision, and they allocate their scarce time and effort to those tasks that maximize their electoral returns. Imagine that the parliament is handed a long and complex international agreement that the median legislator has neither the technical knowledge nor the time to study, yet the legislator must decide how to vote on this agreement. Such a situation is fairly typical, especially in foreign relations. As one Senate Finance chairman, Russell Long, said, "If all members insist on knowing what they are voting on before they vote, we're never going to report this bill" (Hilsman 1993:192).

Lacking the executive's information about the agreement, C will accept any offer that is an improvement over the status quo; we call the set of acceptable offers C's *preferred-to set*. For instance, if $c < q$, the preferred-to set is $(2c - q, q)$. Now C does not know where any offer that has been made actually lies; C, uncertain of the contents of the agreement struck at the international level, can only form beliefs as to its location. These beliefs over the location of the agreement offered for ratification are based on C's prior beliefs about the foreign country's preferences and the type of agreement the executive would negotiate. If C believes that there is a large enough probability that the agreement offered for ratification lies in its preferred-to set, then C will ratify; if, on the other hand, C believes it is unlikely that the agreement falls in its preferred-to set, it will choose not to ratify.

How do P and F respond to this behavior? For given prior beliefs and locations of p and f, the international negotiators know in advance if any offer is going to be accepted or rejected. If C is the optimistic type and ratifies everything, then P and F are not constrained and will offer their NBS for ratification, as in the international game. If, on the other hand, C is the pessimistic type and rejects everything, whatever agreement P and F negotiate will be rejected and the status quo implemented. In either case, then, P and F will choose the unconstrained NBS as their offer, which is accepted or rejected depending on C's beliefs. This result is known as the "pig-in-the-poke result." If one agrees to something sight unseen, the proposer is likely to benefit maximally (Cameron and Jung 1992, Theorem 1).

What does the addition of asymmetric information mean for cooperation? If the status quo point q is close to c, then it is unlikely that the offer lies in C's preferred-to set (which is quite small). Hence, for any beliefs, there is always some interval of qs around c in which C always rejects the offer. However, for qs outside this interval around c, there may indeed be a high enough

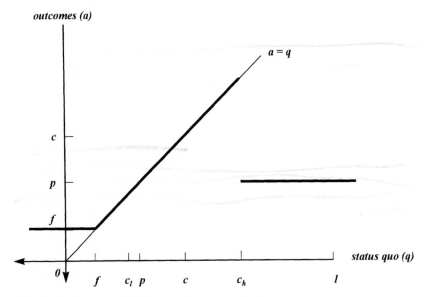

Figure 3.4 Incomplete Information Game, No Endorser

probability that the offer lies in the preferred-to set, and C will accept the offer. This is most likely when q lies far from c (making the preferred-to set very large, occupying almost the entire domain). Hence, for extreme qs, C is likely to accept the offer; for qs around c, rejection is most likely.

Figure 3.4 illustrates the equilibrium outcomes. As depicted in the figure, the status quo outcome occurs whenever C rejects the offer (which occurs between c_l and c_h, and occurs whenever P and F choose q [when there are no further gains to be had by either P or F]).[4] Compared to Figure 3.2, now there is an even larger set of status quo points—(p, c_h) relative to (p, c)—where the status quo is the outcome while mutual gains for the international negotiators simultaneously exist and remain unexploited. Whereas failure to cooperate was possible for some values of q when there was complete information domestically, the addition of asymmetric information makes cooperation *even less* likely. The region in which cooperation fails to occur (agreements to exploit joint gains by P and F are not achieved) expands even further.

When parliament is less informed, it has less impact. There are no circumstances under which C can influence the offer made by P and F. P and F always offer their NBS, irrespective of C, and C behaves accordingly. Thus the distribution of information has a critical effect: asymmetric information impedes cooperation.

[4] Call this interval around c, in which C rejects the offer, (c_l, c_h). This interval is determined by C's prior beliefs about the position of f, C's knowledge of the location of p and q, and the knowledge that P and F bargain to a point consistent with the NBS. Figure 3.4 is drawn for a generic interval; it will be larger and smaller as these determinants vary.

Domestic Politics with Asymmetric Information and an Endorser

What if instead of just voting blindly on the executive's proposal, the legislature could rely on the signals of one or several domestic groups about the nature of the agreement? Suppose the legislature, in order to make its decision, depends on the signal of another actor who has complete information about the agreement; that is, C listens for the endorsement of an actor (from outside the executive's office), obtains information about the agreement from this signal, and then casts its vote. This endorser may be any domestic group other than the executive; it could be an interest group, a legislative committee, other party members, an independent agency, and so on.

The endorser has its own preferences which differ from C's but which C knows. The legislature knows it cannot simply trust the endorser's signal because their preferences differ and thus the endorser may behave strategically. The information the legislature receives is not expected to be neutral; the legislator knows that the endorser has something to gain from the agreement. This endorser communicates its approval of or opposition to the agreement, and the legislature may rely on this signal to decide whether to ratify or reject the executive's offer. The legislature may listen to more than one such endorser. The endorser(s) can only provide limited information since the legislature does not have unlimited time to consider an issue. As Hilsman (1993:191) describes U.S. defense and foreign policy making:

> Almost all [legislative] members try to inform themselves on pending legislation . . . They often must turn to other sources for help in deciding how to vote, and this gives those sources power. Members acquire some information from other members, some from their staffs, some from their constituents, some from the press. Some of the more thorough and accurate information is actually supplied by lobbyists. Throughout the process members struggle to understand the legislation on which they must vote.

Adding another player to the game changes the sequence of moves, making it a three-step process. First, P and F negotiate an international agreement, aware that C must approve it and that C will be listening for the endorsement of some domestic group, called E. Then this agreement is revealed to E, who may or may not have participated in the international negotiation itself. The endorser sends his or her signal to C, which is a yes or no to the agreement. In the third step the legislature hears this signal, updates its beliefs about the agreement, and votes yes or no to ratify it. If the legislature votes no, then q is the outcome and no cooperation the result.

With asymmetric information, multiple equilibria are associated with each structure of preferences. The logic behind the equilibria is as follows. We proceed by backward induction to reveal the best strategies for each

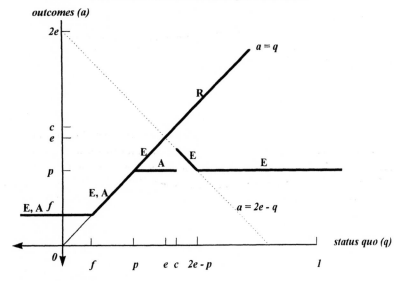

Figure 3.5 Incomplete Information Game with $p < e < c$

player, given what the others are doing and their current beliefs. Consider Figure 3.5, drawn for the case where the endorser is less hawkish than the legislature, $p < e < c$. If $q < e$, then C knows that E will endorse only proposed agreements that also meet with C's approval. But C also knows that E will not endorse some agreements that C prefers to the status quo—that is, those between E's indifference point and C's indifference point. E's endorsements cover only a subset of proposals that C would like to ratify. Hence when C hears an endorsement, C will know to ratify the agreement. When C hears no endorsement, C has to guess where the proposal lies. If C thinks it is close to his preferred policies, it should be ratified anyway (C is accommodating). If C believes it to be far from c, then C will reject it in favor of q (C is recalcitrant).

P and F will take C's beliefs into account when offering a proposal. If P and F know that C requires an endorsement before ratification is possible, the closest ratifiable agreement is q itself. So P and F offer q, which is endorsed and ratified. Hence q is the outcome, as evidenced by the thick line at the 45° angle. If, on the other hand, P and F believe that C will accept any offer, regardless of whether it is endorsed or not (as C might indeed do if C believes that P and F are not likely to offer an unacceptable proposal), then P and F will offer p, which is accepted. The outcome is p, as evidenced by the thick horizontal line at p in Figure 3.5. Hence P and F will either play it safe and offer a proposal that E will ratify or P and F will offer their unconstrained NBS point in the hope that C will ratify it anyway.

E: Endorsement; A: Accommodating; R: Recalcitrant

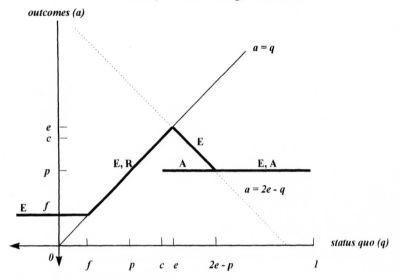

Figure 3.6 Incomplete Information Game with $p < c < e$

If $q > c$, and P and F believe that an endorsement is necessary for ratification, they will offer e's indifference point $2e - q$, as evidenced by the thick part of the line labeled $a = 2e - q$. As we move q further to the right, at some point $2e - q$ becomes equal to p. P and F then will offer p, which will be ratified and accepted. This is indicated in Figure 3.5 by the continuation of the flat line at p when q is large enough. If, on the other hand, P and F believe C is recalcitrant and unlikely to ratify any offer, endorsed or not, P and F will offer p in the vain hope that C might ratify in error. C, however, will reject the offer, implementing the status quo. This is indicated by the continuation of the thick 45° line, as q gets large.

When $e < q < c$, then C will never listen to the endorser and, depending on C's beliefs about the nature of the agreement, C will either accept the proposal or reject it no matter what E says. In this case E cannot be trusted since E's interests are diametrically opposed to C's. P and F know all this and will always offer their unconstrained NBS point. Depending on C's prior beliefs, one of two outcomes occurs. The offer may be accepted, resulting in p, or it may be rejected, resulting in q.

In the opposite case where E's preferences are more hawkish than C's, or $p < c < e$ (as in Figure 3.6), C's preferred agreements are only a subset of those E will endorse. Thus if E fails to endorse a policy, C will know to reject the agreement for certain. But if E endorses the agreement, C will be uncertain about what to do, since the agreement may lie in the area outside C's indifference point but within E's. When $q < c < e$, then if C is pessimistic, he will reject any agreement even though it was endorsed. P and F know all this and will either play it safe by offering a proposal that will be endorsed in the hope C will listen to the endorser or offer their unconstrained NBS point, knowing it will not be endorsed and that C will reject any proposal in any case. In either event q will be the outcome, and this is shown as the thick 45° line in Figure 3.6. For $q > e > c$, an endorsement equilibrium is possible: P and F offer $2e - q$ (or p if $p > [2e - q]$) which is endorsed and ratified (the thick line that descends along $a = 2e - q$ and at p in Figure 3.6). An accommodating equilibrium is also possible when $q > c$, where C ratifies even in the absence of an endorsement. This is evidenced by the thick line at p in Figure 3.6 over this region.

Does the endorser encourage cooperation? Consider the regions of cooperation in the endorser case. As with all three of the previous cases, when $f < q < p$, the status quo is always the outcome. No new agreement is the outcome since there are no joint gains to be achieved. At $q < f$, f is the outcome; this, too, is the same as the prior three cases. For $p < q < c$, p is a possible outcome in Figure 3.5; for $c < q < (2e - p)$, outcomes that differ from q are possible in both Figures 3.5 and 3.6. Hence in these regions (where cooperation was impossible without the endorser) cooperative outcomes are reestablished; agreement to exploit mutual gains is possible.

If a noncooperative point is one where there is no possibility for an agreement to exploit existing mutual gains, the no-cooperation region is (p, c) in Figure 3.6 (where $p < c < e$); in Figure 3.5 (where $p < e < c$), the no-cooperation region is empty. Recall that with no endorser (Figure 3.4), the region of no cooperation was (p, c_h), which is a larger interval than the no-cooperation interval with the endorser. Hence the no-cooperation region shrinks when the endorser is added to the game. Cooperation is facilitated by E's presence: *In the presence of asymmetric information, international agreement is more likely with an endorser than without.*

What does the endorser do that improves the chances for cooperation? At times C will rely on E. When E sends useful information, C ratifies. We call this an *endorsement equilibrium*. When q lies between c and $2e - p$ (for Figure 3.5) or when q lies between e and $2e - p$ (for Figure 3.6), cooperation is possible when P and F agree to send $2e - q$ to the endorser for endorsement. P and F would have preferred to send their unconstrained NBS point p but realize that such an offer would not receive an endorsement from E, an endorsement that is necessary for ratification.

When P and F propose $2e - q$, E will endorse such an offer (it leaves E indifferent between accepting the offer and rejecting it in favor of the status quo), and C ratifies on hearing E's endorsement. Hence there is an area where the endorser constrains the outcome; P and F are unable to negotiate the agreement they would most prefer. P and F compromise in order to achieve a cooperative agreement.

More surprising is the next result: *Incomplete information with an endorser increases the likelihood of international agreements even when compared to the full information domestic game.* In other words, cooperation is more likely in Figures 3.5 and 3.6 than in Figure 3.2. Note that in Figure 3.2 over the range $p < q < c$, international agreement is impossible to achieve. But in Figure 3.5, cooperative equilibria are possible in this range: between $p < q < c$, international agreement at P's ideal point is a possible outcome. In Figure 3.6, however, agreement is never possible over the range $p < q < c$.

The presence of less-informed actors is usually seen as hindering cooperation. Such uncertainty is often portrayed as the major problem causing actors to miss opportunities to cooperate and leading them to conflict. The results here contradict this assertion. Under certain circumstances asymmetric information on the domestic level about international agreements makes their ratification more, not less, likely, as long as the legislature is able to consult informed (and interested) actors about the contents of the agreement.

Not only does the endorser make ratification more likely, it also increases the legislature's influence. In fact the legislature does no worse with the endorser than when it has the same information as the executive. How could this be so? Isn't the median legislator, C, simply deceived into accepting agreements he would not accept if he had complete information about the agreement? Doesn't the legislature lose its influence when it lacks the same information as the executive has? Surprisingly this is not necessarily the case. For instance, in Figure 3.6, when $e < q < (2e - p)$, the legislature may do better than in the full information case (when $q > (2c - p)$ in Figure 3.2); P and F may be constrained by the endorser to offer an agreement at $2e - q$, rather than at p. This agreement is closer to the legislature's ideal point than is P's and F's preferred agreement. In Figure 3.5, however, C will never be better off under incomplete information but may not be any worse off either. It is possible, then, for C to gain (in equilibrium) from not having full information and having to rely on the endorser. The logic is that E provides useful information to C, and that in doing so E constrains P and F. Because of E's existence, P and F are more likely to propose agreements closer to C's ideal point, and C is more likely to accept these agreements.

However, when the endorser provides no useful information to the legislature, the legislature may end up worse off, and never any better off, than in the complete information case. Hence one can see that the endorser, when he or she provides information, can aid the legislature. *The endorser can allow the median legislator to obtain at least as much utility from an international agreement as the legislator could have were complete information available.* This proposition is illustrated in Figure 3.7 for the case where $c < e$. It plots the highest available utility (in an informative equilibrium) to C under the regimes of complete and incomplete information with and without the endorser. As can be seen, the equilibrium utility is the same at low

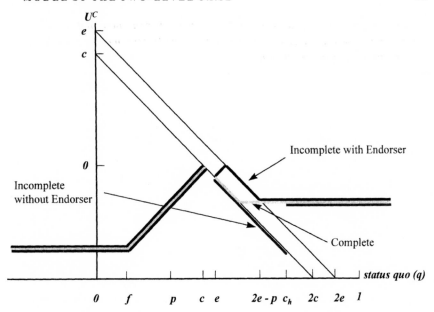

Figure 3.7 Returns to the Legislature under Complete and Asymmetric Information, with and without Endorser

and high levels of q, but the asymmetric information regime with the endorser dominates the no-endorser regime when q lies between e and c_h and dominates the complete-information regime when q lies between e and $2e - p$. Note that no equilibrium utility is presented in this diagram when $c < q < e$, since no informative equilibria exist in this region.

The legislature's reliance on E may be an efficient mechanism for making choices. The costs of gathering information are reduced, and C's utility is at least as high. Additionally, when the endorser E is an outlier $(p < c < e)$, E helps C the most. This, too, is surprising. One might think that when the endorser's preferences were closer to both the executive and the legislature, the endorser might be the most useful. But this is not the case. As others have also shown (Calvert 1985), the more biased the information provider (up to a certain point), the better the results for the legislature making the choice. However, when the endorser is closer to P $(p < e < c)$, international agreements become more likely. Under certain conditions, the introduction of asymmetric information does not necessarily hinder international agreements, and it does not necessarily lower the utility of the group lacking information, the legislature. Having an endorser may enable the legislature to accomplish its task more efficiently.

Interest group signaling has both distributional and informational effects. Interest groups may be able to exert influence over the negotiation process in their role as signalers. This is evident in the cases where the indifference point of the endorser $(2e - q)$ constrains the outcome of the international negotiations. Unlike in either the two-player, unitary actor international game or the complete information domestic game, in the asymmetric information game the endorser can alter the equilibrium outcome under certain conditions. The agreement's distributional consequences are thus changed.

Second, and no less important, the interest group endorser can provide information to the legislature which makes it better able to obtain an agreement it wants. The interest group gives influence to the legislature and helps it in the strategic game with the executive. The need for an endorsement forces the executive and the foreign country to negotiate an agreement that is better for the legislature. Informationally, the endorser may improve the terms of the agreement from a domestic point of view. As others have shown in different models, interest groups need not be just a distributional problem for political actors; they may provide low-cost information that improves the outcomes for the domestic actors (McCubbins and Schwartz 1984; Gilligan and Krehbiel 1987; Epstein and O'Halloran 1993).

This may be one reason why legislatures are keen on having interest groups involved in international negotiations. Although the role of interest groups in international negotiations is usually portrayed as co-opting them into accepting the agreement crafted (Winham 1986), our argument is that the legislature wants the interest groups to be part of the negotiations so they will serve as useful information providers about the agreement. For the legislature, then, having the interest groups involved is an efficient method to check and balance the executive. Where parliaments are strong, one would expect them to provide endorsers in the form of legislative committees and their reports or votes (Krehbiel 1991). Where parliaments are weak—that is, not in the United States—the role of the domestic interest groups will be more pronounced. Their signals will be a crucial mechanism to constrain the executive. Interest groups thus bring informational benefits, even if they also have distributional costs. Our model suggests that interest groups should be seen in a different light in two-level games.

Divided Government with Asymmetric Information and the Endorser

In the complete, symmetric information case, more divided government meant that failure to cooperate was more likely and that the executive had to compromise more with the legislature. In the asymmetric information case without the endorser, increasing divisions mean that C is becoming more pessimistic in its beliefs about the agreement and hence that ratification is less likely. The legislature's beliefs about the agreement depend on how distant its preferences are from those of the executive; the more distant they are, the more likely C is to believe that the executive would never negotiate an agreement that C liked. Divided government has no effect on the nature of the agreement since P and F always offer their NBS, but it does make ratification even less likely.

The effect of divided government when an endorser is present depends on whether the endorser's preferences are assumed to remain constant or to change with the degree of divided government. When preferences are $p < e < c$ as in Figure 3.5, if e remains constant along with p and f but c moves away from p, the area where the constraint exercised by E $(c, 2e - p)$ shrinks, until $c > (2e - p)$ when the constraint disappears entirely. Thus the area where E can be most helpful to C grows smaller as government becomes more divided. Or, the area where E's signal is of no help $(e < q < p)$ grows as divided government increases. C simply has to guess what to do given its beliefs about the agreement. This makes the status quo a frequent outcome; it may also make the executive more powerful since C cannot rely on the endorser.

If the endorser moves with c—that is, e moves away from p but keeps the same distance from c—then the area where E constrains P grows as divided government increases. This means that C may do *better* under more divided government.

When preferences are $p < c < e$ as in Figure 3.6, the effect of divided government depends again on what happens to e. If e remains constant with p and f, then the area between p and c will grow, and the likelihood of no cooperation will increase with divided government. The area between c and e will shrink, until c is greater than e. (At this point we are back at the situation described above.) However, the region where E constrains P $(e < q < [2e - p])$ increases; as c diverges from p, then C's and E's indifference lines $(2c - q$ and $2e - q)$ converge. So increasing divisions imply a greater likelihood of failure to cooperate, but when cooperation does occur, the agreement will reflect the legislature's preferences more closely.

When e moves with c away from p, then the constraints on P and F grow ever larger. As the distance between p and c grows, the status quo becomes more likely. And as the area where E constrains P and F $(e < q < [2e - p])$ grows, greater division means more impact for domestic politics. In this case $(p < c < e)$, having a more extreme endorser gives increased leverage to C.

In three of the four scenarios, domestic politics exercises a growing constraint on the international agreement as divided government increases. In these cases P and F are ever more constrained, and C does better. C's influence grows in part because the endorser is becoming more extreme. These results seem to cast doubt on the Schelling conjecture. Divisions internally do not help the executive negotiating the international agreement. What has been overlooked in other studies is that the other domestic actors may have different preferences than the executive. The more divergent these preferences are, the less likely the executive is to realize her preferred policy. Both the executive and the foreign country will be pulled away from their ideal points and thus will end up worse off as government becomes more divided.

In one case, however, asymmetric information even with an endorser increases the leverage of the executive. This result arises largely because the legislature is unable to depend on the endorser. Endorsers are valuable to the legislature, and endorsers who have more extreme preferences are more valuable.

Multiple Endorsers and Asymmetric Information

Domestic politics is often characterized by the competing signals of multiple interest groups. The legislature is likely to obtain information from interests on opposite sides of the issue. For example, in trade negotiations protectionist groups will lobby against trade liberalization whereas internationally oriented groups will press for it (Magee, Brock, and Young 1989; Milner 1988; Rogowski 1989). In this section we consider multiple endorsers, beginning with the case of two endorsers whose preferences are to the right and left of the median legislator's.

Call the ideal points of the two endorsers l and r and assume they lie on opposite sides of the median legislator's. After international negotiations, they each get to send a signal of yes or no about the agreement. The legislature now acts on the basis of a vector of signals. Basically when multiple endorsers exist the original results still hold. By choosing which endorsers to listen to, the legislature maximizes its ability to constrain the executive and to achieve an agreement closest to its ideal point.

Again multiple equilibria exist in this case depending on the legislature's beliefs about the foreign country and the agreement the executive made with it. Imagine a structure of preferences like $q < l < c < r$; what are the equilibria? (The other preference structure has completely symmetric results.) If an offer is made that gets L's endorsement, then it also always gets R's endorsement. No matter what C's beliefs are, it will endorse the offer in this case. If an offer is made that only R endorses, ratification fails if C's beliefs about F and the offer are pessimistic (C is recalcitrant). If, however, C is optimistic in its beliefs, then the endorsement from R alone can enable ratification (C is accommodating). If neither endorser signals yes, then ratification always fails.

Hence the legislature requires at least one endorsement before ratification is possible. An endorsement from the group nearest the status quo is sufficient (but not necessary) for ratification; an endorsement from the group

farthest from the status quo invokes ratification only if the legislature's beliefs are optimistic. Thus the endorser nearest the status quo exerts the
greatest influence over the median legislator. This endorser has the smallest
preferred-to set; therefore a positive signal from this endorser sends more
information than if the signal came from the other.

Three conclusions can be drawn. First, *ratification will not occur without
at least one, and often two, endorsements*. This confirms the single-endorser
results which also show that endorsers can play a critical informational role
for the legislature. The need for this endorsement affects the agreement
made as well, since it means that the executive may have to modify the
agreement to satisfy at least one endorser.

Second, *the legislature is able to use both pieces of new information to
improve knowledge about the agreement and to obtain one closer to its ideal
point.* The legislature makes a critical decision about the quality of the information provided, and hence about the usefulness of the endorsements. For
example, when the median legislator faces a group that is more protectionist
and one that is more free trade, he gathers information from both but the
final choice depends on the legislator's beliefs and, most important, on what
the endorser closest to the status quo signals. A yes from this endorser is
sufficient for ratification; but with enough optimism the legislature may also
ratify as long as the less informative endorser says yes.

Third, *increasing the number of endorsers beyond two does not add to the
analysis*. In this class of games, Theorem 4 of Cameron and Jung (1992) establishes that the legislature need consider at most two endorsers, the one closest to its ideal point on the right and the one closest on the left. When there
are many endorsers on one side of the legislature's ideal point, the legislature
only listens to the closest one since this one provides the most informative
signal. Hence the legislature, when more than one endorser exists, chooses to
listen either to the closest one or to the two closest ones on each side of the
legislature's ideal point; these are the two cases developed here.

One might be tempted to think that the legislature listens to the endorser
who is most likely to say something C wants to hear or who otherwise supports C's uninformed beliefs about the agreement. Instead C rationally
chooses to listen to the endorsers that provide the most information. Moreover, when the legislature is pessimistic about the foreign country and the
agreement made, its best bet is to listen to the endorser closest to the status
quo and not the one that is necessarily closest to the legislature's ideal point.
Multiple endorsers, then, allow the legislature to extract more information
and to choose which groups the legislature wants to listen to; they also provide an even greater constraint on the executive. Increasing polyarchy by
increasing the number of players in the game complicates life for the executive, limiting her autonomy ever more and making greater compromise with
the legislature likely.

Conclusions

This chapter presented the logic behind the major hypotheses advanced in this book. It explored how domestic factors affect the international negotiations over cooperation and demonstrated how and why the structure of domestic preferences and the distribution of information internally affect the possibility and terms of international agreements. The logic behind the hypotheses was established through a formal two-level game that incorporated an explicit model of domestic politics as well as one of international relations.

The model here is general enough to represent many different countries and issues. A Realist game is used to represent the international level, and an agenda setter, TILI model is adopted to model the domestic one. Our main conclusion deals with the comparison of bargaining among unitary states versus bargaining in the presence of polyarchy. How does the introduction of domestic politics affect the likelihood and terms of international cooperative agreements? In the pure international game with states modeled as unitary actors in an anarchic environment, the results are that, much as a Realist would expect, cooperation is difficult. It becomes increasingly difficult as the countries' preferences diverge. However, introducing polyarchy domestically, so that the legislature and executive must share decision-making power, makes cooperation even less likely. Failure to consider domestic politics means that international relations theorists—even Realists—overestimate the likelihood that countries will cooperate. Furthermore, they will be unable to explain the terms of international agreements. The introduction of legislative ratification changes the type of agreements that can be implemented. The balance of power among the states only partially accounts for the terms of any agreement. Domestic politics in the countries will also shape these terms.

Our results shed light on two other issues: (1) How does the structure of domestic preferences affect the likelihood and terms of any international agreement? In particular, how does divided government affect international negotiations? (2) How does the distribution of information domestically influence international negotiations?

When domestic groups share power and have different preferences, then internal politics begins to intrude into the international negotiations under certain conditions. When the legislature is the most hawkish player ($f < p < c$), domestic bargaining will change both the likelihood of agreement and the nature of any agreement that results. In particular, when the status quo is closer to the domestic players ($p < q < [2e - p]$), then the domestic ratification game dominates. The international negotiators will be constrained by their internal situations. They will have to alter their agreement from what they would otherwise accept in order to obtain ratification. Compromise to meet the legislature's preferences becomes the order of the day.

The effects of divided government on the two-level game are also important. The results tend to show that the more divided the government, the less likely international cooperation is but the better off the legislature will be in any agreement that can be made. This may not be surprising, but it does cast doubt on the Schelling conjecture which posited that internal divisions increase the external leverage of the executive. Indeed the model suggests that as divisions grow, the problems of the executive mount. She will have a harder time getting any agreement ratified and will be forced to negotiate agreements that meet the legislature's preferences.

Introducing asymmetric information at the domestic level has unanticipated consequences. Rather than always leading to less cooperation, it may improve the chances for cooperation under certain conditions. Since it is widely assumed that uncertainty promotes conflict rather than cooperation among nations, this is an important finding. Asymmetric information at the domestic level when tempered by the presence of informed domestic groups may enhance the prospects for international cooperation, similar to its effects in a purely domestic setting (McCubbins and Schwartz 1984; Cameron and Jung 1992; Austen-Smith and Wright 1992; Lupia 1992; Banks 1993; Epstein and O'Halloran 1993). Although asymmetric information alone increases inefficiencies by making cooperative deals less likely, in the presence of an endorser such inefficiencies are greatly reduced.

The political advantages of private information are also reduced by the presence of an endorser. Asymmetric information need not mean that the legislature is worse off. Cooperation does not occur just because the international negotiators are able to deceive the legislature into ratifying an agreement it otherwise would not. Because of the endorser, the legislature obtains information about the proposed agreement and knows that the endorser in certain circumstances constrains the international negotiators into making agreements that are better for the legislature. Without the endorser, the legislature would reject these agreements out of fear of being deceived by the executive and the foreign country. The endorser, which can be any domestic group except the executive, thus provides a service for the legislature.

With multiple endorsers the legislature can do even better. In such cases if the executive wants an agreement to be ratified, she must obtain the endorsement of at least one informed group to whom the legislature listens. Failure to obtain an endorsement means failure to ratify; on the other hand, obtaining two endorsements from groups closest to the median legislator ensures ratification. The executive and the foreign country are thus forced to modify their proposal to obtain the endorsement of informed domestic groups. This compromise leaves the legislature better off and makes ratification more likely.

Informed domestic groups give the legislature important information about international agreements in a cost-effective way. For the legislature, then, having various domestic groups involved in international negotiations is an efficient method to check and balance the executive. Where parliaments are particularly weak, interest groups should play an especially important role as a mechanism to constrain the executive. This may explain why legislatures tolerate corporatist arrangements. When corporatist groups signal disapproval of the executive's proposals, then the legislature receives a "fire alarm" alerting it to the fact that the executive's proposed policy may be far from that favored by the legislature and their constituents. As McCubbins and Schwartz (1984:175) argue, legislators favor fire-alarm systems of oversight since they are more efficient than police patrols: "Citizens and interest groups can be counted upon to sound an alarm in most cases in which the [executive] has arguably violated Congress' goals. Congress has not relinquished legislative responsibility to anyone else. It has just found a more efficient way to legislate." Interest groups thus bring informational benefits, even if they also have distributional effects.

This model generates a number of hypotheses that will be examined in the case studies:

1. If the executive must share decision-making power with the legislature and the two have even slightly different preferences, then cooperation will be less likely than in the pure international game with unitary states.

2. The more divided the government, the less likely cooperation is, the greater the likelihood of ratification failure is, and the more influence the legislature tends to exert over the terms of the agreement.

3. The greater the asymmetry of information and the less likely are informed endorsers, the more likely is ratification failure. But it also becomes more likely that any acceptable agreement will reflect the executive's preferences.

4. In situations of asymmetric information, if the legislature can depend on informed endorsers, cooperation becomes more likely and more responsive to the legislature's preferences. With multiple endorsers the executive will have to obtain the endorsement of at least one for ratification to occur. If both endorse, then ratification always occurs; if neither endorses, it never occurs.

These hypotheses form the basis for understanding the role that domestic factors exert in negotiating international cooperation.

In sum, polyarchy makes cooperation less likely. Factors that induce increased polyarchy, such as divided government, further decrease the chances of cooperation while improving the outcome of any cooperative agreement that is ratified from the legislature's point of view. Leaving the world of states portrayed as unitary actors means understanding that international agreements will now reflect internal political struggles and compromise. Domestic politics reduces the possibility of cooperation, even below the level that Realists expect. It also means that the terms of an international agreement will reflect each country's domestic situation in addition to its international influence.

Four

Political Institutions and International Cooperation

DOMESTIC political institutions determine how power over decision making is allocated among national actors. How power is shared affects whose preferences are most likely to dominate policy making. Thus the institutional relationship between the executive and the legislature in democracies is of central importance in understanding the domestic side of international cooperation. Variations or changes in this institutional relationship influence the probability and terms of international cooperation.

The previous chapter explored the effect of the structure of domestic preferences and the distribution of information on international cooperation. This chapter examines the effect of domestic political institutions on cooperation. In the last chapter the model held these institutions constant, while varying preferences. The executive, it was assumed, negotiated with the foreign country and then the legislature had to ratify without amending the agreement. Hence the executive held agenda-setting power and the legislature controlled only ratification. It could not set the agenda, offer amendments, or change these procedures. The results of the model in chapter 3 depend on the institutional relationship that is assumed between the executive and the legislature. Here I vary the institutional arrangements and examine how this affects the possibility and terms of international cooperation.

This chapter asks what happens to the agreement when the legislative powers of decision making are distributed differently between the executive and the legislature. How do changes in the distribution of these powers between the two affect international cooperation? In the process of making legislation, at least five distinct elements exist in the decision-making process: agenda setting (or initiation), amendment, ratification or veto, use of referendums, and side payments. In different political systems and on different issues, the distribution of these powers between the executive and the legislature varies. If one actor possesses them all, then the unitary actor model of the state is most appropriate and domestic politics does not matter. If multiple actors possess at least one of these powers, then decision making is shared and the polyarchic model of politics is more appropriate.

These powers give actors control over the process of creating and implementing laws and other policies; thus they are legislative powers (Shugart and Carey 1992:131–48). In addition to these legislative powers, the balance of power between the executive and the legislature is affected by what are called "origin and survival" powers. These powers determine who can appoint and censure cabinet members, whether the executive can dissolve the legislature, and whether and under what conditions the legislature can vote the executive out of office. These conditions usually emanate from the constitution and are thus more structural, affecting the relationship between the legislature and executive at all times. They act as background conditions setting the broad parameters for executive-legislative interaction. But on any particular issue, control over the process of making policy—that is, over legislative powers—may be more important.

The classic distinction between parliamentary and presidential systems is drawn on the basis of differences in origin and survival powers. Presidential systems tend to separate the origin and survival of the executive and the legislative branches, whereas parliamentary systems fuse them. Such a broad distinction is useful at some level but, as I will argue, the distinction between these systems often obscures more about them than it illuminates. The differences in terms of legislative powers among parliamentary and among presidential systems are often more salient than the supposed similarities in each system's origin and survival powers. Indeed, I will argue that variations in the distribution of legislative powers reveal more about the relationship between the executive and the legislature on any particular issue. Such variations result in distinct policy choices, since different actors' preferences will be privileged by each distribution.

In this chapter I discuss the five legislative powers and how control over them affects decision making with regard to international cooperation. I demonstrate how four specific distributions of these powers determine whose preferences dominate policy making. In addition, I lay the basis for two hypotheses about the effects of domestic political institutions on international cooperation. First, the probability of a successful cooperative agreement is highest when decision-making power is concentrated in the most dovish domestic political actor. Second, the dispersion of legislative powers from the executive to the legislature alters the terms of cooperation, making them more favorable to the legislature. Hence both the likelihood and terms of international cooperation depend on the balance of powers between the legislature and the executive.

Finally, in this chapter I examine why the ability to make changes in the distribution of legislative powers is the ultimate power. If actors have preferences about policies, then they should also have preferences about institutions since certain institutions will make the realization of their preferences as policy more likely. How policy is made should be contested when the actors who control policy making differ in their preferences. This implies that the choice of procedures to devise and "ratify" cooperative policies should be an object of contest itself. Thus the logical foundation is laid for a third hypothesis about the effects of political institutions, which argues that changes in the ratification procedures, especially after international negotiations are completed, make cooperation less likely.

The chapter acknowledges that the political institutions of a country play an important role in determining how domestic politics affects international cooperation. It also shows that institutions matter but only in conjunction with preferences.

Five Legislative Powers

The balance of power between the executive and the legislature depends in part on which one controls key elements of the legislative process. The more control any one actor has, the more that actor is able to implement his or her preferences as policy. In other words, when the executive controls the main mechanisms of legislative power, she will be able to devise policies that closely resemble her ideal point. As these powers are increasingly distributed to the legislature, its policy preferences will come to dominate legislation. As noted above, such power sharing only matters when the actors' preferences differ.

In chapter 3 the model assumed a particular distribution of legislative powers. The executive had control over agenda setting, while the legislature could ratify the agreement but could not offer amendments. In this setup the executive had no need for a veto nor the ability to propose either referendums or side payments. Although this model is appropriate for many foreign policy issues, different distributions of powers are possible. Here I demonstrate that these institutional variations affect the outcomes of the model but only within certain parameters; that is, variations in legislative powers between the executive and the legislature change the equilibrium outcomes by moving them between the executive's ideal point (p) and that of the legislature (c). When institutional power is concentrated in the executive, outcomes lie closer to p; when such power is more dispersed, outcomes lie closer to c. Preferences matter ultimately because the range of outcomes generated by changes in the distribution of powers is determined by the preferences of the executive and the legislative majority. The ideal points of the executive and the legislature define the boundaries within which domestic political *institutions* can affect the outcomes.

Here I review the five major legislative powers: agenda setting, amendment, ratification or veto, referendum, and side payments. I discuss the role of each in the legislative process and how they give power to the executive or the legislature. The next section shows how changes in the distribution of these powers alter the equilibrium outcomes of the model in chapter 3.

Agenda Setting

The ability to set the agenda in politics has long been recognized as a powerful capability. Keeping certain issues off the table and putting others on can affect the policy choices made later in the game. "The patterns of public policy . . . are determined not only by such final decisions as votes in legislatures, or initiatives and vetoes by presidents, but also by the fact that some subjects and proposals emerge in the first place and others are never seriously considered" (Kingdon 1984:2). Indeed, Bachrach and Baratz (1962) long ago recognized the potency of agenda setting, calling the ability to keep issues off the agenda the "second face of power." Even earlier Schattschneider (1960:68) deemed it "the supreme instrument of power."

Agenda setting usually refers to both the list of topics or issues that are raised for consideration, in our case for international negotiation, and the alternatives posed to deal with these issues. Both the specific topics themselves and the set of proposed solutions are included on the agenda. Although some (Kingdon 1984) separate these two elements of agenda setting, it is best for the discussion here to combine them, as many studies do (e.g., Riker 1993; Baumgartner and Jones 1993). Influence over legislation is conferred by the capacity to identify both certain topics (and not others) as "political issues" and certain proposals (and not others) to deal with these issues. In the context here, this includes both initiating negotiations with a foreign country over a particular issue and defining the proposals to be advanced at those negotiations.

How does agenda setting confer power on the holder of this capability? Control over the agenda allows a player to set the terms of debate. The agenda setter defines the problem or issue to be addressed, thus ruling out many other issues. The actor can define the alternatives available, ruling out those he or she does not prefer and structuring them so the one he or she prefers is most appealing to others. The agenda setter may be able to select the sequence in which options are considered, which is another way of inducing others to adopt the agenda setter's preferred policy. This capacity to define the problem, structure the alternatives to deal with it, and sequence the consideration of problems and alternatives gives the agenda setter great power. As one evaluation of the executive's various powers makes clear, "The bottom line is that when [executives], or ministers who are exclusively accountable to [them], are allowed to initiate legislation on their own, they are generally among the primary forces in the legislative process" (Shugart and Carey 1992:139).

Rational choice models have also demonstrated the agenda setter's power (e.g., Romer and Rosenthal 1978, 1979; Baron and Ferejohn 1989b; Ferejohn and Shipan 1990). This literature establishes that the median voter's or legislator's preferred outcome does not usually prevail; rather, the agenda

setter tends to have the power to shape outcomes in favor of its own preferences. Other actors, however, are not without influence; there are limits on
the agenda setter's autonomy. First, if other actors can amend the agenda
setter's proposal, the latter will be incapable of deviating much from the
median voter's position (Baron and Ferejohn 1989b). Second, even without
amendment power, the agenda setter's proposal can be rejected if the other
players have ratification power, thus forcing a reversion to the status quo.
This reversion point—the outcome in the absence of an agreement—sets
the limit on the degree to which the median voter or legislator is prepared
to compromise. The farthest he can feasibly be pushed by the agenda setter
is to a point that returns as much utility as the reversion point does. If the
proposal is further from the median voter's or legislator's preferred point
than is the reversion point, he will rationally reject the proposal. This
agenda-setter game with ratification is the basis for the model in chapter 3.

Who tends to hold agenda-setting power, the executive or legislature?
Among democracies, parliamentary systems tend to allocate agenda-setting
power to the prime minister. "In more than 50 percent of all countries,
governments introduce more than 90 percent of the bills" (Tsebelis
1995:304). Usually the executive and the majority party in parliament initiate legislation, according to the party program. But some parliamentary systems do give agenda-setting power to their legislatures. In Italy, for example, "the two [legislative] Chambers control their own timetable and agenda
and can amend government proposals almost without restriction. There is
considerable scope for backbenchers and for parliamentary party leaders to
propose their own bills" (Furlong 1990:62). Among presidential democracies, initiation power varies widely (Shugart and Carey 1992:139–40, 155).
Often legislatures can initiate, but sometimes and on certain issues the executive has the exclusive right of initiation.

Most interesting for this book, foreign policy issues tend to be an area
where the executive, even in presidential systems, dominates the agenda-
setting process. Since relations with foreign countries are involved and the
expertise for this lies in the executive branch, presidents may initiate foreign
policy legislation as frequently as prime ministers do. In general, then,
agenda setting, especially on complex issues and matters of foreign policy,
tends to fall into the executive's domain. Where it does not, the legislature
yields important power over the executive.

Amendment Power

The ability to amend any proposal the agenda setter makes is a powerful
capability. If amendment is allowed, then, it is not simply a vote on the
agenda setter's proposal versus the status quo but rather a vote on the pro-

posal versus the amendment to it.[1] This implies that the one amending can alter the agenda setter's proposal to bring it closer to the former's ideal point; maximally the amender can change the proposal to its ideal point. As noted before, amendment power trumps even the strong powers inherent in agenda setting. "Compared to the closed rule [that is, no amendments allowed], the opportunity to make an amendment under an open rule dramatically reduces the agenda power of the member recognized first and results in an outcome that more evenly distributes the benefits among the winning majority" (Baron and Ferejohn 1989a:1200). Further, the authority to amend is not an all-or-nothing power. Political systems tend to use restrictions on the types and number of amendments allowed or on other aspects of the amendment process; these often vary by the issue under consideration. Restrictions on amendment power should weaken the amender and strengthen the agenda setter.

Who tends to hold amendment power, the executive or legislature? In most parliamentary systems, the executive tends to be the agenda setter and the parliament usually has full power of amendment. (In addition, sometimes the government can introduce amendments into the legislative process.) In some systems, however, the government can prevent amendments or severely restrict the nature or time allotted for amendments; the French Fifth Republic is a good example: "The package vote and the guillotine, then, are both institutions that force the [French] National Assembly to make an 'up or down' choice on a policy package determined by the government" (Huber 1992:676). Whether the legislature's power of amendment is used depends on various circumstances. The extent of the executive's majority in the parliament matters: a weaker government may face more amendments. More controversial issues may prevent governments from using a closed rule. Parliaments that are well organized into committees tend to amend more. Indeed, the degree to which legislatures amend government bills is often used as a measure of the legislature's strength relative to the executive (Copeland and Patterson 1994:43, 72). A stronger legislature is one that amends more. Note that amendment power may be a better index of legislative influence than the legislature's acceptance rate of government bills, another frequently used measure. If legislatures have amendment power, then, they should rarely if ever reject a government bill; they will simply amend it to their liking. Rejection should occur infrequently, if at all, and this infrequency is not an indication of the legislature's weakness.

In presidential systems where the executive initiates, the legislature should desire amendment power. This power gives legislatures great

---

[1] The process of making and voting on amendments takes many forms and can itself be very complex. For instance, the process can move backward—that is, amendments are voted on in reverse order of presentation—or it can move forward—that is, each amendment is voted on in order against the status quo (Browne and Hamm 1996:167–68 fn).

influence since they can simply amend the president's bills to reflect their own ideal point; in this case the next power discussed, veto power, becomes important in restricting the legislature's control. Thus one would expect that legislatures would fight hard to keep amendment power, rarely relinquishing it where they controlled it. But in some cases legislatures do constrain themselves and allow the president to call for take-it-or-leave-it votes on its proposals. For example, the U.S. Congress has often agreed to relinquish amendment power on international trade policy (O'Halloran 1994). Several reasons have been suggested for why legislatures might opt for a closed rule. If amendment is allowed, the costs of delay and the difficulties of holding together distributive deals if they involve multidimensional issues may grow, making closed rule appealing at times (Baron and Ferejohn 1989a, 1989b; Shepsle and Weingast 1984; Krehbiel 1991). Thus, although one might expect that legislatures would never relinquish their right to amend freely, it may at times be rational for them to do so.

In presidential systems where the legislature introduces legislation and the president is not the agenda setter, the legislature should not be concerned about its right to amend. Holding both initiation and amendment power is redundant for an actor. However, if agenda setting arises within a small group of the legislature (e.g., a committee) or in one legislative chamber, then amendment power for the entire legislature (i.e., the floor or both houses) may still be desirable from the median legislator's point of view. Again, whoever wields unrestricted amendment power can significantly affect the outcome since that individual will amend the proposed policy to his or her own ideal point. As the amendment game in the next section shows, amendment power is very consequential.

In international negotiations, however, domestic amendment power is a difficult issue. If, after international negotiations successfully conclude an agreement, any legislature begins to rewrite that agreement through amendments, the international bargain may collapse. If the foreign country finds the amendments unacceptable, then international negotiations may have to recommence. Under complete information, of course, this should not occur. Executives at home and abroad should correctly anticipate the legislature's preferences and craft agreements that are acceptable to it; amendment should never occur. Nevertheless, executives in this area should desire control over legislative amendments; foreign countries may also want home executives to have this control, depending on the domestic actors' preferences. Whether legislatures will relinquish such control should depend on the cost of delay involved in renegotiation, the difficulties in maintaining distributive coalitions, and the differences between the majority's preferences and the executive's. If delay and renegotiation are costly, package deals are hard to maintain, or if their preferences are similar, legislatures may well choose to relinquish amendment power over international agreements.

Ratification or Veto Power

Ratification or veto is defined broadly here. It implies that some actor other than the agenda setter must approve the agenda setter's proposal by (some) majority. Whether this means a formal vote giving majority approval of a bill or a tacit showing of majority support depends on the issue and the country. If the executive is the agenda setter, then the legislature often has the ability to ratify, that is, vote for or against the executive's proposal. If the legislature sets the agenda, then the executive may have the right to veto its proposal. Ratification power may thus rest in the hands of either the legislature or the executive. It may also reside with societal actors, such as in corporatist systems where capital and labor groups must approve national wage settlements. As Tsebelis (1995) shows, such "veto power" is important because it limits the agenda setter's ability to change the status quo. The number of "veto players" and the difference between their preferences and those of the agenda setter are key; the more veto players and the greater the differences in preferences (i.e., the more government is divided), the less likely is a change from the status quo.

Ratification is interpreted broadly here. In some countries international agreements must be ratified by the legislature; for instance, in the United States the Senate must ratify treaties. In Denmark all treaties require majority parliamentary ratification, and all legislation involving transfer of power to international organizations requires either a five-sixths majority vote in the Danish parliament (the Folketing) or a majority Folketing vote and public approval in a referendum (Gjørtler 1993:357; Fitzmaurice 1988:284). Even where parliament does not have the right to ratify, international agreements usually affect domestic laws, budgetary expenditures, or even the constitution, and parliament will always need to approve these new or changed laws and constitution. Votes on these matters will in effect be motions to ratify or reject the international agreement. In the United Kingdom, for example, Parliament does not have the right to ratify international agreements, but agreements must be translated into domestic laws which do require legislative assent. Furthermore, the United Kingdom has employed another form of ratification on international issues; it used a popular referendum for dealing with European integration in the 1970s and may do so again. As will be discussed later, in some countries the parliament is bypassed and popular referendums are required for ratification.

In all cases anticipated reaction is at work: the agenda setter(s) and/or amenders will always try to craft bills or negotiate agreements that the executive, a majority in parliament, and/or the public will ratify afterward. As Morgenthau (1985:167) points out, "Popular support is the precondition of the President's stewardship of foreign policy. The creation of a public opinion supporting him, even at the sacrifice of some elements of foreign policy, is a task which a President can only shun at the risk of losing office and, with it, his ability to pursue any foreign policy at all." Not only are the terms of international agreements affected by ratification power but the decision to start international negotiations also depends on the chances for ratifying an agreement at home. Executives decide whether and how to negotiate internationally always keeping the ratification process in mind. They will only negotiate if they believe that some agreement, acceptable to them and the foreign country, is ratifiable at home. Hence they must always anticipate the reactions of domestic groups, such as their legislatures and important societal groups that have ratification power.

Ratification is a central element of chapter 3's model. The executive and the legislature share power because a majority in the legislature must approve the proposed international agreement that the executive submits to them. The executive and the foreign country know this in advance and realize that any proposed agreement must survive this domestic test before it can be implemented. If the legislature does not have the power to amend the proposed agreement, rejection of it means reversion to the status quo. This reversion point—the no-agreement outcome—sets the limit on the degree to which the legislature is prepared to compromise. The farthest the agenda setter can feasibly push the legislature from its ideal point is to a point that returns as much utility as the reversion point. If the proposal is further than the reversion point is from the median legislator's preferred point, the legislator will rationally reject the proposal.

Ratification or veto power is important for it constrains the agenda setter. Amendment power is more significant, however, since the amender can move the proposal to its ideal point and the ratifier cannot. The ratifier or vetoer must accept greater compromise from its ideal point than the amender; it will accept any proposal that is better for it than the status quo. Amendment power is more important than ratification, but it is also more costly. Amending a bill or agreement requires time and information that ratification may not. For one actor to have both amendment and ratification (or veto) power is redundant since after amending he or she will always ratify (as long as the amender represents the same majority as the ratifier). Hence depending on how costly amending is—and it may be very costly in international agreements—actors will desire either amendment or ratification power if they do not have agenda-setting abilities.

Who has ratification or veto power? In parliamentary systems, since the executive is usually the agenda setter, the legislature controls ratification. Government proposals require a legislative majority. As Laver and Shepsle (1994:3) claim, "One of the main jobs of the legislature in a parliamentary democracy is to sit as a court passing continual judgment on the record of

the executive, and continuous sentence on its future." In single-party majority governments ratification is usually taken for granted, unless party discipline is poor. In minority or coalition governments ratification requires the
assent of the legislative coalition supporting the executive. In such cases
ratification may be far more constraining for the executive. Since most governments are made up of coalitions, this makes the ratification game of
prime importance. In parliamentary systems, the executive's use of a veto is
fairly rare. Having agenda-setting power lessens the need for a veto.

In presidential systems, veto power for the executive is more common. If
legislatures control the agenda, then it is important for presidents to have
the veto as it allows them to constrain the legislature. Even when the president initiates an agreement, veto power is significant because it allows the
president to constrain the legislature's power to amend the agreement. Although all presidents do not have veto power, all are required to take some
action on legislation passed by their legislature within a prescribed time
(Shugart and Carey 1992:133–35, 155). Veto powers also vary in their scope:
package vetoes limit the executive's power; partial or item vetoes increase it
since only offending parts of a bill need be vetoed; and pocket vetoes greatly
enhance it since simply by doing nothing the executive gains control of the
last move in the legislative game. As the recent U.S. debate over changing
from a package to a line-item veto makes clear, the balance of power between the executive and the legislature largely hinges on the distribution of
legislative powers (e.g., Pious 1979). To complicate matters, legislatures can
often override executive vetoes, usually by some supramajority. Such override again limits the executive's veto power.

Ratification or veto power is thus important and variable across political
systems. Again, in foreign policy—especially international negotiations—
the executive, whether in presidential or parliamentary systems, usually initiates policy. If the legislature cannot amend, then its ratification power is
important and the executive has no need for a veto. If the legislature can
amend, then its ratification power is less important and the executive's veto
power could be critical. But amending international agreements may be
tantamount to demanding their renegotiation internationally. Hence legislatures may refrain from such amendments and focus on their ratification powers, as chapter 3 presupposes. Later I show what happens when the legislature can amend and the executive can and cannot veto.

Proposal of Referendums

Referendums are votes by the public either approving or rejecting a government policy proposal. They tend to be take-it-or-leave-it votes. Frequently
the executive controls the proposing and wording of referendums, rendering

them equivalent to a vote on the executive's popularity or a ratification of her proposals. Such control over referendums enables executives to get approval for policies that the legislature is hesitant to approve, thus diminishing the legislature's influence. Because referendums tend to pass, executives use them precisely to obtain public support for executive proposals (Butler and Ranney 1978; Pierce, Valen, and Listhaug 1983; Lijphart 1984:30–32).

In some countries, however, referendums are not under the executive's control. Often, as in Switzerland, they are required by the constitution for various policy changes. Sometimes actors other than the executive have the right to call for referendums on the government's policy. In Denmark, for instance, a minority of sixty members of the Folketing can demand a referendum (Fitzmaurice 1988:283). In these cases the executive, whether she desires it or not, is forced to seek popular ratification of her proposals. The public becomes the ratifier. Knowing this, the executive must anticipate the median voter's preferences and craft international agreements to secure the median voter's approval. In this case, either in addition to the parliament or instead of it, the median voter becomes the ratifier of government proposals. Here referendums are less a source of government influence and more one of public constraint on the executive.

Who controls referendums affects how they are used. They may be a source of executive power when they allow the executive either to bypass or override the legislature. When successful, they represent a vote of confidence for the executive and buttress the executive's power vis-à-vis the legislature. Where referendums are mandated by the constitution or can be called by actors other than the executive, both the executive and the legislature may be weakened. In these cases the public checks the executive and may usurp the legislature's power to ratify government proposals. All these types of referendums are equivalent to a ratification game. The only difference is that the ratifier is now the median voter, not the median legislator. This is the same game as shown in chapter 3's model, except that the public takes the legislature's role.

Side Payments

Side payments refer to a broad range of tactics that have one common element. As the name implies, side payments involve an actor giving up value on one issue in exchange for other actors giving up value on another issue. Thus side payments may be viewed in a broader sense to include such practices as logrolling, vote trading, compromise, concessions, reciprocity, bribes, and issue linkage. All these tactics involve the same general principle that is the centerpiece of side payments: an actor gives up value on one issue of lesser importance in order to gain value from others on an issue of greater importance.

For example:

Vote trading is the same as logrolling in much of the literature. Vote trading implies that a politician trades away his vote on one particular issue for the votes of others on some other issue of more concern to him and his constituents. Sometimes logrolling is applied to situations where all deals go into one omnibus package bill to be voted on simultaneously; and vote trading as applying to deals that are voted on separately. But they can be used interchangeably.... Logrolling arises due to differences in voter [preference] intensities. If a minority group supports y very strongly but cares much less about whether z or w prevail and another minority strongly wants w to win over z but cares less about whether x or y wins, then a coalition of y and w can secure joint victory and it is in their interest to do so. (Stratmann 1992:1162)

The critical factor for side payments is that individuals have different preferences or different intensities of preferences across issue areas. As Riker (1962:125) and others (e.g., Miller 1977) have pointed out: "If all intensities of preferences are identical over all individuals and over all issues, no trading of votes is possible. In this case the individual feels as strongly on one issue as on any other, and he will never rationally agree to exchange his vote for reciprocal favors."

Although many recent studies either disagree or implicitly treat logrolling, vote trading, issue linkage, reciprocity, and concessions as distinct tactics, the early literature on side payments explicitly recognize their commonality. In their seminal contributions Luce and Raiffa (1957), Riker (1962), and Buchanan and Tullock (1962) point out the functional equivalence between all these maneuvers.

However, these tactics differ in other important aspects. First, they may represent an exchange that is concluded either simultaneously or sequentially. One often thinks of a "package deal" or a logroll as being a single measure where issues have been bundled together for the purpose of making compromises across them. In contrast, vote trading often occurs sequentially, such as when different issues are voted on in a particular order over a certain time period.

Second, side payments can be implicit or explicit. Actors involved often do not want their offer of or compliance with side payments to be explicitly negotiated or publicly acknowledged. This behavior may be illegal (one thinks of bribes), immoral, or just offensive to others. When actors interact frequently on many different issues, implicit deals are more likely. Reciprocity, a favorite strategy under such circumstances, also embodies the principle of side payments (McGinnis 1986:165; Dixon 1986).

Third, side payments, all of which involve the transfer of utility from one actor to others, can be made in different "currencies." Money, votes, future policy choices, political appointments, back-scratching, territory, or almost any other good or service that has value to one of the actors involved can be used as a side payment.

Finally, side payments may involve either promises or threats, a point that is not well accepted. Side payments are frequently assumed to imply only promises. Actor 1 promises to give actor 2 a concession on issue A in exchange for actor 2's giving in to 1's demands on issue B. This notion of mutual gains from side payments, or issue linkage, is prevalent in the literature. Many separate this from the "leverage" function of side payments (e.g., Sebenius 1983; Mayer 1992; Friman 1993). For example, Tollison and Willett (1979:448) make the following argument:

> Our theory stresses issue linkages as a means of overcoming distributional obstacles to international agreement where direct sidepayments among countries are not a politically feasible alternative. Th[is] mutual benefit theory contrasts with and supplements the traditional rationale for linkage in terms of extending one's leverage in one area of negotiations to other areas. Integration of these two approaches is not attempted in this paper, but we believe it is an important task for future research on issue linkage.

These two functions should be seen, however, as one and the same. Side payments are a means of exercising power, whether through negative or positive sanctions (Baldwin 1989; Oye 1992). They are intended to make an actor do something he would not otherwise do. Both threats and promises serve this function; they differ principally in the way they alter the recipient's baseline of expectations. As Riker (1962) and Stein (1980) rightly point out, threats are also a form of side payment: "At one extreme a leader may so manipulate events that he is able to threaten members of the body with reprisals if they do not join his proto-coalition. The side-payment then consists of a promise not to carry out the threat and the gain of the follower is simply escape from prospective misfortune" (Riker 1962:109). Lest one think this is purely an international phenomenon, Riker goes on to say, "But even in the most thoroughly democratic societies . . . , this kind of side-payment is frequently offered and accepted"; the example he uses is party discipline (109). In the situation involving a threat, then, actor 1 threatens to do something negative to actor 2 on issue A if actor 2 will not give in to actor 1's demands on issue B.

Both threats and promises involve the exchange of values between actors across different issues when the actors value those issues differently, that is, they embody the core principle of side payments. Hence side payments can involve explicit transfers of money from one actor to another as part of a promise simultaneous with the other actor's behavior, as when a legislator "sells" his or her vote. Or they can involve an implicit threat to veto all future policies in an area an actor desires unless the actor goes along on the issue at hand, as the Greek government tried to do in the European Union (EU) over the issue of recognizing Macedonia (*International Herald Tribune*, December 17, 1993, p. 1). In other words, side payments comprise a broad group of tactics that are pervasive in politics, both internationally and domestically.

Side payments here are conceived as domestic in nature, that is, they are promises or threats that executives make to interest groups or legislators. They are not international—from one government to another. This argument is distinct from Realist claims about side payments as international tools of influence. For Realists, side payments are a means of equalizing the gains generated in agreements between states. One government employs side payments (compensation, linkage) vis-à-vis another to arrive at a "balanced" deal, so that no state achieves relative gains (Morgenthau 1985; Waltz 1979; Grieco 1990). For Realists, side payments are part of the international game.

According to my argument side payments are part of the domestic game, used by the executive to affect her ratification game with the legislature. Side payments can be given to legislators or targeted toward interest groups in order to obtain these groups' ratification of the executive's proposal. Side payments, then, represent another power that is available largely to the executive. At the end of the game the executive may be able to make an unratifiable agreement palatable by offering side payments to legislators and/or interest groups. For example, in the NAFTA agreement President Clinton was able to secure legislative votes in the final days of negotiations by offering exemptions from the agreement to various producers in important congressional districts. As noted above, party discipline can also be thought of as a type of side payment; it often takes the form of a threat or promise by the executive to a legislator from the executive's party. For instance, in the United Kingdom a three-line whip invokes the threat of expulsion from the party and hence from office if legislators do not vote the government line.

Side payments can also be a critical tool in the hands of an executive desiring to ratify an international agreement. Instead of having to renegotiate the parts that legislators do not like, the executive may be able to "buy" increased support for the agreement through concessions on other issues.

Distributions of Legislative Powers and Policy Outcomes

Political systems distribute legislative powers between the executive and the legislature in various ways. Moreover, the distribution may vary according to the issue. As Tsebelis (1995:307) claims, "Generally, the number of veto players varies by issue." These institutional differences affect the outcomes of our game. This section discusses how distinct combinations of the

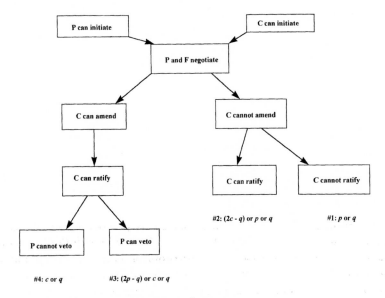

Figure 4.1 Equilibria in Four Institutional Games, $q > p, c$

first three powers—agenda setting, amendment and ratification, and veto—affect the two-level game presented in chapter 3. The use of referendums and side payments are not considered since the former are treated as a form of ratification and the possibility of the latter always exists, giving the executive the last move in the game.

Using the complete information game from chapter 3, I show that the executive's and legislature's preferences bound any equilibrium outcome in the game, no matter what the distribution of powers. In our spatial model (chapter 3), the region where the institutional balance between the executive and the legislature matters is in the area where the status quo is greater than either the executive's or the legislature's ideal point (i.e., $q > p$ or $q > c$). When the status quo is less than the foreign country's ideal point $(q < f)$, then f always dominates. (Note that when F has domestic politics this changes the outcome, symmetrically as in the home country case.) When q is between f and the most dovish home actor $(f < q < p, c)$, then no agreement is possible; q dominates. Only when the status quo is greater than either p or c does its domestic institutional structure matter. Hence for the discussion here I refer to the area where $q > p$ or $q > c$. In this region as the distribution of legislative power shifts from the executive to the legislature, the legislature's ideal point becomes more likely to be the equilibrium outcome. Conversely, when power is concentrated in the executive's hands, the executive's ideal point dominates the equilibrium outcomes.

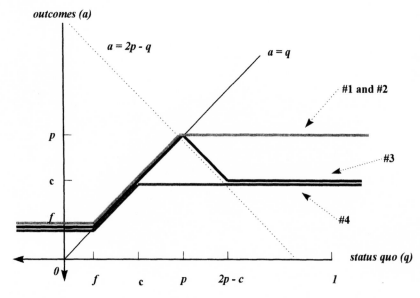

Figure 4.2 Four Institutional Games, $c < p$

Figure 4.1 shows a mapping of the possible combinations of three legisla-tive powers between the executive and the legislature. These combinations result in four different games. In the first—the no amendment-no ratifica-tion game, illustrated by following the arrows at the farthest right of the figure to outcome #1—the executive dominates, as the legislature cannot amend or ratify. Even if the legislature can initiate under these circum-stances, the executive is always able to implement her own preferences in negotiations with the foreign country. Whenever $q > p$, P's ideal point is the outcome.

Figures 4.2 and 4.3 show the (complete information) equilibrium out-comes of the games when different institutions are present; in Figure 4.2 the executive is the hawk ($f < c < p$), and in Figure 4.3 the legislature is the hawk ($f < p < c$). In the no amendment-no ratification game (#1), it does not matter whether the legislature is a hawk or a dove; the executive's prefer-ences dominate since she need not satisfy the legislature. Where legislatures are this weak, domestic politics will be less salient. This situation reduces to the unitary actor model, where P and F negotiate by themselves. But note that in Figure 4.3, when the legislature is a hawk, cooperation is more likely when the executive dominates than in the other three games. In the area $p < q < c$, cooperation is not possible under the other three institutional arrangements; however, it is possible when the executive has a concentra-tion of legislative powers. In this situation the foreign country always prefers a distribution of powers that makes the executive dominant. Not surpris-

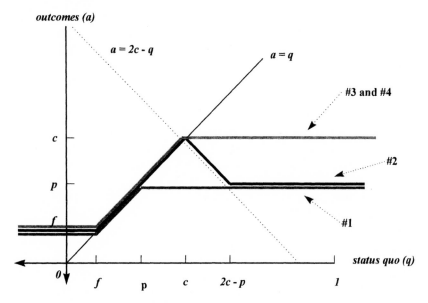

Figure 4.3 Four Institutional Games, $p < c$

ingly, when the legislature is a hawk, concentration of powers in the hands of the dovish executive makes cooperation most likely.

The second game is the ratification game. This is where P or C initiates, P negotiates with F, and C cannot amend but can ratify.[2] It is represented by outcome #2 in Figure 4.1. This is the game used in our model in chapter 3. As the equilibria for the ratification game in Figures 4.2 and 4.3 show, the executive dominates over much of this space (when $q > p$). Sometimes though, when the legislature is hawkish, the executive is forced to moderate her proposals to obtain C's ratification (when $c < q < [2c - p]$). In the ratification game the legislature has some influence over the international agreement and so at times is able to extract a better deal for itself from the executive and the foreign country. But when the legislature is hawkish, this increased influence means that cooperation is less likely (when $p > q > c$) than in the executive dominance game (#1) above. But the legislature is still weak here; indeed, when the legislature is a dove relative to the executive in the ratification game, its influence is imperceptible. The concentration of legislative powers in the executive's hands again produces outcomes closer to those the executive prefers, and in one instance renders the legislature without influence.

[2] It does not matter whether P or C initiates because P must negotiate with the foreign country. In those negotiations P can do what she likes—in effect, P can amend any proposal by C; C's powers after the negotiations determine what P does during them. For instance, if P knows that C can neither amend nor ratify, P always selects her ideal point, or q. But if P knows C can ratify, P will sometimes have to moderate her negotiated position to ensure that C ratifies.

The third game is the amendment-veto game, illustrated by outcome #3 in Figure 4.1. This game shows the progressive movement of the equilibrium outcomes toward the legislature's preferences as the distribution of legislative powers comes to favor it. In outcome #3, P or C initiate, P negotiates with F, C amends the proposed agreement, and P can still veto it afterward. (Note that ratification for C is not important if it can amend; it will amend the proposal to its ideal one and thus always ratify what it amends.) Figures 4.2 and 4.3 show the equilibrium outcomes of the amendment-veto game, relative to those of the three other games. What is obvious is that the outcomes now are closer to the legislature's preferences than they were in the no amendment-no ratification game (#1) and in the ratification game (#2). In Figure 4.2, even though C is a dove, it is now able to influence the outcomes because of its amendment power. In the ratification game C was irrelevant as a dove. With amendment power, as a dove C can extract better outcomes for itself as well as for the foreign country; that is, when $q > p$, the outcomes are no longer p as in the two previous games but now move toward C's ideal point. The same is true when the legislature is a hawk; in Figure 4.3 when $q > c$, the outcome becomes c, rather than p as in the two games above. When the legislature is a dove as in Figure 4.2, the foreign country would definitely want the home legislature to have amendment power. In Figure 4.3, however, the legislature is hawkish and hence the foreign country does not want it to have amendment power since this will move outcomes away from f and toward c.

The fourth game is the amendment-no veto game, which is the outcome illustrated at the far left of Figure 4.1. It represents the maximum influence for the legislature. In outcome #4, C can amend but P cannot veto. This distribution of powers represents the weakest point for the executive. Basically the executive may be able to initiate and negotiate internationally, but since C can amend without recourse from P, P is relatively powerless. The equilibrium outcome (when $q > p$) is always C's ideal point. (Note that when $c < q < p$, the outcome can be either q or c depending on whether P or C initiates or whether C can "amend" to create an agreement P does not prefer to q.) When C is a hawk, the outcome is the same as in the amendment game with a veto (#3), as shown in Figure 4.3. When C is a dove and P cannot veto, the outcome changes slightly from the amendment-veto game (#3), as shown in Figure 4.2. The legislature's ideal point dominates now through the entire range of outcomes ($q > p$). The legislature becomes most powerful here relative to the other three distributions of powers. Note that when C is a dove, the foreign country, F, will want the executive to have as few legislative powers as possible.

Institutions clearly matter for the *terms* of cooperative outcomes. As the executive gains control over legislative powers, the equilibrium outcome moves toward the executive's preferred policy. As power is dispersed toward the legislature, its preferred policy becomes more likely as an outcome of the two-level game. Domestic actors' preferences nevertheless set the boundaries for these institutional effects. No matter which institution is in place, the equilibrium outcome (when $q > p$ or $q > c$) is always between P's and C's ideal policy. Whatever the actors' preferences are, though, they always desire a concentration of legislative powers in their own hands since the policy chosen then will be closest to their own ideal point. Thus actors, if their preferences differ, should also differ over the best institutions to have in place; the distribution of legislative powers should matter for the actors and should be an area of contestation.

The *probability* of cooperation is also affected by the institutional arrangements in place. Cooperation becomes more likely whenever powers are concentrated in the hands of the most dovish domestic actor. As Figures 4.2 and 4.3 show, when the legislature is a dove (Figure 4.2), concentration of legislative powers in the legislature makes cooperation more likely. When the executive is a dove (Figure 4.3), concentration of powers in the executive's hands makes cooperation more likely. Hence dispersion of legislative powers into the hands of the legislature need not undermine international cooperation. It all depends on the domestic actors' preferences. Institutions matter, but preferences are primordial.

Presidential and Parliamentary Systems

The model here would be simplest if presidential and parliamentary systems each had associated with it a particular distribution of legislative power for the executive and the legislature. This, however, is not the case. Comparative studies of these two systems used to take the United Kingdom and the United States as paradigmatic cases in representing parliamentary and presidential systems, respectively. But more and more the dichotomy based on these two systems has been rejected. First, many came to recognize that parliamentary systems differed significantly from the British model as well as from one another. For instance, Lijphart (1984) and others (e.g., Laver and Schofield 1990) have distinguished between majoritarian systems, like the one in Great Britain where single parties control governments, and "consensual" systems, where multiparty government is necessary. Or as Weaver and Rockman (1993:8) note: "There is no 'typical' parliamentary system that can be compared with the U.S. presidential system: differences are especially pronounced between parliamentary systems using proportional representation and single-member-district plurality systems as typified by the Westminster model. Moreover, the way that power is distributed in parliamentary systems may change over time even when basic institutional arrangements do not change." For them, comparing the

U.S. presidential system with parliamentary systems makes no sense since "policy structures and processes in parliamentary systems can vary tremendously across countries and over time. Indeed, comparing parliamentary systems and the American separation-of-powers system is less a matter of comparing apples and oranges than of comparing apples with all other fruits" (19).

If differences among parliamentary systems are now well accepted, differences among presidential systems are becoming better understood. As Shugart and Carey (1992:1–2) claim:

> [Presidential] regimes differ from the common parliamentary type in that there are two agents of the electorate: an assembly and a president . . . [T]here are myriad ways to design [presidential] constitutions that vary the relationship of the voters' two agents to one another, as well as to the electorate. Regimes with elected presidents vary in the ways in which the president may check, cajole, confront, or simply submit to the assembly majority. We even find some systems that give the president so little power relative to the assembly that they are effectively parliamentary. We thus do not see a presidential regime as being the polar opposite of parliamentarism, as much of the literature implies.

Shugart and Carey (1992) and Baylis (1996) also examine the intermediate case of semi-presidential systems, where an elected president sits beside a prime minister who is responsible to the legislature. They show that these types of systems also vary greatly: "There are, however, significant differences in constitutional details in the six [semi-presidential] countries: how the presidents are chosen, what formal powers are accorded them, the circumstances under which prime ministers and cabinets can be forced from office, and so on. . . What can be said in all of these cases is that the question of the actual distribution of executive power has by no means been settled" (Baylis 1996:300). As much of the recent literature concludes, the distinction between presidential and parliamentary systems is often unhelpful, usually impossible to defend, and a poor guide to the relationship between the executive and the legislature.

The distinction between presidential and parliamentary forms of government is made in terms of their origin and survival powers. As Lijphart (1984, 1992) has argued, two central differences exist between them:

> Parliamentary government, or cabinet government, can be concisely defined as the form of constitutional democracy in which executive authority *emerges from*, and is *responsible to*, legislative authority. The two crucially important characteristics of parliamentary government which distinguish it from presidential government are italicized in the definition. First, in a parliamentary system, the chief executive . . . and his or her cabinet are responsible to the legislature in the sense that they are dependent on the legislature's confidence and that they can be dis-

missed from office by a legislative vote of no confidence or censure. In a presidential system, the chief executive . . . is elected for a constitutionally prescribed period and in normal circumstances cannot be forced to resign by a legislative vote of no confidence. . . . The second difference . . . is that presidents are popularly elected . . . and that prime ministers are selected by the legislatures. (1984:68)

Lijphart argues that only these two differences are fundamental because there are empirical examples that defy every other commonly cited difference between them (1984:71–74). Thus the contrast is between a *separation* of executive and legislative powers of origin and survival in a presidential system and their *fusion* in a parliamentary one.

What does this formal distinction mean for the balance of power between the legislature and the executive in the legislative game of crafting policy? It is often felt that because of the fusion of survival of the legislature and executive in parliamentary systems, executive dominance is such that the parliament plays an insignificant role. If the executive completely dominates the relationship, then they do not actually share control over decision making and the unitary state model becomes more appropriate. In terms of the balance of power between the executive and the legislature, in Figure 4.1 outcome #1 represents such executive dominance; here the executive controls initiation and the legislature cannot amend or ratify. In this situation the executive controls international negotiations, and thus agreements reflect the executive's preferences and those of the foreign country.

Although executive dominance may characterize the British system when party discipline is high, it is not a defining characteristic of all parliamentary systems. These systems vary widely in the balance of power between the executive and the legislature. Just as presidential systems may vary in the powers of the executive vis-à-vis the legislature, so may this relationship vary in parliamentary democracies. Parliamentary systems can be divided into at least two groups: those tending toward executive dominance and those with greater legislative-executive power sharing.

The executive's predominance is most assured in what Lijphart calls "Westminster" or majoritarian systems, that is, parliamentary systems with two parties, plurality voting, and single-party majority governments, as in the United Kingdom and some of its former commonwealth countries (1984:16–19). In these systems, because the legislative majority comes from the same party as the executive, the legislature may appear to play a very minor role in decision making:

A parliamentary executive with a secure basis of support among a majority of the assembly can legislate in a virtually unimpeded manner. That is, nearly all proposed laws may be initiated by the cabinet and supported without amendment after their official reading before parliament. It would be folly, however, to infer

from this situation that the parliament is powerless and that the regime is therefore a "facade democracy." . . . In the hypothetical majority party parliamentary
case just sketched, a clear equilibrium stems from the constitutional balance of
powers between the executive and assembly. To the extent that the majority party
can come to agreement internally on policy matters, cabinet proposals will reflect
the general position of the party at large. (Shugart and Carey 1992:132)

But even in this case of clear executive dominance, the legislature still has
a role. "From time to time, . . . the executive may deviate from the intended
policy direction of the mainstream of the party or parties that constitute the
assembly majority . . . The requirement of parliamentary confidence means
that the [majority] can wield their ultimate sanction, voting for censure and
thereby bringing the downfall of the government" (Shugart and Carey
1992:132). The ability to vote no confidence always gives the legislature a
say in the ratification of policies. But it does so at a high cost, since bringing
down the government may necessitate new elections for the legislature.
However, not all votes against the government are cast as votes of confidence; this too depends on the system. A recent study of the confidence
vote procedure concludes that an executive with unilateral control over the
procedure wields much influence but that in general "the 'confidence relationship' between governments and parliaments is a two-way street. Members of parliaments can certainly attempt to control policy outcomes by sub-
mitting, or threatening to submit, votes of no-confidence in the government.
But the prime minister and the cabinet can also take the initiative by demanding that parliament participate in a vote of confidence in the government" (Huber 1996:269). Hence even in two-party, single-member plurality
systems, the executive may be powerful but even there must maintain the
confidence of the legislative majority.

Only 13 percent of parliamentary governments in the postwar period have
been single-party majorities (Laver and Shepsle 1991). This small group is
represented by the majoritarian (Westminster) systems—as in the United
Kingdom, Canada, New Zealand, and Australia. Among them the polyarchic
model used here might not hold. In these cases the prime minister and the
cabinet dominate policy making; the legislature shares little authority in this
process. "Because the cabinet is composed of a cohesive majority party in
the House of Commons, it is normally backed by the majority in the House
of Commons, and it can confidently count on staying in office and getting its
legislative proposals approved" (Lijphart 1984:7). The cabinet's ability to
"blackmail" the parliament into approving its proposals by using the threat
of new elections is particularly strong (Schlesinger 1992:91). In these cases
the executive rarely needs to worry about the legislature's approval of policies and does not face the problem of divided government, as long as party
discipline holds (Crossman 1972:31). Under a single-party majority govern-

ment, "The executive's partisan control over the legislature will ensure that there is no legislative impediment to executive decision-making" (Laver and Shepsle 1991:253). Power over decision making will not be shared, and a unitary model of domestic politics is more appropriate.

Among parliamentary systems, on the other hand, multiparty proportional representation (PR) systems, which Lijphart labels "consensus" models, necessitate greater power sharing between the executive and the legislature. What propels this power sharing is the need for coalition government. In these multiparty PR systems a single-party majority government is rare. Instead, the government is usually created by a coalition of parties or a minority party. In a minority government where the executive must find a majority in the legislature for support on each issue, the power of the legislature is apparent. In a coalition government the prime minister represents one party in this coalition, whereas the cabinet is formed from the entire coalition. Within the government the parties must negotiate over the policies the executive proposes. The cabinet and its legislative majority will thus share decision-making power. Lijphart (1984:25) draws on Belgium to make this general point:

> Belgium has a parliamentary form of government with a cabinet dependent on the confidence of the legislature as in Britain. Nevertheless, Belgian cabinets, largely because they are often broad and uncohesive coalitions, are not at all as dominant as their British counterparts, and they tend to have a give-and-take relationship with parliament. . . . Although Belgium has a parliamentary system without a formal separation of powers, its executive-legislative relationship may be regarded as an informal or semi-separation of powers.

Thus the game between the legislature and the executive greatly depends on how decision-making powers are allocated between the two branches.

The vast majority of advanced industrial democracies are multiparty parliamentary systems. Only a few presidential or semi-presidential systems (the United States, Finland, and the Fifth Republic of France) and a few two-party parliamentary systems (the United Kingdom, New Zealand, and Australia) exist. In all multiparty parliamentary and presidential systems, the legislature and executive share power. The legislature's influence varies significantly within and across constitutional systems. For example, Italy and the Fourth French Republic are viewed as having strong parliaments, whereas the United Kingdom is seen as having a weak one, with Germany's Bundestag falling somewhere in the middle (Norton 1990a; Furlong 1990; Saalfeld 1990). "In parliamentary systems, the dominance of the cabinet in Britain may be contrasted with the classic example of legislative supremacy and weak cabinets in the French Third and Fourth Republics. Among contemporary democratic regimes, Italy is another, but much less extreme, example of imbalance in favor of the legislature" (Lijphart 1984:79). Hence although similar in their powers of origin and survival, parliamentary systems, like presidential ones, differ in the balance of power between their legislatures and executives.

Thus at least three types of systems need to be distinguished: two-party parliamentary, multiparty parliamentary, and presidential (Shaw 1990; Lijphart 1984; Powell 1982). Each has a different power-sharing relationship between its legislature and executive. "Constitutional systems based on the Westminster [two-party parliamentary] model presuppose that political executives will operate within the legislature and lead it; constitutional systems based on the [presidential] model presuppose that political executives will be separated from the legislature; constitutional systems based on the [multiparty parliamentary] model presuppose a range of 'parallel' executive-legislative relationships tending to fall at various points between 'fusion' and 'separation'" (Shaw 1990:251). The executive is most powerful and autonomous in the two-party parliamentary case.

On the other hand, the legislature may be at its peak of influence in some presidential systems. As Lijphart (1984, 1992) and others note, "There is no doubt that constitutional separation of powers tends to give the legislature more strength and independence vis-à-vis the executive than does fusion of powers. In particular, the Unites States Congress is a strikingly powerful legislative body compared with the parliaments of all of the parliamentary systems discussed in this book" (1984:78). This separation of powers, however, does not necessarily imply legislative dominance; some presidential systems—for example, Mexico—have weak legislatures, as Shugart and Carey (1992:156) show.

In general, then, in multiparty parliamentary and presidential systems, the legislature will share more authority over policy making than in the two-party parliamentary ones. Thus the presidential-parliamentary distinction appears less helpful than the categorization of executive-legislative relationships by the distribution of legislative powers. For our purposes, how these powers are distributed between the executive and the legislature on the issue at hand will have a greater effect on how the game is played domestically than will the presidential or parliamentary nature of a regime.

Change of Ratification Procedures

The distribution of powers between the executive and the legislature has important consequences for both the possibility and terms of international cooperative agreements. The ability to change this distribution is therefore an important power resource. If domestic actors have different preferences over policy, their preferences regarding the institutions used to choose policy should also vary. Actors ought to be concerned not just with the policy choice itself but also with the distribution of legislative powers in each issue area. Conflict internally over which policies are chosen should translate into conflict over which institutions are used:

> In the end, therefore, institutions are no more than rules and rules are themselves the product of social decisions . . . One can expect that losers on a series of decisions under a particular set of rules will attempt (often successfully) to change institutions and hence the kind of decisions produced under them . . . Thus the only difference between [preferences] and institutions is that revelation of institutional disequilibria is probably a longer process than the revelation of disequilibria of [preferences] . . . [I]nstitutions are probably best seen as congealed tastes. (Riker 1980:444–45)

Institutions embody actor's tastes—what I call *preferences*—and thus contests over preferred policies necessarily spill over into contests about institutions.

The institutional process used domestically to accept an international agreement plays an important role. These procedures determine who initiates, amends, and ratifies the agreement. As the previous sections show, who controls these processes affects the terms and probability of agreement. The domestic debate over international cooperation should also include the definition of these procedures. The following discussion focuses on only the power of ratification since it is the one used in the model in chapter 3. But in theory all elements of the legislative process should be amenable to the same dynamics. Actors should be concerned about who controls not only ratification but also initiation, amendment, and veto power.

The model in chapter 3 focused on a ratification game. Here I argue that who this ratifier is determines both whether international negotiations on an issue ever begin and what the terms of an agreement on the issue look like. In thinking about international cooperation, the executive must estimate whether any agreement is possible and which agreements will be ratifiable domestically. The decision to start international negotiations depends on the chances for ratifying an agreement at home. Negotiators must anticipate the reactions of their legislatures and of important societal groups.

Rationally a leader will always seek to negotiate agreements that can be ratified at home; if no agreement exists that the legislature will approve of, then international negotiations should never begin. It is costly for executives to negotiate an international agreement only to have it turned down domestically; this may in fact be the worst outcome from an executive's view.[3] Leaders' reputations for being able to conduct foreign policy abroad are damaged, and at home they appear weak and constrained by their legisla-

---

[3] An executive might wish to be seen as trying to cooperate, while not actually being interested in cooperation. This would imply that the costs of the effort were less than the benefits of being seen as trying to cooperate. The argument here is that these costs of trying and failing may be quite high.

tures, not to mention their loss of time and effort in negotiating. Hence the decision to begin negotiations should indicate that the executive believes the legislature will indeed ratify some agreement, which the foreign country will also accept.

The process of ratification also matters because it determines the median voter from whom the executive must secure approval. The form the ratification vote takes influences the terms of the agreement made. Whether ratification takes place through a simple legislative majority, a supramajority (like a two-thirds majority) or a popular referendum affects which groups will decide the outcome. The ratification process determines which actors count, thus determining the structure of domestic preferences. For example, the preferences of the legislator who represents the winning vote in a simple majority contest may be closer to those of the executive than are those of the legislator who represents the winning vote in a two-thirds majority contest in the same legislature. This change in the preference structure will change the nature of the agreement that the executive can get ratified and thus will affect the agreement made, as chapter 3 demonstrates. Under different ratification institutions, the median voter differs. Thus the executive's calculations about what type of agreement can be ratified domestically will also differ.

The rational executive will thus agree to certain terms in international negotiations given her beliefs about the ratification process. If the executive begins the international negotiations believing that ratification will occur as a result of a simple majority vote in the legislature, the executive will negotiate an agreement that the median legislator will support.[4] A different means of ratification logically implies a different agreement. The structure of preferences domestically will change, and new actors will be involved in the ratification game.

A problem for the executive arises when the institutions of ratification are changed after the fact; that is, if after the agreement is made, it is decided that a referendum is necessary instead of a parliamentary vote, the executive is faced with a dilemma. The agreement negotiated, which the median legislator would support, may not be one that the median voter will support. Indeed it is likely that this agreement will be rejected because these two groups may have different preferences. Thus any change in the institutions of ratification after an agreement is reached will make ratification, and thus international cooperation, less likely.

This may be one reason why the domestic opponents of an international agreement often concentrate their ire on the ratification procedures. For them, one way to defeat an international agreement is to try to change the

---

[4] Can the executive be expected to know the median legislator's preferences? In parliamentary systems and in systems with high party discipline, the executive is quite likely to know them. Party affiliation will determine the legislator's vote.

institutions of ratification after the fact. It is thus anticipated that domestic opponents of an international agreement will try to alter the ratification procedures so that actors with preferences closer to theirs become the median voter in the ratification game. Ideally they would like to become the crucial voter, but any change may be sufficient to cause an agreement to fail domestically. When such opponents are successful, the probability of international cooperation will decline.

The ratification procedures should be a subject of contention in the cooperation process; they may be disputed before, during, and after the international negotiations. Both the executive and the other actors know the importance of the ratification procedures. Thus they will realize even before the international negotiations begin that choosing these procedures will have a major impact on the possibility of any agreement and on its terms. Establishing the procedures for ratification should be a major element of the domestic game.

Ratification procedures are issue-specific, which means they tend to vary according to the issue at hand. An international trade agreement is likely to have different ratification procedures connected to it than is an agreement on monetary union. The central actors in each should differ, and hence so should the domestic ratification game. In some cases ratification procedures may be fixed constitutionally; that is, the actors are forced by the constitution to use a particular process. For instance, in the United States all agreements called treaties must be ratified by a two-thirds majority in the U.S. Senate, whereas in Denmark all treaties must be ratified by a majority in parliament. In Germany all constitutional amendments require ratification by two-thirds of both houses of parliament, whereas in the Fifth French Republic the ratification of constitutional changes requires either majority votes in both houses of parliament and a popular referendum, or a three-fifths majority of a joint session of the legislature, or a national referendum alone (Lijphart 1984:191).

Although these fixed procedures may lock the actors into a certain game, in many cases political actors still have the ability to select the means of ratification. The dispute in these cases actually becomes transformed into one over whether the agreement is a "treaty," or a "constitutional amendment," respectively. Not surprisingly, views on the character of the agreement tend to correlate with the actors' preferences. Although there may be nationally prescribed institutional means for ratifying an international agreement, even these will be amenable to the political actors' manipulation. The institutions of ratification may therefore vary more by the issue under consideration than by the country concerned.

Ratification procedures are a part of the domestic game. They may even be endogenous to that game. In particular, they may be seen *in part* as a function of the nature of the power-sharing relationship between the executive and the legislature and the structure of domestic preferences. In an issue area where the preferences of major domestic actors are quite far apart, attempts to alter the ratification procedures should be more likely. More divided government should produce the same effect. When an issue is contentious—that is, when the legislature, executive, and/or interest groups have very divergent preferences—one would expect an intensified struggle over the procedures used to ratify it. The more contentious the issue, the more disagreement over the ratification procedures. In contrast, when general agreement reigns over a domestic issue, one would expect debate over the ratification process to recede.

Furthermore, the actors' preferences concerning the means of ratification should follow from their preferences about the issue. For instance, before international negotiations begin, opponents of an international agreement should attempt to make the ratification procedures more difficult or make themselves the median voter; or, after the fact, they might simply try to change the procedures to derail the agreement. Supporters of the agreement will oppose these efforts and try to design procedures that make ratification easier or make them the median voter; they should also oppose all attempts to change the process after the fact. In the United States, for example, the creation of "fast track" procedures to ratify trade agreements has been a product of the supporters of trade liberalization and has been challenged by its opponents (Destler 1992).

In Great Britain contention over European cooperation has been so strong that it has produced many fights over ratification procedures. In 1975, after years of fierce debate, the British government took the highly unusual step of holding a national referendum on the issue—the first referendum ever in British history (Lijphart 1984:15). In 1994 opponents of the European Monetary Union, believing the British public would not support these measures, once again pushed for a national referendum against the prime minister's wishes (*Financial Times*, May 11, 1994). The institutions of ratification for each issue should depend on the nature of power sharing between the legislature and executive and the structure of domestic preferences surrounding that issue. As stated above, the more contentious the issue, the more debate over the procedures. And the actors' positions in the debate over the means of ratification should be linked to their preferences on the issue.

The procedures for ratification of an international agreement are both a factor influencing the domestic game and one influenced by it. As noted before, the relationship between institutions and preferences is difficult to disentangle. The structure of preferences affects which institutions are used, and the nature of pre-existing institutions affects which actors and preferences are important for the ratification game. What has been emphasized is that actors can make institutional choices. How an agreement is ratified is an important variable; it is part of the domestic actors' game. The procedures for ratification should not be seen as a constant for each country; rather, they will vary by issue area and by country.

The choice of ratification institutions becomes endogenous to the domestic game. This is not a problem for the model elaborated on in chapter 3. The model is very general; all it requires is that the median actor of some group have a say afterward in approving the international agreement crafted by the executive and the foreign country. The actor giving approval may be the legislature, the voting public, or some other entity. Who this group's median voter is —that is, the one whose vote is necessary for approval—is also not specified. By allowing the actors' preferences to vary in the model, we can see the effects of assuming different median voters. Changing the median voter from a simple legislative majority to a two-thirds majority alters the structure of preferences. Variation in the ratification procedures, then, does not affect the utility of the model here. In fact it can demonstrate what happens to the domestic game when these procedures change.

Conclusions

Political institutions have an important impact on decision making domestically. Institutions determine which actors have greater influence in the policy process and hence affect whose preferences the policy chosen most reflects. I am particularly concerned with institutions that determine the power-sharing relationship between the executive and the legislature. In contrast to the unitary state assumption, the assumption that states are polyarchic systems implies both that domestic actors share power over decision making and that their preferences differ. Polyarchic systems make policy and negotiate internationally differently than unitary states do.

This chapter examined how different distributions of legislative power between the executive and the legislature affect the outcomes of international negotiations. It made four claims:

1. For understanding international cooperation, the distinction between parliamentary and presidential systems in terms of the origin and survival powers is less important than the distribution of legislative powers.

2. Key legislative powers include the ability to set the agenda, make amendments, ratify or veto proposals, call referendums, and deploy side payments. Control over these powers gives actors influence in the legislative process. When control over these powers is concentrated in the executive, the executive's preferences prevail. When control is dispersed to the legislature, its preferences will come to the fore. The model in chapter 3 used the ratification game, which tends to favor the executive. In systems that concentrate all powers in the hands of the

executive—that is, where the legislature cannot ratify—then our model will underestimate the executive's influence. On the other hand, in systems where the legislature is more powerful—say, having sole control over amendment and ratification—our model will overestimate the executive's power; outcomes will favor the legislature. The probability of agreement is also greatest when legislative powers are concentrated in the hands of the most dovish domestic actor.

3. Changes in the institutions by which international agreements are considered domestically after international negotiations conclude will negatively affect the possibility of international cooperation.

4. Issue areas matter greatly. Control over legislative powers often varies significantly by issue and if actors have preferences over issues, they should also have preferences over the institutions they desire for considering each issue. In emphasizing issue areas, this book joins a long debate about the relative importance of issues versus national characteristics (Lowi 1964; Zimmerman 1973; Evangelista 1989). National political institutions set broad parameters within which the domestic game is played, but the game may vary substantially within these parameters. The particular issue under consideration determines the structure of preferences and shapes the debate over the institutions of ratification that are used. In turn the process of ratification selects which actors will be the median voters from whom the executive must obtain support, thus determining the domestic ratification game.

Institutional factors shape the power-sharing relationship between the executive and the legislature and are an important set of variables that must be considered when analyzing the domestic game. Institutions affect both the probability and terms of international agreements, but they do so in conjunction with the actors' preferences. Chapter 3 showed how preferences matter, holding institutions constant. This chapter varied those institutions to see their effect, holding preferences constant. What both chapters demonstrate, however, is that preferences and political institutions (as well as the distribution of information) jointly determine how domestic politics shapes international relations.

Part Two ————————————————————

THE CASE STUDIES

CHAPTERS 2 through 4 presented the theory of two-level games used to understand international cooperation. The main argument was that the nature of power sharing between the executive and legislature and the structure of domestic preferences conditioned the possibility and terms of international agreements through their effect on the domestic ratification game. A number of hypotheses follow from the analysis in these chapters. Here I present these hypotheses and examine the cases in light of them.

First, of key importance are the domestic actors' policy preferences. The structure of these preferences is a central independent variable explaining both the probability and terms of international cooperation. Chapter 3 lays out two hypotheses about the effect of the structure of preferences on international cooperation. First, in the ratification game domestic politics exerts its greatest influence when the legislature is the hawk domestically. Ceteris paribus, the possibility of cooperative agreement declines in this situation. But the terms of any agreement that is ratifiable favor the legislature more. Second, divided government spells problems for cooperation. More division means less cooperation; however, where agreement is possible again it favors the legislature more.

Second, chapter 4 focuses on the role of political institutions in influencing international cooperation. Political institutions matter for they allocate power over policy making among domestic actors. Thus they condition whose preferences are most closely adhered to in cooperative agreements. Chapter 4 lays out two hypotheses about the effects of political institutions on the probability and terms of international cooperation. First, where political institutions concentrate decision-making power in the hands of the executive, outcomes will be different than where they disperse such power between the legislature and executive. The ratification game will produce outcomes other than those that result from the amendment game. The latter gives greater power to the legislature, rendering cooperative outcomes closer to its preferences. Moreover, when the institutions vest greater powers in the more hawkish domestic actor, cooperation becomes less likely. Second, changes in political institutions during or after international negotiations lower the possibility of a successful agreement.

Third, chapter 3 also focuses on the role of information in two-level games. The distribution of information domestically affects the ability to make international agreements and the terms on which they are made. Information asymmetries create inefficiencies and political advantages. Two hypotheses about the domestic distribution of information can be adduced. First, the presence of incomplete or asymmetric information (without endorsers) makes cooperation less likely and advantages the executive. Second, the endorsement of the proposed international agreement by at least one informed signaler, usually an interest group, is a necessary condition for cooperation in the presence of asymmetric information. Such endorsers make cooperation more likely and more favorable to the legislature.

Four factors reduce the possibility of cooperative agreement. First, divided government and increasing divisions in it are key problems for any agreement. Greater divisions mean less chance of cooperation. Second, lack of endorsement from at least one major interest group involved in the issue reduces the likelihood of cooperation in that area. The role of domestic groups as information providers is essential. Third, the interaction of preferences and institutions is another factor that may undermine the possibility of cooperation. In countries or on issues where legislative power is concentrated in the hands of the most hawkish player domestically, cooperation will be least likely. Political institutions also variously affect the probability of successful cooperative agreement. Fourth, any change in these domestic institutions during or after the international negotiations spells trouble for the international agreement.

The goal of part 2 of this book is to explore these hypotheses about domestic politics through a series of case studies. The propositions of the alternative theories presented in chapter 1 are briefly examined in each case, but this does not constitute a test of them, given the means used to select the cases. These alternative hypotheses highlight the potential role of international systemic factors and raise other issues about the cooperative effort.

As noted in the introduction, I analyze eight cases. These are paired and presented in four chapters. The pairing involves using the same countries over the same time period to examine instances of successful and failed cooperation. Cases where cooperation was never initiated are not examined explicitly; thus there is a bias in the cases studied. A means of correcting for this is to ask why other countries did not join in the cooperative efforts undertaken. For example, in the two European cases from the early 1950s, one should ask why Britain failed to join. What was it about British political leaders that made them uninterested in European economic integration, especially when they were initiators of Atlantic security cooperation?

On the other hand, cases of both failed and successful cooperative agreements are presented. The central question is why countries reached cooperative accords in some cases but not in others. Whether the agreements were fully carried out as specified and whether they had good or bad results is not addressed here. The expectation is that the hypotheses presented here can help answer when and why cooperative agreements among nations can be crafted.

I have chosen these cases for various reasons. First they involve different issue areas and different countries. Hence both the structure of preferences and the political institutions vary in each case. The areas of cooperation I have chosen include monetary and exchange rate, trade, industry, and defense policy. Different political institutions also characterize the sample of countries examined. The countries include the United States with its two-party, presidential system; the United Kingdom with its (largely) two-party, parliamentary system; France in the Fourth Republic with a multiparty proportional representation (PR) system and in the Fifth Republic with a semi-presidential system; and West Germany with a multiparty PR system. Including such variance gives us leverage on the impact of institutional variables.

Another reason I have selected these sample cases is that the same countries can be compared at the same time periods on different issues. Each pair of cases includes a failed cooperative effort and a successful one. This allows us to hold constant the international situation and elements of the national political system while varying the issue and the outcomes. With this method of comparison we can judge whether these cases support the arguments adduced in the first four chapters. Moreover, it allows us to address more directly the key question of why cooperation fails or succeeds.

The final set of cases follows a somewhat different pattern. It involves different countries on different issues at the same time and with the same outcome. In the cases of both NAFTA and the Maastricht Treaty, cooperative agreements were achieved even though the implementation of their terms may not yet have been. Unlike the other cases, these two occurred at a different time. The first six all occurred within a decade of the end of World War II, when U.S. hegemony was important and the cold war was just beginning. The last two cases occurred recently: after the end of the cold war and with U.S. hegemony reduced from that of the 1940s and 1950s. Inclusion of these two final cases provides a comparison with the earlier ones. What effect did U.S. hegemony have on the argument presented here? Were domestic politics of more, less, or the same importance when the United States was dominant as when it was less so? Similarly, what effect did the cold war have? Was domestic politics as important to relations between countries during the height of the cold war in the 1950s as it was after the cold war ended? Thus the cases also allow for comparison over time.

Five

The Bretton Woods Monetary Agreement and the International Trade Organization, 1943–1950

DURING the final stages of World War II the British and U.S. governments attempted to create a new world economic order. Their efforts mainly concerned international trade and monetary relations but also involved petroleum and civil aviation issues, which are discussed in the next chapter. The countries were successful in negotiating agreements to govern the monetary and aviation areas but failed to develop such arrangements in trade and petroleum. Given that these negotiations largely involved the same countries during the same time period, why were some cooperative agreements reached and others not? This chapter focuses on identifying what factors differentiated the failed from the successful agreements. It also examines the terms of the agreement and which actors' preferences were most closely followed in the agreement. In particular, it examines these cases in light of the hypotheses presented above. Three variables seem especially important in explaining the outcomes: the degree of divided government, the endorsement (or lack of it) by domestic groups, and changes in ratification procedures.

Beginning with negotiations over the Atlantic Charter in August 1941 the United States and the United Kingdom embarked on a journey to revive the international trade and payments system, which depression and war had severely damaged. In 1943 the two nations started negotiations over international monetary relations by discussing their respective national plans for creating a stable monetary system, the White and Keynes Plans. After a year of intergovernmental bargaining, the two reached a tentative agreement on plans for a fixed exchange rate system, the International Monetary Fund (IMF), and the International Bank for Reconstruction and Development (IBRD). In July 1944 the United States, Great Britain, and forty-two other countries (including representatives from the Soviet Union) met at Bretton Woods, New Hampshire, to revise this agreement, which they then signed. It took the United States about a year and the United Kingdom about eighteen months to obtain ratification of the agreement domestically, longer than it took the two nations to reach an agreement between themselves (Van Dormael 1978; Gardner 1980).

Trade negotiations began at the same time as those over monetary matters in 1943; indeed, trade was the central issue in dispute in Article 4 of the

Atlantic Charter in 1941 and Article 7 of the Mutual Aid Agreement in 1942. But the trade talks stalled for nearly two years as disagreements fueled by domestic pressures persisted. In late 1945 negotiations resumed, and by the end of the year the United States publicized its "Proposals for an International Conference on Trade and Employment." In February 1946 negotiations resumed in the context of a United Nations-sponsored conference in London, which resulted, in October of that year, in the Charter for an International Trade Organization (ITO). In the spring of 1947 the United States, the United Kingdom, and twenty-one other countries met in Geneva to discuss the Charter and to negotiate tariff reductions under the interim General Agreement on Tariffs and Trade (GATT), which embodied a small section of the ITO Charter relating to trade and tariffs on manufactured goods. Negotiations concluded in October 1947 with limited reductions achieved. A new conference, equivalent to the one in Bretton Woods, began in Havana, Cuba, in December 1947 to finalize the ITO Charter. In March 1948 the agreement reached at this conference set new rules and procedures for a wide range of trade and investment issues. In 1948 the agreement was introduced into the U.S. Senate for ratification but failed to receive enough support and died in 1950. Without ratification by the United States, other countries—especially those where domestic support was weak, like the United Kingdom—refused to consider the ITO. Hence the ITO agreement, the analogue in the trade area to the Bretton Woods monetary agreement, could not be achieved.

Why could a cooperative agreement be negotiated in the monetary area but not in the area of trade? This outcome is especially puzzling because negotiations in both areas occurred at about the same time and involved roughly the same countries. Negotiations in the monetary area took place between 1943 and 1946; those involving trade between 1943 and 1949. The two sets of negotiations primarily involved the United States and the United Kingdom, but a number of other countries also participated in the latter stages of both, including many Western European states and lesser developed countries (LDCs). As one study of international policy coordination points out, "The groundwork for both the monetary and the commercial policy institutions was substantially an Anglo-American affair" (Artis and Ostry 1986:23). Both negotiations occurred during the final stages of the war and concluded in its aftermath. Many of the most prominent theories of cooperation, especially those at the systemic level, cannot explain these two different outcomes. Rather, they would predict that similar systemic conditions at the time should lead to similar outcomes. The global balance of power and U.S. hegemony in the West remained fairly constant over this period. The rise of the Soviet threat and continued U.S. hegemony should have induced cooperation in these cases, according to many of these theories.

Before examining these cases, it is necessary to determine whether their outcomes are in fact different. Although the ITO failed, revitalization of world trade in a liberal, multilateral system occurred through the GATT. Moreover, even though the Bretton Woods agreement was signed in 1946, it failed to operate as it was intended until the late 1950s. While these are valid issues, two points should be noted. First, the GATT failed to deal with a wide range of international trade and investment issues that the ITO was intended to regulate. Hence cooperation beyond tariff setting for industrial goods was not achieved at all. Second, the GATT, which was never ratified by the United States or other countries, served less as the basis for trade barrier reductions in its early years than did national laws. Cooperation in reducing tariffs occurred as a result of bilateral, reciprocal negotiations, many of which were conducted under the Reciprocal Trade Agreements Act (RTAA) in the United States. The RTAA provided the framework for the trade talks to a greater extent than did the GATT, at least until the Kennedy Round in the 1960s. Without the RTAA, the United States would not have been able to participate in the international tariff-cutting negotiations. Without the GATT, on the other hand, the United States could have achieved similar reciprocal tariff reductions.

As others have noted, "The chapter on commercial policy of the ITO charter on which the GATT was based included familiar provisions that had been developed in earlier [U.S.] bilateral agreements" (Vernon and Spar 1989:45). Hence "cooperation" in trade was not centered around an international agreement, as Bretton Woods provided in the monetary area.[1] Rather, tariff reductions resulted from the widespread use of unconditional most-favored-nation (MFN) treatment and American willingness to bargain away its tariffs reciprocally. Thus the GATT before 1960 does not fit the definition of cooperation very well. It required much less of an adjustment of U.S. policies in return for, or anticipation of, the adjustment of other states' policies than the ITO would have required. To an important extent the United States was pursuing a policy and following rules it would have pursued even in the absence of the GATT. These two points undercut the argument that the same level of cooperative agreement was achieved in the trade and monetary cases. Even if one admits that some cooperation resulted from the GATT in the trade area, it was less substantial than that achieved in the monetary area through the Bretton Woods agreement.

---

[1] After the 1950s the GATT became more like the Bretton Woods agreement, embodying a set of rules and norms for behavior. Ironically, the GATT system continues today, whereas the element of a fixed exchange rate of the Bretton Woods system has disappeared. Moreover, the recent GATT Uruguay Round agreed on a new World Trade Organization with greater responsibilities and more formal structure, much like the ITO.

The ITO and the GATT

Domestic Preferences and Institutions

During World War II the United States and the United Kingdom began both monetary and trade negotiations. The trade negotiations arose largely as a result of U.S. initiative, unlike the monetary negotiations where Britain took the lead initially. U.S. preferences concerning trade policy were divided. On one side stood the executive branch, led by Secretary of State Cordell Hull and President Franklin D. Roosevelt, and export-oriented U.S. firms, who desired tariff reductions in exchange for greater access to foreign markets. On the other side were the protectionists: most of the Republican Party, agriculture, and domestically oriented U.S. firms.

The interest of the executive and internationally oriented firms in trade liberalization predated the war. The international trade negotiations were intimately connected with earlier changes in U.S. trade policy and the internal politics surrounding them. As mentioned above, the president's choice to adopt the RTAA signaled a change in the direction of trade policy. Without this prior unilateral policy change, neither the ITO nor the GATT would have been possible.

The RTAA recognized the importance of exports for the prosperity of the U.S. economy and gave the president the ability at renewable periods to negotiate reciprocal tariff reductions. As the economist who coordinated the administration's international commercial policy in the 1930s said, "American domestic prosperity cannot be secured by exclusively domestic programs. Domestic prosperity depends upon the wheels of production . . . ; and such continued activity is in turn dependent upon the maintenance of foreign markets in order to utilize to the full our productive capacity" (Sayre 1939:10). Roosevelt, like most presidents since, recognized that foreign markets were important to the health of the U.S. economy; trade liberalization in the eyes of political leaders has always been about the creation of jobs and profits and the electoral benefits they bring. Hull even acknowledged during hearings on the RTAA that "the whole purpose [of the bill], of course, is to promote our domestic prosperity; that is the primary and paramount purpose" (U.S. Congress, House Ways and Means Committee 1934:12).

For Roosevelt the interest in trade liberalization rested on the calculation that the home benefits of protection had become very small while the negative externalities generated by other countries' protection reduced U.S. prosperity. The reconstruction of a multilateral system of world trade thus became the Roosevelt administration's key objective in international economic affairs after World War II (Gardner 1980:13). The U.S. State Department led by Cordell Hull had been the most vigorous proponent, since the 1930s, of the goals of "multilateralism" and the end of preferential trade relations. This was not the same as a free trade system. It meant a system in which barriers to trade in industrial products were nondiscriminatory and lowered to moderate levels; agriculture would be exempt from any such cuts, given the strong political opposition to its inclusion. For Hull this meant negotiating trade agreements that put nondiscrimination first and trade barrier reduction second (15–16).

U.S. business support for nondiscrimination also depended on changes in U.S. trade policy begun before World War II. The adoption of unconditional MFN treatment at the end of World War I (in 1921) made U.S. industry "the most vigorous champion of nondiscriminatory trade"(Gardner 1980:16). By 1919 the United States had become a large exporter of mass-produced industrial goods, and it needed markets abroad for them. The principal barrier to U.S. exports was the preferential trading blocs set up by the Europeans, especially the British. Bitter complaints by American producers, who desperately needed foreign markets in the 1930s to offset domestic depression, encouraged Hull to begin the battle against the British preferential system in the wake of the Ottawa agreements in the early 1930s, which closed many Commonwealth markets to U.S. producers (19).

The second and subordinate element of U.S. policy involved reducing trade barriers. Many in the U.S. government and business community opposed government intervention in economic affairs; they wanted some elimination of trade barriers but few wanted their complete elimination. Many domestic producers—including almost all of agriculture—still demanded protection (Gardner 1980:20). There were also political divisions, the most salient being that between the political parties. The Democrats generally favored some liberalization whereas the Republicans were usually opposed to it.

American actors' preferences, then, were represented by two positions. No domestic group, except professional economists, preferred purely free trade. Rather, the executive and internationally oriented business groups favored "selective, reciprocal, and moderate reduction[s]"(Gardner 1980:22) in trade barriers, largely to stimulate exports. Congress, when Democrats were in the majority, could be relied on to support the executive as long as he did not go too far. During the first part of the trade negotiations, the Democrats controlled both houses and the presidency. Unified government existed, then, from 1943 to 1946. However, the Republicans gained control of Congress from 1947 to 1948, leaving the government divided. This division had important consequences because the Republicans' and Democrats' preferences over trade differed significantly. Domestic business, agriculture, and the majority of Republicans opposed any trade liberalization. Thus the majority in Congress was always somewhat more hawkish about trade liberalization than were Democratic presidents in this period, but after 1946 Congress became extremely hawkish.

The institutional arrangements for setting trade policy in the United States had undergone a substantial change since the mid-1930s. The U.S. Constitution grants Congress the power to initiate and formulate policy in the trade area. Before 1934 the U.S. Congress exercised this right exclusively. The Reciprocal Trade Agreement Act of 1934 changed this ruling and has served as the basis for U.S. trade policy since then (Haggard 1988; Goldstein 1988). An interesting note is that the RTAA became law under a Democratically controlled Congress, the first instance of unified Democratic control since 1918 (O'Halloran 1994:85). The RTAA, by delegating authority to the president to negotiate reciprocal trade agreements with foreign countries, allowed for the periodic transfer of control over trade policy making to the president and away from Congress. Congress would allow the executive to negotiate tariff barrier reductions up to a certain level and proclaim these as law. Although this process substantially strengthened the executive's hand, the process of delegation limited executive control. Because Congress forced the president to renew this authority every two or three years, Congress in effect maintained a veto over international trade negotiations. This ex ante delegation power served as a form of ratification vote; Congress, if it did not like the results of the previous negotiation, could eliminate or reduce the president's future authority to negotiate.

As O'Halloran (1994) shows, the RTAA did not give the president a free hand in trade policy; moreover, the discretion Congress gave the president varied with the current structure of preferences. When government was divided, Congress tended to rein in the executive, limiting her negotiating ability and including other procedures to protect industry. Indeed, at a major stage in negotiations over the ITO, divided government hindered the executive:

> In 1947, for example, with the election of the Republican-controlled Eightieth Congress, protectionist concerns called for repeal of the trade agreements program and postponement of the ongoing General Agreements on Tariffs and Trade multilateral negotiations in Geneva. . . . GOP pressure forced President Truman to agree to an "escape clause" in all future trade agreements . . . In October 1947, Truman signed the GATT, which defined the protocol for conducting multilateral negotiations on international commerce. But Congress continued to restrict the president's negotiating authority to bilateral trade agreements and to only those provisions consistent with domestic statutes. As a result of this protectionist sentiment, Truman never submitted the GATT agreement to Congress for formal ratification. (88)

The RTAA did transform the institutional process of trade policy making by giving greater powers to the executive. But this institutional transformation was limited for domestic reasons. According to Gardner (1980:22), there was "no other approach [for] securing political support for a programme of tariff reduction" in the United States. By the 1940s most of the U.S. administration was committed to multilateralism and trade liberalization, supported by its international business community but opposed by more domestic-oriented industries that remained well represented in Congress and the Republican Party. Internationally oriented business was, however, a key element in Roosevelt's political coalition; its support was essential for successful pursuit of his other domestic and international policies (Ferguson 1984; Frieden 1988).

The structure of British preferences differed in two respects from that in the United States. First, the British government retained an interest in lowering trade barriers but had little enthusiasm for multilateralism because a large part of its trade was with the Commonwealth. For Britain, "multilateralism remained a controversial public issue. British opinion was sharply divided on the merits of an open, nondiscriminatory trading system"(Gardner 1980:24). Moreover, the executive in the United Kingdom was isolated in its desire for trade liberalization. Within Britain, business was opposed to the abolition of the Imperial Preference system (30). "British business groups showed no signs of abandoning these policies in their planning for the post-war period. In notable contrast with their American counterparts, they urged widespread government controls and the development of more effective private agreements to control the movement of prices and the flow of trade"(32). In 1942 the London Chamber of Commerce, in contrast to the Americans, suggested an international trading system based on bilateral clearing; the leading British association of industries, the FBI, also advocated the use of bilateral clearing and quantitative restrictions—both of which were anathema to the Americans (32). "[The] most obvious form of right-wing opposition to multilateralism came in passionate defense of Imperial Preference" (33). Much of British industry was devoted to the preference system, which sheltered their Commonwealth markets from competition and, since the Dominions were not a competitive threat, kept competition at home to a minimum.

Imperial Preference also had its supporters in the British government during the war. Within the cabinet itself there were two leading proponents of Imperial Preference: Amery, Secretary of State for India, and Lord Beaverbrook, Minister of Supply. In addition, many in both political parties opposed trade liberalization and the end of discrimination. The Labor Party—both the left-wing Socialists and the Keynesians—identified free trade with unemployment and British decline, whereas the Conservatives supported the demands of industry and agriculture for protection. "On neither Left or Right, therefore, was there much enthusiasm for economic liberalism"(Gardner 1980:31).

The British Labor government, then, had two postwar goals. The first was to maintain historic *Commonwealth ties* after the war: "In short, the British Government could not support any American programme which seemed to be aimed indiscriminately at weakening Commonwealth ties" (Gardner 1980:36–37). Second, for electoral reasons, the government felt it had to protect the domestic economy and to promote full employment. Safeguards would be necessary to prevent even limited trade liberalization from creating another depression in the United Kingdom. As Gardner stated, "Any future projects for the revival of multilateral trade would have to have an expansionist bias, with safeguards to protect [the United Kingdom] from fluctuations originating abroad" (37). Neither Britain nor any other country at the time accepted the American goal of multilateralism. For most nations, fear of American competition and the desire to retain the foreign markets they already had meant that multilateralism was not economically and hence politically advantageous.

The structure of preferences in Britain at the time was such that the government favored lowering tariffs, especially abroad, and restoring world trade. But neither the government nor Parliament nor business favored multilateralism or the end of Imperial Preference. Business was even less interested in trade liberalization than the executive was. The Labor government, which maintained a majority in Parliament throughout the negotiations (1945–51), was thus more dovish than the rest of its domestic actors. But its preferences were far from those of the U.S. executive. The British government needed to secure a majority in Parliament in order to pass the ITO or any modifications to Imperial Preference, and this put limits on how much it could compromise with the Americans.

Several points are worth noting about the trade talks. The United States was clearly the economic hegemon by the end of World War II, especially given Britain's postwar economic situation. However, America played more of a coercive than benign role as it tried to pry open British markets around the world. It did not initiate trade talks out of fear of another country or alliance. The cold war had not yet begun; the U.S. administration even invited the USSR to participate in the trade negotiations. Large differences over trade policy existed even between the most dovish domestic actors in both countries, that is, the executives. Although many economists were united on the virtues of free trade, there was no agreement in the policy community on what trade policy should look like. Even Keynes did not favor trade liberalization; at times during this period he advocated bilateral clearing and trade restrictions. Although others (e.g., Ikenberry 1992, 1993) argue for the existence of an epistemic community in this period, it is difficult to find one among all the disagreements between and within each government.

Terms of the International Agreement

International negotiations over trade continued on and off from 1943 until 1948. The United States and the United Kingdom made little progress, the same issues continuing to divide them. In September 1943 the first meetings between U.S. and British negotiators achieved broad agreement on several issues. Both sides wanted to eliminate quantitative restrictions, reduce tariffs, and create an international trade organization to settle disputes. Three key areas of contention remained. First, the relationship between employment and trade barrier reduction was debated. Basically the British demanded that full employment take priority over trade liberalization (Gardner 1980:105–6). Second, the British wanted to eliminate quantitative restrictions but to be able to use them in the event of short-term, balance-of-payment problems. The United States opposed this, fearing it would lead to their continuous use. Third, both parties in principle wanted to eliminate trade barriers and preferences. The United States, led by the State Department, wanted to end the Imperial Preference system but Britain, not surprisingly, rejected this. Thus the two countries focused their attention on tariff cutting. The British proposed making an across-the-board percentage reduction but the Americans, because of domestic politics, rejected this. There would be "very grave difficulties in gaining Congressional approval for any plan embodying a ceiling on tariff levels and . . . for any across-the-board formula [for cutting them]" (109).

While negotiations on monetary issues proceeded throughout 1944 and 1945, trade negotiations were at a stalemate because of domestic problems in both the United States and the United Kingdom. The British were divided over the merits of proceeding, given America's emphasis on the elimination of Imperial Preference (Gardner 1980:145). In late 1945, however, the two countries negotiated a series of compromises that culminated in the creation of a set of "proposals for consideration by an International Conference on Trade and Employment." These compromises involved the three issues of contention described above.

First, the link between trade and employment policies was acknowledged by including two separate proposals, noting the intimate connection between the two areas and urging that measures in the two not be allowed to conflict. The agreement had to be vague because of the irreconcilable differences between the two nations. The U.S. government, having recently rejected the full employment provisions of the Full Employment Act in 1945, could not accept an agreement that promised full employment as a goal. In turn the British, who had accepted full employment as their primary domestic goal, could not allow trade policy to drive their domestic economic program (Gardner 1980:147). Moreover, once the Labor government took control in July 1945, it rejected any reductions in trade barriers that could affect its domestic reconstruction plans (156).

Second, both countries agreed to eliminate quantitative restrictions, but, as the British desired, they agreed to allow them in times of balance-of-payment difficulties. In return for keeping this exception rather loose, Britain allowed the United States to retain quantitative restrictions for agriculture, which the U.S. government had to demand for domestic reasons (Gardner 1980:149–50).

Finally, on the most contentious issues of tariff reductions and preferences, the two countries compromised. Since the United States refused to reduce tariffs across the board, as the British wanted, Britain in turn refused to give up the preference system. Instead, the United States agreed to a series of bilateral tariff negotiations on many goods simultaneously, and the United Kingdom, after certain exceptions were made, slowly accepted the principle of relinquishing Imperial Preference (Gardner 1980:151–52). This compromise reflected domestic pressures in both countries. The U.S. government, because of congressional opposition, could not agree to across-the-board tariff cuts; similarly, the British government could not accept the end of Imperial Preference because of the strong support for the system in business circles, Parliament, not to mention the Cabinet itself. "Parliament," according to Gardner, "would not permit the elimination or even the substantial reduction of Imperial Preference" (156). The only way a compromise could have been reached was if the Americans would give up their high levels of tariff protection, but domestic politics prevented this. "British opinion was not prepared to eliminate Imperial Preference except in return for a very substantial quid pro quo—in Churchill's words—'a vast sweeping reduction of tariffs and trade barriers and restrictions all over the world'"(158).

Not only was the U.S. government unable to offer such reductions, it was forced to add an escape clause to any tariff cuts agreed to in negotiations because of domestic pressures (Gardner 1980:158–59). All these measures were necessary to garner enough domestic support so the eventual agreement could be ratified by the U.S. Congress. Ratification was the key issue on which the Truman administration focused, and tried to anticipate, during the international negotiations. The administration's problems in obtaining renewal of the RTAA alerted it to the potential difficulties an international trade agreement could face in Congress. Because of domestic pressures, the British and American negotiators ended up in a stalemate over tariff cutting and preferences (160–61).

In late 1945 the question of a U.S. loan to Great Britain raised new hopes in the United States for reaching a trade agreement. The U.S. government tried to link the loan with trade, a link also promoted because of domestic pressures. With the end of the war the American public, Congress, and business no longer supported generous foreign aid, and business was eager for access to British commonwealth markets. Many in the U.S. administration "could not contemplate further financial assistance to the British unless it received firm promises that the British would ratify the Bretton Woods institutions and participate in the establishment of an International Trade Organization" (Gardner 1980:191). All major U.S. business organizations pushed the administration to get the British to relinquish Imperial Preference in exchange for the loan. "The linking of multilateral policies and transitional aid was urged not only by the business community but also by dominant opinion in the American Congress" (197).

Finally, in October 1946 the British and American negotiators met to draw up the Charter for ITO. The United States and the United Kingdom remained the central players, but other countries now joined in the discussion. Three main issues were on the table. The countries agreed to accept unconditional MFN treatment, except where preferential areas already existed. They also agreed to begin negotiations to cut tariffs in Geneva in the spring of 1947 (Gardner 1980:270). Second, in terms of the relationship between trade and employment, Britain and other countries prevailed by getting the United States to accept the proposal that exceptions to trade liberalization were allowed in cases of severe unemployment and balance-of-payment problems (276, 284–85). Third, Britain and other countries succeeded in getting the Americans to accept the use of quantitative restrictions in cases of balance-of-payment problems (282–83).

With this Charter the countries began two sets of simultaneous negotiations. In Geneva they negotiated over specific tariff cuts and the reduction in preferences in the spring of 1947, while in Havana they negotiated over the International Trade Organization and other aspects of trade. In Geneva the U.S. government, for domestic reasons, pushed for the end of Imperial Preference. The Republican victory in the 1946 congressional elections put great pressure on the Democratic administration to eliminate preferences without lowering tariffs. Thus divided government in the United States began to hinder the trade agreement. In fact the State Department was forced to pledge, in congressional hearings, that it would ensure the end of preferences if Congress renewed the State Department's RTAA authority (Gardner 1980:148–49). The State Department failed completely to get the British to end their preference system, however.

In the United Kingdom support for Imperial Preference had grown over time. By the spring of 1947 no majority in any British party would support the abandonment of Imperial Preference (Gardner 1980:351). The British were firm in their unwillingness to give up preferences because they were certain the United States could not make major tariff cuts because of domestic opposition. A coalition of Conservatives and left Labor party members in Parliament forced the government to declare that the Imperial Preference system would not be touched during the Geneva negotiations (354). In the Geneva Round the United States finally gave in and agreed to some tariff cuts without any change in the Imperial Preference system (361).

Negotiations over the ITO Charter in Havana in 1947–48 were more complicated. Many issues were involved, ranging from economic development to treatment of foreign investment. In most areas the United States was outvoted by the Europeans and developing countries, so that the final agreement contained broad but complex rules allowing discrimination in trade and investment often for economic development reasons (Diebold 1952; Gardner 1980:361–68). The British government refused to seek ratification of the Charter after its approval, claiming that it would wait until the United States had done so. Many in the United Kingdom did not like its terms. As Gardner (1980) claims, "It was doubtful that Britain would ratify the ITO, even if the U.S. should choose to do so" (371). The Truman administration for its part submitted the agreement to Congress for ratification in the spring of 1948, with a Republican majority to convince.

To sum up, the trade negotiations were difficult and lengthy because of divisions in preferences between and within the two negotiating countries. The executives in both countries, who were in fact the most dovish actors, had distinct ideas of how the trade system should operate. Both hoped that the high existing trade barriers would be lowered, but each preferred lowering the type of barriers that protected the other country most. The United States wanted to end the Imperial Preference system, and the United Kingdom wanted to reduce tariffs. In the end, the United States gave in, agreeing to reduce industrial tariffs and allow preferential arrangements to continue. This proved to be a mistake, however; it undercut crucial U.S. domestic support for the agreement. The protectionist, domestically oriented industries opposed tariff reductions, and internationally oriented business lost interest once the preferential trade arrangements were not eliminated. Business opposition to such an agreement had prevented the U.S. side from agreeing to it in the first years of negotiations. But the exclusion of U.S. business interests from the Havana conference allowed the American negotiators to make such a deal (Diebold 1952:24). In Britain the government realized that neither the cabinet nor Parliament would approve any agreement that relinquished preferences; thus it refused to change its position.

Thus, although the British prevailed in setting many terms of the agreement, later this proved fateful. The British bargaining position was stronger than the American one since no group in Britain favored multilateral trade liberalization. Preservation of Imperial Preference and protectionism were the preferred policies for all the major British actors domestically. Unity at home seemed to be helpful in the international negotiations, contrary to the Schelling conjecture. Moreover, the British position was closer to the reversion point; that is, in the absence of a trade agreement, the situation would look more like that preferred by the British—Imperial Preference would remain in place and multilateral tariff reductions would not occur. Thus, even though one might suspect that the superior resources and international position of the United States after World War II would enable it to dominate negotiations, Britain's internal politics and the proximity of government preferences to the reversion point gave Britain the advantage. U.S. hegemony was no match for a protectionist and pro-Imperial Preference Parliament and business in the United Kingdom.

Failed Cooperation and Domestic Ratification

Domestic politics not only played a major role in shaping the international negotiations over trade, it also drove the ratification process, which ultimately determined the fate of the international trade agreement. As others have argued, "When the American delegates returned from Havana in the spring of 1948, their most difficult struggle was still ahead of them" (Gardner 1980:371). The gradual loss of critical domestic support for the agreement meant that in the end the United States failed to ratify the agreement, and the British might have done so as well given the chance. The ratification process, then, was the critical turning point for international cooperation in trade. The election of a Republican majority in Congress in 1946 divided the government and endangered the agreement, especially since the Republicans were more protectionist than the Democrats (Cox and Kernell 1991:3). Not even the growth of the Soviet threat after 1947 could prompt Congress to support the agreement (Gardner 1980:373; Diebold 1952:5–6). "The opposition to Soviet policy that had helped pass economically enlightened measures like the British loan and the Marshall Plan did not generate support for the ITO" (Diebold 1952:6).

But the crucial variable was the loss of business support. "The ITO might still have been saved had it not been for the defection of that critical portion of the American business community whose cooperation had made possible the passage of the Bretton Woods and the British Loan Agreements" (Gardner 1980:375). During the congressional hearings on the ITO in 1949–50, all major U.S. business groups testified against the agreement. In their eyes the ITO represented a step away from trade liberalization. They objected to the maintenance of Imperial Preference and other forms of discrimination, the exceptions granted for quantitative restrictions and controls on investment for reasons of economic development (375–76). Internationally oriented businesses, which should have supported the agreement, thus came to oppose it, largely because in their view "it was inconsistent with the very multilateral objectives for which the American government had fought so hard" (376).

This loss of business support affected the chances of ratification by making Congress far less willing to follow the president's lead. Congress looked to business groups as "endorsers" in trying to decide how to vote on the agreement, and the signals sent by internationally oriented business against the agreement convinced many in Congress to vote against it. "The fact that the merchant and export groups who regularly supported the Trade Agreements Act were split over the ITO removed an important prop on which the Administration's case with Congress would otherwise have rested" (Diebold 1952:9). The Republican gains in the 1950 Congressional elections also spelled trouble for the accord; Congress remained in Democratic hands but only by a small majority. Realizing this, Truman withdrew the ITO Charter from Congress on December 6, 1950. This action killed the ITO. Thus only the GATT negotiations, based on the American RTAA, survived as a result of the years of international negotiations over trade policy. Even the GATT was left in a perilous position, since Congress never ratified it and the Republicans often attacked it.

Even though the British and American executives ultimately reached an agreement, this failure to achieve domestic ratification of the ITO dealt a critical setback to international cooperation in trade. The United States could not ratify the ITO agreement for two domestic reasons. First, important constituents failed to endorse the agreement. The model in chapter 3 shows that the legislature, when it lacks complete information about a proposal, may depend on the endorsements of informed domestic groups in deciding whether to ratify. If none of the key groups endorses an agreement, ratification should always fail. If both groups endorse it, it should always succeed. If only one endorses it, ratification may occur depending on other factors. The loss of all business support and the vigorous opposition of protectionist groups caused many in Congress to oppose the ITO agreement. Failure to negotiate an agreement that at least international business would endorse was a major stumbling block for the administration. The second reason ratification failed was divided government. Republican gains in the late 1940 elections meant that the Democratic administration lost control of the majority in Congress. The Republicans, as isolationists and protectionists, opposed trade liberalization and the ITO (Watson 1956:679–81). Lack of endorsement and divided government thus defeated the ITO in the United States.

The Bretton Woods Agreement

Domestic Preferences and Institutions

The second set of negotiations between the United States and the United Kingdom involved the international monetary system, which, like the trade negotiations, began in 1943. Initiated by the British, these negotiations also had their origins in national planning documents and earlier informal negotiations. The structure of preferences on both sides was similar to that in the trade negotiations. In both countries the median legislator was more hawkish than the executive, and actors were more divided on the American side. In Britain the cabinet, Parliament, and major interest groups were all united behind the British plan, devised by John Maynard Keynes, for an international monetary system. In the United States, once again isolationist, protectionist Republicans, supported by groups in Congress and traditional banking interests, argued for a more hawkish position than did the Democratic president, legislators from his party, and international industrial interests. Thus the U.S. executive's plan for an international monetary system—the White Plan—suffered much criticism from these opposing groups.

The British government, as the major global financial player and growing debtor, knew that it needed to reestablish a stable monetary system. It was supported by the banking industry in this. The way the British handled their war debts would have a major impact on the domestic economy. The government feared a repeat of the 1930s and did not want to subject the domestic economy to deflationary pressures from the international economy. "But Britain could not live under autarchy even with the aid of the Commonwealth. Her existence—or, at least, her standard of living—depended upon her export industries, her shipping, and her foreign financial connections" (Mallalieu 1956:11). International cooperation thus appealed to British leaders as a way to promote the domestic economy and avoid the deflation and massive unemployment of the 1930s.

Britain's success in dealing with its heavy war debts required monetary cooperation internationally. Maintaining a flexible exchange rate system with its new debtor status was not a desirable outcome; the country's debtor position was likely to drive down the value of the pound, thus undermining Britain's dominance over international financial markets and importing inflation. A system of perfectly fixed rates was also undesirable since this would mean that external balance took priority over internal growth. The stability provided by fixed rates together with various means of insulating the domestic economy from the pressures of external balance was a more ideal outcome for British banking interests and the government.

Based on this assessment of its preferences the British government commissioned Keynes to devise a plan for its monetary system after the war, and "by the end of April [1941], Keynes' draft [for an International Currency Union] had . . . become government policy" (Van Dormael 1978:9). The British government then presented this plan to the Americans in early 1942, after the war cabinet voted for it (Van Dormael 1978:6–10, 51).

The British government and the private sector of the economy were now major international debtors, and the government was most concerned with ensuring domestic prosperity. As major debtors, the British desired an international environment that would allow them to retain their preeminent place in world financial markets but also to avoid sacrificing the domestic economy to the deflationary demands of international markets and institutions. In Britain, the city and its financial interests had long enjoyed a privileged position in government policy circles (Blank 1978). Britain's new debtor status had to be accommodated with its financial industry's preference for international leadership. Keynes's plan was a means of achieving these somewhat incompatible goals. Reflecting these goals, Keynes's plan for an International Clearing Union (ICU) prioritized the idea of providing liquidity in times of balance-of-payment crises and forcing creditors even more than debtors to change policy in the event of such disequilibria. The ICU was expansionist in effect and was intended to prevent deflation pressures common to the prewar gold standard system. The plan reflected the British preoccupation with domestic full employment. It contained an inflation bias, which was vigorously opposed by the American administration and bankers (Gardner 1980:80).

On the other hand the Americans were the largest world creditors, and the government and financial interests wanted a stable monetary system in order to maintain the value of their loans. White's plan for an International Monetary Fund to stabilize currencies was similar to Keynes's ICU but much smaller in size, $10 billion compared to $26 billion (Van Dormael 1978:69–71; Gardner 1980:74). Unlike Keynes's plan, White's strategy put the onus of adjustment on the debtor, requiring the debtor to pay strict obedience to the IMF in order to receive funds. White also proposed a Bank for Reconstruction and Development, which would lend money to promote those two goals.

Because of domestic politics, the American plan gradually became less oriented toward reconstruction lending and more toward monetary stabilization (Gardner 1980:75–77). The IBRD fell in importance and the IMF rose. Although the Treasury Department wanted to promote government control over financial markets in order to prevent a repetition of the 1930s, other domestic actors opposed the extension of government control at the expense of private financial actors. Accordingly the government's role in the plan was reduced in early 1943, as a result of the Republican gains in the 1942 congressional elections which meant that the "balance of power on economic issues was shifting to a conservative coalition of Republicans and Southern Democrats" (Gardner 1980:77; Eckes 1975:74–75). These groups were supported by American bankers who did not like the Treasury's plan. This change in the U.S. position moved it further from the British stance. The U.S. executive was able to resist even more hawkish positions largely because Congress and the presidency remained under Democratic control throughout the process (1943–45), unlike in the trade case.

In early 1943 formal negotiations commenced, using the two national plans as their basis: the British plan Keynes drew up and the American one developed by White in the Treasury. Although drawn up separately, the two plans had much in common. They also differed substantially, however, because of the two states' distinct international economic positions (Van Dormael 1978:69–71). There were basically two central differences in the plans. First, the British proposal was far more generous in terms of the liquidity it would make available through the ICU. The White Plan had only $5 billion in liquidity built into the Stabilization Fund; Keynes's ICU called for $26 billion (Gardner 1980:87). Second, the proposals differed on the question of who should adjust in the event of disequilibrium. Both wanted fixed exchange rates and an end to exchange controls but they disagreed over who should adjust domestically: the creditor or the debtor. Keynes's plan put the burden on the creditor, not surprisingly. White's plan, on the other hand, proposed that the burden be borne more by the debtor (Gardner 1980:90–95).

The executives in both countries had little leeway to change their positions in these two areas because of domestic opposition. Many in the British Labor and Conservative Parties viewed the American plan as a return to the Gold Standard, which was strongly opposed because of the problems associated with it during the interwar period. They felt that British domestic policy would be too constrained by such a system. This was especially true of the Conservative Party and its Beaverbrook wing. The other major objection involved the role of the Stabilization Fund in domestic policy. The American plan envisioned the Fund requiring changes in domestic policy in return for aid; such interference in a country's internal affairs was opposed by all major British actors who did not want the Fund dictating domestic policy—deflationary policy, in all likelihood—to the government (Gardner 1980:96).

The Keynes proposal met with even stronger opposition in the United States. "If the White Plan spelled financial orthodoxy and deflation to the British critics, the Keynes Plan spelled reckless experimentation and inflation to the Americans" (Gardner 1980:97). The isolationists close to the Republican Party opposed the plan. Worse, financial groups who wanted a return to monetary orthodoxy also opposed both plans. The banking community, led by the major East Coast banks, opposed White's plan as well as Keynes's (Odell 1988:302–3; Eckes 1975:83–88; Van Dormael 1978:97–98). These groups urged a return to the Gold Standard. Because of this domestic opposition it was not clear whether the U.S. government could even get enough congressional support for the White plan, let alone for a compromise with the Keynes plan. The U.S. Treasury would have to "hedge [the plan] about with sufficient safeguards to neutralize the opposition of conservative financial and political opinion" (Gardner 1980:99).

By April 1943 the U.S. and British governments were negotiating over two proposals, each one reflecting their international economic positions and domestic political constraints. As described above, concerns over the domestic economy drove both countries' interest in international monetary cooperation. The British realized that international cooperation was needed to handle successfully their heavy war debts because the way they dealt with their debts would have a major impact on the domestic economy. The Americans realized that their creditor position would only be safeguarded if a stable system could be established. If creditor status is connected to being a hegemon, then the American motivations might be tied to its role as an ascending hegemon in the monetary arena. Other external threats seemed to have played little role, if any, since the agreement was reached long before the cold war began. Executives in both countries were motivated by a mix of domestic and international economic goals, but each had different goals as a result of their differing financial positions. A major international monetary agreement in both countries would require legislative ratification, but compromise internationally was likely to make domestic ratification even more problematic.

The Terms of the International Agreement

The international negotiations began in September 1943. In April 1944 the two countries reached a compromise, and in July 1944 the Bretton Woods conference approved the international monetary agreement.

The international negotiations centered on three issues. First, the liquidity problem was resolved when a compromise was reached granting the Fund $8.8 billion, which was much lower than the British wanted but slightly higher than the Americans had initially offered (Van Dormael 1978:166; Gardner 1980:112–14). On the adjustment issue, the British government pushed for greater exchange rate flexibility to ensure that domestic policy would not be constrained to support external balance. The government wanted to have the right to alter the exchange rate if it faced severe balance-of-payment difficulties. The British also demanded inclusion of a "scarce currency" clause, under which countries in difficulty could put restrictions on the scarce creditor country's currency. Both these measures were intended to prevent deflationary pressures in the external economy from being transmitted to the domestic economy. The U.S. government opposed both, knowing the measures would fan opposition at home and fearing they would undermine its goal of currency stability. In the end, however, they accepted the proposals since the British government refused to budge (Gardner 1980:115–16). Third, the problem of providing aid to make the transition to a new monetary system was raised. Because of congressional and financial opposition, the U.S. government greatly reduced its initial offer for loans from the IBRD (Gardner 1980:117). The Bank was made into a conservative lending organization, where ability to repay became important. The British objected to this and were able to loosen the constraints on the Bank, giving it more ability to fund long-term reconstruction and development.

The international negotiations over the monetary system were long and difficult but more rapid than those over trade. In particular, once the U.S. and British governments reached an agreement, the other countries largely accepted their terms. The contrast between the Havana and Bretton Woods conferences is striking. As in the trade negotiations, however, the U.S. negotiators did give in on major issues but were also able to secure a few of their key positions. Although the two governments had serious disagreements on principles for guiding the monetary system, they were able to find compromises that satisfied important domestic interests. The U.S. government was also careful to make sure to include key domestic players in these negotiations and to take domestic preferences into account (Eckes 1975:83–88, 115–17; Odell 1988:304). These factors made ratification easier than in the trade case.

Unlike in trade, the monetary agreement represented more of a compromise between the two countries. The British prevailed on some points, but on other issues the United States was able to secure an outcome more favorable to its preferences. Despite U.S. economic hegemony and its creditor status, however, the British were able to resist many American pressures to alter their position. Britain's influence may have flowed from the British actors' more unified position and their adamant refusal to let international balance dictate domestic policy. In contrast, the U.S. government's position was bolstered by the fact that it lay closer to the reversion point; that is, in the absence of a monetary agreement the international economy would continue with limited liquidity, a flexible exchange rate system, and no means to borrow in case of an exchange rate shock. This system would be less deleterious for the United States as a creditor with a strong economy than for the British as weak debtors.

Successful Cooperation and Domestic Ratification

Immediately after the United Kingdom and the United States had achieved a compromise in early 1944, the ratification debate began in each country. Reaction to the agreement in Britain was largely negative. The Left, led by the Labor Party, opposed anything that appeared similar to the Gold Standard. They desired a monetary system that placed domestic economic priorities first. More damaging was the opposition of the Conservative Party's right wing and of financial interests (Van Dormael 1978:127–34; Gardner 1980:112–13). Financial groups and Conservatives in favor of Imperial Preference all opposed the accord. They thought it gave too much control to the Americans. "On the Right . . . these projects [Bretton Woods and the ITO] were regarded as a threat to domestic industry and to Imperial economic arrangements; on the Left, as a menace to full employment and the welfare state" (Gardner 1980:228–29).

This opposition led to a bitter debate in the House of Commons in the spring of 1944 (Gardner 1980:124). Keynes and the government defended the plan, but Parliament demanded further clarifications and other measures before it would ratify (Gardner 1980:143–44). In 1945 the ratification debate grew more bitter. By then the Bretton Woods agreement had been linked to the U.S. loan. The U.S. government demanded that the British approve the international monetary and trade accords in exchange for the loan. The British resented this pressure (Van Dormael 1978:270–75; Gardner 1980:229). Although the Labor Party had a large majority in the House of Commons, the House of Lords was controlled by the Conservatives, who could thus delay the vote on the agreement (Gardner 1980:225–26). With strong party discipline in place in the House of Commons, the Parliament approved the agreement in December 1945 after a bitter struggle. As one analyst notes, "Bretton Woods had been approved by Parliament because the government controlled the majority, and because party discipline had been maintained" (Van Dormael 1978:281). The House of Lords finally approved the agreement after much delay as well, largely because without it there would be no U.S. loan.

In the United States unified Democratic control of Congress and the presidency from 1943 to 1945 helped to make the ratification process easier than in the trade case. President Roosevelt sent the accord to Congress for ratification in January 1945. Opposition to the agreement came from two different groups: "a strange coalition of mid-western isolationists and eastern bankers" (Gardner 1980:129). The compromises made to secure British approval caused problems in the United States. The scarce currency clause and provisions for changes in the exchange rate caused many to question the amount of stability and debtor discipline the agreement would provide (Gardner 1980:129–31). In addition, opponents argued that the British would never be able to live up to the plan for currency convertibility. John Williams's "key currency" proposal, which was the main alternative to the Bretton Woods agreement in the United States, focused on this problem. However, it was rejected by the U.S. Treasury.

Faced with this opposition, the U.S. government sold the bill to a skeptical Congress by means of side payments. In order to garner support it made a series of assurances to Congress and to important financial interests. The U.S. government also forced several alterations in the accord after the fact, all designed to supplement American control over lending (Van Dormael 1978:256; Block 1977:50–58; Gardner 1980:134). The American Bankers Association (ABA) lobbied hard for changes in the agreement. They succeeded in forcing the executive branch to alter it by limiting the scope of the IMF's operations and having an advisory council, composed in part of bankers, formulate the U.S. position in the Fund and the Bank (Odell 1988:305; *New York Herald Tribune*, June 11, 1945; *Journal of Commerce*, May 2, 1945; Block 1977:50–55). In other words, the ABA's ability to force changes in the agreement quelled its opposition. In addition, the administration gave a series of assurances to Congress to alleviate its worries and those of the bankers (Gardner 1980:133–40). The administration felt it needed the support of the banking community to achieve a ratifiable accord. These side payments split the opposition to the agreement. The Republicans eventually came to favor the accord, as did many groups in industry and finance who endorsed the agreement (Gardner 1980:142). In June and July 1945 the House and Senate passed the Bretton Woods agreement with large majorities (Van Dormael 1978:262–64; Gardner 1980:142–43).

Conclusions

This concluding section addresses two questions. First, what can the two-level game elaborated here contribute to our understanding of the cases? Second, can it explain why the ITO failed and the Bretton Woods agreement passed?

The terms of both international agreements were strongly constrained by domestic pressures, as the model suggests. In the trade case, neither government could move far beyond its initial position because of legislative opposition. The British Parliament voted not to accept the end of Imperial Preference, and the U.S. Congress refused to authorize across-the-board tariff reductions. These stances reflected the positions of domestic interest groups. Both governments tried to work around these constraints. The British government was least able to, however; its majority depended on maintaining Imperial Preference. The U.S. government, on the other hand, negotiated an agreement at Havana that lacked the support of both international business and the Republicans. This neglect of domestic preferences proved fatal when the Republicans took control of Congress.

In the monetary negotiations the United States was hamstrung by Congress in the amounts it could offer the Fund or the Bank, and it was forced into a more conservative financial position because of domestic financial interests. As large international creditors after the war, American banks and their political allies demanded an orthodox monetary system; Keynes's plan and part of White's were anathema to them. Opposition in Britain on both the Left and the Right to the return to "orthodoxy" (i.e., fixed exchange rates) forced the British government to seek major concessions from the United States, including the scarce currency clause; without it, the British government could not muster the majority it needed to pass the agreement.

Political leaders during negotiations were severely constrained by domestic politics and by concerns over the ratifiability of the agreements reached. Each side modified its position to accommodate domestic opposition, and the final agreements reflected these internal pressures.

The biggest difference between the two cases is that the United States and Britain ratified the Bretton Woods agreement but not the ITO one. In both cases domestic ratification was a major issue. The governments always had to negotiate with domestic considerations in mind. In the trade case the governments failed to adequately anticipate their legislatures' and interest groups' reactions. What made the trade case different? First, the structure of domestic preferences contributed to the different outcomes. In the monetary case ratification occurred in the United States in 1945 when the Democrats had majority control of Congress. Government was not divided as it was in the late 1940s during the trade debate. With Republicans in the majority the ITO had no chance of ratification. As the model suggests, divided government was a critical problem for the trade accord.

Another element involved the role of interest groups and their effect on the legislature's position. The model in chapter 3 demonstrates that an agreement that is not endorsed by either of the informed groups providing information to the legislature will always fail to be ratified. If it receives the endorsement of one group, it may be ratified; if both groups endorse it, it will always be ratified. With regard to the ITO, the U.S. government failed to negotiate terms that at least one group of industries would support. Indeed neither the domestically oriented industries nor the internationally oriented group endorsed the agreement. The Bretton Woods accord, on the other hand, received the endorsement of financial interests. Interest groups, in their role as information providers, exercised a major impact on ratification and on the terms of the international agreements.

Using side payments and anticipating the preferences of financial interests, the Roosevelt administration was able to secure the endorsement of U.S. financial interests for the Bretton Woods agreement. The Truman administration, on the other hand, lost the endorsement of international business for the trade agreement, a critical loss. As many analysts agree, "It was . . . more devastating to the Administration's campaign for the ratification of the [ITO] Charter that those organizations which represented industries particularly interested in free trade and the expansion of foreign trade reacted vigorously against the Charter" (Kock 1969:59). Or, as Gardner (1980:375) claims, "The ITO might still have been saved had it not been for the defection of that critical portion of the American business community whose cooperation had made possible the passage of the Bretton Woods and the British loan Agreements." The compromises made at Havana to secure the assent of other countries so changed the ITO proposals that internationally oriented U.S. business lost interest in the ITO. The objections of this group (and of the protectionists) influenced Congress, undermining Senate support for the treaty. Since international business was also a core support group for the Democratic administration, this group's opposition also weighed heavily on the executive branch. Even had the Democrats controlled Congress at the time, it is debatable whether Truman would have pushed this agreement and risked alienating this element of his electoral coalition. Without the endorsement of international business the ITO was in trouble; add to that a divided government and it was doomed.

In general, the variables that the two-level game focuses on help to explain the two cases. Similarities between the two issue areas account for the initiation of cooperation. For both governments the economic and political advantages of cooperation were apparent. The home benefits of maintaining unilateral policies of protection and flexible exchange rates in both areas, respectively, were outweighed by the negative externalities generated by such policies; cooperation could help reduce these externalities. Following on the RTAA the U.S. government recognized the economic importance of exports and the difficulties of unilateral trade policy, whether protectionist or liberal. The British administration understood its vulnerabilities in international financial markets and the preferences of its financial interests for a stable monetary system. But it could never again agree to relinquish its domestic monetary autonomy for the sake of international balance. Finally, the existence of divided government and the failure of important interest groups to endorse the trade agreement differentiate it from the monetary case. Overall, domestic politics variables help explain the terms of the international agreements and the factors that made ratification possible in one case but not in the other.

Six

The Anglo-American Oil Agreement and the International Civil Aviation Agreement, 1943–1947

NEGOTIATIONS between the United States and Britain for managing the world petroleum market and the international civil aviation system played an important role in constructing the new post-World War II system. These negotiations took place roughly between 1943 and 1947. Their outcomes established the practices and norms for these industries for much of the postwar period. Today the Chicago Convention and Bermuda Principles, set in the mid 1940s, still regulate international civil aviation, and the arrangements made at that time guiding the world oil market were in operation until the early 1970s.

These negotiations are worthwhile to compare since one was a failure and one a success. The Anglo-American oil agreement died in the late 1940s as a result of "involuntary defection" by the United States. It was never ratified by the U.S. Congress, and in its wake the major international oil firms organized their own system for controlling oil. In contrast, the negotiations over civil aviation set the terms for the system over the postwar period. The first negotiations in 1944 led to the Chicago Convention, which laid down the basic framework for the international civil aviation system. This conference, however, failed to settle many specific issues about the system. A later bilateral negotiation between the United States and Britain in Bermuda in 1946 settled many of these issues and became a model for future bilateral arrangements.

This chapter addresses the puzzle of why the two negotiations had such different outcomes. Why were the same two countries in the same period of time unable to agree on the oil issue yet able to agree on aviation? Differences in the ability to cooperate are often attributed to differences in the prevailing international conditions. But the international environment surrounding these two sets of negotiations was similar. They occurred almost simultaneously, involved the same countries and often the same decision-makers, and were affected by the same changes in the global balance of power. In both cases the United States was replacing British hegemony and held the ascendant position. Its "hegemony," then, does not seem to be the key variable explaining its capacity to devise cooperative agreements with other countries. The disparate outcomes are even more puzzling because the conflicts separating the two countries in the aviation area were greater than those surrounding the oil issue. In both cases the primary issue centered on the degree to which each industry would be regulated internationally. There was a greater overlap in British and American answers to this question in oil than in aviation, but cooperation in oil proved more elusive.

The explanation to this puzzle lies in domestic politics. Domestic politics in both countries strongly affected their governments' ability to negotiate international agreements and to ratify them successfully. Two domestic factors played a key role: the endorsements (or lack of them) by important domestic groups and changes in the ratification process.

The Anglo-American Oil Case

Domestic Preferences and Institutions

The idea for a bilateral, intergovernmental agreement to control world oil markets was initially raised by the British government in 1943. Major actors on both sides of the Atlantic had similar preferences for such cooperation. The British and American governments and the international oil firms in both nations desired an accord to regulate international prices and supplies of oil. Only in the United States did strong opposition exist. The domestic oil producers, backed by their representatives in Congress, opposed the idea. Unified government existed in both countries throughout the period involved, but British actors were more unified in their preferences than the Americans.

The British proposal was in part an indirect response to U.S. policy. In 1943 President Roosevelt approved the plan for a Petroleum Resources Corporation (PRC), which was to be a state-controlled oil company to promote the "orderly" exploitation of foreign but mainly Middle Eastern oil fields. The PRC, fashioned after the Anglo-Iranian Oil Company (AIOC), which was the British national oil company, would buy a direct interest in Middle Eastern oil by purchasing parts of some American firms. This unilateral domestic policy choice created the conditions for the beginning of the Anglo-American oil negotiations. Much like the RTAA in trade policy, the PRC signaled a change in the executive's policy preferences and made international negotiations possible.

This domestic policy initiative, begun before international negotiations, was crucial in two respects. First, it sparked British interest in a cooperative bilateral deal as a way to derail the PRC, which the British saw as an attack on their position in the Middle East. Indeed, the PRC's creator, Secretary of the Interior Harold Ickes, even claimed that "the real purpose of the [PRC] proposal had been to get the British to talk" (Anderson 1981:102). Second, the policy initiative raised strong opposition on the part of the domestic American oil industry and those international firms that refused to be part of any agreement involving a governmental plan, including bilateral coopera- tion. Thus the international firms who were not involved began to look around for other ideas on how to deal with Middle Eastern oil.

In the wake of the PRC plan the international oil firms and governments in both countries realized the convergence of their preferences around the idea of a bilateral, intergovernmental arrangement. All four groups—the Brit- ish and American oil "majors" and both governments—had a common inter- est in some sort of cartel that regulated supplies and promoted the "orderly" marketing of Middle Eastern oil worldwide. Organizing Middle Eastern oil production appealed to both sides because the U.S. government worried about petroleum shortages in the future, and the British feared an oil glut. Beyond this, their interests diverged. The Americans hoped to alter the exist- ing "property rights" set by the British during their hegemony, and the Brit- ish wanted to check the rising tide of American influence and retain their position in the Middle East. The AIOC sided with the British government, while the American oil companies envisioned cooperation only if they could obtain antitrust exemptions and advance their position in the Middle East.

The preferences of the leading actors in the oil industry and the two gov- ernments were important. The U.S. oil industry was divided into two groups. One was made up of five large international firms (the majors) who after World War I developed extensive foreign operations (Anderson 1981:14). The other group were the domestic producers (the independents) who were small, numerous, and well represented politically. Unlike the majors, the independents derived their profits from domestic production and were un- able to control oil production and prices without government help. After more domestic oil discoveries in the 1930s, fears of an oil glut led the domes- tic independents to rely on the Texas Railroad Commission to regulate oil production in order to keep domestic prices high (Sampson 1975:89–90).

The domestic firms' preferences were intrinsically opposed to those of the majors. The former opposed the importation of large quantities of cheap foreign oil, since this would drive oil prices down and put domestic produc- ers out of business. The independents and their representatives in Congress feared that international regulation would upset their own domestic regula- tory schemes; through regulation at the international level, the majors would take over the task of setting U.S. oil prices. In terms of chapter 3's model, the domestic independents and their backers in Congress were hawks. The in- ternational firms, on the other hand, made vast profits from cheaply pro- duced foreign oil; although not wanting to undermine high oil prices, they led the movement to "conserve" domestic oil by replacing it with foreign oil (Blair 1976:156–65; Anderson 1981:10–13). The preferences of these two groups were mixed; cooperation was necessary to maintain high prices, but conflict over how much of whose oil—foreign or domestic—would be sold was endemic.

During World War II the Roosevelt administration realized that petroleum was a vital, strategic resource; control over oil became "an instrument of national survival" (Miller 1980:62). In addition, interest in access to foreign oil—especially the vast resources of the Middle East—heightened. Although U.S. domestic production had grown dramatically, fear of oil shortages became foremost in many policy makers' minds. Thus the promotion of foreign oil production, particularly that of the Middle East, became a central goal for U.S. policy makers in the early 1940s. The State Department and the Department of the Interior, the Joint Chiefs of Staff (JCS), and the Petroleum Administration for War (PAW) all saw the need to exploit Middle Eastern oil and "conserve" U.S. domestic supplies (Miller 1980:63–64; Painter 1986:47). These goals were similar to the oil majors' interests and conflicted with those of the small independent oil firms. A key issue for the government, however, was how best to achieve these ends, and in this choice of approaches lay the potential for conflict with the majors.

The U.S. government pondered three approaches to ensuring the "orderly" development of Middle Eastern oil markets: direct government control of the industry, international cooperation, and a private global cartel. The first, involving direct government participation in the oil industry, was favored by the JCS and by Harold Ickes, Secretary of the Interior and head of PAW. It was modeled after the British government's approach, which involved having a majority position in the Anglo-Iranian Oil Company. Ickes and the navy argued that the U.S. government should protect its oil interests abroad by owning a direct stake in them; it should have a "chosen instrument" to pursue its goals. With a government-owned firm, they reasoned, the British would not be able to restrict or take over U.S. oil concessions in the Middle East. Ickes thus developed the plan in 1943 for the government-owned PRC (Miller 1980:73–78, 96; Anderson 1981:50–55, 80–82; Painter 1986:52–59).

The idea of a government-run oil company, such as the PRC, generated widespread opposition. Although Ickes was able to get President Roosevelt's support, he met with opposition from the domestic independents, some of the majors, Congress, the British government and AIOC, and the State Department. The domestic independents felt that the PRC was government intervention at its worst. Not only did they not want federal intervention that might challenge their system of regulation—that is, the Texas Railroad Commission and other state-run efforts to set oil prices—but they also saw this intervention as favoring the majors. The PRC would, in their opinion, flood the market with cheap imported oil that had been produced or subsidized by the U.S. government. Conservation by promoting cheap Middle Eastern oil was not in their financial interests (Miller 1980:97–98). Many in

Congress—including a group in the Democratic majority—also opposed the PRC. Some were just opposed to government intervention in principle; others were against any efforts to extend executive privileges (anti-New Deal); and still others responded to domestic oil producers' complaints about the damage the PRC would do to their state's interests. In response, Congress set up a committee to investigate the PRC. Thus even though Congress and the presidency were controlled by the same party, differences in preferences between the two branches were already posing problems for the executive.

Finally, the majors were not happy with the PRC and preferred bilateral international cooperation. The firms that would not directly benefit from the PRC—SONJ and Socony-Vacuum—opposed it as giving unfair advantages to SOCAL and Texaco. Instead they sided with the domestic independents. SOCAL and Texaco, however, not wanting to lose their profitable interest in Saudi Arabia to the U.S. government, negotiated long and hard with Ickes over the deal, giving the PRC's opponents time to mobilize. Hence, by the time SOCAL and Texaco reluctantly agreed to sell their interest to the PRC, Ickes faced so much opposition that he ended negotiations (Anderson 1981:62–63). Thus the PRC died in late 1943, and with it the government's first option for promoting its goals via direct federal intervention.

The other two options—intergovernmental cooperation with the British and a private cartel run by British and American international firms—remained to be explored. Between these two options, the majors preferred an intergovernmental accord but only under two conditions: that it allow cooperation among the U.S. firms and that it end British domination of the international oil market. Without these conditions, they preferred a private cartel. The search for a solution to domestic problems over oil policy thus led to the international negotiations; cooperation was a means of pursuing domestic political goals.

The Roosevelt administration preferred a bilateral, intergovernmental deal to a private cartel. But it is unclear to what extent the Roosevelt administration shared the international firms' desire to alter British restrictions and concessions in the Middle East. The U.S. government's philosophy opposing discrimination against U.S. firms abroad and pushing for an "open door" implies that this goal may have been part of the government's position initially. However, this goal was the core of the U.S. oil majors' position, and when the government failed to include it as part of the agreement, the majors lost interest. In general, the views of the oil firms were neglected throughout the negotiations (Anderson 1981:77). This would have grave consequences since the terms of the agreement failed to satisfy the main concerns of these powerful domestic actors. Both the independents and the majors proved unwilling to endorse the agreement, and this made Congress less likely to approve it.

The structure of British preferences was less divided than in the United States. The British had two oil firms. One, half Dutch, was the giant international firm of Royal-Dutch-Shell; the other was the AIOC, created by the British government (Sampson 1975:65–67, 74). These two companies wanted to control the international supply of oil in order to keep prices high and to prevent other firms, especially those in America, from getting access to international oil fields. Like the U.S. majors, these two counted on their government's support. But there was a close relationship between the British government and these firms—especially the AIOC, which was 51 percent government-owned (67). The government saw the firms as a way to promote its national interest in having a large, secure supply of oil, since Britain had no domestic reserves at the time. Thus, unlike the U.S. oil industry, the British one was well established worldwide, internally unified as a long-running cartel, and in close relations with the government.

The British government had long been concerned with both oil and the Middle East. Even before World War I the government had begun to promote the development of a secure oil supply in the Middle East (Sampson 1975:52, 61–67). It founded the AIOC—its chosen instrument—to control a monopoly interest in Iran, and it helped both the AIOC and Shell to develop production in other areas, such as Iraq and Kuwait. The British government and firms viewed the United States as a threat and wanted to ensure that the Americans would respect their oil interests in the Middle East. But the British also realized that the balance of power globally was changing, that the Americans were growing stronger daily, and that in time the British would have to make concessions.

Thus by 1943 the British government came to prefer a cooperative solution to managing the world oil situation. Both the government and the firms favored a binational commission to control oil since this could help prevent overproduction and check the rising dominance of U.S. firms. Because the U.S. oil firms, for antitrust reasons, could not negotiate as a group, the British firms realized that only an intergovernmental agreement would suit their purposes. Most important, the British government and firms did not want the United States to take unilateral action, as in the PRC plan. Allowing the United States to continue its unilateral control of oil policy had high negative costs for the British government, whereas giving up unilateral control cost the government little.

But the British feared that the Americans would use the international negotiations to usurp Britain's position in the Middle East. Establishment of the PRC had convinced them that "the American intent was competitive and hostile" (Anderson 1981:85). Although desiring bilateral cooperation to regulate oil prices and supplies in order to avoid price wars, the British companies and the government were intent on preventing any changes in the favorable, existing pattern of Middle Eastern oil concessions. Thus the British refused to negotiate unless and until the Americans assured them that their position in the Middle East would be respected. By doing so, however, the U.S. government undercut the American majors' interest in the agreement. Hence, although this action brought the British to the negotiation table, it undermined support for the agreement among the U.S. majors.

It is interesting that the British initiated the bilateral negotiations while the hegemonic U.S. lagged behind. Moreover, the "threat" motivating the British was none other than the Americans; no external, third party propelled the two countries to seek cooperation. Rather, the pursuit of domestic political goals motivated the executives on both sides to start negotiations. After the unilateral attempt to start the PRC, the British realized the negative externalities the Americans could impose on them and their industry. No longer did the home benefits of an independent global oil strategy outweigh these externalities. Instead, cooperation that would keep the Americans in check was preferable. Beyond agreement between the two governments and their international firms that a policy should rest on "regulating" Middle Eastern oil prices and supplies, much disagreement over policy was apparent. Probably this disagreement was as great internally as it was between the two countries, especially in the United States. Compromise at the domestic level was imperative for international cooperation to be viable.

The Terms of the International Agreement

The international negotiations took less than a year to conclude. As indicated above, all sides, except the domestic independents in the United States, favored the idea of a binational commission to regulate oil markets in the Middle East and hence throughout the world. This overlap in the positions of the two governments ensured that the international negotiations were rapid and successful.

The first round of negotiations from April to May 1944 went smoothly. The United States proposed the creation of a joint petroleum commission to regulate the development, supply, and availability of oil worldwide. The British government succeeded in having the Americans make the commission advisory rather than regulatory. They got the Americans to agree not to disturb existing concessions, although conceding that in the future oil development should not be impeded by government restrictions. They prevented the Americans from mentioning the Middle East, so that the agreement seemed to refer to oil production globally. In short, the British made no specific commitments, gave little away, and agreed to a vague set of principles for a bilateral commission to guide petroleum development (Miller 1980:102–4; Stoff 1980:155–56).

They did make one concession. The British wanted to insert a clause to enable them to restrict British oil imports to those paid in sterling rather than dollars in times of balance-of-payment difficulties. The United States objected, seeing this as a discriminatory device. The U.S. team convinced the British to drop this proposal by pointing out that the U.S. majors would oppose any such clause and veto the entire agreement if this restriction were included (Anderson 1981:90–91; Stoff 1980:165–66). On this objection the British backed off, but they generally prevailed in the initial negotiations.

The initial negotiations in May 1944 resulted in a "Memo of Understanding." Although the British and U.S. governments reacted favorably to the memo, opposition within each country arose. Within the British cabinet, the memo created dissension. Lord Privy Seal Beaverbrook, its most bitter opponent, objected to the overall memo and specifically to the failure to include a balance-of-payment exception for "sterling oil" (Anderson 1981:92). In the United States, two problems emerged. First, the international oil firms' support for the agreement hinged on the inclusion of an antitrust waiver. The operation of a binational oil cartel would receive the majors' cooperation only if they were protected from the government's own laws designed to prevent such collusion (Anderson 1981:91). This antitrust immunity was uncertain; it depended on both the Justice Department and Congress since it involved overturning existing legislation. Second, the independents saw the agreement as one more attempt at federal government intervention in the industry; they opposed it on the same grounds as they had opposed the PRC (Painter 1986:62; Anderson 1981:96–99). Worse, they feared that the joint commission might take over the role of the various state commissions—such as the Texas Railroad Commission—that regulated supply domestically. For these reasons, the independents were hawks on the oil agreement, refusing to endorse it and urging their representatives in Congress to veto it.

Despite growing domestic opposition in both countries, the negotiations resumed in late July 1944 and proceeded smoothly. The British raised three objections, dropping two of them after American insistence. But the final point was the old issue of "sterling oil." After U.S. negotiators resisted this clause, the British dropped the issue but added a letter containing their position on it. On August 8, 1944, the two nations signed the agreement (Anderson 1981:93–94).

The international negotiations were rapidly concluded. Before the meetings the negotiators had all agreed on the basic objective: a binational commission to regulate Middle Eastern oil. No reference was made, however, to changes in British control over the oil fields in the Middle East, which created a major problem since such changes were a prime demand of the American majors. The views of the American oil companies were generally not taken into account during this phase. Arriving at an agreement without their support proved problematic, as the argument predicts. Without at least the majors' endorsement, the agreement should not have been viable in Congress.

The accord more closely heeded the terms preferred by the British government. Again, as in the trade and monetary cases, two factors help to account for this. First, the British were more united internally; their preference that no changes be made in their control over Middle Eastern oil was intense. Second, the British government's preferences lay closer to the reversion point; that is, in the absence of a binational agreement the oil market would be controlled by a cartel that included the two British firms. This would allow the British to maintain their control over Middle Eastern oil and avoid a price war with the Americans. Given this set of preferences, the British had less to lose from a failure to agree than the Americans. America's rising power was worrisome to the British government and oil firms, but it played a lesser role in these negotiations than one might have expected.

Failed Cooperation and Domestic Ratification

The Anglo-American oil agreement was never ratified by the U.S. Congress. Domestic opposition killed it. Although the agreement was negotiated in less than seven months, it was debated in Congress for more than a year before being withdrawn and disappearing. The agreement's fate was also linked to the unsuccessful domestic attempt to create the PRC. This unilateral initiative raised opposition in the United States to any form of government intervention in the oil industry. International cooperation was tightly linked to domestic politics. In the end, then, the domestic ratification process proved more difficult than the international negotiations.

The Anglo-American oil agreement ran into intense, immediate opposition in the United States. Even its initial supporters became unenthusiastic and finally turned against it. The domestic independents, who hated governmental activism, railed against it as they had against the PRC. They felt the binational accord would challenge local, state control of domestic oil. The domestic independents felt it favored the majors, since it would flood the U.S. market with cheap foreign oil and thus erode their profits (Anderson 1981:96–99, 104; Stoff 1980:181). As they had successfully done in the PRC case, the independents urged rejection of the agreement and used Congress to undo it. They had an ace up their sleeve since the head of the Senate Foreign Relations Committee was from one of the largest oil-producing states, Texas. As head of this key committee, Tom Connally, a Democrat, fought for the independents.

Other domestic groups also objected to the agreement. Within the executive branch opposition mounted. The Justice Department thought the antitrust clause inserted at the majors' request was too general and intervened to write a narrow exemption. Thus the majors were no longer given antitrust immunity, which had been their sine qua non for supporting the binational accord. At this point the agreement lost its only U.S. domestic supporters—the majors. Although never enthusiastic about the agreement since it did not end British restrictions on Middle Eastern oil production, the majors had supported it as a means of forming a government-sanctioned cartel—their second choice. Once antitrust immunity was questionable, they lost any interest in fighting the domestic independents over the agreement (Anderson 1981:105). Had the executive branch offered the majors broad antitrust immunity the firms might have fought for the agreement in Congress. As in the ITO case, the loss of the international firms' endorsement proved deadly for the agreement, for now both sides of the oil industry refused to endorse it.

Much also depended on the ratification process. Were the agreement treated as an executive agreement, then the independents and Congress would have less voice in its ratification. If it were a treaty, then the opponents of international cooperation would have greater veto power through their influence in Congress. Initially the State Department had planned to submit the agreement as an executive one, and throughout the proceedings the government negotiated with such a ratification process in mind. In late August 1944, however, after the agreement was signed, Connally and the Senate Foreign Relations Committee pressured the president and the State Department to change the agreement's designation to a treaty, requiring the advice and consent of two-thirds of the Senate (Anderson 1981:95, 103). Since opposition to the agreement was centered in the Congress, this change in ratification procedures proved to be the kiss of death for the agreement. This change in ratification procedures enlarged the veto power of the independents.

Although agreement with the British was achieved, the terms were unacceptable to key domestic actors in the United States. After a cold reception in the Senate, the State Department withdrew the treaty for revision in January 1945. In consultation with senators and the oil industry, Ickes revised the agreement. But conditions had changed by the time it was again ready for submission for ratification. Roosevelt's death and Ickes's and Hull's departure from the government further undercut any support for it. Nevertheless, the idea of a binational cooperative agreement lived on for another two and a half years before the majors constructed their own private cartel (Stoff 1980:185–94). With the agreement's demise, the third option of a private industry-run cartel (the "Seven Sisters") emerged as the solution to America's postwar problem of managing the world oil market (Yergin 1991).

Lack of interest group endorsement and changes in the ratification process proved crucial for the rejection of cooperation. Failure of the executive branch to muster internal support through the use of side payments ensured that the agreement could not be ratified. The opposition of the entire U.S. oil industry meant that no key group would endorse the agreement, thus making Congress more likely to reject it. The change in the ratification process after the fact had a damaging effect since it altered who the median legislator would be. Despite the successful international negotiation process, the domestic political game proved fatal for the Anglo-American oil accord.

The Civil Aviation Case

Domestic Preferences and Institutions

Before World War II international civil air transport was a new industry that lacked organization. National sovereignty over the air was the central norm; that is, each state controlled who had access to its air space and landing rights, and each was free to negotiate away these privileges (Jonsson 1987:26–31). This resulted in a crazy patchwork of agreements between countries. In contrast to ocean commerce where "freedom of the seas" prevailed, in international air commerce restrictions on travel were the norm. During the war many countries acknowledged the need for a better system for organizing the world's air space. In 1943 the British, backed by their dominions, called for international negotiations to create an organization to oversee civil aviation and to organize the industry (Dobson 1991:138). The two central issues were the same as in the oil case: how the industry should be organized internationally (how much regulation) and what role governments should play (private versus governmental regulation).

As usual, preferences in the United States were more diverse than in Britain. Although Congress was controlled by the president's party throughout the period, divisions existed within the industry and these were reflected in the Congress. The U.S. civil aviation industry was divided into two groups, much like the oil industry. On one side was Pan American Airways (PAA), the only U.S. airline with international routes before World War II. At the prodding of the U.S. government PAA had monopolized international air routes in Latin America and Asia by the early 1940s and had become the U.S. government's "chosen instrument" (Thayer 1965:33–34; Smith 1950:4–36, 69). But when PAA attempted to open an air route across the Atlantic it ran into trouble. Because European states had their own airlines, PAA could no longer negotiate its own unilateral agreements for access to these markets. The European airlines wanted reciprocal access to American air space and fields, which could only be granted by the

U.S. government. PAA had to depend, then, on the U.S. government to negotiate the Atlantic air routes. This raised the issue of whether the government would continue to allow PAA to exert monopoly control as its "chosen instrument" or whether it would encourage competition for international air travel.

The second group in the U.S. airline industry consisted of the other eighteen domestic airline companies. Before World War II these firms did not operate abroad, but many were eager to do so since the international market looked lucrative. These firms opposed PAA's attempt to retain its monopoly, and they urged the government to allow competition in world travel. Seventeen of these airlines formed a political association, the Airlines Committee for U.S. Air Policy, to influence U.S. policy and counterbalance PAA (Smith 1950:207–10). This group's preference for regulated competition aligned them with the executive branch in opposition to PAA and its congressional allies.

The executive branch had changed sides by 1940. Although initially promoting PAA as its "chosen instrument," the Roosevelt administration later adopted competition as its preferred course. To fight Pan Am, the "administration went so far as to form a new alliance with the domestic airlines to break PAA's seeming monopoly in the international field, even if the action was delayed by the war" (Thayer 1965:37). During World War II the administration used its wartime policy instruments to overturn PAA's monopoly by awarding foreign air routes to U.S. military bases to other domestic carriers (Smith 1950:269–77). PAA had strong ties in Congress, which it used to resist this action. PAA lobbied for a single international airline and got the Senate Commerce Committee to develop a bill, the McCarran bill, to force the administration to follow such a plan.

Because the domestic airlines and the administration strongly opposed the bill it failed to become law, and PAA's monopoly was broken (Thayer 1965:68–72). The result was to foster competition among U.S. airlines in international routes, but also to throw American regulation of these routes into chaos. The U.S. industry and government both realized the necessity of international agreements over air rights by the middle of the war and began thinking about a plan for the postwar system.

The U.S. government's international negotiating position grew in part out of this domestic battle with PAA and its congressional allies. Although the Roosevelt administration recognized the need for international agreements to organize the world's air routes, it preferred a competitive approach to air travel. The administration sought to extend the open-door principle to this issue area. Since U.S. planes dominated world travel, an open-door policy would guarantee that U.S. companies remained dominant. The government opposed discrimination against U.S. carriers and wanted to help them obtain access globally.

The American administration thus advocated the "Five Freedoms": (1) the right to fly across another country without landing; (2) the right to land in another country for refueling or repairs but not to take on or let off passengers; (3) the right to carry passengers from its own country to another; (4) the right to carry traffic from a foreign country home; and (5) the right to carry passengers from one foreign country to another. Without the adoption of these freedoms, the U.S. industry would be in a disadvantaged position. "The Five Freedoms became part of U.S. civil aviation policy because it was believed that unrestricted traffic was the only means by which Americans could take advantage of their special aviation assets to build up a truly worldwide service" (Smith 1950:117).

The central issue, then, facing the U.S. government—which was analogous to that in the oil case—was how the international aspect of civil aviation would be organized and what role the government would play in this. The executive branch opposed a government-supported monopoly, arguing instead for competition. It garnered support for this position from the alliance of domestic airlines. On the question of international regulation of air travel, the executive branch opposed any regulation of routes, prices, or frequency of flights, pushing for an "open skies" approach based on the Five Freedoms. The domestic airlines approved of the Five Freedoms approach, but wanted to combine this with price regulation. PAA, on the other hand, wanted exclusive access to foreign air space and international regulation in order to continue its monopolistic practices. PAA preferred having a government-supported monopoly, as did its supporters in Congress.

The other, related issue involved who was to do the regulating. Was it to be done by intergovernmental agreement or by an industry-run cartel? The executive branch preferred the former whereas the domestic airlines and PAA preferred the latter. All the major U.S. actors supported the opening of international air space according to the Five Freedoms, but they disagreed on the extent of international regulation versus competition in air travel (Smith 1950:129–48). The search for a domestic solution to the organization of the aviation industry thus led to the international negotiations.

The preferences of the British government and its civil aviation industry greatly overlapped. The British air transport industry was weak after World War II. Although a leader in air transport before the 1940s, the British agreed to build only jet fighters during the war and to let the United States produce air transport (Smith 1950:70–71; Thayer 1965:75–76). Hence at the end of the war they faced a U.S. aircraft industry that had superiority in transport development and global airlines already operating. Indeed, by 1943 the United States controlled 72 percent of world air travel while the British held only 12 percent (Smith 1950:109). The British industry consisted of one government-owned corporation, the British Overseas Airways Corporation (BOAC), born in 1939 out of the remains of the ailing Imperial

Airways company. Like the AIOC in oil, BOAC was the government's "chosen instrument," much as PAA had been for the United States in the 1930s. It was "the weapon of the British in their fight for a share of postwar air commerce" (Smith 1950:101, 107).

The promotion of British international aviation was essential for Britain's foreign policy and economic goals. International air connections could help keep control over Britain's far-flung colonies and to exercise influence abroad more generally (Thornton 1969:21–22). Maintaining an aviation industry could also promote British trade and help its balance of payments. For these reasons and because of pressure from aircraft and parts' manufacturers, the government decided to promote British aviation by subsidizing the industry domestically. But in order to create a viable domestic industry, the British needed global regulation of the industry in order to contain American competition. To advance its domestic policy, the British government advocated an international regulatory scheme—something like the American CAB (Civil Aeronautics Board) for the international market (Smith 1950:110; Thayer 1965:75–76; O'Connor 1971:27–29; Little 1949:31–33; Dobson 1991:136–38). BOAC, as the major beneficiary, supported this idea.

After the war, in their weakened competitive position, the British government and BOAC felt that only in a regulated system could their industry withstand U.S. efforts to monopolize the world market. Their goal was to develop an international regulatory organization to monitor rates and routes that would control the Americans. Thus the British opposed America's Five Freedoms plan. They particularly objected to the fifth freedom, which they envisioned America using as a means to "snatch all of their traffic" (Smith 1950:117). The British government and BOAC wanted to develop their own international aviation industry but realized this could only be accomplished with U.S. cooperation. As the world's two main rivals in air transport, the United States and Great Britain had to cooperate or else third countries would play them off each other and they would both have to pay more for access to foreign markets. The convergence of preferences in the United Kingdom again contrasted with the divisions present in the United States.

Before their call for negotiations, the British coordinated their policies with the Commonwealth countries. This alliance preferred a multilateral agreement, involving an international regulatory mechanism and the reciprocal exchange of air rights. In 1943 they called for a multilateral conference on civil aviation. The United States initially refused, claiming it did not yet have a sufficiently developed national proposal and that presidential elections were too close (Jonsson 1987:31; Dobson 1991:136–38). Finally, in September 1944, Roosevelt agreed to a multilateral conference and invited fifty-four nations, including the Soviet Union, to Chicago for that purpose (Dobson 1991:161).

As in the oil case, the weakened British initiated cooperation rather than the ascending hegemon, the United States. To pursue its domestic goal of creating a viable civil aviation industry, the British required cooperation from the United States. The U.S. government and firms also needed cooperation since acquiring landing rights abroad could only be negotiated. No set of common norms or rules existed in this area; indeed, the negotiations were about creating such a common understanding. Finally, threats from external sources, like the Soviet Union, played no part in this cooperative venture; the Americans posed the greatest threat to the British.

The Terms of the International Agreement

The negotiations to organize the civil aviation industry commenced in Chicago in November 1944. Before World War II national sovereignty over landing rights prevailed, and access to foreign airspace and airports had to be negotiated bilaterally. The Chicago Conference, intended to develop a better system for organizing the world's air space, was only partially successful by its conclusion. This necessitated a second round of international negotiations, held in Bermuda in February 1946, in order to devise a fully developed international civil aviation system. International agreement was difficult to reach in this area because of the two governments' diametrically opposed positions.

In 1943 the British and their dominions agreed on a plan to control international civil aviation, which would set up an international authority to guarantee the first four freedoms advocated by the United States and to regulate routes, rates, and frequencies of flights. They opposed the fifth freedom and wanted it only to be negotiable bilaterally.

The U.S. position called for complete freedom of the skies. It advocated acceptance of the Five Freedoms and creation of an international organization with limited and noncompulsory powers. The U.S. government opposed any attempt to regulate the skies; unlike its domestic system, it wanted no regulation of rates, frequencies, or routes (Hackford 1947:492–93; O'Connor 1971:20–23; Thayer 1965:75; Gardner 1964:270–75). U.S. airlines were less opposed to international regulation but were divided on whether a single airline (the "chosen instrument") or all domestic lines should be allowed to compete internationally.

The conference that began in Chicago in November 1944 to discuss these matters quickly turned to narrowing the differences between the U.S. and British proposals. The countries agreed on the need for technical and safety cooperation and on the first two freedoms of the skies. To cover these points of agreement, the conference drew up two agreements. The first, the Convention on International Civil Aviation, embodied a general set of rules and created the International Civil Aviation Organization (ICAO) to monitor the system and enforce technical and safety regulations. The second, the International Air Transit Agreement, enshrined the first two freedoms and thus ensured free navigation around the globe. It involved a significant relaxation of previous restrictions on air transit and was a multilateral accord (Smith 1950:163–204; Cooper 1947:157–96; Hackford 1947:493–95; O'Connor 1971:41–45).

The conference had more difficulty with the other three freedoms and the issue of regulation. After much disagreement, a third agreement providing for recognition of the third, fourth, and fifth freedoms—the International Air Transport Agreement—was drawn up. But few countries—only the United States, Sweden, and the Netherlands—signed it; most important, Britain refused. Hence the conference ended with no agreement on these last freedoms. The major point of contention was the fifth freedom, which allowed a carrier from country A to transport passengers from country B to country C. This freedom put foreign international carriers into direct competition with national ones. The British and others opposed it, then, because they feared that the United States, given its substantial lead in civil aviation, would use this "freedom" to drive other countries' airlines out of business. This fifth freedom had direct commercial advantages for U.S. industry. The British and others wanted to restrict this freedom and to regulate rates and frequencies to ensure that their airlines survived U.S. competition (Hackford 1947:494–95; O'Connor 1971:30–36, 41–45). With no agreement over the fifth freedom or on the issue of regulation, the conference ended. Some cooperation was established at Chicago, but key issues were left undecided.

In the wake of this conference, the United States decided that organization of the air routes was crucial and must proceed even without a multilateral agreement. New negotiations in Bermuda in February 1946 covered the same issues as the Chicago Conference. The key issues were the regulation of rates and frequencies and the fifth freedom. After much haggling, the Americans agreed to allow rates to be regulated but only by an association of international airlines, IATA. In exchange, the British agreed that frequencies of flights would be left to each state to decide. On the last issue, both compromised. Britain accepted the fifth freedom in principle, but both agreed it could only be used "reasonably." Hence the U.S. government's quest for an unregulated system was denied (Hackford 1947:496–99; O'Connor 1971:45–49; Smith 1950:257–60; Little 1949:34). This bilateral negotiation settled the key issues on civil aviation for the two countries.[1]

---

[1] A multilateral accord was not initially achieved. But over time, as more and more countries negotiated cooperative arrangements exchanging landing rights, a multilateral-like system emerged. Since many countries chose to use the Bermuda agreement as the formula for their bilateral accords, the regime that emerged has had standardized terms, which made it similar to a multilateral system (Little 1949:39–40). Dobson (1991) disagrees to some extent.

This agreement, as most assessments concur, contained terms closer to the preferred policies of BOAC and the British government than to those of the Americans (Smith 1950:257–63; Thornton 1969:154–57; Jonsson 1987:46,48). Once more, despite U.S. hegemony, the British government was able to obtain terms closer to its preferences, in part because the British actors were more unified than the Americans. In addition, the status quo favored the British; that is, if no agreement had been concluded, the situation would have remained one of restricted access to foreign air space—far from the Five Freedoms proposed by the United States—and bilateral bargaining. This reversion point was closer to the British government's preferences than to those of the Americans.

The international negotiations were a bitter struggle between the two countries. Because of the different conditions of their air transport industries, they had opposing policy preferences. The U.S. government used the international negotiations to pursue its domestic strategy of promoting competition in the skies at home and abroad. Similarly, the British government used the international agreement to promote its domestic policy of supporting an aviation industry. Cooperation was another means of pursuing domestic goals for both countries.

Successful Cooperation and Domestic Ratification

The aviation agreements required legislative ratification in the United States and the United Kingdom. Ratification of the agreements, although troublesome, eventually was successful. But the agreements almost suffered the same fate as the Anglo-American oil agreement. Opposition to the Chicago and Bermuda agreements crystallized after their conclusion. Some in Congress felt that the British had gained the upper hand in the negotiated settlement. PAA and its congressional allies also objected to certain terms in both the Air Transport Agreement of Chicago and the Bermuda agreement. The airline wanted to retain its status as a monopoly. Many Senators shared PAA's view and, hoping to derail the agreement, claimed it should be ratified as a treaty, not as an executive accord. Unlike in the oil case, the agreements regulating air traffic were supported by all the domestic airlines and the executive branch. The domestic group of airlines opposed to PAA endorsed the agreements and lobbied Congress strenuously to ratify them. Unlike in the oil case, then, the aviation agreements were endorsed by an important industry group, and this convinced many in Congress to support them.

The agreements had strong domestic supporters in the United States. This support was gained in part through the executive's use of side payments. By allocating international routes to the domestic airlines shortly before the accord was finalized, the executive branch ensured that they would have an interest in an open skies system. With gains available through these new routes, the domestic airlines were willing to lobby Congress and battle Pan Am for the agreements. Ratification of the International Convention of the Chicago Conference and the Bermuda accord, however, hinged on gaining support from the key Senators involved in aviation. Even though Congress was controlled by the president's party, the president had trouble building a majority.

Pressure from the domestic airlines plus an adroit strategy by the executive branch gained this senatorial support and saved the agreements. But domestic politics still had a major effect on the agreements made and implemented. Many in the Senate, because of Pan Am's pressure, intended to veto the International Convention of Chicago, establishing the International Civil Aviation Organization, which required Senate ratification as a treaty. In order to forestall this, the administration made a deal with Congress. It agreed to renounce the Air Transport Agreement, which included the controversial fifth freedom and was signed by only a few countries, if Congress would pass the Convention. The concerns of the legislature were alleviated with this move, and the Senate ratified the Chicago Convention. The Congress also agreed to maintain the Bermuda agreements as executive accords (Smith 1950:196–202, 262–68, 322–23; Hackford 1947:499–500).

The British also had troubles with ratification. By the conclusion of the Bermuda accord in February 1946, the Labor cabinet was still unhappy with the agreements. They desired more regulation of the industry, as did BOAC. The cabinet was divided in its view of the accords, and only pressure from the prime minister made the cabinet accept the agreements, which ensured parliamentary approval since the Labor party also controlled the legislative majority (Dobson 1991:197). Ratification, although difficult in both countries, ultimately ended successfully. The adroit use of side payments by the U.S. executive induced endorsement of the agreements by the domestic airlines, which in turn helped ensure that Congress would ratify them.

Conclusions

This final section addresses two central questions. First, can the hypotheses advanced by the two-level game explain the terms of the two agreements? Second, what explains the different outcomes in the two cases? How can one solve the puzzle of why intergovernmental cooperation in oil failed to emerge, whereas cooperation was possible in aviation. The emergence of cooperation is often explained by international systemic conditions. But since the two sets of negotiations occurred at the same time, external conditions were basically the same (i.e., the end of the war, U.S. economic hegemony, and growth of the Soviet threat); thus it is difficult to explain the divergent outcomes in the two cases in this way.

Domestic political variables provide some answers. Interest in cooperative solutions was related to other domestic policy initiatives; that is, prior, unilateral domestic policy decisions often made a cooperative solution more appealing. In the oil case, the U.S. government's development of the PRC created an interest in greater coordination with the United Kingdom and also heightened Britain's interest in cooperating with America. The British were made aware of the high externalities of unilateral U.S. policy making in oil; combined with the low home benefits of a unilateral industrial policy, this peaked their interest in cooperation. In the airline case, the British government's prior decision to subsidize the creation of a national aircraft industry made air transport a key issue. Likewise, the Roosevelt administration's decision to promote competition in air transport had a major effect on its approach to the international negotiations. Once again the British saw that trying unilaterally to develop their airline industry would have low home benefits and high externalities, if the United States pursued a unilateral course as well. Prior domestic policy decisions that increased policy makers' demand for cooperation occurred in the trade, aviation, and oil cases. National leaders who believe that their domestic policy success depends to some extent on international cooperation will be more willing to pursue it. International cooperation thus served as the pursuit of domestic politics by other means.

Why did negotiations in the aviation case succeed and those in the oil case fail? Two features of the domestic politics argument can explain this. First, the willingness of domestic actors to endorse the two agreements differed. The model in chapter 3 predicts that at least one of the two (or more) informed groups who serve as information providers to the legislature must endorse an agreement before a legislative majority will agree to ratify it. If both groups endorse, then the legislature should always ratify; if neither does, then the legislature should never ratify. In the oil case, the lack of endorsement from either the majors or the domestic independent firms was a crucial problem. The U.S. executive branch could not obtain a majority in Congress largely because the entire U.S. oil industry opposed the agreement. Whereas the domestic independents and their congressional allies denounced the idea from the start, the international firms lost interest only when their minimum conditions were not met. By 1946 they preferred a private cartel to the binational accord. Had the accord done more to alter the status quo in the Middle East and had it given them antitrust immunity it might have prompted their endorsement and been ratified. The strong influence of the independents in Congress was also important. As the model points out, perhaps even with the endorsement of the majors, the agreement might have failed owing to the independents' opposition. However, without backing from either segment of the industry, the intergovernmental agreement was doomed.

In the aviation case, the U.S. executive obtained an endorsement of the accords from part of the airline industry. All domestic groups in the U.S. industry favored an international agreement of some kind to regularize air transport. The industry was thus united in its desire for international cooperation but divided on the best terms for it. But the fact that a well-organized group of domestic firms in the industry endorsed the plans negotiated by the executive branch at Chicago and Bermuda made a difference. In the compromise that the governments crafted, the domestic segment of the U.S. industry was the biggest winner; its most preferred terms were the closest to the compromise position. They lobbied Congress for approval and counterbalanced PAA's opposition. Thus allied with the executive branch, these domestic firms used their influence as both pressure groups and information providers to make ratification possible; the signal they sent to Congress was necessary for ratification.

Second, changes in the ratification process were important. How an agreement is to be ratified shapes which actors will matter and hence whose preferences are key. As argued in chapter 4, changes in the ratification procedures after the fact matter most. What helped kill the oil agreement in Congress was its change from an executive agreement to a treaty. As an executive agreement, the Anglo-American oil accord might have been ratified because the independents would have had less influence. But as a treaty the accord was subject to a two-thirds majority vote in the Senate, and hence the independents had plenty of chances to derail it. Of course they knew this and encouraged the Senate to force the government to change procedures. As argued in chapter 4, opponents should try to alter the ratification process to make it harder, and one expects that their success in this will make ratification much less likely. In the airline case, the opponents also tried to change the ratification procedures. PAA demanded that Congress force the administration to treat the Chicago and Bermuda agreements as treaties. The airline's allies in the Senate could then fan opposition to the treaties. The active lobbying of the domestic airlines against PAA and their endorsement of the agreements dissipated PAA's influence in Congress and prevented any change in procedures. Hence a central feature that distinguishes the two cases is that in the oil one the ratification process was altered after the negotiations concluded, whereas procedures for the aviation agreements were not changed.

The strategies the executive used to construct support for an international agreement are important. In the oil case the executive's failure to adopt two strategies was critical. First, it chose not to include the oil industry and its congressional allies in the preparation for the negotiations or in the talks themselves. This made even the more sympathetic elements of the industry, the majors, suspicious of the agreement and unwilling to endorse it. The British, in contrast, included their firms and had less trouble with ratification. The inclusion of the domestic actors could have had beneficial effects. Their preferences would have been taken into account to a greater degree in the international negotiations, and they might have endorsed the final agreement. As a result their inclusion might have made Congress less hostile to the agreements. The U.S. negotiators in the airline case used this strategy. Representatives from the airlines and Congress were consulted regularly and included in the negotiations. Even early opponents, such as Senator Brewster, were involved and later endorsed the agreements.

In addition, the U.S. administration failed to employ side payments to increase internal support for the oil accord. In fact its biggest mistake was to fail to produce antitrust immunity for the majors. After this, no domestic group was willing to endorse the agreement and oppose the independents in Congress. In contrast, in the airline case the executive increased support from the domestic airlines by giving them stakes in international air routes they desired. The strategies pursued domestically by the executive made an important difference to the ratifiability of the agreements.

These domestic factors, then, help to explain the failure of cooperation in the oil case and the success in the civil aviation one. The lack of endorsement by key interest groups and changes in the ratification process were critical in the failure of the oil agreement. In the civil aviation case, the U.S. executive was able to garner interest group support and prevent any changes in the ratification procedures.

In both these cases divided government per se played no role. The executive and the legislature were controlled by the same parties in both countries during the period when the cooperative agreements were in consideration. Party discipline was a problem in the United States, however. The Democratically controlled Senate, led by Tom Connally as head of the Foreign Relations Committee, forced the president to submit the Anglo-American oil agreement as a treaty rather than as an executive agreement. In the United Kingdom, stronger party discipline and greater convergence of preferences among the domestic actors facilitated ratification of the agreements and helped them negotiate agreements closer to their preferences.

Seven

The European Coal and Steel Community and the European Defense Community, 1950–1954

IN THE EARLY 1950s six Western European nations began efforts to create a European Community, negotiating cooperative agreements in two different areas. The European Coal and Steel Community (ECSC), the first agreement, laid the basis for a common market in coal and steel among the six nations. The other, the European Defense Community (EDC), attempted to create a European army from the six countries' forces. The two were similar; indeed the EDC was modeled explicitly after the ECSC. Both were viewed as precursors to a larger European Community, embracing all economic sectors and political relations. These accords formed the background for the 1957 negotiations for the Treaty of Rome which established the European Economic Community (EEC).

An interesting puzzle regarding these two attempts at international cooperation is that the ECSC was successfully ratified, whereas the EDC was not. As in the cases discussed earlier, the countries reached international agreements in both instances but only in the ECSC case were they able to obtain domestic ratification in all six countries. In the EDC case, the French National Assembly refused to ratify the treaty and the Italian legislature never even considered it. The central task here is to show why the countries succeeded in cooperating in the ECSC and failed in the EDC. What factors distinguished the two?

This chapter also seeks to examine what the two-level game model can contribute to our understanding of the agreements' terms. The evidence suggests that domestic politics was central to the cooperative process, and that the reasons for the different outcomes rest with two variables: the degree of divided government and the endorsement (or lack of it) by key domestic groups.

As in the previous two chapters, what makes the different outcomes surprising is the strong similarities between the two cases. The ECSC and the EDC were negotiated at roughly the same time by the same countries. Robert Schuman, the French Foreign Minister, presented his plan for the ECSC, aptly named the Schuman Plan, in May 1950. In October of the same year, Pleven, the French Premier, announced the plan for the EDC. International negotiations for each occupied approximately one year and involved the same six countries—France, the Federal Republic of Germany, Belgium, the Netherlands, Luxembourg, and Italy. In both cases the main players were France and Germany. Great Britain chose to remain aloof from both negotiations, a point to be explored later. The two treaties were signed one year apart—the ECSC agreement in April 1951 and the EDC in May 1952.

Ratification of the treaties by domestic parliaments, however, took place about two years apart. The countries ratified the ECSC treaty quickly, so that by early 1952 it was operational. For the EDC, though, ratification was drawn out, especially for the French. Although the French National Assembly voted to accept the ECSC in December 1951, a mere eight months after its signing, the Assembly took more than two years to even consider the EDC because of political problems with the treaty. Not until August 1954 did it cast its vote, and then, on a procedural motion, it rejected the agreement. Events between 1952 and 1954 hurt the EDC's chances, but other fundamental differences surrounding the treaties also affected their separate outcomes.

Although the two cases concerned different sectors, they dealt with similar issues. One was how to deal with Germany in the postwar period. Both treaties represented attempts by France to devise a new relationship with the Federal Republic, so that Germany could regain its sovereignty and France could retain its security. Accomplishing this meant sharing control over aspects of domestic politics and the economy; the disputes concerned who would control what. A second issue related to the role the governments would play relative to other domestic forces. After the re-creation of new democratic governments in these countries at the end of the war, their relationships with industry, the military, and other domestic groups had to be forged anew. Intergovernmental cooperation in these areas implied greater subordination of private industry and the military, respectively, to political control by the government.

The central issue in both negotiations was whether countries would agree to turn over control of critical elements of domestic sovereignty to a supranational body. The Schuman Plan called for the countries and their firms to relinquish control of two vital economic sectors, coal and steel, to a supranational "High Authority" (HA). Since these sectors undergirded the rest of the economy and provided the means to make war, control over them was not just an economic issue but had important security implications as well. Once these sectors were integrated internationally, it was felt, war between these countries would never again be possible.

The EDC was modeled consciously after the ECSC. It envisioned the same types of supranational institutions to control the countries' armies. The key issue again was the relinquishing of national sovereignty over a critical element of the polity. The EDC had clear security implications; once in place, it would mean that the countries could not use their armies independently. It also had economic implications. The EDC required that the countries' military budgets be controlled supranationally and that their defense industries be subjected to supranational integration and control.

Some might argue that it is no surprise the EDC failed since it involved "high politics," that is, security, whereas the ECSC succeeded because it only affected the economy, considered to be "low politics." As noted above, however, both had important security implications; no West European country could wage a war without an independent coal and steel industry, nor could it do so without an army (Dell 1995:15). Moreover, both implied similar solutions to the same "high politics" problem—containing a sovereign Germany. What distinguishes the two cases, then, is not the nature of the issue involved; both meant giving up national control over sectors with essential economic and security functions for the sake of gaining control over the other country's sectors.

Defeat of the EDC, it could be claimed, was not surprising because it took place in a different environment than did the ratification of the ECSC. The two-year gap between the ratification attempts may account for the different outcomes. Systemic-level arguments would focus on the differences between the international situation in 1951–52 and in 1953–54. The claim would be that the international pressures for European cooperation were greater in the earlier period. Changes in U.S. hegemony are unlikely to be the cause here, since no noticeable change in U.S. dominance occurred during these two years. Moreover, U.S. pressure for ratification was a constant in both cases and may have been exerted even more strongly in the EDC case.

The international atmosphere surrounding the two cases was also similar. They both occurred at the height of the cold war, just after the Berlin crisis of 1949 and the start of the Korean War. The increased sense of threat from the East and the growing need to find an allied solution to the German problem drove the Europeans and Americans to the idea of the common coal and steel pool and the European army. Although no change in the balance of power occurred, the sense of threat from the Soviet Union decreased between 1952 and 1954. Stalin's death and the end of the Korean War both in 1953 and the end of the war in Indochina in 1954 may have created a temporary thaw in the cold war (Rioux 1987:195). However, if tensions did cool in the 1953–54 period, why did the Europeans accept German rearmament in NATO in late 1954? In general, antagonisms and suspicions between the Europeans and the Soviets ran high throughout the first half of the 1950s.

Another problem with this argument regarding international systemic factors is that the reason the ratification process for the EDC stretched into 1953 and 1954 hinged on domestic politics, as mentioned above. Like the ECSC, the EDC treaty could have been voted on in 1952. But objections to the EDC in France forced the government to seek revisions to the treaty and to delay debate on it for two years. The international negotiations over the EDC concluded in 1952; had domestic opposition been weaker, ratification could have taken place the same year, as it did in the ECSC case. What factors, then, account for the successful ratification of the ECSC and the failure of the EDC? Two domestic variables are key: the degree of divided government and the endorsement (or lack of it) by important domestic groups.

The European Coal and Steel Community

Domestic Preferences and Institutions

The ECSC was initiated by the French government in order to deal with its long-standing quarrel with the Germans over the border separating them and to ensure the success of their domestic economic modernization plans. Although six states were involved, France and Germany were the key players. "Without France and Germany, there could be no Coal and Steel Community . . . From the beginning it seemed that if France and Germany accepted the Coal and Steel Community the other signatories would be bound to follow" (Diebold 1959:104–5). Preferences among the major French actors with regard to the ECSC were quite divided. The prime minister and the cabinet, backed by their centrist parties, and the nationalized coal industry and other steel-using industries all favored cooperation to create a common market. The private steel industry opposed intergovernmental cooperation, preferring a private industry-run cartel with the Germans. The left-and right-wing parties—the Communists and Gaullists, respectively—also opposed the ECSC idea, although for different reasons. The French government became increasingly divided after 1951, as these hawkish groups gained power. In contrast, the Germans became more unified. The Christian Democratic government, the coal and steel industries and their unions, all favored a common market; they simply objected to the French terms for controlling it. Only the opposition party, the Social Democrats (SPD), actively fought the ECSC.

The major force behind the ECSC was indeed the French government. Announced by Foreign Minister Robert Schuman in May 1950, the coal and steel community would pool the coal and steel capacity of the six European countries and subject them to a central supranational authority, the High Authority (HA) mentioned above, who would make decisions about production, exports, investment, and prices in these sectors. Decisions in the two industries would no longer be the sole province of private firms or national governments. In addition, a common market in coal and steel would be created among the six countries; trade barriers and other forms of government intervention would be eliminated and delegated to the HA. Efficient production for a large European market would be promoted.

The French government favored this plan for the ECSC because it would solve numerous problems. The disputes over coal- and steel-producing areas along the French-German border—the Saar, Rhine, and Ruhr areas—promoted tensions and at least three wars between the two countries. At the end of World War II France and Germany were still quarreling over these areas, and Americans and Europeans alike realized that long-term peace depended on a durable solution to the coal and steel issue. French postwar attempts to control these areas had failed: the effort to internationalize the Ruhr had been defeated by the late 1940s and the attempt to maintain control over the Saar was becoming increasingly untenable. In 1949, when the British ended their occupation of the Ruhr, the International Authority for the Ruhr (IAR) was established with an international board to control the region's coal and steel industries. Although it performed poorly (Gillingham 1991:161–62; Diebold 1959:32–35), it gave the French the idea for a supranational coal and steel pool. "Recognition that the Ruhr Authority was a weak reed undoubtedly made Schuman's new approach more acceptable in France" (Diebold 1959:34). With the ECSC, control over the Ruhr and Saar would no longer be a concern. War between France and Germany would be ruled out since neither could fight without an independent coal or steel industry. Thus the ECSC would constrain Germany and enhance French security.

The French government's interest in cooperation was also fueled by the need to promote domestic economic reconstruction. The creation of a common market would spur economic growth in Western Europe, aiding in its reconstruction. It would create a Europeanwide market which would aid French industry in its modernization. By 1949 the French government, through its Modernization Plan (the Monnet Plan), had dedicated much capital to revitalizing its steel industry, and its profitability now depended on access to export markets. The idea of a large common steel market in Europe thus appealed to both the French steel industry and the government. Success for the Monnet Plan rested on access to *European* markets for French coal and steel (Shonfield 1965; Kuisel 1983). The decision to move ahead with the Plan, then, was an essential prerequisite for French interest in building a European coal and steel community.

Finally, by 1949, widespread fears of steel overproduction existed. Industrialists thus discussed renewing the old interwar steel cartel (Milward 1984:399–402; Diebold 1959:19–20). The U.S. and French governments, steel users, and left-wing parties in Europe all opposed a private cartel. The high steel prices, resistance to modernization, and control gained by German heavy industry in such a cartel were anathema to them. The High Authority would prevent the reemergence of a private industry cartel. The ECSC seemed to solve several problems and provide a variety of benefits for the French government (Gerbet 1956:532–38; Grosser 1961:234–37).

The French government's preferences primarily reflected those of Foreign Minister Schuman and Jean Monnet, the head of the French Modernization Planning Commission. From 1950 to 1951 Schuman remained part of the government as premiers and parties changed. Schuman and Monnet were dedicated to the idea of a strong supranational High Authority to make the ECSC work. For them, the HA served three purposes. They "wanted the coal-steel pool to protect French security through international control of the Ruhr and with this aim in mind designed a powerful directorate to regulate European heavy industry" (Gillingham 1991:229). Strong controls over Germany's ability to make war had to be instituted to maintain French security. Second, Schuman and Monnet realized that France's attempt to modernize its industry would be thwarted if the steel industry could once again cartelize itself (Gerbet 1956:538–41; Gillingham 1991:230–31). Government efforts through the Planning Commission to regulate and rationalize industry would be lost if traditional ways of doing business in France returned. Moreover, in order for the French Planning Commission's strategy to work, the steel industry would need to increase its exports, and a common market in Europe would greatly facilitate this (*Financial Times*, June 5, 1950; Milward 1984:385; Lynch 1984). Third, the two felt that the ECSC would be the nucleus of a larger European organization of industry and politics in the future. European unity would allow Europeans to play a greater role in world affairs, one closer to that of the two superpowers. For these reasons, Schuman and Monnet advocated a highly supranational ECSC and resisted efforts to weaken the High Authority.

Fearing strong domestic resistance, the French cabinet unilaterally and secretly developed the Schuman Plan and immediately presented it publicly (Gerbet 1956:544–46, 552–53; Gillingham 1991:228–29, 235–36; Rioux 1987:142). It anticipated that the steel industry and various political parties would react negatively to its plan. Business preferences were important but divided. The French steel industry opposed the Schuman Plan vigorously. Run before the war by the Comité des Forges, the steel industry had been a powerful cartel with great influence on the government. After staving off nationalization in 1945, the industry had no desire to be controlled by some supranational body, like the ECSC's High Authority. It preferred a return to the prewar situation, where a national cartel would determine production, price, and investment levels (Ehrmann 1957:407–10; Gillingham 1991:293–94). Firms in the industry also worried about the end of protection implied by the common market (Willis 1968:95–97). Thus the steel industry called for new terms for the ECSC, including a weakening of the HA, less emphasis on decartelization, and an escape clause to maintain some protection (Diebold 1959:88–90; Ehrmann 1953:467–69). These changes would have allowed the industry to arrive at its preferred position: "a return of the Cartel, secure home markets, and no increase in governmental supervision" (Milward 1984:402).

The battle over the ECSC was part of a war between the domestic industry and the government over who would control the steel industry. As one study of the ECSC noted:

> In the [French] steel industry the complaint [against the ECSC] was frequently made that the Treaty would subject producers to *dirigisme* of a sort they were trying to escape at home. Many arguments centered on this theme: the powers given the High Authority were too great; it would be a "technocracy," not subject to political control . . . the rules on cartels and restrictive practices were unrealistic, dangerous, and a reflection of American ideologies instead of European experience . . . First, the steel industry wanted to be able to regulate its own affairs in a manner to which it felt accustomed. . . . Second, to the extent that there had to be governmental regulation the industry preferred to deal with the French government. Under the Schuman Plan power over the industry would be wielded by a body that was not French, that was not subject to the known pressures and considerations of a French government, that would see French industry in a different context from that seen by any French government, and that might be much more remote from the reasoning, values, and pressures of the French industry. (Diebold 1959:89–90)

The steel industry was joined in its opposition to the ECSC by the chemical and engineering industries and the organization for small and middle-sized businesses, the CGPME. With these groups behind it, the steel industry also obtained the backing of the national organization for industry, the CNPF. Shortly after Schuman announced his plan, the CNPF, led by the steel industry, began a loud campaign against it (Diebold 1959:85; Gillingham 1991:235–37). Their main concern was the plan's supranational aspect, which they feared would eventually spread to their sectors (Ehrmann 1953:479; Willis 1968:94–95).

Other elements of the business community supported the ECSC plan. Schuman mobilized three important sectors behind it. First, the nationalized industries, led by coal, the railroads, and the auto producer Renault, favored the ECSC since these industries were major steel consumers. Other industries dependent on steel also supported the plan, for they too opposed an industry-run cartel that would elevate steel prices and restrict their supply. Finally, the powerful agricultural producers organization, the COFACE, agreed with the idea of a common market and hoped it would soon be extended to agriculture (*Le Monde*, June 9, 1950; Willis 1968:98–103; Ehrmann 1953:472–75). Because the farm bloc controlled an important segment of votes in the parliament, its endorsement, along with that of the other groups, helped Schuman in his effort to ratify the treaty.

In order to implement the ECSC treaty, Schuman needed a majority vote from the French National Assembly. Under the Fourth Republic, the government was made up of a coalition of at least three parties and often more. From 1947 to 1952 so-called Third Force governments prevailed; these included two of the largest parties, the Socialists (SFIO) and the Christian Democrats (MRP), and several centrist parties, such as the Radicals, the Moderates, and the Independents. Excluded were the extremes: the Communists (PCF) on the Left and the Gaullists (RPF) on the Right (Rioux 1987:158–60). This constellation of parties was a positive factor for the ECSC. The biggest supporters of European cooperation were, not surprisingly, Schuman's own party, the MRP (Grosser 1961:126–27). The Socialists in the early 1950s also supported European unity as well as favoring governmental control of industry (Grosser 1961:118–19). The smaller centrist parties, too, accepted one of Schuman's main arguments for the ECSC—that it would provide the spark for European unity which France needed to regain a power status equal to that of the two superpowers (Becker and Knipping 1986:164, 180–82; de Beaumont 1983:58–59; Diebold 1959:84–87). In contrast, the Communists and Gaullists bitterly opposed European unity and the ECSC. For the PCF, the plan meant the creation of a capitalist bloc against the Soviet Union. For the Gaullists, it meant the loss of French sovereignty and hence a further blow to French power status.

Fortunately, until 1952 "the proponents of Atlantic alignment and European unity; that is, the MRP, [were] firmly in control of foreign policy; the bulk of the Socialists . . . plus of course the Radicals, Moderates, and the Right [were] all the elements of Third Force governments" (Rioux 1987:138). From 1951 on, this constellation of governing parties began to disintegrate. First, the Socialists declined electorally and had to leave the government as it implemented economic austerity plans. Then the MRP suffered electorally, and the governments moved steadily to the Right. The entry of right-wing parties and finally of the Gaullists into the government by 1954 shifted the government majority away from support for European unity. But the Third Force governments lasted through 1951, the crucial ratification period for the ECSC.

Because the ECSC centered largely around Germany and France, the Germans' preferences are important. The German government—led by the Christian Democrats of Konrad Adenauer and the Free Democrats—and heavy industry concurred in their views of the ECSC. They disliked elements of the plan—basically the same parts that the French steel industry and CNPF objected to. The German government and industry liked the idea of a coal and steel common market but opposed the strong supranational High Authority. They preferred that European industry be run by traditional cartel methods. Like the French steel industry, they desired a privately run heavy industry cartel free from supranational control, especially if France directed the High Authority.

The Germans thus suggested an alternative approach: "The Federal Republic wanted a High Authority too weak to interfere with the restoration of the Ruhr or its traditional methods of operation . . . The German [idea] assigned those powers stripped from the High Authority to producer associations . . . The new [German] language shifted the emphasis from the politics of federalization à la Monnet to the economics of location favoring the Ruhr" (Gillingham 1991:240–41). Neither the government nor industry opposed the ECSC completely, however. Both saw the plan as a means to end occupation controls, terminate the discriminatory IAR, regain German sovereignty, and revive the steel industry through a new cartel. The ECSC with alterations to erode its supranational controls was their preferred policy.

In Germany the only group to express outright opposition to the ECSC was the Social Democratic Party. Under the leadership of Kurt Schumacher, the SPD attacked the ECSC as a new guise for an international steel cartel. The party wanted nationalization of industry. Interestingly, the union movement eventually split with the SPD over the ECSC. The unions, especially in the coal and steel industries, supported the industries' position against the plan initially. They opposed the supranational High Authority and the anticartel provisions of the treaty. In the end Adenauer gained their support for the ECSC by promising to include codetermination for the unions in the two industries (Gillingham 1991:287–89). This was a crucial side payment that enabled the unions to endorse the treaty and thus helped ensure greater legislative support for it.

In general, the Germans were fairly united in their view of the Schuman Plan. Unlike the SPD, the government, industry, and unions liked the idea of a common market but objected to the supranationalism and anticartel aspects of the plan. "These views [embodied in the German alternative] were by no means those of only the smokestack barons: There was a solidarity of fact among industry, the ministries, and the West German government which, by the time the Schuman Plan was concluded, also embraced the coal and steel unions and a good portion of the social democratic movement" (Gillingham 1991:242). Unlike the French, then, the Germans presented a united front at the international negotiations over the Schuman Plan.

The ECSC had been initiated by French political leaders and hence was intimately connected to their domestic political goals. The successful modernization of the French economy through the Monnet Plan depended on access to the coal and steel of the Ruhr area. As Milward has claimed, "The Schuman Plan was invented to safeguard the Monnet Plan" (1984:395). Peaceful relations with Germany also required a mutually satisfactory solution to this problem. The Schuman Plan thus appealed to French leaders as a means for resolving both domestic and foreign difficulties. Neither the Soviet threat nor U.S. hegemony seem to have had much to do with the plan; as in the other cases, cooperation chiefly involved the countries who were threatening each other the most, in this case Germany and France. Indeed, when Schuman announced his plan he stated that participation was open to all European countries—Eastern ones as well—and to the Soviet Union; he explicitly stated that he did not want the plan to be a weapon in the cold war (Dell 1995:112). The plan was as much a continuation of domestic politics as it was a part of foreign policy.

Terms of the International Agreement

Shortly after Schuman announced his plan for the ECSC in May 1950, the six countries opened international negotiations in July of that year. Two sets of issues faced the negotiators. First, the four smaller countries objected to the plan. With highly inefficient steel factories and coal mines, especially in Belgium and Italy, these governments would have had to close many of these factories and mines and face rising unemployment as a result of a common market. This was politically impossible for these weak governments. Thus they demanded that their industries be protected for a long transitional period. The French and Germans agreed, developing complex plans to help the small states' industries and delaying a true common market for several years (Gillingham 1991:247–50; *Manchester Guardian*, February 21, 1951).

The second set of issues concerned the High Authority and its powers. The small countries and the German government opposed a strong HA, and the Dutch and Belgians were especially outspoken in their efforts to weaken it. They introduced the idea of a European Assembly that could vote no confidence in the HA, thus forcing its members to resign. They also proposed a Council of Ministers to serve as a national check on the HA; it could monitor the HA's decisions about prices, investment, and so on, and would hear countries' or firms' complaints about the High Authority. The French accepted both these restraints on the High Authority. "Thus the supranational authority [was] surrounded with many more checks and balances than the original French plan proposed" (*New York Times*, January 7, 1951).

In addition, the German government and industries and the French steel industry objected to the plan's strong anticartel provisions; they wanted these weakened so that private industry would control the pool. The French government could not accept these conditions, for its "delegates knew that unless some limitations were imposed upon the future formation of cartels, fear of German recovery would defeat the [ECSC] treaty in the National Assembly" (Schmitt 1962:72–73).

The French faced an uphill battle to preserve the powers of the High Authority and the anticartel provisions. After yielding to German and other pressures to weaken the HA, in early 1951 negotiations came to a standstill. U.S. intervention then helped to force a compromise. The United States threatened to impose its own decartelization program on the Germans through its occupation powers unless they accepted the ECSC as negotiated (Diebold 1959:72–75; Gillingham 1991:255–62, 280–82). To avoid this outcome, the German government agreed in March 1951 to the draft treaty for the ECSC. German industry opposed this but was unable to stop Chancellor Adenauer. The German government did soften the blow, however, by proposing the Investment Aid Law of 1952, which contained large subsidies and huge tax credits for the coal and steel industries (Gillingham 1991:284–86). Again, this crucial side payment by the German government helped secure industry endorsement for the plan and eased any ratification problems in the legislature. After less than a year of negotiations, the six countries had all agreed to the ECSC treaty. At this time, in March 1951, each country needed its national parliament to ratify the treaty.

In the end the Schuman Plan of 1950 looked remarkably different from the ECSC treaty of 1951. In the final document the High Authority's powers had been weakened, new institutions had been added to check its supranationalism, and its means of operation were left largely undefined (Schmitt 1962:68–71; Milward 1984:408–13; Gillingham 1991:228). "The original design had been drastically altered: the centralizing reformist directorate was, by stages, turning into a corporate economic community" (Gillingham 1991:298). These modifications were necessary to satisfy the demands of governments and especially industries in the other five countries; the original Schuman Plan could not have been adopted because these governments feared the electoral consequences of massive changes in their large steel and coal industries. The French, then, yielded much to the other countries in order to arrive at an agreement. French influence was weak partly because of internal divisions, especially the objections of their own steel industry, and because of the reversion point. Failure to arrive at a treaty probably meant the reconstruction of a private cartel, the preferred outcome of the German government and the German and French steel industries.

Successful Cooperation and Domestic Ratification

The ratification process was relatively painless for the six countries involved in the ECSC. In Germany the governing coalition of CDU and FDP members controlled the legislature and cabinet and favored the agreement. The coal and steel pool faced easy ratification since there was little opposition, except for the minority of SPD members. Side payments by the chancellor to key domestic groups turned them into supporters, who endorsed the treaty and helped induce legislative ratification. The promise of codetermination to the unions and the Investment Aid Law for industry had appeased both these groups, making them supporters.

Satisfying the industries and unions at home in order to obtain ratification was important in all six countries. In the smaller countries, for example, ratification, executives believed, hinged on obtaining continued subsidies and exemptions to delay transition to a common market for the two industries. These measures were necessary especially in Belgium and Italy where weak and divided governments feared for their electoral prospects if massive unemployment accompanied the coal and steel pool. With these modifications to the treaty, industries in the smaller countries supported the agreement, and its ratification enjoyed majority support in the four smaller countries.

The ratification debate for the French was more interesting. ECSC ratification by the French parliament took almost as long as the international negotiations. In December 1951, eight months after the treaty was signed, the French National Assembly approved the pool by 337 to 233. Opposition to the treaty came from the Communists and the Right, principally the Gaullists of the RPF (Grosser 1961:237–38; de Beaumont 1983:72–73). The MRP, Socialists, and center-right parties all united in favor of the ECSC. With the French public largely indifferent to the treaty (close to a third had no opinion about it), the parliament paid most attention to the industry groups it affected (Willis 1968:98).

The Assembly's views were shaped by the information and pressures of these groups. The treaty was too complex and abstract to draw much attention in parliament: "The walls of incomprehension between a complex, technical project [like the ECSC] and Paris parliamentarians were all but insurmountable . . . [Only] a minute fraction of politicians . . . actually read the treaty" (Schmitt 1962:73). Instead they depended on industry information and endorsements to form their reactions. The CNPF and steel industry had access to the right-wing parties; "During the parliamentary debates conservative deputies and senators drew heavily on materials which the employers' movement had distributed to all members of parliament" (Ehrmann 1957:241). The vehement opposition of the steel industry and CNPF was mitigated by two factors. The French parliament passed an amendment to the treaty that pledged increased access to investment funds for the coal and steel industries as well as a package of favorable loans and credits (Lerner and Aron 1957:40–41; Baum 1958:260–62). This amendment, giving side payments to the industry and thus reducing their opposition, helped to induce wavering members of right-wing parties to vote for the treaty.

The Assembly was also pressured by another group of industries to support the ECSC. The nationalized industries and steel users endorsed the treaty and argued for its positive effects on France. Several studies suggest that it was the support of these groups that ensured the treaty's passage. "Had the coal and railroad industries still been in private hands, ... the treaty might not have had the necessary support in parliament. As it was, the managers of the nationalized coal mines and the state railroad system, highly respected for their professional competence, brought their expert testimony to show that the advantages of the common market outweighed its dangers" (Ehrmann 1953:473). As another study claimed, "It was the backing of the nationalized industries—the Charbonnages de France, the SNCF and the Régie Renault, all important consumers of steel—which allowed Schuman and the planners to surmount the opposition" (Rioux 1987:143). Endorsed by the more dynamic French industries and critically linked to the domestic project of economic modernization, the ECSC found majority support in parliament. As the model in chapter 3 showed, endorsement from at least one of the key domestic groups involved in an agreement was necessary for its legislative ratification.

Ratification in the ECSC was achieved as a result of two factors. First, the executive negotiated an agreement and made side payments so that at least one, if not both, key groups involved in the ECSC could endorse the treaty. In both France and Germany the industries and labor unions involved in the agreement were divided over its merits. Failure to endorse by both the unions and industries would have doomed the agreement if the model here is correct. Endorsement by the unions and industry in Germany and by the unions and coal and other industries in France was crucial for ratification. These positive signals made the legislature more likely to ratify the agreements.

Second, a low degree of divided government was present in the French and German states. The lack of serious divisions in the French and German governments at this time made ratification easier. Although both were coalitions, neither contained parties who opposed European cooperation. The Third Force governments in control in France during this period were solidly behind the ECSC. Endorsements from key domestic groups and lack of divided government made ratification, and hence cooperation, possible in the ECSC case.

The European Defense Community

Domestic Preferences and Institutions

Although the French government initiated the EDC, internally the French were very divided over the plan, even more so than in the ECSC. The government, led by the MRP, was the agreement's main supporter. Opponents included both the military and the Gaullist party on the Right and the Communists on the Left. In addition, unlike the ECSC, the centrist parties, other than the MRP, were divided on the merits of the EDC. Many members of the Socialists, Radicals, and Independents, parties that were part of the government, opposed the defense community. The loss of electoral support in the early 1950s by the centrist parties and the growth in power of the hawkish Gaullists made the French government increasingly more divided and less interested in the EDC. On the other hand, the Germans, although less enthusiastic than the French about the EDC, were more unified. The CDU-FDP coalition government, led by Adenauer, and the military preferred rearmament within NATO first but, absent that, accepted the need for the EDC. Only the Social Democrats, who were in the minority, opposed the EDC.

The French government modeled the EDC after the ECSC, which had been announced several months earlier. It "was the twin of the Schuman Plan . . . , and it applied to the problem of arms the same principles being tried for coal and steel" (Rioux 1987:144). The EDC called for the pooling of the countries' armies into an international force that would be directed by a supranational Commissariat. The countries would contribute to a common defense fund and would coordinate their arms production industries. Policy over the use of force, the budget, and arms production would be made by the supranational Commissariat with the same three bodies overlooking it as in the ECSC: the Council of Ministers, the European Assembly, and the Court of Justice (Fursdon 1979: ch. 5).

The French government had several purposes in proposing the Pleven Plan. Domestically, it could help solve the government's difficult relations with the military. A multinational army would give political leaders greater control over the military. Second, the French hoped to avoid the creation of an independent German national army. The outbreak of the Korean War in July 1950 made German rearmament imperative, from the British and American points of view. Soon thereafter, both U.S. Secretary of State Dean Acheson and President Harry Truman demanded that Germany arm at least ten divisions as soon as possible (Willis 1968:130–31). Faced with this situation, the French responded by proposing a European army as a means of preventing the creation of an independent German national army. They hoped to use the popular idea of European unity to constrain the Germans, while also satisfying the U.S. demand for German participation in European defense. The EDC was "an attempt to apply the Schuman Plan method to the settlement of the problem brought up by the American demand for German rearmament. The European idea was popular [in France]. Its popularity could bring about the acceptance of the obviously unpopular remilitarization of Germany" (Lerner and Aron 1957:4).

Finally, the EDC also served to derail the idea of German rearmament within NATO. At the same time that the idea of the Pleven Plan was being devised, the Allied powers were negotiating at the Petersburg Conference from January to June 1951 over German rearmament and its relation to NATO. These latter negotiations failed because France refused to allow German rearmament in any form acceptable to the Germans—that is, in ways that did not discriminate against the Germans. Because of these failed negotiations, the British and Americans were convinced that the French proposal for the EDC was the only option available and thus deserved their strong support (Fursdon 1979:105–11, 114–20). "By the middle of 1951 the hopes of the majority of the Western Allies that a German military contribution could be contained within the NATO framework had been dashed by the failure of the Petersburg Conference. There was growing acceptance that . . . 'the NATO solution' [was] dead" (120). With the death of the NATO option, serious negotiations over the EDC began in September 1951.

As in the ECSC, the major actors in these negotiations were France and Germany, although the other four Western European countries participated and the United States and Britain played key roles. Opinion among almost all groups in France was enormously divided over the EDC, divisions that were also reflected in public opinion. One-third of the public had no opinion on the EDC; another third favored it; and the remainder opposed it (Lerner and Aron 1957:83–87). But although the EDC generated much public controversy, it was not much affected by it. The public "is unlikely to have played a significant part in the parliamentary vote [for EDC], since the European-minded third . . . which supported EDC was matched by another third that disliked it, while an equal number was undecided. All sections of the country were too evenly divided for any one part to be able successfully to influence [the ratification process]" (Tint 1972:58). The only preference common to all in France was "resistance to the reconstruction of a German army and General Staff" (Rioux 1987:144).

The most important group to oppose the EDC was the French military. Like the ECSC, the EDC would shift control over a critical sector of French life from the national sphere to a supranational body. The EDC would mean a fusion of national forces into a fully integrated European army. The French military and its veterans opposed this vehemently. To them, it meant the end of the French army, increased political control over the military, and the demise of a major symbol of national pride. High-ranking officers both inside and outside the government protested against supranational control over the army. Who would control the French army was the EDC's major issue, and the military led the opposition to the supranational EDC (Lerner and Aron 1957:24–25; Fursdon 1979:131; Gillingham 1991:263–64).

The EDC also provoked great divisions among and within the French political parties. The Communists opposed the EDC for the same reason they had the ECSC. Being against German rearmament as well as the creation of a Western bloc against the Soviet Union, they saw nothing to be gained in the proposal. The Gaullists, at the other end of the political spectrum, shared in this opposition to EDC. For them, the worst feature was loss of national control over the army. They were so opposed to the supranational aspect of the plan that they even preferred German rearmament (Lerner and Aron 1957:7, 131). The Communists and Gaullists, then, were allied in a strange coalition against the EDC.

The only party that was internally united in favor of the EDC was the MRP, Schuman's party. For them, the promotion of European unity, greater control over the military domestically, and the restraint of German military might within a European framework were the prime benefits of the Pleven Plan. Other parties experienced serious internal divisions over the proposal. The Socialists generally supported European unity but opposed any form of German rearmament because this would fix the division of the Continent. The EDC was less preferred than an unarmed Germany. For the other center-right parties, the issues were somewhat different.

Opposition to the EDC within the Independents and Radicals centered on the view that it was insufficient to control the Germans without the British and Americans and that its supranationalism meant the demise of the French army. These groups feared that while the EDC rearmed the Germans, it dismantled the independent French army (Lerner and Aron 1957:10–11). Supporters in these parties countered that the EDC furthered European unity and Franco-German reconciliation and that it was preferable to an independent German army. The EDC's supranationalism and its consequences for the nature of German rearmament divided these parties, as they did the public.

Party preferences toward the EDC differed from those toward the ECSC and grew more hawkish over time. In the coal and steel case, the MRP could count on strong support from the Socialists and center-right parties. In the EDC, the MRP was bereft of such allies but still had to face the united opposition of the Gaullists and PCF. Not only was the "Third Force" coalition less favorable toward the EDC in general, but after 1952 these parties no longer controlled the government, as they had during the ECSC process. During 1951 and 1952 the MRP and Socialists lost seats in parliament. By March 1952 the Socialists were no longer in the government and now parties of the Right were predominant. In January 1953 the Gaullists entered the government and forced Schuman out. By mid 1954, when the Mendès-France government submitted the EDC treaty for ratification, the pro-European party that proposed it—the MRP—was no longer part of the government and was now part of the opposition (Willis 1968:145–80; Rioux 1987: chs. 7, 8). As one study notes, changes in French domestic politics over the course of the four-year EDC controversy were critical:

> The initiative for the EDC had come from a third force government, presided over by M. Pleven and supported by a majority in which 160 deputies of the MRP played the leading role. The final decision was taken by a completely different

Assembly, a government presided over by M. Mendès-France and supported by the [Gaullists], the Radicals and the Socialists. The so-called "European party" in power at the early stages of the [EDC] enterprise[—i.e., the MRP—]was in opposition during the last phase." (Lerner and Aron 1957:2)

Thus the composition of the French government changed over these four years in ways detrimental to the EDC. Increasingly divided government made ratification of the agreement, and of virtually any domestic policy, difficult (Williams 1966). Many have claimed that the EDC could have been ratified in 1952 and perhaps even in 1953. The same majority that approved the ECSC would have supported the EDC. At that time (late 1951 or early 1952), the MRP remained in the government; the Socialists were more supportive of EDC; and the Gaullists were outside the governing coalition. Over the course of 1953 and 1954, the majority for the EDC slipped away (Lerner and Aron 1957:134–35, 145–48; Rioux 1987:202–3; Willis 1968:145, 161–84; Tint 1972:55). Changes in domestic politics thus shifted the governing majority against the EDC.

In addition, the preferences of the government itself changed over the four years. In 1951 and 1952 the government was led by Pleven, Schuman, and a strong MRP presence in the cabinet. Pleven and Schuman in "an internal conspiracy" developed the idea for the EDC in secret and presented it as a fait accompli that set the agenda for the negotiations (Gillingham 1991:263). As with the Schuman Plan, they were able to take the initiative and avoid diluting the proposal to satisfy domestic opponents. But they were unable to see the treaty through to ratification. By 1954 both were out of the government and in the opposition. Worse yet, the new cabinets contained individuals hostile to the EDC. After March 1952 none of the French Premiers was a strong advocate of EDC. All seemed ambivalent at best, and Mendès-France, many believed, may have actually opposed it (Rioux 1987:224–30; Willis 1968:163–84; Lerner and Aron 1957:19). In addition, his government contained four Gaullist ministers, including the National Defense Minister General Koenig who vehemently opposed the EDC. Between 1952 and 1954 not only had the parliament's preferences toward EDC changed, so had the French government's. The government was increasingly divided, as it came to depend on a wider spectrum of parties, many of whom were hawks on the EDC.

German preferences surrounding rearmament were less mixed. In general, the CDU-FDP coalition government, led by Adenauer, preferred the option of rearming within NATO. NATO was preferred because it linked the Americans inextricably to the defense of Europe (Fursdon 1979:96–97). Once it became apparent that the French refused to accept the NATO solution, Adenauer and his government were willing to agree to a European army as long as it meant the end of all occupation controls and the complete return of German sovereignty. For the German government, the quid pro quo for acceptance of the EDC was Germany's return to equal political status (Willis 1968:134–35, 154). The German military accepted this solution as well. Unlike in France, the German military supported the EDC.

German opposition to the EDC came from two sources. The Social Democrats opposed it because they viewed any form of German rearmament as eroding the possibility of reunification and promoting the cold war. In addition, much of the German public opposed rearmament because of memories of the war (Willis 1968:145–54). These groups were sizable, but, unlike in France, the substantial German governmental majority in favor of the EDC persisted throughout the ratification period.

French political leaders thus initiated the EDC, as they had the ECSC. They were not pressured into this by the reigning hegemon, the United States, or even by the regional hegemon, the United Kingdom. The EDC was in fact not preferred by the British or the Americans at any point, but they did eventually promote it. The Soviet threat and the Korean War were important in stimulating interest in the EDC and German rearmament in general. The French plan represented a novel way to deal with Germans. It also served domestic goals by enabling the French government to control its military better. Intergovernmental cooperation thus served as another means of promoting domestic goals. Unilateral German rearmament was the worst outcome from the French point of view; the government saw the costs of continued unilateral control of its own military as being less significant than the negative externalities created by unilateral German action. Hence French political leaders saw the EDC as a means to solve both domestic and external problems.

Terms of the International Agreement

The international negotiations over the Pleven Plan lasted from February 1951 until May 1952. The key issues in the negotiations had less to do with the text of the treaty than with supplementary problems. None of the countries involved in the EDC negotiations, except France, believed the European army to be the best solution. They all preferred German inclusion in NATO to the supranational EDC (Fursdon 1979:96–97). Indeed, the British refused any participation in the EDC because of its supranationality; they too favored NATO. The other countries were willing to accept the EDC as long as supplementary conditions were added.

For the Germans the EDC became linked to the issue of occupation controls. They proposed a series of contractual agreements that would end Allied involvement in German affairs. France's acceptance of these agreements was the price for German approval of the EDC. In May 1952 the Allies signed the agreements, but they would only be enforced, as the

French demanded, after ratification of the EDC (Fursdon 1979:125; Willis 1968:135–37). The other smaller countries involved, as well as various parties in France, refused to sign the EDC treaty without supporting agreements that linked the United States and Great Britain to the EDC. The EDC's supranationalism bothered them because it was both too strong and too weak, so strong that it infringed on their sovereignty and too weak ever to contain Germany. To facilitate German rearmament, the British and Americans also agreed to provide guarantees to these countries (Willis 1968:137–38; Fursdon 1979: chs. 5, 6). With the conclusion of these agreements in May 1952, the six countries signed the EDC treaty and took it home to be ratified.

Thus negotiations for the EDC were difficult. Few of the countries liked the idea of a supranational body directing their military. As with the ECSC, the norm of supranational control was not well accepted. Many of the compromises in both negotiations involved weakening the supranational bodies that the French originally proposed. The EDC's final text, however, was closer to French preferences than was that of the ECSC. The French, although internally divided, were better able to influence the outcome here because the reversion point was more favorable to them. In the absence of the EDC they threatened to veto German rearmament, either unilaterally or through NATO. French leverage depended on what the most likely alternative was to the EDC. At this point, most countries believed French cooperation was necessary for any form of rearmament. The international negotiations over the EDC did result in an agreement that satisfied most of the countries, and international agreement was more rapid than was domestic ratification.

Failed Cooperation and Domestic Ratification

Ironically the French, who had proposed the EDC, had the hardest time obtaining domestic ratification. Unlike the ECSC treaty, the EDC could not gather enough domestic support in France to obtain parliamentary approval. Although international events influenced the process, the reasons for this lie largely in domestic politics: the increasingly divided government in France and the failure to obtain the French military's endorsement of the treaty.

In May 1952 the French government began its attempt to ratify the EDC treaty. Although the government had received a majority vote from the National Assembly in favor of the principles of the EDC in February 1952, by May internal politics in France had begun to change. Because of domestic issues, governmental coalitions began to collapse rapidly and the center of gravity in successive governments shifted to the Right. Governmental coalitions became broader as they had to include more right-wing parties to

maintain a legislative majority. Thus each government became more dependent on right-wing parties and the Gaullists, who opposed the EDC. To
obtain their support to form a government, the initiating party had to agree
to moderate its support for the EDC and/or to attach conditions to its acceptance. Attempting to ratify the treaty without these conditions would mean
the government's downfall, which each premier sought to avoid.

Thus, from March 1952 on, each French government had to ask its international partners to agree to attach new conditions to the EDC. As each
government became more divided and dependent on the Gaullists for its
majority, the conditions became more onerous. Up to 1954, France's partners accepted all of these new understandings. But when Mendès-France,
in August 1954, proposed a virtual rewriting of the entire treaty at the Brussels Conference, the other countries flatly refused (Willis 1968:161–84;
Lerner and Aron 1957:15–19, 151–62; Fursdon 1979:207–9). Stalling was no
longer an option, and Mendès-France was compelled to take the treaty to
parliament for a vote.

From 1952 to 1954 the composition of the French government and its
parliamentary majorities, then, became increasingly unfavorable to ratification of the EDC. "The decline of [EDC] started on the day when, for domestic political reasons, the Socialists deserted the majority; the day when the
Right, Gaullists, Moderates entered the governmental majority with all their
votes and influence" (Lerner and Aron 1957:163–64). An important question
is why the government postponed ratification for so long. The reasons are
largely domestic. By the second half of 1952, even Schuman was hesitant to
raise the EDC issue in parliament for fear of losing a vote of confidence.
"[T]he stalling was a result of the government's dependence on the votes of
the defecting RPF [Gaullist] deputies, who, though they had voted it into
office, remained loyal to De Gaulle in their hostility to the EDC" (Rioux
1987:202).

For the Mayer government, from January to May 1953, the problem was
acute. "Mayer had always been a supporter of the principle of the EDC, but
it was a condition of the necessary Gaullist (RPF) support for his candidature
that he would negotiate new protocols on the EDC to preserve the integrity
and unity of the French armed forces" (Fursdon 1979:207). Later, in the
summer of 1953, "there was no hope of a favorable majority in the Assembly
for the EDC, and the new Laniel government had no wish to incur defeat by
putting the measure forward. It [thus] maintained its position by repeating
that any ratification vote must be preceded by the fulfillment of three preconditions" (Fursdon 1979:221–22). It is unclear, however, whether any set
of conditions would ever have satisfied the Gaullists and allowed ratification.
The attachments to the EDC treaty were a means for each French government to postpone bringing the issue to a parliamentary vote, which in the
likely event was negative would mean the fall of the government (Rioux
1987:203–6).

The other domestic factor undermining ratification was the French military's role. Had the military been in favor of the EDC, it might have been ratified. With the military's endorsement, fears that the EDC was undermining the integrity of the French army would have been assuaged. Allaying these fears might have persuaded more parliamentary members of center-right parties to vote for the treaty, since their greatest concern was the effect of its supranational elements on the French army. Unfortunately, Britain's rejection of the EDC also had important domestic consequences in France, providing a powerful weapon for the treaty's French opponents. They pointed out that the British also saw the treaty's supranationalism as a threat to British military autonomy and thus French objections to the EDC's supranationalism were valid (Fursdon 1979:127–28). Military support of the EDC might have convinced the Radicals and Independents to vote solidly for the treaty as they had for the ECSC. Had that been the case, the EDC would have passed (Lerner and Aron 1957:162; Fursdon 1979:295–7). But that was not the case. Rather, the French military did everything it could to block the EDC, especially in 1954 when the vote seemed near. In April 1954, when the Laniel government was considering bringing the EDC to parliament, a leading French general, Marshall Juin (the French general to NATO), vehemently denounced the EDC, for which he was forced to resign. This added vigor to antigovernment protests, and any plans for the EDC's consideration in the Assembly were shelved (Rioux 1987:204; Fursdon 1979:248).

The military's objections also led the National Assembly's National Defense Commission, which was studying the EDC, to vote heavily against the treaty. Committees in the French Fourth Republic were very strong, and a negative endorsement from a National Assembly committee was a damning signal to the rest of the legislature (Williams 1966: ch. 18). This vote in June 1954 helped set the tone for the Assembly's later consideration of the treaty. Finally, in August 1954, when Premier Mendès-France had decided to submit the treaty for a vote, three of his key ministers, led by General Koenig, resigned in protest (Rioux 1987:229; Lerner and Aron 1957:18). These signals from the French military helped undermine support for the EDC in parliament. The failure to endorse the treaty by both the military and the National Assembly's National Defense Committee spelled legislative disaster for the EDC. As demonstrated in chapter 3's model, lack of endorsement from all key players tends to lead to legislative rejection of proposed agreements.

International issues also affected the treaty's ratification. Stalin's death and the end of the Korean War both in 1953 raised hopes of an end to the cold war and delayed consideration of the treaty (Lerner and Aron 1957:8). In addition, the French war in Indochina delayed the EDC vote. The disaster at Dien Bien Phu in 1954 brought down the Laniel government and rendered consideration of the EDC impossible until the war was concluded. Difficulties in ending the war made French governments sensitive to military opinion. They needed the military to endorse the EDC to help get it ratified, but the military refused. When the new government of Mendès-France finally signed an armistice in July and turned to the EDC problem, he too was constrained by his governing coalition, which included many Gaullists who opposed the EDC. To satisfy them, Mendès-France proposed a new set of conditions that reduced the EDC's supranational character and gave France special treatment. The other European countries rejected his modifications, and Mendès-France was forced to bring the treaty to parliament, where in August 1954 on a procedural vote it was turned down 319 to 264 (Rioux 1987:230).

Increasingly divided government in France contributed much to the EDC's defeat. As the majority in favor of it slowly passed from the government, the treaty's ratification chances fell. Military opposition and lack of endorsement from the parliamentary committee charged with defense matters were also negative factors for the EDC. Without either of these two groups' endorsement, a majority in the Assembly could not be built to ratify the EDC. Increasing divisions in government and lack of endorsement prevented cooperation in this area.

Conclusions

This section assesses what the model presented here can contribute to our understanding of these two cases. How can we explain the terms of these two cooperative agreements? In addition, why did the outcomes in the two cases differ? Why in Western Europe in the early 1950s was cooperation possible in coal and steel and not in defense? Two elements are identified that might account for this differential outcome: the degree of divided government and the presence or absence of endorsement from important domestic actors.

Domestic politics undid the EDC. Two factors stand out for their role in the different outcomes in the two cases. One major difference involved the lack of endorsement from key domestic actors in the EDC and the presence of such endorsements in the ECSC. In the ECSC case, the existence of an important group of French domestic actors that endorsed the treaty—the nationalized industries and the steel users—was crucial. In the EDC case, French military opposition and the negative vote of the National Assembly's Committee on National Defense spelled trouble. Failure to obtain endorsement from at least one key domestic group that is informed about an issue tends to make legislative ratification impossible.

Governmental strategies also help explain why endorsements occurred in the ECSC and not in the EDC. In the case of the ECSC, the French Premier—and the German Chancellor—successfully employed side payments.

They targeted the key domestic actors involved in the ECSC and offered them aid. This helped silence critics and made their legislatures more willing to ratify the agreements. Internal side payments were not evident in the EDC case in France. The government never seemed to try to win the support of the military. Had it successfully converted the military to the side of the EDC, the National Assembly might have followed suit and agreed to the defense community. Skillful use of side payments could have generated military support of the EDC, thereby promoting legislative ratification.

Second, increasing divisions in the French government over the course of two years were a major problem for the EDC. The composition of the French government changed over the years between 1951 and 1954 in ways detrimental to the treaty. The EDC, many have argued, could have been ratified in 1952 and perhaps even in 1953. The same legislative majority that approved the ECSC would have supported the EDC. Over the course of 1953 and 1954, however, the majority for the EDC slipped away.

The French National Assembly in 1950 and 1951 was controlled by the Third Force parties—the Socialists, the MRP, and the center parties (the Radicals and Independents)—who strongly backed Schuman and his European policies. The Third force coalition controlled more than half the votes in the Assembly; thus the median voter was probably from a center party like the Radicals or Independents, who favored European cooperation. This coalition, then, was able to approve the ECSC. In contrast, a more divided government came into office in 1953–54. Dependence on the Gaullists for a majority meant that the coalition government was unable to cobble together a majority in the Assembly to approve the EDC. Hence, by 1954, the preferences of the parliament's majority had moved away from the European solution. The preferences of its median member now lay closer to the military's position than the government's. Increasing divisions in government thus undermined the parliamentary majority for the EDC.

Finally, it is interesting to speculate why the British did not join either agreement. Having the continent's largest economy, military, and population, Britain was the regional hegemon in Europe in 1950.[1] But not only did they not initiate either agreement, they also refused to have anything to do with European cooperation. Basically, the British government opposed European cooperation for two reasons. First, it did not fit with the government's domestic goals and plans. Nationalization of the coal and steel industries had been a major policy decision intended to help ensure full employment goals; loss of British government control over them in the ECSC would hinder achievement of this goal (George 1991:35–39). No longer would the government control these sectors; the High Authority would be

---

[1] IMF statistics show that in 1950 the British GNP was $37.184 billion; the French GNP was $28.151 billion; and the West German GNP was $23.143 billion, or 60 percent as large as Britain's (*International Financial Statistics* 13, no. 12 (December 1960): 126–32, 264–66).

making decisions with great import for the British economy. As Dell (1995:20–21) describes:

> Britain's perspective was different. It had nationalized coal. It had legislated, much more controversially, to nationalize steel. At the time it produced one-half of the coal and one-third of the steel of the seven countries that might participate in the Schuman proposal. Coal and steel were believed to be the commanding heights of the economy. Was public power over them to be surrendered to a supranational authority whose decisions would be binding and which would itself be a staging post to a European federation? . . . But what could Britain gain to justify participation in a scheme that apparently went to the roots of national economic sovereignty by establishing an authority that could bind governments?

The ECSC in Britain, unlike in France, was not seen as being economically or electorally beneficial.

Furthermore, the British opposed the EDC because it did not fit with their domestic or foreign policy plans. It would not involve the United States and hence might be seen as a pretext for the United States to leave Europe, which the British wanted to avoid at all costs. (Ironically, the U.S. administration strongly supported the ECSC and were angry at the British for refusing to participate, which made the British even less interested in the treaty [Dell 1995:106–9].) Further, endorsing the agreement would mean long-term British military involvement on the Continent and all the costs that would entail. European cooperation, then, did not fit with British political leaders' domestic goals and hence, even though they were the regional hegemon, they had no interest in such cooperation.

Eight

The North American Free Trade Agreement and the Maastricht Treaty on European Monetary Union, 1989–1993

THE EARLY 1990s saw the conclusion of two major cooperative agreements. In 1992 the United States, Canada, and Mexico signed the North American Free Trade Agreement (NAFTA). In 1993 the Maastricht Treaty, proposing monetary union among the twelve European Community countries, came into effect.[1] These agreements represented significant cooperative measures. In both, the countries involved agreed to relinquish various policy instruments and coordinate their economic policies, thus giving up a measure of policy autonomy and national sovereignty. The central questions are why political leaders in these countries chose to cooperate, and why they were able to reach agreements in both cases.

First, why did political leaders initiate these negotiations, given the costs of such far-reaching economic change as the accords involved? Free trade agreements in North America and monetary union among the EC countries had been attempted before but had failed. The 1911 free trade agreement between Canada and the United States suffered from a defeat at the Canadian polls. The 1980 accession of Mexico into the General Agreement on Tariffs and Trade was called off by Mexico. And the 1970 Werner Report, which was signed by the EC countries and called for monetary union, died in the turbulent decade that followed. Although other leaders were in power by the early 1990s, these events should have alerted them to the potential problems and high costs involved. Second, given the end of the cold war and the economic difficulties of the late 1980s and early 1990s, factors one might have expected would undermine interest in international cooperation, why was agreement among the countries possible?

Finally, the chapter asks what made domestic ratification possible. Political leaders who negotiated each of these agreements had to obtain the approval of either their legislatures or electorates. Ratification proved to be a problem in both cases. The NAFTA accord faced a difficult fight in the U.S. Congress, and then the new Canadian prime minister almost vetoed the agreement. It took two years to ratify the Maastricht Treaty: Denmark failed to pass it the first time; Britain and Denmark passed it only with significant

[1] This chapter looks only at the monetary agreement within the Maastricht Treaty.

amendments; France barely ratified it in a popular referendum; and the Germans, the last to ratify it, did so only after a constitutional court ruling. The model here points to three factors that might provoke such problems: increasingly divided government, lack of interest group endorsement, and changes in the ratification procedures. Were these conditions present in the two cases?

Unlike the other paired case studies, these two represent successful cooperative agreements. In both, the international and domestic negotiations proved fruitful, although often after much travail. Whether the terms of the Maastricht Treaty on European Monetary Union (EMU) are ever fully implemented is of less concern here; the countries have signed it and have begun implementing its first two stages. These cases were chosen because they represent contemporary attempts at cooperation. In the cases discussed previously, U.S. hegemony, the end of World War II, the beginning of the cold war, and the Soviet threat served as background factors. Here, these factors have essentially disappeared. Do these changes in the international environment alter the process of cooperation?

The key question explored here is whether the two-level game model developed earlier can help us understand why cooperation was possible in these two cases. In terms of initiation, were domestic economic and electoral concerns a primary issue for national political leaders? Did domestic constraints shape the terms of the international agreement; that is, were the international negotiators focused on obtaining domestic approval for what they negotiated internationally? I expect the structure of preferences and the reversion point to affect the terms of the agreement. Finally, why was ratification (relatively) successful in these two cases? Do the three key variables that explain the other cases help here? In the earlier cases, the degree of divided government, endorsement of the agreement by key domestic groups, and changes in the ratification process all played major roles in determining the fate of attempts at international cooperation.

Like the other cases, these two, as we shall see, confirm the importance of domestic politics. The decision to cooperate was related to domestic politics first and foremost. Prior, unilateral changes in policy were essential prerequisites for the agreements. The domestic ratification processes were long and difficult—certainly longer than the international negotiations and probably more difficult. In September 1990, at Mexico's behest, the United States, Canada, and Mexico launched negotiations for a free trade area in North America, which would eliminate all trade barriers between the three countries over the course of several years. In August 1992, after fourteen months of negotiations, the NAFTA treaty was signed by the three countries, each one then having to ratify it.

Ratification proved difficult in both the United States and Canada. The Mexican government required a simple majority vote of its Senate. Since the party controlling the government (the PRI) also controlled sixty-one of sixty-four Senate seats, ratification proved easy. In the United States, national elections intervened. The election of Bill Clinton in November 1992 forced renegotiation of parts of the treaty but meant an end to divided government in the United States for awhile. After a long battle throughout 1993, Clinton secured final approval of the agreement late in that year. For Canada, the NAFTA accord also proved difficult. Poor economic conditions and unpopularity doomed the Conservative government in the spring of 1993. Elections brought a new government into power, controlled by the Liberal Party. After threatening to veto it, this government eventually approved it. In January 1994, after at least sixteen months of domestic negotiations to ratify the agreement, NAFTA came into force.

Discussions about monetary union in Europe began shortly after the conclusion of the Single European Act in 1987. The French began pushing for greater cooperation in monetary affairs and, in particular, for a European Central Bank (ECB) and single currency. The French government's unilateral decision to deregulate its own financial markets in the early 1980s provided the impetus for the government to proceed with EMU. In 1988 the French Finance Minister, Edouard Balladur, proposed negotiations on monetary union. This proposal was favorably received by all the EC countries except Britain. The Delors Committee, headed by EC Commissioner Jacques Delors and largely involving central bankers, began work on drafting an implementation plan for EMU; its plan was submitted in April 1989. In December 1990, after revision and approval of the Delors Committee report, the EC initiated a series of intergovernmental conferences (IGCs) to negotiate the details of the treaty on monetary union. This occurred almost at the same time as German reunification. A year later, at the Maastricht Summit of EC leaders, despite British opposition all the countries signed the treaty, which now included many issues in addition to monetary union.

The next phase involved ratification in the twelve countries. Ratification problems had arisen even earlier, but for nearly two years—from early 1992 until the end of 1993—they dominated the agenda. Each of the countries required a vote to enact the treaty, but the methods used varied. Some employed popular referendums (Denmark, Ireland, and France); some a simple majority vote of parliament (Portugal, Britain, Netherlands, Italy, and Greece); and others required a special parliamentary majority, usually two-thirds, to enact constitutional revisions (France, Luxembourg, Spain, Belgium, and Germany).

Unfortunately, the first attempt to ratify the treaty—the Danish referendum—failed in June 1992. This event set back ratification in the other countries, as did worsening popular opinion about the treaty. Problems then arose in Ireland, France, Britain, and Germany. In late June 1992 a small Irish majority approved the treaty. France faced a battle within parliament and then a popular referendum, which approved the agreement by the thinnest of margins in September 1992. Simultaneously, the first currency crisis of the EMS occurred, driving the British pound and Italian lira out of the system, forcing reevaluations of other currencies and threatening the system's viability and the EMU. The British government put off a final vote until late 1993. By this time another crisis of the EMS had occurred, and the mechanism linking countries' exchange rates had to be loosened, thus damaging the EMS fundamentally. The German government won its ratification battle in parliament in late 1992 but faced increasingly hostile public opinion and a constitutional court challenge, which it finally resolved in October 1993. In November 1993, then, the Maastricht Treaty was formally adopted by all the EC countries. As with NAFTA, the domestic bargaining over ratification required a greater effort and a longer period of time than did the international negotiations. The reasons for this are explored in this chapter.

NAFTA

Domestic Preferences and Institutions

In early 1990 Mexico and the United States began discussions about a possible free trade area (FTA). The idea for bilateral negotiations between Mexico and the United States came from the successful conclusion in 1988 of the Canadian-American Free Trade Area (CAFTA) agreement, which served as a prototype for the NAFTA negotiations (Whalley 1993:357). The NAFTA negotiations were a Mexican government initiative; in September 1990 Mexican President Carlos Salinas de Gortari officially asked the United States to begin negotiations on a bilateral treaty (*Financial Times*, September 10, 1990; Pastor and Wise 1994). The official negotiations, however, could not begin until June 1991, following U.S. congressional approval of their start and of the "fast-track" ratification process that the president wanted. Canada was also slow to join the process since CAFTA had been a major battle for its government. In large part, domestic divisions in each country slowed down the process.

In all three countries, deep internal divisions over trade policy were apparent. In general, support and opposition to free trade did not follow Left-Right distinctions or party lines. The executives in power in each country and their internationally oriented business sectors supported trade liberalization. In contrast, domestically oriented business, labor unions, sectors of agriculture, and more nationalist politicians—often in the legislatures—opposed it. In all three countries the political parties were split internally over the merits of freer trade. However, the greatest divisions appeared in the United States, as divided government held sway from 1990 to 1992 with the Republicans in control of the presidency and the Democrats controlling Congress. Owing to divisions within the parties, though, dovish executives were faced with more hawkish legislatures in all three countries.

As the initiator, Mexico and its structure of preferences are of particular interest. Of utmost importance was the change in preferences of its government and long-governing party, the PRI. For practically the entire twentieth century, the Mexican government, which was controlled continuously by the PRI, employed a protectionist system of import-substituting industrialization (ISI) as its central development strategy to avoid increased economic dependence on the United States. The FTA went completely against these long-held principles.

Interestingly, the end of Mexico's protectionism and ISI strategy commenced before the NAFTA negotiations. Unilaterally, the Mexican government began a massive economic reform program in the early 1980s. After the debt crisis of 1982 and the second oil shock, Mexico in 1983 launched a comprehensive reform program that by the end of the decade eliminated virtually all quotas and reduced its high tariffs to around 10 percent on average (Schott 1989:255–60). Mexico also decided to join the GATT in 1986 in the midst of this reform process. In the absence of this internal decision to liberalize trade, Mexico would have had no interest in NAFTA. Indeed, NAFTA became the logical next step. As one analyst noted in 1989, "Considering the rapid pace of Mexico's import liberalization, . . . it is hard to imagine an immediate movement toward a freer trade regime without some concessions on the part of Mexico's main trading partner" (Schott 1989:267). Moreover, NAFTA provided a means to lock in the trade liberalization strategy that had been undertaken unilaterally. By joining an FTA, Mexico could not unilaterally change its policies and return to protectionism, at least not without incurring substantial costs. "NAFTA could help cement the trade reforms already implemented in Mexico by better allowing its policymakers to resist protectionist pressures at home" (Calvijo 1993:386). This increased the credibility of its policy moves and hence their effectiveness.

Mexico's unilateral trade liberalization policy from 1984 to 1988, which preceded the initiation of NAFTA, was a central catalyst for the free trade agreement. Its decision to join the GATT in 1986 was also a product of a change in the governing PRI's preferences. Interest in both stemmed from the same considerations. Many agree that by 1982 the Mexican economy was in shambles; there was little growth, high inflation, capital flight, and low productivity. These economic problems in turn caused political crises for the ruling party. Challenges to the PRI's unbroken rule were arising as the economic situation deteriorated; indeed, the PRI barely won the 1988 presidential election. Given this set of conditions, a free trade strategy seemed one of the few ways to revive the economy and to ameliorate the PRI's political problems. By the early 1980s, "with a low price for oil and with the absence of foreign funds that followed the debt crisis, a more open foreign trade strategy seem[ed] to be one of the few options for attaining a rapid and sustained resumption of economic growth in Mexico" (Schott 1989:258).

Trade liberalization and NAFTA were favored in part because of the extensive openness of Mexico's economy. "The Mexican economy is too small to support an efficient industrial sector under an autarkic scheme. Some specialization and foreign trade is thus necessary to attain an efficient scale of production in many industries" (Schott 1989:257). Moreover, an agreement with the United States was particularly important since most of Mexico's trade (70 percent) was with the United States. For the PRI leaders, trade liberalization appeared as a primary means to revitalize the economy and hence their political fortunes.

The PRI's support for free trade was backed by most major business associations in Mexico (Poitras and Robinson 1994). Large firms, and especially those located near the American border, the ones more likely to export, favored trade liberalization by the late 1980s. Indeed, some have suggested that the PRI tried to win back business support by proposing the FTA, hoping thus to undermine their support for the rising conservative party, PAN (Poitras and Robinson 1994; Pastor and Wise 1994). This party was also a supporter of freer trade.

In opposition to NAFTA were groups mainly on the Left in Mexican politics. Traditional elements of the PRI objected to it, and many, including President Salinas, worried that loss of their support would divide the PRI permanently. Labor unions, peasants, protected industry largely in the center of the country, and the left-wing party, the PRD, strongly opposed NAFTA (Poitras and Robinson 1994; Heredia 1994). Despite these divisions, Salinas was able to move forward because of two factors. His party controlled a large majority in the legislature, and its discipline was quite strong. In addition, the Mexican president has traditionally been a very powerful actor, able to initiate and execute policy without much interference from the legislature (Shugart and Carey 1992:155–60). Needing only a majority vote from its Senate for ratification, the president was relatively free to negotiate NAFTA as he desired, given the large PRI majority (Nacif-Hernandez 1995).

In the United States, preferences over trade policy were similarly divided, but President Bush had a harder time than Salinas. His problems arose because of divided executive-legislative control, for the U.S. Congress was controlled by the opposition party, the Democrats. The Bush administration nevertheless believed that there were economic and political benefits to be gained from NAFTA. The U.S. executive branch saw NAFTA as "crucial to a more efficient, competitive and export-oriented economy"(*Wall Street Journal*, August 7, 1992). The administration was counting on it as "a vote-winner for President Bush" (*New York Times*, August 12, 1992, p. 1). Bush was supported in his efforts by internationally oriented business in the United States. Firms, like American Express and Kodak, and business associations, like the National Association of Manufacturers

(NAM), were strong proponents of NAFTA, seeing access to the Mexican market and its cheap labor as important competitive advantages.

Opposition to NAFTA arose from a strange alliance of groups. As one would expect, domestic industries under import pressure, especially from Mexico, such as textiles, opposed the agreement, as did organized labor in the United States. Traditionally connected to the Democratic Party, these groups pressured their Democratic representatives in Congress to oppose NAFTA. Unexpectedly, however, groups of environmentalists, consumer and human rights advocates, and conservatives—like Patrick Buchanan and Ross Perot—opposed NAFTA vigorously. Opposition thus cut across party lines, uniting left- and right-wing groups.

Because of the institutional structure of trade policy making in the United States, much of the battle over NAFTA was fought before the international negotiations took place. Because Congress constitutionally wields control over trade policy, the president must request authority to negotiate trade liberalization. Since the RTAA in the mid-1930s, the president had traditionally been delegated limited authority to do so. Beginning in 1974, however, he had to obtain congressional approval after the fact for any international agreement (O'Halloran 1994). To negotiate successfully with other countries, presidents devised a "fast-track" system. Under this procedure both houses had to give majority approval for the international agreement without amendment and within ninety days of its submission. To receive fast-track authority, the president notified Congress of his intent to negotiate; barring a negative vote in either house within sixty days, he could proceed.

In 1990, then, Bush realized he needed new fast-track authority to cover the NAFTA negotiations. The battle over NAFTA began at this point, as its opponents mobilized to block the granting of fast track in Congress. The coalition of labor unions, environmentalists, consumer groups, and domestic industries almost produced enough votes in the Democratic-led Congress to defeat fast track. But after agreeing to separate labor and environmental negotiations and action plans, in mid-1991 the Bush administration won congressional approval to negotiate the agreement and to use fast-track procedures to ratify it. Fast track provided large advantages to the president, shifting legislative power away from Congress. The initiative for trade negotiations was turned over to the executive, and Congress relinquished its ability to amend the agreement. Time limits also reduced legislators' ability to gather full information about the agreement made. Hence legislative power was shifted to the more dovish actor, making an agreement more likely.

In Canada, preferences over trade were also sharply divided. In the early 1980s the policy preferences of large, internationally oriented business and the Conservative Party under Mulroney changed dramatically (Doern and Tomlin 1991:25–33). By the mid-1980s they were ready to negotiate a free trade agreement with the United States. The factors motivating the Canadians were similar to those prompting the Mexicans. The petering out of a nationalist strategy of subsidies and protection in the face of slow growth globally and the rise of protectionism in the United States that threatened Canadian access to its markets prompted both business and the executive in Canada to change their preferences. For Mulroney and his Conservatives, free trade could be an electorally advantageous policy for a variety of reasons:

> The significant partisan advantages that free trade offered the Conservative government also made the option of comprehensive negotiations attractive. Mulroney was determined to offer a clear alternative to the centralizing, interventionist policies of the Trudeau Liberals and to build a lasting power base for his party. A policy that was market oriented and had broad appeal in Western Canada and Quebec served both his ends . . . Free trade offered the prospect of immediate partisan advantage to a government in search of a major policy on which to set sail. (Doern and Tomlin 1991:34–5)

Much the same coalition for the same reasons backed NAFTA, although with somewhat less enthusiasm. After winning the brutal 1988 election fought largely over CAFTA, the Canadian government was less excited by NAFTA. The Canadian government's attitude was shaped by its domestic situation. Its cautious approach reflected the loss of public support for free trade, and its decision to negotiate reflected its electoral strategy. "Like President Bush, Mr. Mulroney is expected to use positive features of the trade agreement in his own bid for reelection" (*New York Times*, August 13, 1992, p. 4).

Opposition to free trade in Canada cut across the political spectrum. Labor unions opposed both agreements, fearing job losses to the south (Doern and Tomlin 1991); the recession of the late 1980s helped turn public opinion against free trade, as the public blamed the recession on CAFTA; and parts of the Liberal Party opposed it. In addition, the coalition of labor and environmentalists that appeared in the United States also arose in Canada. As long as the Conservatives maintained their majority in the parliament, these opponents could not derail NAFTA. But once new elections were called in 1993—in part over NAFTA—its ratification no longer became a sure bet. The new majority in the parliament would have to ratify the agreement, which had been negotiated before the election. Any change in government was likely to affect NAFTA negatively.

National political executives—Mexican President Salinas in particular—initiated the agreement largely because of the economic and electoral advantages it provided. The domestic political and economic consequences of trade liberalization played a critical role for all three leaders. Salinas saw the pact as promoting his party's interests in Mexico. Bush and Mulroney saw it as a vote-attracting strategy. The prospect of increased economic growth, competitiveness, and jobs motivated all the political leaders. Each seemed to believe that in the absence of an international agreement the national economy would fare less well, which would erode the leader's political support. Protectionism, at least in Mexico and Canada, was no longer seen as bringing net home benefits; the costs of retaliation and the externalities imposed on them by other countries' use of protection—especially by the United States—had come to outweigh any benefits from the unilateral use of protection. The prior, unilateral policy changes in Canada and Mexico attest to their executives' change of view about the utility of protection. NAFTA in many ways represented a continuation of domestic politics by other means.

Terms of the International Agreement

Official negotiations over NAFTA occurred over fourteen months—from June 1991 until August 1992—when the three governments signed the agreement. The actual negotiations, however, began earlier, probably in mid-1990. Although the negotiations were originally intended to create a free trade area eliminating all trade barriers between the three countries, the actual result, according to many, was more of a compromise—a free trade agreement with many sectors being exempted or treated specially (Whalley 1993). The negotiators' central concern were these exceptions from the overall principle of free trade.

A number of so-called sensitive sectors were the focus of attention throughout the entire fourteen months, and some even after the agreement was signed. "Autos, textiles, agriculture and petrochemicals are the sectors where negotiations seem to have been the most intense" (Whalley 1993:357–58). For each of these sectors, the problem for the negotiators was domestic politics. In each case, firms, labor unions, and/or the entire industry strenuously objected to trade liberalization in their sector. Political leaders were often forced to listen to these complaints because they needed these groups' support to win legislative approval of the agreement. Hence ratification depended on assuaging these sensitive sectors. The Mexican government faced pressure from its banking, energy, and certain agricultural sectors for continued protection, and the U.S. administration was under strong pressure from its auto, textile and apparel, and various agricultural groups—both labor and management—to obtain exemptions for each of them. These domestic pressures critically shaped the international negotiations. The opposition of domestic sectors and the need for ratification combined to shape the course of the international talks.

In addition, Congress forced the Bush administration, and then Clinton's, to initiate negotiations over issues tangential to the accord in order to secure its passage. "In order to gain congressional approval for fast-track negotiating authority for the talks with Mexico, President Bush submitted an action plan to Congress in May 1991" (Whalley 1993:375). This plan entailed beginning negotiations with Mexico over issues of environmental and labor standards. These issues were important for certain groups in the United States, whose support was necessary for ratification. Since the U.S. government was divided, with the Democrats in control of Congress, President Bush, as a Republican, needed some of their votes. Appeasing American labor and environmental groups would allow some Democrats to vote for NAFTA. But in the process Bush had to be sure to maintain the support of the most pro-NAFTA group, internationally oriented business. Long supporters of free trade, this group was a critical one for the Republicans. Attaching too much environmental or labor regulation would weaken the support of international business, and if the latter did not endorse NAFTA the agreement would never survive a legislative vote in the United States. Once more, the international negotiations were heavily influenced by the domestic politics of ratification.

Given the large number of sectors covered and the variety of non-tariff barriers addressed, it is difficult to assess the NAFTA agreement overall. It certainly provides for substantial trade liberalization in a number of sectors, although some important ones remain protected, at least for fairly long periods (Hufbauer and Schott 1993). Because Mexico had higher barriers to begin with, NAFTA represents a bigger reduction in its barriers. Most estimates see Mexico as gaining the most, although having to face high adjustment costs (Lustig, Bosworth, and Lawrence 1992:9). But because highly protected sectors in the United States, like textiles and agriculture, were included, the United States also compromised a great deal. The compromise nature of the agreement reflects the fact that in the absence of an agreement both countries might have been worse off. For Mexico, unilateral American protection was a constant concern; without NAFTA, Mexico might have had less access to U.S. markets. On the other hand, without NAFTA the American firms would be faced with greater competition in Mexico from third countries and in its own market. Mexico's unilateral reduction of trade and investment barriers meant that third-country firms could export there more easily and could use Mexico as a platform for entry into the United States. Executives in both countries were willing to compromise to get NAFTA, as long as they could protect their most sensitive sectors.

Successful Cooperation and Domestic Ratification

The model here suggests that domestic ratification exerts an important influence not only on the terms of an international agreement but also on its likelihood. Three factors should make ratification, and hence cooperation, less likely: divided government, lack of endorsement from key interest groups, and changes in ratification procedures after the fact. Canada and Mexico both had a unified government and required only simple parliamentary majorities. But in Canada the majority changed dramatically between the initiation of negotiations (1991) and ratification (1993), with a new Liberal government sweeping the 1993 elections. This change should have made rejection more likely. In the United States, divided government was replaced in 1993 by a unified Democratic-controlled government. This should have greatly improved chances for ratification.

Endorsement of NAFTA in all three countries, at least by internationally oriented business, was forthcoming; hence this should have had a positive affect on the chances of ratification. Finally, changes in ratification procedures were avoided in all three countries. In the United States, once fast track was in place, opponents could not change it until after 1993. Thus the model suggests that before January 1993 the United States should have experienced trouble negotiating and ratifying NAFTA; after that, unified government should have made it easier. Nevertheless, the fact that a new majority of more protectionist Democrats controlled the White House after 1992 meant that modifications might have to be made in NAFTA to make it acceptable to them. In Canada, the issue should have been easily dealt with until the Liberals gained control of the government in late 1993. Their more protectionist stance should have also created problems for the agreement, perhaps necessitating renegotiation or side payments.

In actuality, in two of the three countries, ratification was a problem. For the United States and Canada, domestic politics delayed ratification. Until the last minute, no one knew if these two countries would accept the deals they had negotiated internationally. Not only did the international negotiations hinge on the anticipated reactions of domestic groups needed for ratification—as evidenced, for example, in the Bush administration's decision to allocate funds for worker retraining and its plans for negotiating environmental and labor issues with Mexico. But the ratification debate later affected the agreement. The Bush administration, at the conclusion of talks, realized that "the hard part comes next. Having thrashed out the path-breaking accord with America's neighbors, the Bush administration now must sell the deal to a Congress and an electorate that seem more concerned with job losses than with liberalized trade" (*Wall Street Journal*, August 7, 1992).

Clinton, once he was president, took the extreme step of reopening negotiations with Mexico to deal further with these two issues, largely because he needed to appease members of his own party so they would vote for NAFTA. The lack of strong party discipline among the Democrats meant that Clinton, even though his party controlled Congress, had to offer various side payments to gain ratification. Besides these two side agreements and the exemptions for sensitive sectors, Clinton was forced to make other side payments to ensure legislative approval (*New York Times*, November 14, 1993). A large worker retraining package, a development bank, an environmental commission, and promises of continued protection or subsidies to various industries were the price for obtaining majority support in Congress. Despite some of these concessions, the accord was liberal enough to maintain the support of international business. This group's endorsement was critical for NAFTA. Had they opposed the agreement, as they had the ITO in the 1940s, it would have lost legislative support, especially among the centrist Republicans who were necessary for its approval.

Unified government in the United States, with the Democrats in charge of both the executive and the legislature, made ratification more likely as well. Had Bush remained president in 1993, according to the argument here, ratification would have been more difficult, if not impossible. Bush would have had to obtain the support of many Democrats, who were under pressure to reject the accord from their primary supporters. Clinton's election may indeed have been necessary for ratification.

At this point, the Canadians endangered the accord. A change of government in late 1993 brought Canadian ratification into doubt. Only after receiving various assurances from the United States did the new Canadian government pass the accord. The ratification process (sixteen months) took longer than the official negotiation process (fourteen months).

Ratification was a major issue throughout the negotiations and afterward. But the key concerns for the countries having problems were domestic, not international. Few in any country complained that another country was obtaining better terms than it was; rather, they worried about the accord's effects domestically. The concerns in Canada and the United States were that absolute gains were nonexistent. "Much of the focus of public debate, however, has centered on a few broad questions: whether American jobs will be created or destroyed, whether American wages will fall and whether the Federal budget deficit will grow" (*New York Times*, November 14, 1993). This emphasis on domestic issues, especially those connected with jobs, underlines the linkages among international negotiations, electoral politics, and the ratification process.

Four factors are important in explaining why NAFTA was attempted and succeeded. First, initiation depended on the electoral calculations of political leaders. The low home benefits and high externalities of continued protection in Mexico and Canada made trade liberalization feasible. Prior, unilateral changes in preferences and trade policy in both countries were essential prerequisites for the Mexican and Canadian governments' interest in NAFTA. Second, the return of unified government in the United States with Clinton's election made ratification more likely. Third, the endorsement of internationally oriented business in all three countries, but especially in the United States, signaled legislators positively about the treaty, inducing acceptance of the agreement by centrist Republicans. Fourth, the skillful use of side payments helped Clinton "buy" legislative support for NAFTA. These four domestic factors, then, made a crucial difference to the cooperative process.

The Maastricht Treaty and EMU

Domestic Preferences and Institutions

A monetary union in Europe depended on Franco-German agreement, as have most other European cooperative efforts (Milward 1984). Hence this section focuses on German and French domestic politics, and also touches on those in Britain, the other large player in this game. This is not to say that the other nine countries were not important; as shown later, they did play a role. But the initiation and terms of any agreement depended heavily on German and French behavior. Thus the structure of preferences toward monetary cooperation in these two countries is of key importance. Combined with the institutions used to ratify an agreement, this structure determined how difficult ratification would be and what type of agreement was most likely.

In all three countries divisions over monetary union did not follow Left-Right or party lines. No major European party in any of the twelve countries opposed the Maastricht agreement. In general, groups on the far Left and far Right opposed Maastricht, whereas centrists on both sides supported it. This has been a common pattern throughout postwar European integration efforts (George 1991; Featherstone 1988). Preferences over monetary union differed within political parties and created problems because of the processes of ratification used. Although the British would appear to be the least divided since the Conservatives maintained a majority throughout the period, they actually experienced significant problems owing to intraparty divisions. The German government also experienced problems despite its majority coalition, because differences over monetary union were reflected in its independent Bundesbank and its SPD-controlled Bundesrat. Finally, in France cohabitation and divided government gave way in 1988 to a Socialist-controlled government but one that lacked a majority in the National Assembly. As the initiator, the French government is of primary interest; changes in its preferences made monetary union feasible.

In early 1988, the French government, led by Edouard Balladur as finance minister and François Mitterrand as president, began the process that led to the Maastricht Treaty on monetary union. The government presented a report calling for further moves toward monetary integration in Europe, especially creation of a European Central Bank (ECB). This report received a mixed reaction in Germany, as will be discussed later; it was, however, favorably received by the critical coalition partner, the FDP (Free Democratic Party), of the ruling party (the CDU/CSU [Christian Democratic Union/Christian Social Union]). The German foreign minister and leader of the FDP, Hans Dietrich Genscher, also called for an ECB (*Financial Times*, January 21, 1988; February 27, 1988). In June 1988 the twelve EC countries agreed to set up a commission to draft a mechanism for moving toward monetary union. This commission, headed by Jacques Delors, the

EC commissioner, submitted its report in April 1989. After further discussions among the countries and modifications of the Delors report, official intergovernmental negotiations began in December 1990 over the plans contained in the Delors report.

Why did the French government initiate the EMU process? The government's interest in EMU was tied to its domestic situation. Much like the Mexican government in NAFTA, the impetus for cooperation depended on prior changes in the government's preferences, as reflected in changes in domestic policy. In 1984 the French Socialist government announced a major set of policy reforms for the entire financial system, the central one being the elimination of all capital controls by 1990. This decision came in the aftermath of the economic crisis of 1981–83, in which the French government had imposed draconian capital controls to stem its outward flow in the face of expansionary policy. The failure of those controls and the pressure exerted by industrial and financial interests within France against such controls led to the government's reversal of its position (Goodman and Pauly 1993:73–75). Again, as with Mexico and its move to free trade, the French government's decision to open its capital markets represented a major policy shift away from its traditional, long-standing dirigiste direction (Loriaux 1991).

Two points are crucial. First, as many claim, without this unilateral step in 1984 the French government would never have initiated EMU in the late 1980s. "The shift in favor of capital mobility [in France] eventually tied in directly with plans for European Monetary Union, and France became a key promoter of the idea. The freedom of capital movements across member states of the prospective union, indeed, was a prerequisite" (Goodman and Pauly 1993:75; Tsoukalis 1993:117–22). This prior, unilateral French financial reform program was the key event in prompting the government's interest in reviving EMU. Just as the ECSC provided essential support for pursuit of France's internal goal of modernization via the Monnet Plan, so the EMU was viewed as a means of forwarding domestic goals involving the deregulation of the economy.

Second, this reform program had internal roots. It was motivated by concerns among French government officials and businessmen about French competitiveness and jobs:

> More subtle and ultimately more decisive pressure [for financial reform] emanated, however, from the boardrooms of large French firms and financial intermediaries. In the French case, direct threats of exit were muted by the fact that virtually all of these firms were owned or controlled by the state. In this environment, such an option was transmuted into rising concerns of government officials regarding the competitiveness of those firms relative to their rivals. Jobs and investment were seen to be leaving France and migrating to less restricted markets. (Goodman and Pauly 1993:74)

Thus a key supporter for the Mitterrand government in its quest for monetary cooperation was internationally oriented business and finance.

The French government in the 1980s came to realize its country's high exposure to the international, and especially the European, economy. This recognition of increasing openness had three consequences. "In effect, as international financial integration outside France accelerated, French policymakers came to the conclusion that their preference for national monetary autonomy was unrealistic" (Goodman and Pauly 1993:75). As the Mundell-Fleming model shows, in the face of complete capital mobility the desire for fixed exchange rates means that countries must relinquish independent monetary policy. Thus the French government would be forced to choose between stable exchange rates or national monetary policy. The only way to have both was to impose capital controls, which it recognized had become less useful and more costly. Finally, the government realized that financial market regulation reduced the competitiveness of French industrial and financial firms, thereby hurting economic growth and job creation. The experience of 1981–84, when the Socialist government was forced to reverse its policies in the wake of huge capital outflows and trade deficits, brought home the importance of its openness to the international economy. The 1984 program, begun by the Socialists and then continued by both Conservatives and Socialists afterward, was fueled by France's growing acceptance of the fact that economic growth and hence electoral outcomes now depended on cooperation with its neighbors. "The increase in trade and economic interdependence, which would invariably result from the completion of the internal market, should be expected to reduce further the effectiveness of the exchange rate as an instrument for the correction of payments imbalances" (Tsoukalis 1993:206). In this environment, as the French government had discovered in 1981–83, coordinated policy moves were often the only way to realize its objectives.

The EMU had international roots as well as domestic ones. Part of the French interest in EMU may be attributed to its frustration with U.S. policy (Tsoukalis 1993:184). Instability created by inconsistent U.S. policy and the long-term currency misalignments it produced created European sentiment for a zone of stable exchange rates. The EMU may have also represented an attempt by French policy makers to achieve a balance against Germany. Although some disagree, many have argued that Germany held the dominant role in European economic and especially monetary affairs after the early 1970s. "It is generally acknowledged that since the collapse of the Bretton Woods par value system in 1973, Europe has developed into a deutsche mark zone. In other words, multilateral stabilization of European exchange rates is largely accomplished by the non-German states, each of which stabilizes its currency's value on a bilateral basis with the German deutsche mark" (Andrews 1992:13–14; Giavazzi and Giovannini 1989:63–83). France and some

other states saw EMU as an opportunity to alleviate the asymmetric performance of the EMS, which gave Germany a privileged position in Europe
(Gros and Thygesen 1992:325). France, in particular, hoped to negotiate
rules that would constrain Germany's advantage in monetary relations. "The
drive toward EMU came . . . from France and other states that wanted a
greater say in EC monetary policy-making than they enjoyed in the EMS. . . .
In the late 1980s, French leaders chafed under what they saw as German
dominance of the EMS. They proposed monetary union because it would
increase the voice of France in the format of EC monetary policy" (Sandholtz
1993:27). The crisis of the franc within the EMS in 1987 added impetus to the
French decision to push for an EMU. Balancing against the United States
and Germany may have been motivating forces as well.

Political opposition to EMU arose on both the Right and the Left in
France. The Communists, and unions associated with them, opposed it, as
did the National Front and the Gaullist party, the RPR, on the Right. Since
none of these groups was necessary for the Socialists' legislative majority,
their opposition was not much of a problem. Only when Mitterrand made a
late decision to use a referendum to ratify Maastricht did their opposition
and public opinion in general become a factor. Until the referendum, opposition to EMU in France was generally muted. "Thanks to his presidential
powers, Mr Mitterrand has not had to worry much about opinion at home,
where there has been little debate about Europe. The main opposition parties have not said much because they disagree among themselves. The
centre-right Union pour la Democratie Française, like most of the ruling
Socialists, is pro-EC. But neo-Gaullists [RPR] oppose the abandonment of
sovereignty" (*The Economist*, December 7, 1991, p. 52). Unified government with a centrist majority in favor of EMU provided auspicious conditions for its ratification in France.

In Germany, divisions were also muted. All the major parties favored
EMU but only under certain conditions. Initially, even the majority coalition (CDU/CSU-FDP) was divided over the French proposal. Genscher of
the Free Democratic Party supported EMU, but Chancellor Kohl, Finance
Minister Waigel (both from the CDU-CSU), and Bundesbank president
Pöhl were much less enthusiastic, if not overtly opposed. French government pressure, aided by Genscher, placed the issue on the EC agenda (*Financial Times*, January 21 and February 27, 1988). The terms negotiated for
the agreement would be crucial in deciding whether the ruling coalition
could support it. The opposition party, the SPD, generally supported monetary union but was against the proposed terms (*The Economist*, December 7,
1991, p. 52).

The Bundesbank was also a key player in the monetary area. Although it
did not control exchange rates directly, it did control Germany's currency
and money supply. EMU would basically take these powers from the Bun-

desbank and give them to the ECB. Support for monetary union among business and the public depended on the Bundesbank's endorsement of EMU. But the Bundesbank, while never enthusiastic about it, would only support the idea if the ECB functioned like the Bundesbank, making price stability its first goal and economic convergence an essential prerequisite (*The Economist*, September 22, 1990, p. 60; *Wall Street Journal*, October 15, 1990, p. 11). The government needed Bundesbank endorsement, then, to obtain legislative approval. Thus divisions over union were muted in Germany, but the terms of any such union were very important and provoked dissension.

In Great Britain, intra-party differences posed larger problems since groups actually opposed union itself. The British government was controlled by a Conservative majority throughout the period. As in the other countries, the majority in every major party supported monetary union. But in Britain an important group of Conservatives, including Margaret Thatcher, who was prime minister until 1991, opposed it vigorously. This group was large enough to destroy the Conservative's majority, meaning that it would either have to appease them, call a vote of confidence, or rely on other parties for help (*The Economist*, June 15, 1991, p. 58). The opposition Labor Party supported monetary union but refused to help the Conservatives. They elected to abstain or oppose it on any vote. The Liberal Democrats supported it and eventually helped the Conservative government in its search for votes (*Financial Times*, November 2, 1992, p. 16). Internationally oriented business and the financial sector ("the City") also supported EMU (Frieden 1991; *Financial Times*, November 2, 1992, p. 8).

Rising capital mobility, the growing integration of their economies, and the slowing of economic growth posed challenges for European political leaders in the 1980s. In most of the twelve EU countries, all major parties supported monetary cooperation, including union. Internationally oriented business and finance also supported it throughout Europe. Divisions within the three large EU countries were muted; opposition lay at the extremes or cut across parties. Majority governments—either single-party or coalition—in these three countries also helped to mute controversy over the Maastricht Treaty. The institutional process of ratification, however, made a difference. Although simple majorities in each country could ratify EMU, if supramajorities or public referendums were required this would render ratification far more difficult.

The initiation of monetary union would seem to have little to do with the larger political changes in the international system. The end of the cold war and the collapse of the Soviet Union seem less important than various economic changes—such as rising capital mobility—in producing interest in monetary union. Indeed, these political changes may have made cooperation more difficult. Clearly, the existence of the EU mattered. The Single

Market Act and the increasing integration of the countries' economies because of earlier integration efforts had a major impact on the development of government preferences for monetary union. But the claim that the EU initiated the Maastricht Treaty may be overdone. Without the firm support of national political leaders such as Mitterrand, Balladur, and Genscher, EMU probably would have gone nowhere. Delors and the EC Commission played a critical role in moving the idea forward. The Delors Committee report provided the framework for the international negotiations, but it is unclear what independent impact it had on their outcome. The Delors Committee, made up mainly of national central bankers, focused mainly on the *process* of monetary union. The decision to seek union had been made before by the national governments. In addition, central parts of the report were later changed to accommodate national objections (*Financial Times*, September 10, 1990; *The Economist*, September 15, 1990). The idea for monetary union had previously been agreed on within the EC; the Werner report of 1970 set forth an EC agreement to move toward monetary union. This report had lain dormant for almost twenty years, however. National political leaders' interest in monetary union was what revitalized the issue.

The initiation process was most clearly related to domestic politics. French financial liberalization in 1984 was a necessary precondition for EMU. This unilateral move preceded the Single Market Act and was motivated largely for domestic political reasons. It created the dilemma of the "inconsistent quartet" of free trade, free capital movements, fixed exchange rates, and national monetary autonomy, which EMU was designed to resolve (Padoa-Schioppa 1988). The deepening of French and other Europeans states' exposure to the international and European economies in the 1980s prompted them to search for cooperative ways to realize their internal policy objectives. "Economic recovery and European policy are two sides of the same coin. Failure to ratify Maastricht would be a truly massive economic as well as political calamity" (*Financial Times*, November 3, 1992, p. 19). For European leaders, international monetary cooperation was the pursuit of domestic politics by other means.

Terms of the International Agreement

The official international negotiations over EMU lasted one year, from December 1990 to December 1991. The unofficial negotiations began in 1988 when the idea was first broached. The negotiations centered on four issues: the timing of union, the preconditions for union, the status and role of the ECB, and the irreversibility of union. A number of countries, led by Germany and other northern European creditors with good inflation records, preferred a long or unspecified period to effectuate union, with economic convergence prior to union and an independent ECB ruled by a price stability mandate. The other group, led by France and including the Latin countries of southern Europe who were often debtors and had worse inflation records than the other countries, negotiated for a shorter, more specific timetable for union, for a union that was irreversible and preceded convergence, and for a more political ECB controlled by a council of European central bankers. Countries in both groups agreed on the need for union; Britain under Thatcher was the only one that explicitly rejected the idea. National, democratic control of its macroeconomic policy remained a key demand for Britain throughout. In other aspects, though, Britain and Germany shared many preferences about EMU. Despite Britain's resistance, the EC countries signed the Maastricht Treaty in early 1992 after the December summit.

The divisions in the EMU negotiations reflected domestic concerns, particularly worries over ratification. The three countries that were most reluctant to move forward were the United Kingdom, Germany, and Denmark. In Britain, Thatcher and a bloc of Conservative Party members opposed union on the grounds that it would be an unconstitutional relinquishing of national sovereignty; they were "hawks" in our terms. The main fear was that giving up this instrument of national monetary control would make it harder to reach domestic goals, like low inflation, deregulation, and strong economic growth. Thatcher's opposition was attributed by some to domestic electoral concerns (*Europe*, October 26, 1989). As others have pointed out (Gros and Thygesen 1992:256–59; Tsoukalis 1993:214), Britain's economy was less exposed in both trade and monetary affairs vis-à-vis EC markets than were the other major states, and Britain held a preeminent place as a *global* financial center. This implied that, as was demonstrated in the aftermath of the ERM crisis of 1992, Britain could more easily than other EC countries pursue an autonomous monetary policy. Giving up this capability is more costly for the United Kingdom than for other states because it is more useful; that is, for the British government monetary policy may have positive home benefits as well as high externalities. In the negotiations, Britain blocked progress on every move and finally negotiated an "opt-out" clause for itself (*The Economist*, October 29, 1988; *Financial Times*, December 11, 1991, p. 2).

In Germany, too, the concerns of a dominant domestic player affected negotiations. The opposition of the Bundesbank, led by Pöhl, significantly changed the negotiations. The German government realized that it needed the Bundesbank's endorsement for EMU to be ratified. The Bundesbank was thus able to set conditions for EMU, and the German government had to fight for these internationally if it wanted domestic support (*The Economist*, September 22, 1990). The Bundesbank insisted that the ECB resemble itself; that is, that it be politically independent and have the maintenance of price stability as its main goal. In addition, the Bundesbank wanted the national central banks to be made independent before the ECB was created. It also demanded that tough economic convergence conditions be met by all countries before proceeding with EMU (*Financial Times*, November 7, 1991). Much of Germany's behavior in the negotiations over EMU was related to obtaining the Bundesbank's crucial support domestically.

The French government and others opposed these conditions. But they were in a weak position. In the absence of EMU, the German government and Bundesbank would retain major control over all European monetary policy because of the dominance of the deutsche mark. Thus the reversion point in this case was very close to the Bundesbank's most preferred position and to the German government's as well. This gave strong leverage to the Germans in the negotiations. "Other member [countries] understood that Germany would agree to abandon the D-mark only if it won most of the arguments on monetary union, and so it has" (*The Economist*, December 7, 1991, p. 52). In the end, then, since the Bundesbank's endorsement was essential to German support for the agreement and since the no-agreement outcome was closest to the Bundesbank's and the German government's preferred position, the demands it made were largely met in the treaty.

Successful Cooperation and Domestic Ratification

The Maastricht agreement nearly came apart as a result of failed domestic ratification. The ratification process lasted longer than the official negotiations, and it resulted in significant amendments to the treaty. Domestic politics in the countries drove this process.

The model here would lead us to examine three factors to explain the outcomes. Divided government, lack of endorsement from key interest groups, and changes in the ratification process should have made ratification more difficult. The presence of divided government, or increasing divisions in it, should make ratification less likely and should weaken the executive, forcing her to accept new terms for the agreement. Failure of key groups, like international business or finance or the Bundesbank, to endorse the treaty should also raise the probability of failure. In addition, changes in the ratification procedures during or after the international negotiations should create serious problems, again curtailing the influence of the executive and necessitating renegotiation of the agreement.

In early 1992, when the treaty was signed, where would we expect ratification problems? Ratification problems depend on both the structure of preferences and the institutions of ratification. For instance, the German government had a simple majority in the Bundestag, which would have been sufficient to ratify the treaty. But the SPD opposition was able to force the government to treat the treaty as a constitutional amendment. In this situation, ratification now required a two-thirds vote in both houses. The government did not control a majority in the Bundesrat, let alone two-thirds. In effect, the government was divided since it would have to depend on SPD support to pass the treaty. The countries where the structure of preferences and the ratification process created such divided government, that is, dependence on the opposition for support—were Denmark, Belgium, Luxembourg, Spain, Germany, and France.[2] In all these countries we would expect problems with ratification. In contrast, in the United Kingdom, Italy, the Netherlands, Portugal, and Greece, unified government and a simple majority vote meant that these governments should not experience problems.

Lack of endorsement from major domestic groups could also pose problems. The model suggests that at least one such group must endorse in order for ratification to occur. In all twelve countries, internationally oriented business and finance endorsed the treaty. In addition, the central banks in the twelve countries, except in Britain, endorsed the agreement. Thus, once Bundesbank approval was given, we would not expect lack of endorsement to be an issue. Finally, where changes in ratification procedures were attempted or made after the negotiations, we would expect problems. Three countries experienced such changes or attempted changes. In France, the government, after pressure from the opposition, agreed to a public referendum, in addition to the parliamentary vote. In Germany, the Social Democratic opposition forced the government to treat the Maastricht Treaty as a constitutional amendment, which required supramajorities in both houses. Finally, in Great Britain, the Labor Party and hawkish Conservatives also pushed the government to use a public referendum, although they ultimately failed to obtain such a change.

This would lead us to anticipate ratification problems in a number of countries. France and Germany should face the worst trouble since both divisions in government and changes in procedures existed. We might also expect trouble in Spain, Luxembourg, and Belgium, although in those countries the opposition parties all supported EMU. The structure of preferences, then, suggests these countries should have few problems. We should also expect trouble in Denmark. Minority government should have made ratification problematic, but all major Danish parties supported EMU. In addition, Denmark, like Ireland and France, used a referendum to ratify the treaty. Interestingly, Eurobarometer polls showed that in February 1992 public opposition to EMU was a majority position only in three countries: the United Kingdom, Germany, and Denmark (*Los Angeles Times*, June 9,

[2] In Denmark, the government was a minority coalition; in Belgium and Luxembourg, a majority coalition existed but a two-thirds vote was required; in Spain, a single-party majority ruled but again a two-thirds vote was needed; in France, the Socialists lacked even a majority in the National Assembly and a three-fifths vote of both houses was required for a constitutional amendment (*Financial Times*, April 23, 1992, p. 22; *World Factbook* 1993, 1996).

1992, sec. H, p. 1). Given this structure of public preferences, referendums in any of these three nations might have failed. If Denmark, Germany, and France seem to be most problematic, the least trouble should have been in Greece, Portugal, the Netherlands, Italy, and the United Kingdom; none of our three conditions existed in them. In actuality, this prediction is only partially correct. As we will see, problems arose in Denmark, Germany, and France, as predicted, but also in the United Kingdom, contrary to our prediction. The other countries all ratified the agreement without much difficulty, as anticipated.

In Denmark, in 1992, the public rejected the Maastricht Treaty. At the time, the government was divided. It was a minority conservative-liberal coalition, which had won less than a third of the votes in the December 1990 elections (Cameron 1993; *Financial Times*, October 15, 1992, p. 3). Two small parties on the Left—the Socialist People's Party and the Progress Party—were the only ones who opposed EMU, whereas leaders in the other parties and especially in the largest opposition party, the Social Democrats, voiced support. In the referendum, however, Social Democratic voters and the supporters of the left-wing parties overwhelmingly rejected the treaty. The minority government was unable to obtain ratification. Only after it had fallen and been replaced by a majority coalition led by the Social Democrats could the public be persuaded to ratify Maastricht. Before ratification, this coalition also attached new conditions to the treaty, including an "opt out" clause, in order to gain acceptance of the agreement.

In France, the government also had considerable difficulty with the ratification process. Because it needed a constitutional amendment to implement Maastricht, the government had to obtain a majority in both houses and a three-fifths majority in a joint sitting of the parliament. Divided government created problems in France, too. Difficulties arose because the Socialist government lacked an absolute majority in the National Assembly. It had to win the support of other parties in order to ratify. To do this, the government accepted four amendments to the agreement; the key one was a promise that the parliament would from then on have a greater role in debating EC legislation. In return, the center-right UDF-UDC party backed the government, causing a split within the Right since the Gaullist RPR party opposed it (*Financial Times*, May 11, 1992; *Financial Times*, May 14, 1992). Although the government won a three-fifths majority in parliament in June 1992, it faced pressure from EMU opponents to call a referendum and finally decided that because elections were less than a year away a public referendum might be a good way for the government to gain public support and divide the Right. The referendum, however, backfired on the government: the public used it to register their general disapproval of the Socialists. Nonetheless, in September 1992, the government obtained a tiny majority in favor of the treaty (*Wall Street Journal*, September 21, 1992). Thus the French, who had initiated the EMU process, ended up barely supporting it. Divided government and a change in the ratification process delayed and almost derailed the treaty's ratification.

In Germany, political divisions also caused problems. As in France, the government had to amend the constitution to implement EMU and hence needed a two-thirds majority for the treaty. Because of this requirement, which the opposition parties forced on the government, it could not rely on its parliamentary majority. In addition to its partners in the FDP, the government had to obtain support from the SPD and the Länder, who also controlled the upper house, the Bundesrat. Chancellor Kohl was thus forced to include certain amendments to the treaty to garner their support; the central ones were a pledge to give the Länder in the Bundesrat greater control over EC legislation and to give the parliament the final word on monetary union (*Financial Times* April 23, 1992, p. 22; *Financial Times*, May 8, 1992, p. 8; *Financial Times*, June 17, 1992, p. 3). Thus Germany added its own opt-out clause as well, solely as a consequence of the ratification process. In addition, as noted above, the government needed the Bundesbank's support, and this allowed the central bank to impose important conditions on the treaty during its negotiation (*The Economist*, September 22, 1990).

Other parties in Germany who opposed EMU called for a public referendum, since polls revealed that the public lacked enthusiasm for the treaty. When the government rejected this, the opponents launched a Constitutional Court appeal. This further delayed ratification and imposed new conditions on the process. In October 1993, the Court ruled for the government but forced it to consult more with parliament on future EC issues. "The end result is that all agree that the Bundestag and the Bundesrat . . . should in the future exercise stronger democratic control over EC decisionmaking. In the future, German overseeing of Brussels legislation will be similar to that in Britain and Denmark . . . In a considerable tussle with the German government, the two chambers [of parliament] have wrestled constitutional powers to oversee all future Brussels legislation" (*Financial Times*, October 13, 1993). The need for political support for ratification once again affected the treaty; now irreversible movement to EMU, as agreed to in the treaty, would be impossible.

In Britain, the single-party majority government required only a majority in the House of Commons for ratification. This suggests that it should have had little difficulty, but the lack of party discipline among the Conservatives created great problems for the government. In 1992 the Conservatives, led by John Major, had a majority in Parliament. But the party itself was riven by dissension over EMU. A group of about forty Conservatives, led by Margaret Thatcher, opposed the government at every step and shattered its twenty-one-seat majority in the House of Commons (*The Economist*, December 14, 1991; *Financial Times*, October 4, 1992, p. 1). At the Maastricht Summit in December 1991, because of this rebellion within his party, Prime Minister Major was forced to negotiate three side clauses to the Maastricht

Treaty. He obtained an exemption from the social charter on workers' rights, a clause preventing more power from being given to the EC, and an opt-out provision, giving Parliament the right to vote on the move to monetary union before it was achieved (*The Economist*, December 14, 1991).

After the Danes rejected the treaty, the British Conservative rebels were emboldened and they forced Major to postpone the vote on the process of ratification until the fall of 1992. At this point, Major was forced to almost call for a vote of confidence just to obtain support for discussion of Maastricht. Supported by the Liberal Democrats, however, the government won a small majority to move ahead with the ratification vote. The Labor Party voted against the government because of the exemption of the social clause and in order to force a government defeat and new elections. The Labor and Conservative opponents of EMU also called for a popular referendum on the treaty, which Major was able to reject. Without the Liberal Democrats, however, the government would have failed (*Financial Times*, November 5, 1992, p. 1). To get their support, Major promised there would be no vote on the treaty until the Danes had passed it and offered other side payments. Hence the British were unable to ratify Maastricht until mid-1993, and then only after enduring a House of Lords' challenge as well (*New York Times*, May 21, 1993). Lack of party discipline, which created a situation similar to divided government, delayed and encumbered the ratification process.

The structure of domestic preferences and the ratification procedures combined to determine the probability of ratification and the terms on which countries would accept EMU. In those countries with more divided government and with difficult ratification procedures or with changing procedures, new terms had to be attached to the treaty and ratification became more problematic. Unified government and simple majority ratification procedures gave executives freer hands to negotiate the terms they desired. Divisions in government forced executives to attach new conditions to the EMU treaty in order to obtain ratification. Opponents also tried to derail the process by altering the institutions of ratification, as evidenced in France, the United Kingdom, and Germany. The need for domestic endorsements from key groups also shaped the international negotiations, as it forced all the countries to accede to the Bundesbank's major concerns. Not only did ratification prove difficult politically in a number of cases, it fundamentally affected the terms of EMU.

Conclusions

Do the cases lend support to the arguments about the role of domestic politics? What factors helped induce (and impede) the successful negotiation and ratification of the NAFTA and Maastricht accords? How can we explain the terms of the two cooperative agreements? Finally, did the changed international environment of the 1990s affect the role of domestic factors in the agreements? Does the end of the cold war and the decline of U.S. hegemony spell greater or lesser influence for domestic politics in international relations?

The model here is useful for understanding the cases. In each, changes in domestic preferences, as reflected in unilateral domestic policy initiatives, preceded the start of negotiations. For NAFTA, a change in the Mexican government's preferences about trade was critical; Mexican trade liberalization was a necessary precondition. For EMU, French and Italian financial market liberalization were prerequisites. These unilateral decisions were made for domestic political reasons. Heightened international economic openness meant that leaders could do more to improve their economies by seeking joint solutions to their economic problems. Unilateral policy choices played an important role; that is, as many economists argue, the best choice for a country is often to get its own domestic house in order first. But cooperative policy making allowed the countries to advance the pursuit of their unilateral policies, while avoiding some of the costs entailed by these policies. Cooperation was intimately tied to the domestic political calculus of executives.

The domestic ratification game also cast a shadow over the international negotiations. Leaders knew they had to find support internally for their agreements. Endorsements by key domestic groups were pivotal to the process. This search affected the negotiations and the agreements made. The United States had to protect its "sensitive" sectors and to negotiate stronger environmental and labor standards to get Democratic support for NAFTA. Britain, France, and Germany had to obtain the support of the major political groups at home for EMU. Opt-out clauses and changes in the timing of EMU and the role of the ECB were made to win the endorsement of salient domestic groups, such as the Bundesbank in the German case. The domestic ratification game was important throughout the process; concerns over ratification influenced all aspects of the cooperation process, even the international negotiations that preceded ratification.

Finally, the two-level game perspective links electoral calculations, divided government, and international negotiations. Four factors affected the chances for ratification. First, divided government posed a problem for ratification and hence cooperation in both cases, and in a variety of different countries. Despite their different political systems, the United States (divided, two-party system), Denmark (minority coalition), France (majority coalition), Britain (lack of party discipline), and Germany (majority coalition) all faced internal governmental divisions that endangered the ratification process. Moreover, as argued in chapter 4, changes in the ratification process were used by the agreements' opponents to destroy the accords. The British, French, and German governments all faced challenges to the ratification procedures they had chosen by the opponents of EMU.

Third, the need for endorsements by key domestic actors constrained the international negotiators. In NAFTA, Clinton could not concede too much to opponents of NAFTA, lest he lose the crucial support of internationally oriented business. In EMU, gaining the Bundesbank's endorsement was necessary for the German government to have a chance to ratify the agreement. Without either international business endorsement of NAFTA or Bundesbank endorsement of EMU, these agreements probably would not have been ratified by the United States or Germany, respectively. As in the other cases, then, the degree of divided government, the need for endorsements by key domestic players, and changes in ratification procedures after the negotiations were all critical variables for understanding the negotiation and ratification of cooperative accords.

What difference did the changed international environment have on these cooperative negotiations? Unlike the previous cases where U.S. hegemony, the end of World War II, and the cold war served as background factors, in these two cases none of these conditions was present. Did this new international environment affect the way the two-level game was played? This question raises many issues, only a few of which can be addressed here. Two sets of predictions exist. According to one view, cooperation should become less likely as the bipolar structure of world politics erodes and as U.S. hegemony declines. Both Hegemonic Stability theory and various Realists, for different reasons, appear to forecast the erosion of Western cooperation in the face of U.S. decline and the cold war's end (Krasner 1976; Kindleberger 1973; Mearsheimer 1990; Gowa 1994). Systemic theories, however, could argue that NAFTA and the Maastricht Treaty reflected shifts in the distribution of power to regional blocs, one in Europe around Germany and one in North America around the United States (Gilpin 1987:397–400). The model here would not predict any necessary relationship between cooperation and such international systemic factors. Rather, it focuses attention on the structure of domestic preferences and institutions. Cooperation at the international level is seen as part of the domestic game rather than just part of the pursuit of the national interest vis-à-vis other countries. The model here would not anticipate any linear decline in cooperation among Western countries as a result of changes in the distribution of power resources internationally.

A second prediction relating to the effect of changing international power structures on cooperation has been that the period we are entering will be more driven by domestic pressures than before. Again, various Realists and non-Realists both seem to anticipate this growing role for domestic politics (Waltz 1979; Katzenstein 1978). As Katzenstein argued in *Between Power and Plenty*:

> The relative weight of domestic structures in the shaping of foreign economic policy increased during periods of hegemonic decline. As long as the distribution of power in the international political economy was not in question, strategies of

foreign economic policy were conditioned primarily by the structure of the international political economy. But when that structure could no longer be taken for granted, as is true today, the relative importance of domestic forces in shaping foreign economic policy increased. (1978:11)

In contrast to this claim, the argument here would not see domestic politics as necessarily becoming more important as structural forces changed. Instead, it would argue that the weight of domestic forces depends on the issue at hand and the structure of preferences domestically. If important domestic groups shared the same policy preferences, if the executive were able to make agreements without ratification of any sort, or if the ratifying body were less hawkish than the executive, domestic politics would play a much less important role, no matter what the distribution of power internationally. As noted earlier, when there is no power sharing domestically or the actors share the same policy preferences, then the unitary state model is most appropriate and domestic politics fades in significance. These conditions have much more to do with the country's political institutions and the issue at hand than with the character of the international system.

The predictions of the argument here, then, are not that some linear increase will occur in the weight of domestic forces over the period from World War II to the present but rather that the importance of domestic politics will vary by issue and country. If one looks at the eight cases examined here, this prediction seems to hold: domestic politics was just as important in the 1940s and 1950s as it was in the 1990s. Its salience depended more on the structure of domestic preferences and the nature of domestic political institutions than on the distribution of power internationally. One expects this to be the case no matter what the future brings for the international system.

Part Three _____

CONCLUSIONS

Nine

Conclusions

The Argument: The Role of Interests, Information, and Institutions

This book examines the implications of relaxing the assumption that states are unitary actors. This central assumption drives much of International Relations (IR) theory. States are assumed to act as if they were hierarchically organized. Instead of a hierarchical mode of organization, states are assumed here to be polyarchic. They are composed of at least two groups that share power over decision making and have different policy preferences. In contrast, the unitary actor assumption implies either that domestic actors have the same policy preferences or that only one group controls decision making. The assumption of polyarchy means that neither of these conditions holds. No strict hierarchy describes domestic politics; rather it resembles a web of interdependent relations. Changing the unitary actor assumption yields different conclusions about the nature of international politics, as the concluding sections of this chapter detail.

Relaxing the assumption of a unitary state demands a new model of interstate relations. Although the importance of domestic politics to international relations has been noted frequently, a theory of domestic factors is not available. No counterpart exists to Waltz's *Theory of International Politics* for the role of domestic factors. But, as most scholars understand, domestic considerations are intertwined with international factors. Leaving one of them out of the model biases its results. The key goal of this book, then, has been to develop a parsimonious, abstract model of the interaction between domestic and international politics, based on the assumption that domestic politics is polyarchic. A "two-level game" is used as the starting point. Many such games have lacked an explicit theoretical structure, especially at the domestic level (Snyder and Diesing 1977: 510–24; Putnam 1988; Evans, Jacobson, and Putnam 1993; Mayer 1992; Iida 1993a, 1993b; Bueno de Mesquita and Lalman 1992; Mo 1991, 1994, 1995). Chapter 3 presented a formal model showing how domestic and international factors interacted to shape cooperation among nations. In this model, the international level was presented as an anarchic environment, free of institutions, involving competition between two unitary states. The domestic game involved three actors who shared power over decision making. Combining these two levels, the model laid out the logic behind the hypotheses linking domestic politics to the negotiation and ratification of international agreements.

This model was applied to a particular empirical puzzle: why do nations cooperate with one another? More specifically, why does the extent of cooperation vary both across issue areas and over time, as well as among states. Previous arguments answer this question mainly by examining international factors. In the model here, cooperation among nations is less plagued by fears of other countries' relative gains or likelihood of cheating than it is by the *domestic distributional consequences* of cooperative endeavors. International negotiations often fail because of domestic politics, and such negotiations are commonly initiated because of domestic politics. Domestic considerations affect all aspects of cooperation. Existing theories of international cooperation have neglected this influence of domestic politics, and the goal here is to correct this oversight. A theory of domestic influences is needed, especially one that takes into account their interaction with international factors.

A key finding was that domestic politics, even in its simplest form, made cooperation more difficult for countries. Two unitary states operating in an anarchic environment were more likely to find a cooperative agreement than were those same two actors when even one of them had to worry about domestic politics. Domestic politics made cooperation less likely and changed the terms of agreements that could be made. This suggests that even Realists, who are the most pessimistic about states' ability to cooperate, may overestimate the likelihood that they will do so. Making the international game less anarchic might increase the likelihood of cooperation. But this result depends on the domestic political situation. If the domestic environment is the same as it is in the more anarchic setting, then a change in the system's degree of anarchy need not have any effect on the likelihood of cooperation. Whether or not Realists are correct about the international system's degree of anarchy, agreements among countries may be harder to achieve than IR scholars believe. Domestic politics also affects the terms of any international agreement. Focusing solely on the states' relative capabilities will lead to an incomplete understanding of how an agreement is shaped. Thus failure to consider domestic politics explicitly will lead IR scholars and policy makers to be overly optimistic about cooperation among nations and to be unable to understand the terms of cooperative agreements made.

Why does domestic politics have these effects on relations among nations? Three internal factors condition a state's ability to cooperate: *the structure of domestic preferences, the nature of domestic political institutions, and the distribution of information internally*. These factors determine which domestic players are involved in policy making, what powers each has in this process, and how these actors' policy preferences differ. In turn, these aspects of the domestic game combined with the international game determine whether cooperation is possible and what its terms will be.

The first key variable is the *structure of domestic preferences*. This structure refers to the relative positions of important domestic actors' preferences on the issue at hand. How disparate domestic actors' preferences are and how distant they are from those of the foreign country—that is, how hawkish they are—are critical in shaping the domestic game. The three main sets of internal actors here are the political executive (the president or prime minister), the legislature, and interest groups. In other cases, different actors can be added if needed and these three sets of actors deleted. For instance, if the legislature is not important in an issue but labor unions are, then labor can be added to the game and the median legislator deleted. One must know only the actor's preferences relative to the other players and the role he or she plays in proposing, amending, or ratifying/vetoing the policy choice. The model here can be generalized to any set of actors.

The structure of domestic preferences differs by issue area. On different issues, the main actors—who may differ—will have distinct preferences, and hence the distribution of these preferences may vary. No single national structure of preferences exists; rather, this structure will change with the issue area. On the other hand, when actors' preferences are more similarly structured in two different countries, one should expect their domestic games to be more similar.

Two aspects of the *structure of domestic preferences* are critical: the degree of divided government and the preferences of the executive. In the domestic game, the relative positions of the executive and the legislature exercised a major impact on the international negotiations. *Divided government*—the degree of divergence between the median legislator's preferences and the executive's—played a powerful negative role. The more the government is divided, the less likely is international cooperation but the better off the legislature is in any agreement made.

This finding casts doubt on arguments made elsewhere that internal divisions increase the external leverage of the executive internationally, that is, the Schelling conjecture (Schelling 1960; Putnam 1988; Mo 1995). Indeed, as divisions in government grow, the executive's problems should mount. She should have a harder time getting any agreement ratified and be forced to negotiate agreements that meet the other domestic actors' preferences. Although others have shown that divided government in the United States poses problems for the executive in making trade policy vis-à-vis Congress, the argument here is different and broader (O'Halloran 1994; Lohmann and O'Halloran 1994). It applies the notion of divided government to all democratic countries, not just the United States. It also embeds the domestic ratification game within an international bargaining model, so that divided government is shown to pose a problem in international negotiations as well as in a purely domestic context.

In the case studies the relationship between the executive's preferences and the legislature's played an important role. Divided government proved to be a negative factor for cooperation. As their policy preferences diverged,

ratification became more problematic and the executive was forced to accede to terms favored by the legislature. A central reason for the failure of
the ITO in comparison to the Bretton Woods agreement and for the failure
of the EDC relative to the ECSC was the growing divisions in government
in the two situations. Republican control of Congress in the late 1940s made
ratification of the ITO problematic for the Democratic president. The Gaullists' entry into the government in the French Fourth Republic had the same
effect on the EDC. In contrast, with regard to NAFTA, the return of unified
government in 1993 with Clinton's election helped greatly in the ratification
of the agreement. Finally, in the EMU case, Denmark—with its minority
coalition government—had the most divided government of the twelve
countries involved and failed to ratify at this time. Britain's majority party,
the Conservatives, also had major problems ratifying the agreements owing
to its lack of party discipline. Thus divided government made international
cooperation less likely in all cases.

In addition, divisions at home seemed to undermine a country's international bargaining strength. In the Anglo-American oil and civil aviation
cases, the British government and firms were quite united in their preferences and this allowed them to obtain better terms from the Americans. The
Bretton Woods and ITO cases also revealed that the unity of British preferences helped them gain bargaining advantages over the divided Americans.
The ECSC case also showed how the divisions among the French weakened
them in their negotiations with the other European countries. Having a
united home front meant that the intensity with which a government held its
preferences was high and that budging it from its position was much harder
than where domestic groups differed. When domestic groups are divided
over an issue, they can be played against one another. Their divisions can be
exploited and the most dovish home actor can be used by the foreign country to extract better terms for itself. In general, the model and cases here do
not support the Schelling conjecture.

Second, the preferences of political executives (i.e., prime ministers or
presidents) are important. When executives control the initiation of negotiations—whether government is unified or not—the more hawkish they are,
the less likely they will be to ever initiate cooperation. The European
cases—especially the United Kingdom—underlined that when the executive is a "hawk"—that is, when she prefers outcomes that give her country
greater advantages relative to the legislature's preferences, cooperation will
be less likely. The more hawkish the leader, the less domestic advantage she
will perceive in initiating such cooperation. Failure to initiate, rather than
ratification failure, should be apparent in these cases. The non-event used to
examine this was British unwillingness to start or join European cooperation
in the 1940s and its resistance to EMU under Thatcher. When the executive
is the most hawkish domestic player and controls the initiation of negotiations, cooperation is unlikely.

Domestic political institutions define the second key variable. A country's political institutions determine the nature of power sharing domestically. Rarely do these institutions allow domestic politics to function as a pure hierarchy. Instead, actors must depend on one another in the decision-making process and play distinct roles in it; they are interdependent. At the broadest level, whether a country is democratic or not influences how power is shared internally. Democratic countries tend to have representative legislatures that share control with the executive over decision making. Nondemocratic countries usually do not have such formal power-sharing arrangements; rather, various groups, including the military, big business, landowners, and party organizations, are informally involved in decision making.

In democratic countries, at least two groups—the legislature and the executive—share control over policy making. In these countries, the distribution of legislative powers matters. Who controls initiation, amendment, and ratification or veto powers affects whose preferences are most closely followed in policy choices. Different political systems distribute these powers in distinct ways; furthermore, on separate issues within the same country, these powers may be allocated differently. This distribution matters, for it privileges groups in the policy process; that is, if the executive is given most of these powers—for example, she controls initiation and the legislature cannot amend, even if it can ratify—the executive's preferences will shape policy outcomes most of all. Political institutions—formal and informal—determine how these powers are allocated. As noted before, these institutions themselves are thus part of the political struggle domestically. Because they determine whose preferences influence policy most, actors will have preferences for institutions as well as for policy. Not only will the content of international agreements be contested domestically, so will the institutional process used to ratify them.

The nature of power sharing domestically, which is determined by formal and informal political institutions, also shapes the likelihood and terms of international cooperation. The assumption about power sharing here is that the executive and the legislature play a "ratification" game. A broad notion of ratification is used; it refers to any situation in which some domestic actors can exert a veto over the executive's foreign policy, usually ex post facto. Even Morgenthau acknowledges the importance of such ratification: "A contemporary government, especially one subject to democratic control, . . . must secure the approval of its own people for its foreign policies and the domestic ones designed to mobilize the elements of national power in support of them" (1985:164). This ratification game in turn affects the international negotiations through the process of anticipated reaction. The executive proposes policies and the legislature votes them up or down. Although the executive sets the agenda, the legislature has an ex post facto veto, which means that it too influences policy choices. The executive will anticipate the legislature's preferences and propose policies it will ratify.

Anticipated reaction is a crucial element in the ratification game. Political leaders negotiating a cooperative agreement will always be looking over their shoulders at the domestic game and trying to make sure that the agreement is compatible with their domestic constraints. Leaders do not, however, face a completely given domestic situation; that is, they can exercise some influence over their domestic "constraints." Leaders can adopt strategies to win domestic ratification. In particular, they can offer domestic groups side payments in order to obtain their support for ratification of the agreement at hand. The domestic strategies of leaders, however, are a function of the ratification process. The necessity of domestic ratification in its broadest sense means that domestic politics influences all aspects of the attempt to find a cooperative agreement, from its initiation to its international negotiation and, of course, its domestic ratification.

Among the case studies, an important factor distinguishing the failed from the successful cooperative agreements was *the ratification process*. The institutional process of ratification was an important part of the domestic contest over the international agreement. Which actors controlled what elements of the process of negotiating and implementing an agreement was a subject of debate in each case. But where opponents could effect changes in this process, especially after the conclusion of the international agreement, ratification became much less likely. When executives negotiate internationally with a particular ratification procedure in mind, they devise an agreement that is supported by the median legislator (or voter) as defined by this ratification process. Changes in the process that make another actor the median voter will reduce the likelihood of ratification significantly. Hence executives should be concerned with obtaining the most favorable ratification process before the international negotiations begin. Moreover, a key tactic of an agreement's opponents should be to try to alter the ratification process after the fact.

This tactic was clearly used in the Anglo-American oil case and civil aviation cases, as well as in the NAFTA and EMU cases. In the oil case, the American independents, who were the opponents, succeeded in having the agreement changed from an executive agreement to a treaty, thus increasing their influence over it and dooming it. In the civil aviation case, Pan Am tried to have the executive agreements changed to treaties, but it failed. With regard to NAFTA, much of the struggle the United States experienced came early on in the consideration of "fast-track" status for the agreement. In the EMU case, the opponents of the Maastricht Treaty in France, Britain, and Germany all attempted to change the ratification procedures. In France and Germany they succeeded, yet failed by the narrowest of margins to kill the agreement. In the British case, they were unable to force a change. A key difference between the ITO, which failed to be approved, and the GATT, which was successful, was their ratification process. The GATT remained an executive agreement, unlike the ITO. The choice of the ratification process involves strategic behavior on the part of the executive and the opponents of the international agreement. In general, then, the cases suggest that the nature of domestic political institutions plays a critical role in international cooperation, as does the structure of domestic preferences.

Third, the *distribution of information domestically* was also a key factor. An asymmetric distribution had surprising effects: under certain conditions it actually increased the chances of cooperative agreement. When a group has private information, this is expected to lead both to inefficient outcomes—failure to cooperate when joint gains are possible—and political advantages for the more informed actor. When the legislature is uncertain of the exact terms of an international agreement and cannot rely on an endorser, cooperation, as expected, is less likely. The legislature is asked to ratify an agreement that it does not fully understand, and thus it is highly likely to reject the agreement, as the "pig-in-the-poke" result generally suggests. However, when the legislature can depend on one or more informed domestic groups to signal it about the proposal, the situation changes. The presence of such "endorsers" has unanticipated consequences. *Asymmetric information in the presence of an endorser actually improves the chances for cooperation, relative to both the full information and incomplete information situations.* When the legislature can depend on an informative endorser, it may be better off under such asymmetric information and more willing to cooperate. Indeed, the presence of such endorsers can leave the legislature at least as well off as it would be with complete information. Asymmetric information in the presence of endorsers mitigates the inefficiencies and power advantages usually associated with it. These findings are surprising and suggest an efficient way for legislators to deal with policy choices.

Legislators can listen to multiple endorsers, who often have different preferences. With multiple endorsers, the legislature will always ratify the executive's proposal if two opposing groups endorse it. If neither endorses, ratification will not occur. If one endorses, the legislature's vote depends on other factors, such as its beliefs about the executive and the position of the status quo. Thus the role of the endorser is critical for inducing ratification of the executive's international agreements. Since it is widely assumed that incomplete information promotes conflict rather than cooperation among nations, the finding that the probability of cooperation increases with incomplete information and an informed endorser is an important result.

The importance of *endorsers* for ratification was highlighted in the cases discussed. Gaining the endorsement of at least one key domestic group was critical for ratification. Having endorsements from two groups with opposing preferences ensured ratification. As the cases underscore, failure by both sets of endorsers to support an agreement spelled its demise. In the ITO case, both internationally oriented business and domestic groups favoring protection op-

posed the agreement crafted at Havana; their refusal to endorse it made ratification unlikely. In the oil case, where both the domestic independent oil firms
and the multinational ones were opposed to the Anglo-American accord, the
U.S. Congress also rejected the agreement. In the EDC case, the French military and the National Assembly's Committee on National Defense not only
refused to endorse the proposal but were often relentless in their opposition to
the defense community, making ratification virtually impossible.

In the other cases, at least one critical group endorsed the agreement. The
positive signals these groups sent made legislators more willing to approve
the agreements. In Bretton Woods, the American banking community was
initially split over the agreement, although later it became more unified as
even the East Coast bankers relented in their criticisms of it. In the civil
aviation case, domestic airlines in the United States supported the accords
strongly, in opposition to Pan Am. In the ECSC, the coal and steel industries
in France were on opposite sides of the issue, with the coal industry and steel
users being strong endorsers. In NAFTA, the division in the United States
was between domestically oriented industries, who opposed it, and internationally oriented ones, who endorsed it. Finally, in the EMU case, the central
banks—including the Bundesbank—and many private European banks
eventually supported the agreement. Endorsement by at least one major
group was essential for ratification of these international agreements.

This finding suggests a new interpretation for the role of interest groups
in international relations. As argued, interest groups acting as endorsers may
be an important source of information for the legislature about international
agreements. For the legislature, then, having interest groups involved in
international negotiations can be an efficient method to forward its members' interests and to check and balance the executive. Other domestic
groups can also serve as endorsers; legislative committees, independent
central banks, or other independent governmental agencies may all fulfill
that role depending on the issue at hand. Interest groups thus provide informational benefits, even if they also have distributional effects.

In sum, the model highlights three factors that help explain the cases. The
structure of domestic preferences, the nature of domestic political institutions, and the distribution of information domestically played key roles in
the search for international cooperation. Interests, institutions, and information are primary here.

The Relationship between Interests and Institutions

An important element of my argument is the mutual relationship between
interests and institutions. Studies in political science tend to bifurcate between those that emphasize policy preferences and those that emphasize
political institutions. For example, a number of scholars have suggested that

domestic actors' preferences—especially societal ones—play a central role in shaping policy (e.g., Popkin 1979; Bates 1981; Paige 1975; Milner 1988; Rogowski 1989; Frieden 1991; Shafer 1994). Indeed, Marxist analyses have tended to emphasize the preferences of one group—capitalists—to the exclusion of others in their explanation of policy outcomes (e.g., Lenin 1917; Block 1977). In contrast, and in reaction to these preference-based arguments, "new institutionalist" arguments have focused on political institutions, largely to the exclusion of preferences. In the nonrational choice version of institutionalism, scholars have emphasized the role of formal and informal institutions in shaping policy choice (Hall 1986; March and Olson 1989; Haggard 1990; Goldstein 1993; Sikkink 1991). In much of this literature the watchword has been the "path dependence" effect of institutions; that is, past behavior that becomes institutionalized determines future choices made. Once institutions are established, they create a groove, so to speak, out of which it is difficult for policy makers to opt.

The rational choice version of institutionalism has focused on the problem of equilibrium selection. In multidimensional preference space, stable equilibria are almost impossible to find (Plott 1967; McKelvey 1976, 1979). Only when one adds structure to the game does a stable equilibrium become sustainable. This structure is provided by institutions that allocate control over issues to different players, select the players' order of moves, and decide which moves each can make. Institutions determine the allocation of powers among the players, as in the model here. Such "structure-induced equilibria" demonstrate the power of political institutions to determine policy outcomes (Shepsle 1979).

Common sense tells us, however, that institutions and preferences both matter. More interesting is how they interact to produce political outcomes. The arguments made here show not only that both are important but also how they matter. Actors' interests are primordial; from these they derive their policy preferences for different issues. The structure of these preferences exerts a major impact on the domestic political game, which shapes policy choices. These policy preferences also determine actors' preferences about institutions. Actors will desire those institutions that allow them to achieve their most preferred policies. For example, if an interest group prefers protectionism, it should also prefer that power over trade policy be given to that institution in which its preferences are best represented. If legislators tend to be more sympathetic to protection, because, for example, they represent smaller, more concentrated constituencies, then protectionist groups should prefer that the legislature have control over trade policy making.

But institutions are not always malleable. Sometimes the costs of changing an institution may be too high, and so they will not change no matter what groups desire. In these cases, actors face a given set of institutions in which they must operate. These institutions will bias the outcomes; they will favor one group's preferences over another. As chapter 4 showed, when the executive and the legislature play a ratification game, the outcome is different than when they play an amendment game, even when the actors' preferences are the same. In the ratification game—where the executive initiates and the legislature can only ratify, not amend—the executive dominates; policy is always closer to the executive's preferences. In the amendment game—where the legislature can now amend any executive proposal—influence shifts to the legislature; policy choices will be closer to its preferences. Actors' preferences determine the range within which feasible outcomes are possible; the institutions determine where in that range policy actually will be. Hence preferences and institutions are both critical, but they play distinct roles in shaping policy outcomes.

Executive-Legislative Relations and Presidential versus Parliamentary Systems

Part of the argument here is that the distinction between presidential and parliamentary systems is not very helpful in understanding the relationship between the executive and the legislature in two-level bargaining games. Presidential and parliamentary systems vary greatly among themselves in terms of the balance of power between the executive and the legislature. Some parliamentary systems, like in Great Britain, have powerful executives, as do some presidential systems, like in Mexico. On the other hand, some parliamentary systems have strong legislatures, like in Fourth Republic France and post-World War II Italy, as do some presidential systems, as in the United States (Shugart and Carey 1992; Lijphart 1984). Chapter 4 argued that although origin and survival powers are an important element of this relationship, most important for our game is the distribution of legislative powers. Who controls agenda setting, amendment, ratification or veto, and the calling of referendums matters fundamentally for understanding policy choices.

In this light, chapter 4 showed that the distribution of institutional powers shaped the outcome of our game within the bounds set by the structure of domestic preferences. When the distribution of legislative powers was concentrated in the executive's hands, she was better able to dominate policy outcomes. When the legislature held greater powers, its preferences were more influential in policy making. The model, then, generated the following hypothesis: when the distribution of legislative powers favored the more hawkish domestic player, cooperation was least likely and, when possible, more likely to reflect that player's preferences. This points out the interrelationship between preferences and institutions.

The case studies in chapters 5–8 present ten cases of executive-legislative relations: those involving the United States and the United Kingdom in the

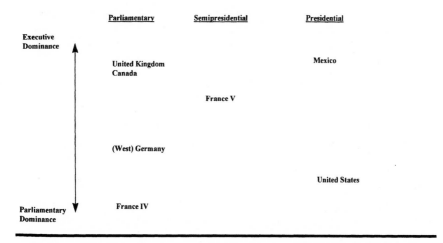

Figure 9.1 Ranking of Executive-Legislative Relations in the Seven Cases*

mid- and late 1940s, West Germany and France in the early 1950s, the United States, Mexico, and Canada in the 1980s and early 1990s, and Germany, France, and the United Kingdom in the late 1980s and 1990s. These cases reduce to seven when we consider that the institutional relationship between the executive and the legislature in the United States, the United Kingdom, and Germany has not changed much over the period. Some scholars claim that the German and British parliaments have become stronger over time, but the importance of this shift is difficult to evaluate (Copeland and Patterson 1994; Norton 1990a, 1990b; Saalfeld 1990; Hancock et al. 1993). Debate in the United States over the direction of change in this relationship has been extensive; hence it is difficult to attribute change in any direction to it (e.g., Cronin 1980; Sundquist 1981). The case of France is different, however. The shift from the Fourth Republic to the Fifth in 1958 marked a dramatic change in the relations between the legislature and executive. From a parliamentary system with a weak executive in the Fourth Republic, the French consciously changed to a semipresidential system with a strong executive (Lijphart 1984; Copeland and Patterson 1994; Frears 1990; Shugart and Carey 1992). The Fifth Republic has a split personality: when government is divided the prime minister is the key figure, whereas under unified government the president tends to dominate (Duverger 1987; Pierce 1991). Thus we have seven cases of executive-legislative relations.

Figure 9.1 ranks these cases in terms of the legislature's strength, given the type of constitutional system. This strength is measured by several variables: cabinet durability (Lijphart 1984); the percentage of government bills

*Executive-legislative relations are ranked according to cabinet durability, the percentage of government bills the legislature rejects, the percentage of bills it initiates, and the percentage of bills it amends.

the legislature rejected (Copeland and Patterson 1994); the percentage of bills the legislature initiated (Copeland and Patterson 1994); and the percentage of bills the legislature amended (Copeland and Patterson 1994). Less durability, more legislative rejection, more legislative initiation, and more amendments signal stronger legislatures. These measures provide a rough gauge of the relationship between the executive and the legislative in these seven cases. The United Kingdom, Canada, and Mexico appear to have the strongest executives, followed by the Fifth French Republic (France V) and Germany. The United States and the Fourth French Republic (France IV) seem to have the most influential legislatures.

This ranking tells us little about policy outcomes, however, without a knowledge of the two groups' preferences. If the median legislator in France IV and the United States were usually more dovish than the executive, then these countries might be quite able to cooperate. When the legislature is more hawkish, however, they should have real trouble making international agreements. Conversely, in Canada, Mexico, and the United Kingdom, when the legislature is a hawk, cooperation will still be very likely since the dovish executive is most powerful. But in these cases a hawkish executive will be disastrous for cooperation. The cases support this. When government is divided and when the median legislator is more hawkish than the executive, the United States and France IV have great difficulty cooperating. The ITO, the Anglo-American oil case, and the EDC confirm this. Likewise, when the executive dominates but is hawkish, as in the United Kingdom during the ECSC and later the Maastricht negotiations, cooperation also becomes much less likely. On the other hand, when the executive is dovish, the Canadians, the British (in the 1940s), and the Mexicans should be able to cooperate far more easily than the other countries, as the cases in chapters 4 through 8 corroborate. Thus one must consider both preferences and institutions when trying to explain policy outcomes. The institutional balance of power between the executive and the legislature matters, but policy outcomes also depend on the structure of domestic preferences.

Political Leaders and Societal Actors

In many earlier studies, a tendency to focus on either political actors or societal ones has been pronounced. Society-based explanations of foreign policy have tended to exclude consideration of political actors, such as legislatures, bureaucrats, and executives (e.g., Milner 1988; Rogowski 1989; Frieden 1991). In contrast, "statist" arguments have tended to downplay the role of societal actors (e.g., Krasner 1978; Zysman 1983; Johnson 1982; Wade 1990). Moreover, one could caricature International Relations by saying that those who study security policy emphasize state actors, and those who study political economy focus more on societal actors. Although not truly accurate—there are numerous exceptions—this categorization has some truth. This bifurcation has had two deleterious effects.

First, it is hard to deny that political and societal actors, especially in democracies, are both involved in creating policy. Political actors—like prime ministers or presidents, legislators or bureaucrats—are more likely to control the formal legislative powers necessary to make policy. But societal actors have numerous means of influencing that process indirectly (through campaign contributions, bribes, capital flight, strikes, and so on) and in some cases are directly involved, as in corporatist systems where representatives from labor and business shape economic policy. Political leaders rarely exist in a vacuum where they can ignore the demands and preferences of all societal actors. Likewise, societal actors rarely have the means to make policy without dealing with state actors. The two groups are most often interdependent, although the degree of dependence will vary from system to system and issue to issue. If this is the case, then, ignoring one group will result in a misleading picture of the policy-making process. If these groups are interdependent, they should be modeled that way, as is done, for example, by Ramseyer and Rosenbluth (1993).

This brings us to the second problem in ignoring one group of these actors. If only one group is examined, the effect of the *strategic* relationship between them is also ignored. But state and societal actors play a strategic game with each other in order to realize their preferences. Each actor's behavior affects and is a response to the other actor's behavior; indeed, each actor's best move always depends on what others are likely to do. Economists have increasingly realized this. In rational expectations models of the macroeconomy, economists have interjected a game between policy makers and societal actors to explore the effects of monetary policy.

> The major thrust of the recent literature on monetary policy concerned with [the issue of credibility] has focused on the . . . strategic aspects. The essential idea here is the interdependence between the behavioral patterns of private individuals and centralized policy makers—in particular, the view of centralized policy making as being conducted in an environment inhabited by sophisticated forward-looking private agents who are attempting to predict the economic policy to be applied (and policy makers' understanding of this). The strategic view of policy making inherent in this lends itself naturally to a *game theoretic* interpretation where the players in this game are the policy makers and private economic agents. (Blackburn and Christensen 1989:3)

In extreme versions of this model, policy makers may end up having no effect on economic outcomes if societal actors anticipate their behavior correctly. These results differ greatly from when policy makers alone are considered to set monetary policy. Strategic interaction between the two groups changes policy outcomes fundamentally.

The model used here tries to capture one form of this strategic game between political and societal actors. It shows how political actors depend on the endorsement signals of societal groups. Executives must craft policies that secure societal endorsement so that legislatures who listen for such endorsements will ratify their policies. Modeling the relationship between political and societal actors as a strategic game can yield interesting insights into the mutual influence these groups have over one another.

International Cooperation as the Continuation of Domestic Politics by Other Means

This book has focused on actors within the state as central to the process of international cooperation, with special attention given to the political executive, a prime mover for cooperation. Other actors within the state, such as the legislature or interest groups, may or may not want cooperation to occur, and their policy preferences matter. But if the political executive is unfavorable toward it, no cooperation is likely, given the executive's agenda-setting role. Chapter 2 analyzed when and why leaders might prefer cooperation to unilateral policy making. One of the main points is that international cooperation is only likely when it promotes the political executive's electoral prospects, and in many cases this implies that it must have a positive effect on the domestic economy, at least in the short run. Although some economists have shown that the economic benefits of cooperation may be quite modest, even small short-term improvements in the economy can help win elections (Oudiz and Sachs 1984). The case studies revealed that cooperation usually followed some prior domestic policy change that leaders had effected in order to improve the economy and their electoral standing.

The desire for a cooperative policy often flowed from prior shifts in an executive's preferences as reflected in unilateral domestic policy changes. Success of the internal policy became more likely if cooperative agreement could be achieved. American political leaders in the 1930s, wishing to open export markets to U.S. industry during the Depression, adopted the Reciprocal Trade Agreements Act (RTAA), which gave the president authority to pursue the reciprocal lowering of trade barriers. This domestic policy change helped promote interest in the ITO and the GATT after the war. This prior, unilateral domestic policy change may have been a necessary condition for interest in the later international cooperative agreements. In the oil case, U.S. policy promoting governmental involvement in the oil industry in the form of the Petroleum Resources Corporation stimulated interest in a joint Anglo-American governmental organization to control global petroleum supplies. Likewise, the Monnet Plan to modernize French industry can be seen as a prerequisite for the ECSC. The decision to modernize French industry became a catalyst for the European coal and steel pool. In the same way, unilateral Mexican trade liberalization in the early 1980s was a necessary precursor to NAFTA. Finally, decisions by the French and Italian governments to deregulate their financial markets provided crucial preconditions for their later interest in EMU.

In all these cases, unilateral domestic policy changes reflected a change in the executive's preferences. Once in place, these new domestic policies created an interest in, and sometimes a need for, international cooperation in order to improve the domestic policies' chances for success. Policy makers sought international agreement in order to promote the domestic policies to which they had already committed because the success of these domestic initiatives often rested on changes in the actions of other governments. International cooperation was used as another means for pursuing domestic goals.

Thus the international realm may be a means for political leaders to promote their domestic interests. They will choose cooperation when it advances these domestic goals, and avoid it otherwise. To paraphrase Clausewitz (1832), one could say that international cooperation was the continuation of domestic politics by other means.

Interest Groups in International Politics: Pressure Groups or Information Providers?

This book has argued that domestic interest groups can be seen in at least two different lights. Interest groups rarely were directly involved in initiating international cooperation. But they did play important roles in the domestic ratification game. They acted as pressure groups and/or information providers. These two roles are important and distinct. Much of the literature in political economy focuses on the former (Olson 1982; Frieden 1991; Milner 1988; Rogowski 1989). Some recent literature about U.S. politics, however, examines the second role that interest groups might play (McCubbins and Schwartz 1984; Epstein and O'Halloran 1993).

As pressure groups, these actors use their position to influence the preferences of the political actors. Legislators, for example, decide on their preferred policies by taking into account the preferences of various interest groups. They do so out of concern for the electoral consequences of failing to do so. Neglect of interest group preferences can mean the loss of their members' votes, campaign funds, or general support. In this pressure group role, they affect the international negotiations by shaping what agreements the legislature will be willing to ratify. A change in their preferences means a change in the legislature's preferences, and thus a change in which international agreements are ratifiable. The presence of such pressure groups has distributional consequences—both domestically and internationally—since they affect the terms of the agreement made, as well as the likelihood of cooperation.

Interest groups can play another role. In addition to shaping legislator's preferences, legislators can use them as sources of information. If the legislature is uncertain as to exactly what an international agreement means, it can turn to various, well-informed interest groups to hear their opinions. Knowing the interest groups' preferences and hearing their views on the agreement, the legislators can then better comprehend what the agreement might portend for them electorally. This informational role can be critical. It provides a means of constraining the executive's behavior without consuming much time or effort. As one study of British politics notes, "Interest groups have strengthened Parliament, making use of select committees to feed in their views on policy and administration. They provide M.P.'s with a constant supply of information and argument, which is deployed in Parliament against the prime minister and government" (Jones 1991:126).

This role may account for why legislators often want interest groups to be involved in international negotiations. It may also explain why, in popular referendums, governments still seek to obtain interest group endorsements of the international agreement. The approval of the Maastricht Treaty by labor union leaders, for example, might signal voters what the treaty meant for them and how they should vote on it. This view of interest groups as information providers is a new formulation for the field of international relations and political economy. It may well be that interest groups perform several political functions at once. They may act as both pressure groups and "fire alarms" in the political arena. One should be open to the multiple roles that interest groups might play in two-level games.

The Value of Rational Choice Theory: Anticipated Reaction and Its Failure

The ideas in this book are based on the assumption that actors are rational. The utility of rational choice theory is a much debated issue. Many scholars of International Relations theory (and others) find its flaws serious and its utility limited (e.g., Green and Shapiro 1994). Even its proponents admit that it has serious problems (Elster 1979; Kreps 1990). Rational choice theory should be seen as a tool for aiding in social science inquiry; it is not a miracle cure. The test of the theory should be whether it provides valuable insights and helps produce testable hypotheses to explain real world phenomena.

Like all models (rational choice or not), the one here is not a realistic representation of reality; it is an abstraction used to generate hypotheses about how two-level games might work. It is also not the last word on models of two-level games. Many different types of models can be built, and I hope they will. The model here is a starting point, not a finality.

Can the use of rational choice theory promote social science inquiry? Although keeping the limits in mind, this approach offers several benefits. First, the assumptions used are stated clearly and explicitly. The results flow ineluctably from these assumptions. Changing the assumptions, then, can change the results; sometimes it will do so more than others. But the explicit changing of assumptions and comparison of the results can bring cumulative progress to the field. As Kreps (1990:88–89) states in discussing game theory in particular, "It contributes . . . the ability to push intuitions into a slightly more complex context [by changing the assumptions]; and the means of checking on the logical consistency of specific insights, and . . . a way of thinking through logically which of our conclusions may change drastically with small changes in the assumptions."

This aspect of rational choice theory has been a main strength in the field of economics. Exploring different assumptions can open new areas of knowledge. Keynes's change of assumptions about the relationship between demand and supply energized a new version of macroeconomics; changing assumptions about the rationality of economic actors created the new brand of rational expectations macroeconomics; and altering assumptions about perfect competition led to the new trade policy models, termed *strategic trade theory*. These new departures—whether one calls them progress or not—came from scholars understanding the assumptions of previous models and changing them to see the results.

This book alters a central assumption of the field, namely, that the state is unitary.[1] Instead, it assumes that states are polyarchic—composed of at least two actors who must share power over decision making. Altering this assumption has important consequences for International Relations theory. The book also makes other assumptions about the situation the actors face. These may be more or less well justified. It is hoped that others will alter these assumptions and examine the results. The point is that a rational choice model enables one to perform this type of controlled experimentation.

A second advantage of rational choice theory is the way it aids inquiry even when it fails to predict accurately. In fact, failure of its predictions can be, and often has been, the catalyst for advancing our understanding. For example, the bargaining literature in game theory has advanced in this fashion. The central conclusion of early bargaining models that used the assumption of full information was that actors should reach immediate agreement and exploit all opportunities for agreements that provide joint gains. There should be no delays in bargaining and no failed agreements. This obvious inaccuracy has led to the creation of new models using incomplete information and signaling that have produced interesting results (Keenan and Wilson 1993).

---

[1] Note that it does not alter the assumption that the international system is anarchic.

In the model here, we expect political leaders to anticipate their legislature's and interest groups' reactions to the agreements they are making. In the complete information version, this implies that leaders should never have their agreements rejected domestically. They may not be able to reach an agreement because they know it will be rejected, but they should not have to suffer through rejections. They will anticipate them and not start the international negotiations. As the cases have shown, this expectation is incorrect. Political leaders do get their agreements rejected. If one believes that the full information assumption is reasonable, then the cases generate anomalies for the model. Executives often fail to anticipate correctly their domestic constraints.

If one believes, however, that the complete information assumption is only useful as a starting point for comparison, then the model must incorporate asymmetric or incomplete information. This can be introduced in a number of ways. The asymmetry of information examined here assumes that the legislature is uncertain about the foreign country's preferences and hence unsure about the exact terms of the international agreement. Most interesting here is that even though the executive knows the legislature's preferences, rejection of international agreements can still occur. In this case, the model shows that even anticipated reaction may not prevent domestic rejection of international agreements.

Thus, by using a rational choice model and making explicit assumptions, one can generate clear expectations and see what happens when the assumptions are changed. This picks up on both points made above. The complete information case did not help account for why domestic rejection of international agreements could occur. Changing the assumptions by adding asymmetric information generated new expectations and provided a way to understand this fact. Thus the model calls attention to the fact that the distribution of information *domestically* may affect how the domestic and international games are played. This somewhat surprising result lends importance to a variable that has otherwise been ignored. International Relations theories, especially those at the systemic level, have tended to ignore the problem of information. The ones that do note it, usually those more concerned with decision making, tend to focus on the distribution of information among states at the international level, as is apparent in studies of misperception and regime theory (e.g., Jervis 1976; Keohane 1984).

The domestic distribution of information has been even less studied. Even the major study of two-level games (Evans, Jacobson, and Putnam 1993) notes that its empirical cases raise the issue, but then it never examines this factor systematically. Attention to the international effects of domestic asymmetries of information is, however, the central theme of several recent studies (Fearon 1994; Downs and Rocke 1995). Assuming complete information, then, may generate results that are patently at odds with empirical evidence. Altering this assumption may produce better explanations as well as interesting new findings. Notwithstanding all its problems, then, one of the values of rational choice theory may be its incorrect predictions.

When Should We Expect States to Cooperate?

The message of this book for international cooperation is a pessimistic one. Although Realists believe that states' concerns over cheating and relative gains are the fundamental impediments to cooperation, the model here shows that even more problematic is domestic politics. Actors' worries about the domestic distributional implications of cooperation make cooperation even less likely. The model shows that the assumption of polyarchy never makes cooperation more likely than it is in the anarchic game between two unitary states. The addition of domestic politics has negative consequences for international cooperation. Hence when cooperation is unachievable, one should not simply ask what the problem was between the states; one should also ask what domestic political problems each executive faced and was unable to overcome.

What is it about domestic politics that is so deleterious for cooperation among nations? First, internal divisions are a negative factor for cooperation. Whenever the main actors who share control over policy making have different preferences, cooperation is unlikely; the more those preferences differ, the less likely cooperation is. Divided government, where the median legislator's and the executive's preferences differ, is only one example of this. As the model and cases show, the more divided a government is, the less able it will be to cooperate and the more it will be constrained by domestic pressures in the terms it can accept. One would expect the least cooperative behavior from minority parliamentary governments and divided presidential ones. Thus one would anticipate that the French should have had more trouble cooperating in any issue area in 1986–88 and 1993–95, when their government was divided, than in 1989–93. One would also expect the minority Japanese government of Tatsumo Hata (1994) to be less able to cooperate than the majority governments preceding and following it. Changes in party control over the legislature and executive because of elections may have important effects on the prospects for international cooperation.

But political leaders' preferences also matter. If the public elects prime ministers or presidents who have "hawkish" preferences, then the likelihood of cooperative behavior will drop. Since these political leaders must initiate cooperation, their preferences are crucial. Britain's ex-prime minister, Margaret Thatcher, was a prime example. Her strident opposition to most European cooperation throughout much of the 1980s caused serious problems for the EC countries. The election of a Le Pen or Séguin in France or a Conservative Euro-skeptic in Britain could have negative implications for European cooperation in the future. The election of more isolationist politicians in the United States would also bode ill for America's engagement with other nations. The popular election of leaders with such hawkish preferences makes cooperation much less likely even if the legislature and a majority of the public generally favor it.

Will increasing exposure of a country to the international economy affect the likelihood of international cooperation? Increasing openness should make leaders more interested in cooperation, create more domestic groups who see cooperation as desirable, and even, perhaps, as Rogowski (1987) argues, stimulate countries to alter their political institutions in ways that favor more cooperative behavior. In general, this would lead us to expect a linear relationship between openness and cooperative behavior, ceteris paribus. It is the phrase "all other things being equal" that is most important here. Changes in other variables, such as political leaders' preferences and divided government, can work against this trend. Moreover, the structure of domestic preferences in the issue area matters because it shapes the domestic ratification game. All these other factors are not necessarily linked to increases in the country's exposure to the international economy. Thus growing openness, all other things held constant, should promote political leaders' interest in cooperation. But other factors—including those identified here—can rarely be held constant; hence the model does not anticipate a linear trend toward greater cooperation.

Finally, one should not expect to see cooperation across the board among a set of countries. It should vary by issue area. For any country, some issues will prove more amenable to cooperation, and others less so. Although international-level theories, such as Hegemonic Stability Theory and balancing, cannot predict the issue areas in which one will see cooperation when a hegemon exists or when balancing occurs, my argument predicts that different structures of domestic preferences and power-sharing arrangements will make issue areas differentially susceptible to cooperation. Conversely, one would not expect that a breakdown of cooperation among nations would occur simultaneously in all issue areas. The prospects for cooperative outcomes should vary more by issue area than by country, if the argument here is correct.

Most important, international cooperation should be a function of domestic politics. As argued above, international cooperation often seems to be a continuation of domestic politics by other means. When domestic policy changes in ways that make cooperative endeavors more profitable for political leaders, the likelihood of cooperation should grow. For instance, a country's pursuit of unilateral trade liberalization policies should mean that it is likely to become more interested in cooperating with other countries in order to lower trade barriers. Conversely, when political leaders change policies domestically in ways that make coordinated policy making problematic, one should expect less cooperation. Hence the adoption of a series of domestic agricultural policies intended to protect and support American farmers in the late 1940s and 1950s meant that trade liberalization in agriculture became anathema for America's political leaders and farmers; they banished it from the GATT negotiations. In contrast, the domestic political decision to support farmers but the lack of national resources to do so made the French in the 1950s eager for European cooperation in this area. Thus unilateral, domestic policy changes may be harbingers for cooperation among nations. Ultimately, only when political executives feel that international cooperation will serve their domestic goals will it be attempted, even if all the international concerns about cheating and relative gains have been overcome.

The Unitary State as Actor and International Relations Theory

A central difference between the theory presented in this book and other theories of international relations involves the assumption that the state is a unitary actor. The key assumption in many International Relations theories, especially Realist ones but also its main rival—neoliberal institutionalism—is that the state can be treated as if it were unitary (Waltz 1979; Keohane 1986, 1989). These theories posit that the state, like an individual, has a single-preference ranking and hence the ability to add up its gains and losses from a policy into a net evaluation. There is a national interest for these arguments.[2]

For the theory here, however, no such entity as "the state" exists. Instead, the actors are different groups within the state with distinct preferences and goals. For instance, the legislature and the executive often have distinct policy preferences, even though their overall goals (reelection) may be the same. Depending on who reelects them, they may evaluate any policy differently; in effect, each policy option provides them with a different level of utility. These varying levels of utility cannot merely be summed up to find the policy that is most in the national interest, for two reasons. First and foremost, the actors are in a strategic game to realize a policy closest to their own preferences; a mathematical summation of their utilities cannot capture the political consequences of this game. Actors' utilities do not translate directly or simply into outcomes. Second, these different levels of utility cannot be added together because this involves the interpersonal compari-

---

[2] Similarly, those using this assumption also assume one can total up a state's absolute gains and compare them against those of another state in order to measure their relative gains (Grieco 1990). This is contingent on the unitary actor assumption.

son of utility. Thus there is no single set of national policy preferences, no single national preference ranking on any issue, and no single national "interest." At times actors will differ over the goals a country should pursue; usually this involves how the trade-off between goals should occur—for example, more security or more growth? But there will often be goals on which all actors within the country can agree—for example, economic growth and security. Even when this is the case, internal conflict can still erupt since the actors will prefer different policies—which involve choosing different *means*—for realizing these goals. These differences in policy preferences constitute the heart of domestic politics.

Although the assumption of polyarchy may be more realistic, does it provide a parsimonious and powerful explanation of events? Waltz (1979:65) makes the strongest objection to relaxing the unitary actor assumption. As he claims, and it is worth citing him in detail,

> It is not possible to understand world politics simply by looking inside of states. If the aims, policies, and actions of states become matters of exclusive attention or even of central concern, then we are forced back to the descriptive level. . . . If the situation of actors affects their behavior and influences their interactions, then attempted explanation at the unit level will lead to the infinite proliferation of variables, because at that level no one variable, or set of variables, is sufficient to produce the observed result. So-called variables proliferate wildly when the adopted approach fails to comprehend what is causally important in the subject matter. Variables are added to account for seemingly uncaused effects. What is omitted at the systems level is recaptured—if it is recaptured at all—by attributing characteristics, motives, duties, or whatever to the separate actors. . . . There is, however, no logically sound and traceable process by which effects that derive from the system can be attributed to the units.

For Waltz, without the unitary actor assumption, one can only describe, and not explain, international politics. His objections are problematic. First, there is confusion about who the units are. If one looks inside the state, the unit and system levels change. The state is no longer the actor or unit of analysis; rather, domestic groups become the actors, and "the state" becomes the system. Hence Waltz's third sentence remains correct even when thus amended: "If the [domestic political] situation of actors affects their behavior and influences their interactions, then attempted explanation at the unit level [i.e., by looking at each domestic group] will lead to the infinite proliferation of variables." The problem is in the next step. Waltz assumes a unitary state enmeshed only in an international system, rather than a series of domestic groups enmeshed in a domestic *and* an international system. For some reason, the international system is given priority, to the neglect of the domestic political system. Why should one system in which the actors operate be privileged over the other? Only by assuming that a unitary state is the sole actor in politics, an assumption he returns to in the rest of the quote, can he maintain that the only system that matters is the international one.

This is connected to a second problem. Waltz asserts: "In the history of international relations, however, results achieved seldom correspond to the intentions of actors. Why are they repeatedly thwarted? The apparent answer is that causes not found in their *individual* characters and motives do operate among the actors collectively" (1979:65). This may be true, but it provides neither justification for the unitary state assumption nor support for ignoring the domestic political system. The question is who are the actors. If one assumes they are domestic groups, then the domestic political system may account just as much for these unintended consequences as the international system does. The next sentence clarifies that Waltz means that states are the sole actors he is discussing. But if one conceives of the actors as legislatures, executive branches, and interest groups, then the unintended outcomes of international politics may have as much to do with their domestic bargaining game as with the international system.

An analogy to the study of human beings can be made. Say that one wanted to understand human emotions. Clearly, an important aspect of this would involve understanding the larger social system in which human beings are enmeshed. Their relative position vis-à-vis other humans—economically, politically, amorously, and so on—should have an important impact on their emotional state. But to stop there would be to see at most half the picture. Their emotions also depend on the physical system they inhabit—the human body. Their genetic makeup and biochemical system affect their emotional states in important ways. Focusing on only the larger social system—analogous to Waltz's international system—gives us only part of the picture, as the debate over nature versus nurture makes clear. Moreover, it is not apparent why one should prioritize the larger social system over the internal physical one. In fact, Sigmund Freud (1961), often seen as the epitome of this approach, believed that ultimately we would understand that human behavior was more rooted in and responsive to the body's biochemical system.

Waltz's assertion advances a preference for looking at systems rather than studying the actors within them; but it contains no logical argument about which systems are to be preferred. He presumes that states are unitary actors, and thus the only system around them is the international one. But if one rejects the notion of a unitary state, one can still study systems. This time the actors are surrounded by more than one system—the international and the domestic one; the actors confront a two-level game, which can be understood without an infinite proliferation of variables. Failure to understand the actual actors in world politics and the multiple systems in which they are involved can only limit the field.

The Implications of Polyarchy for Theory and Practice in International Relations

What are the implications of this view for International Relations theory and practice? How does domestic politics affect international politics? When one rejects the unitary actor assumption, can one still parsimoniously study international relations? Adopting the assumption that states are polyarchic retains parsimony and improves explanatory power. Assuming polyarchy implies that international relations operate differently. It means that all policy (foreign policy, too) will be the result of an internal compromise, reflecting the preferences and power of domestic groups. The executive does not always prevail, as Realism and statism imply (Waltz 1979; Krasner 1978). In most nations—and in all democracies—no single group or actor decides policy single-handedly. Domestic groups share power, and thus they vie to have their most preferred policy adopted; they in effect play a strategic game against one another. The executive never dictates, even in nondemocracies. Usually in nondemocracies, the political ruler depends on various groups, such as the military or civil service, for support. These groups often have the implicit right to ratify the executive's major policy choices. Even dictators must cajole, bargain, and induce support from key domestic groups. Even in nondemocracies, then, polyarchy is important. Only if the executive can rule without any other groups' support will she be free from the ratification constraint. Otherwise, internal compromise will shape policy choices, including foreign policy.

Polyarchy seems a likely characterization for most countries. If a country contains actors with different policy preferences, then these actors will seek to realize those preferences—and this will create a bargaining game internally. If the country also has institutions—formal or informal—that allow more than one actor to affect the decision-making process, then policy choices must reflect this bargaining process. Even before the rise of democracy and advanced industrial economies and militaries, most states were polyarchic. Machiavelli's The Prince, for example, deals first and foremost with the leader's struggle to maintain power at home. This domestic struggle to stay in power and a leaders' need to raise tax revenues in order to wage wars implies that leaders constantly faced groups with different preferences and confronted an internal bargaining game over their policy choices (Tilly 1975, 1990). Many monarchs' foreign policy behavior was strongly affected by these internal struggles. As Weingast and North (1989:324) observe about British monarchs in the aftermath of the Glorious Revolution: "In exchange for the greater say in government, parliamentary interests agreed to put the government on a sound financial footing, that is, they agreed to provide sufficient tax revenue. Not only did this remove a major motive underlying the exercise of arbitrary power, but for the new King William it meant he could launch a major war against France."

The assumption of polyarchy applies to security issues as much as to political economy ones. For instance, Morrow (1991) and Miller (1984) show the importance of domestic politics to arms control negotiations. Moreover, if international crises represent situations where the unitary actor assumption seems most likely, then finding that domestic politics mattered in crises provides strong support for the assumption of polyarchy, as Peterson (1996) suggests. Snyder and Diesing (1977:357), for example, show that of the sixteen security-related crises they studied, the large majority of domestic "decision-making structures" (twenty-eight of forty-one states) were characterized by more than two actors bargaining over policy choices and involved situations where executives depended on the support (or ratification) of other groups. Even in these cases of rapid, tense crisis only nine states (of forty-one) were found to have one or two lone decision makers acting by themselves.

As Snyder and Diesing (1977:74–75) conclude:

> Our crisis bargainers however were committees or hierarchies, or even competing groups within a government. The preference functions of these groups, bureaus, or committee members differ greatly and are sometimes direct opposites. Some may have preferences closer to members of the opposing side than to some of their own colleagues. Consequently, the preferences of the whole bargainer vary according to the shifting power distribution of his component parts and may in fact shift suddenly as a former minority coalition becomes predominant. An example is the shift of French policy in 1922–1924 as Briand was replaced by Poincaré, who in turn was replaced by a Left coalition. Sometimes components of a bargainer are also internally divided, for example Japanese navy leaders in 1941 and the West German foreign office in 1961. *Consequently the crisis bargaining process is as much a struggle within governments as between them.* The preferences, specific objectives, . . . and strategies are not given at the start of bargaining but are determined and changed during it. The moves of a dominant group within a government may be directed as much to maintaining or improving their internal position as to winning against an opponent or ally. (Emphasis added.)

Retaining the assumption that the international system is anarchic while assuming domestic politics is polyarchic changes our understanding of international politics. No longer do unitary states single-mindedly seek to balance other states. Rather than the struggle for state survival always taking priority, the struggle for internal power and compromise now dominates. This internal struggle may even lead domestic groups to act in ways that threaten the survival of their own state. For instance, the struggle for power within Czechoslovakia in the early 1990s (as well as in the late 1930s and again in the late 1940s) led to the breakup of the country. Or in France in the early 1940s the Vichy French aided the Germans in the dismantling of the French government. Preoccupation with internal struggle can lead to the destruction of a country. In the extreme, civil war, which is often more prominent and deadly than external conquest, is possible. Thus in polyarchic systems the struggle for internal power and compromise can produce behavior that appears less than rational from an international systemic standpoint. This behavior is nonetheless rational but only when the perspective of the domestic political system is added.

What do these internal struggles imply for conflict and cooperation internationally? In general, is cooperation more likely if the state is unitary or polyarchic? As noted above, the model produces pessimistic conclusions about cooperation. Domestic politics makes cooperation even less likely than does a pure international game among unitary states. Polyarchy, on balance, will make cooperation less likely. Aspects of domestic politics that make a state more polyarchic, like divided government and weak party discipline, constrain the executive further, making her less able to negotiate acceptable agreements with foreign countries. In general, polyarchy, as compared to more hierarchic domestic relations, hinders the search for international cooperation.

Interestingly, polyarchy should also hinder the outbreak of conflict among nations. As the democratic peace literature has argued, democracies tend to be more pacific vis-à-vis themselves than are other forms of government. The arguments for this range from the culture of democracy toward conflict resolution (Russett 1993) to the costs imposed by the public on policy makers for waging war (Doyle 1986) to the greater credibility of threats and promises in democracies and hence the lesser need to challenge them (Fearon 1994). A different and broader argument can be made. It would suggest that the more polyarchic the government, the less likely it would be to initiate war. This should hold whether the government is democratic or not because initiating war requires that the executive obtain the support (or ratification) of other groups with which she shares power. The more polyarchic the state, the harder it is to obtain a change of policy that moves one from the status quo. If democracies are likely to be more polyarchic than nondemocracies, however, their probability of war with each other should be reduced. Hence the probability of two democracies fighting should be lower than the probability of two nondemocracies or a democracy and a nondemocracy fighting.[3] But this argument also helps to explain why democracies are not generally less warlike than nondemocracies. Both nondemocracies and democracies will vary in their degree of polyarchy, and hence in their proneness toward war. For example, from 1900 to 1986, nonde-

---

[3] This assumes it takes a decision by both sides to initiate a war, as most analyses of the democratic peace presume.

mocracies like Peru and Taiwan participated in fewer wars than did democracies like Canada, the Netherlands, and Australia (Mansfield 1996). The argument here is that differences in the extent of polyarchy domestically in each country might help to explain this.

While cooperative agreements between more polyarchic states are harder to realize, so are conflictual policies. It is not democracy per se that matters, but the degree of polyarchy. A dictatorship that was more polyarchic (i.e., that depended on more groups with more diverse preferences) than a democracy should be less likely to initiate conflict as well. In general, the more groups internally with which an executive must share power and the more the preferences of these groups differ, the less likely it is that cooperation or conflict will occur. Polyarchy can prevent both cooperation and conflict.

Lessons for Policy Makers

The arguments here have more than theoretical value. Policy makers can draw four lessons from them. First, when evaluating one's own policy options, policy makers should make sure to understand their own domestic situation. When the implementation of policy depends on the behavior of other actors internally, then lack of attention to the preferences of these actors will spell disaster for the policy. The need for ratification by other domestic groups before a policy can be implemented means that policy makers must anticipate whether these groups will accept the proposed policy. For example, to start a war without one's legislature's consent, tacit or otherwise, when the legislature must appropriate funds for the war is likely to lead to an inability to prosecute the war successfully if one's legislature disagrees with it. Anticipating the reactions of other groups who share control over a policy area is essential for policy makers in the executive branch whether in foreign or domestic policy. Lesson 1: Find consensus at home first.

Second, when assessing other countries' behavior, policy makers should make sure they understand the domestic situation their foreign counterparts face. For example, much behavior that appears as delaying tactics or aggression may simply be the result of internal problems. Delays in responding to foreign actions may occur because of an inability to find consensus internally, rather than because of indifference, weakness, or appeasement. Behavior that looks aggressive from a distance may be more attributable to the consequences of a particularly nasty domestic game. For instance, China's aggressive policies in the early 1990s can be viewed as the result of a bitter internal power struggle for control of the country; thus China, rather than being a fundamentally belligerent power, once the battle for succession is concluded, may become more pacific in its foreign relations.

To understand other states' behavior, it is essential to look not just at their capabilities or intentions but also at their domestic political systems. Indeed, this may be especially important since political psychology shows that decision makers regularly tend to overestimate the degree of centralization and unity in other states (Jervis 1976:319–42):

> The perception of greater coherence than is present leads the actor astray in three ways. First, taking the other side's behavior as the product of a centralized actor with integrated values, inferring the plan that generated this behavior, and projecting this pattern into the future will be misleading if the behavior was the result of shifting internal bargaining, ad hoc decisions and uncoordinated actions. . . . Thus states make sophisticated, and often alarming, inferences from the policy that the other pursues in one issue-area without giving sufficient consideration to the possibility that the coalition that decides the policy in that area may not be the one that establishes other policies . . . Second, the effectiveness of attempts to influence the other's policy will be reduced because the importance of internal conflict will be underestimated. . . . Third, illusory incompatibility [between the states] is created because duplicity rather than confusion is perceived when the other's policy is inconsistent. (Jervis 1976:338–41)

Thus ignoring domestic politics in other states is likely to mislead, rather than facilitate, decision making. Lesson 2: Learn about the domestic situation of other governments. In particular, the preferences of key actors, their political institutions, and the distribution of information in the other country should be of paramount importance.

The third lesson is that domestic signals matter. The importance of signals sent from one country to another has long been recognized (Schelling 1960; Jervis 1970; Baldwin 1985). But the value to policy makers of understanding the signals sent among groups *within* other countries has only recently become more appreciated (Fearon 1994). If groups internally do not fully understand their domestic situation, they will send signals to one another to indicate their preferences, degrees of commitment, and so on. Foreign policy makers can benefit from trying to read these internal signals. Lesson 3: Learn to read the signals sent among actors within other countries.

Fourth, power in international politics springs not just from one's material resources. The balance of power among countries derives not just from their relative resources but also from the history of their relationship. The proximity of one's preferred policy to the reversion point—what occurs in the absence of a mutual accommodation in policy—is also a source of influence; that is, the actor whose preferred outcome is closest to the reversion point is often the most powerful because that actor can reject any outcome and still remain the best off (Lax and Sebenius 1986:46–51). When the reversion point refers to the status quo ante, this means that history matters greatly. Previous interactions among the states will determine what the status quo at any time is. When the reversion point is different from the status quo ante, then the ability of states to change this point becomes of crucial interest. Altering what happens in the absence of cooperation can be a powerful instrument to make other states prefer cooperation. Lesson 4: Remember that the player who has the best alternative to an agreement may be the most powerful.

The model here leads to fundamentally different lessons for policy makers and for scholars than do other theories of international relations, most especially Realism. Indeed, many Realists reject the lessons counseled here. For them, domestic politics should be ignored because it interferes with the pursuit of realist principles of foreign policy. For these Realists, domestic politics is part of the problem facing statesmen (e.g., Morgenthau 1985; Carr 1946). For example, Morgenthau vividly counsels that statesmen must rise above public opinion and sometimes disregard it for the sake of the nation's best interests: "The temptation is overwhelming for an administration to seek to gain electoral advantage by catering to the preferences of public opinion, regardless of foreign policy. Thus one requirement of the statesman's act is to steer a middle course in between respect for the perennial principles of sound foreign policy and the fickle preferences of public opinion" (1985:165–66). Carr also associates the desire or willingness of political leaders to allow public opinion to affect foreign policy as part of the dreaded utopianism against which he rails, even blaming it for World War II (1946:31–36). For some Realists, then, domestic politics needs to be overlooked because it should not interfere with the statesman's pursuit of the national interest. But this seems a utopian dream. No political leader can afford to ignore domestic politics—at home or abroad—when contemplating foreign policy choices. What goes on within states cannot be neglected for it shapes all their behavior toward other states.

Appendix _____

COAUTHORED WITH B. PETER ROSENDORFF

There are four players in this game: the foreign country, F, specified here as a unitary actor, and three domestic players in the home country. Internally, there is the executive, P (president, prime minister, or the proposer), the legislature, C (the chooser), and, in the incomplete information case, a domestic group, E (the endorser). Our focus here is on international trade negotiations between two countries (or between one country and the rest of the world), but the model can be generalized to any policy space.

Define τ^* in $[0, 1]$ as the average tariff rate levied by F on all goods entering its economy. Similarly, τ in $[0, 1]$ is the tariff levied by the domestic country. Then $Q = (\tau_Q^*, \tau_Q)$. Each F, P, and C will have ideal tariff levels that maximize its electoral returns: (τ_i, τ_i^*) for $i = $ F, P, C. The endorser E also has its preferred tariff rate (τ_E, τ_E^*). To simplify the analysis, we will reduce the dimension of the agreement space to an interval on the real line. Any agreement (τ, τ^*) can be expressed as the difference between the tariff rates. Let $t = \tau^* - \tau$. Then $t \in T = [-1, 1]$, and the ideal points are $j = \tau_i^* - \tau_i$ for $i = $ F, P, C, and E, and $j = f, p, c$, and e, respectively, and the status quo is $q = \tau_Q^* - \tau_Q$. Each player attempts to obtain a tariff differential as close as possible to its ideal point, and utility decreases linearly as the implemented policy deviates from the ideal: $U^i(t) = -|t - j|$ for $j = f, p, c, e$.

A strategy for the proposer is a function from the space of possible ideal points, T (the type space), to the set of possible proposals that is also T, i.e., $\pi : T \to T$. Similarly, there is a strategy for F specified by $\phi : T \to T$, where $\phi(t)$ is a proposal sent by an F of type t. Denote any realized agreement selected by F and P and offered for ratification as $a \in T$. In equilibrium we require $a^* = \pi^*(p) = \phi^*(f)$.

The International Level: The Nash Bargaining Solution: (NBS)

Bargaining takes place between P and F independent of domestic or informational constraints. Once agreement is found, the game ends. Consider the set $S^* = \{(s^P, s^F) \in R^2 : (s^P, s^F) = (U^P(a), U^F(a))$ for $a \in [-1, 1]\}$. S^* is compact, contains the disagreement point $d = (U^P(q), U^F(q))$ and there is a point $s^* \in \Delta(S)^*$ such that $s^{*i} > U^i(q)$ for $i = $ P, F. For a finite (or compact) set D, $\Delta(D)$ denotes the set of probability distributions over

D. *S** is convex; hence a bargaining problem has been established (Rubinstein and Osborne 1990:17). Therefore the Nash solution to the bargaining problem (S^*, d) is a^* where

$$a^* = \pi^*(p) = \phi^*(f) \in \text{argmax}_{a \in T}[U^P(a) - U^P(q)][U^F(a) - U^F(q)].$$

LEMMA A1.1: $a^* = a_T$ where

$$a_T = \begin{cases} p & \text{if } f < p < q \text{ or } q < p < f \\ f & \text{if } p < f < q \text{ or } q < f < p \\ q & \text{if } p < q < f \text{ or } f < q < p \end{cases}$$

PROOF: Define $N(a; p, f, q) = [U^P(a) - U^P(q)][U^F(a) - U^F(q)]$ and $a_T = \text{argmax}_{a \in T} N(a; p, f, q)$.

If both P and F have ideal points that lie to the same side of q, then the ideal point closest to q is chosen as the solution to the Nash bargaining problem and becomes the agreement offered for ratification. If P and F have ideal points that straddle q, then q is chosen as the solution. This is shown in Figure 3.1.

The Domestic Level: The Multiple Agenda-Setter Model

The chooser, C, after seeing the agreement struck by P and F makes a ratification decision $r \in R = \{0, 1\}$, rejecting (0) or accepting (1) the agreement a. A strategy for the chooser is the function $\gamma : T \rightarrow \Delta(R)$. Denote the probability that C accepts the treaty after observing agreement a as $\gamma(1; a)$. An equilibrium (a^*, γ^*) has P and F choose strategies as before, but now they are restricted to the set of *ratifiable treaties*: $T' = \{a \in T \mid \gamma^*(1; a) > 0\}$, and C is choosing from the set R in order to maximize utility at every node.

DEFINITION: *Define the "pivot point"* $\underline{j}$ *as the point such that* $U^i(\underline{j}) = U^i(q)$ *for* $i = F, P, C$.

For each player, there is a point in the action space T for which that player is indifferent between it and the status quo. For example, C's pivot point is $\underline{c} = 2c - q$. These are plotted as the straight lines in Figures 3.2, 3.5, and 3.6. C's preferred-to set (the set of points that yield as much or more utility than q, the status quo point) is

$$\Gamma = \begin{cases} [q, \underline{c}] & \text{if } c > q \\ [\underline{c}, q] & \text{if } c \le q \end{cases}$$

PROPOSITION A1.I: *The equilibrium to the multiple agenda-setter domestic game is*

$$\gamma^*(1, a) = \begin{cases} 1 & \text{if } a \in \Gamma \\ 0 & \text{otherwise;} \end{cases} \quad \text{and} \quad a^* = \begin{cases} a_T & \text{if } a_T \in \Gamma \\ \min \Gamma & \text{if } a_T < \min \Gamma \\ \max \Gamma & \text{if } a_T > \max \Gamma \end{cases}$$

PROOF: C approves any offer in Γ. P and F are both constrained to offer the NBS (a_T) in exactly those instances when the NBS lies in C's preferred-to set. If the NBS does not, P and F are constrained to offer the closest ratifiable treaty — either q or $\underline{c}$. In the instance where q is the closest ratifiable treaty, we allow P and F to offer a_T by a trembling-hand argument. Hence P and F are operating as required.

The outcomes here are represented in Figure 3.2 for the case where $f < p < c$.

Domestic Politics and Incomplete Information

Information Structure.

The location of f is treated as uncertain by C: consider f a random variable drawn from the bounded support T with distribution Ξ and everywhere positive density ξ. This distribution is common knowledge. After observing the treaty, a, struck in period 1, the endorser, a new player, with ideal point e selects a message $m \in M = \{0, 1\}$, where the message 0 (1) is interpreted as endorsing the status quo, q (the treaty, a, respectively). A strategy for the endorser is a function $\epsilon : T \to \Delta(M)$. Then $\epsilon(m; a)$ is the probability that the endorser sends message m, given the observed agreement a.

The chooser, C, after seeing the message m makes a ratification decision $r \in R = \{0, 1\}$, rejecting (0) or accepting (1) the (unobserved) agreement a. A strategy for the chooser is the function $\gamma : M \to \Delta(R)$. Denote the probability that C accepts the treaty after observing message m as $\gamma(1; m)$. Expected utilities, then, can be expressed as follows. The chooser's payoff using strategy γ given message m is

$$U^C(\mu, m, \gamma) = \gamma(1; m) \int_T U^C(\pi(t)) \mu(t; m) \, dt + [1 - \gamma(1; m)] U^C(q).$$

For the endorser, given agreement a and the strategy of the chooser γ, the payoff to the endorser of sending message m is $U^E(a, m, \gamma) = \gamma(1; m) U^E(a) + [1 - \gamma(1; m)] U^E(q)$. Therefore

$$U^E(a, \epsilon, \gamma) = \sum_{m \in M} [\gamma(1; m) U^E(a) + [1 - \gamma(1; m)] U^E(q)] \epsilon(m; a).$$

The proposer of type p agreeing with F on a can expect $U^P(a, \epsilon, \gamma) = \sum_{m \in M}[\gamma(1; m)U^P(a) + [1 - \gamma(1; m)]U^P(q)]\epsilon(m; a)$. Similarly, for the foreign country,

$$U^F(a, \epsilon, \gamma) = \sum_{m \in M}[\gamma(1; m)U^F(a) + [1 - \gamma(1; m)]U^F(q)]\epsilon(m; a).$$

Equilibrium Concept

The equilibrium concept we employ is a modified version of sequential equilibrium (Kreps and Wilson 1982), the imperfect information analog of the subgame perfection equilibrium used in the previous section.

DEFINITION: A *modified sequential equilibrium* to this game is a quadruple of strategies $(\phi^*, \pi^*, \epsilon^*, \gamma^*)$ and posterior beliefs μ^* that together satisfy

(i) $\forall p, f \in T$, $a^* = \pi^*(p) = \phi^*(f) \in \text{argmax}_{a \in T}[U^P(a, \epsilon^*, \gamma^*) - U^P(q)][U^F(a, \epsilon^*, \gamma^*) - U^F(q)]$

(ii) $\forall a \in T, \epsilon^*(m; a) > 0$ whenever $\forall m' \in M$, $U^E(a, m, \gamma^*) \geq U^E(a, m', \gamma^*)$

(iii) $\forall m \in M$, $\gamma^*(r; m) > 0$ whenever $\forall r' \in A$, $U^C(\mu^*(m), m, r) \geq U^C(\mu^*(m), m, r')$.

(iv) $\mu^*(\cdot ; m)$ satisfies Bayes's rule given the prior beliefs ψ, π^*, ϕ^*, and ϵ^*. That is $\forall m \in M$ such that

$$\int_{t \in T} \epsilon^*(m; \pi^*(t))\psi(t)\, dt > 0, \quad \mu^*(t'; m) = \frac{\epsilon^*(m; \phi^*(t'))\psi(t')}{\int_{t \in T} \epsilon^*(m; \phi^*(t))\psi(t)\, dt}.$$

An equilibrium has four properties. First, the executive and the foreign country are constrained (as before) to offer for ratification a point in the set of treaties that is also the Nash Bargaining Solution to their treaty negotiation. For any equilibrium $(\phi^*, \pi^*, \epsilon^*, \gamma^*)$, we redefine the set $S^* = \{(s^P, s^F) \in R^2 : (s^P, s^F) = (U^P(a, \epsilon^*, \gamma^*), U^F(a, \epsilon^*, \gamma^*))$ for $a \in [-1, 1]\}$ and the disagreement point $d = (U^P(q, \epsilon^*, \gamma^*), U^F(q, \epsilon^*, \gamma^*))$. Again a bargaining problem has been established. Second, the endorser endorses with positive probability only in those instances that are optimal; and third, the chooser ratifies only those treaties that are optimal given its beliefs. Fourth, beliefs are consistent with Bayes's rule and the messages that are sent.

Notice that the posterior μ is derived not from the prior Ξ, but from Ψ. Recall that C is not informed of the relative position f. However, C knows p and that f is drawn independently from Ξ over the support [-1,1], and that once drawn, P and F bargain to the Nash solution in the set of ratifiable treaties. What, then, constitute the prior beliefs of C over proposed *agree-*

ments? We write the reduced form of these beliefs over proposed agreements as the distribution function Ψ where this is derived from Ξ using the common knowledge that P and F pick the NBS from the set of agreements; that is, $\Psi(a')$ represents the chooser's prior beliefs that P and F have bargained to a policy that is a' or less with probability $\Psi(a')$. This way we reduce the belief structure from types to agreements or from preferences to policies. The density of this reduced form is written ψ. Recall, however, that the Nash Bargaining Solution is determined in expectation: P and F bargain all the time cognizant that their offers will be subject to scrutiny by the endorser, and that the chooser, i.e., the legislature, will optimize with respect to that endorsement. Therefore Ψ is a statement of beliefs about the proposal before any endorsement is made. But after bargaining has taken place, it is no longer a statement of *prior* beliefs nor of *posterior* beliefs. These beliefs do, however, take on the role of the priors in the definition of the sequential equilibrium; for this reason, we might call them the *interim* beliefs.

Pig-in-the-Poke Result.

When the game is played with imperfect information but without the endorser, the equilibrium is as follows:

PROPOSITION A1.II: *The equilibrium to the multiple agenda-setter domestic game with imperfect information and no endorser is*

$$\gamma^*(1) = \begin{cases} 1 & \text{if } \int_T U^C(t)\psi(t)\,dt \geq U^C(q) \\ 0 & \text{otherwise;} \end{cases} \quad \text{and} \quad a^* = a_T$$

PROOF: See Cameron and Jung (1992), Proposition 2.

Returning now to the game with the endorser, we will look only at those equilibria where the endorser does not use pooling equilibria whenever a better nonpooling equilibrium strategy exists (Banks 1990, 1991). Following Cameron and Jung (1992), the endorser is following a *pooling strategy* if in the equilibrium $(\phi^*, \pi^*, \epsilon^*, \gamma^*)$, $\forall a, a' \in T, \epsilon^*(m; a) = \epsilon^*(m; a')$. A strategy is *babbling* if the endorser uses a pooling strategy in which all messages are used with positive probability. If the strategy is not pooling, then we say that an endorser is *willing to send* information. The endorser *sends useful information* in the equilibrium if he or she is willing to send information and $\gamma^*(1; m) \neq \gamma^*(1; m')$ for $m, m' \in \{0, 1\}$ and $m \neq m'$; that is, information is useful only if that information changes the chooser's behavior. Pooling equilibria always exist in costless signaling games, and we are interested in how the information that is transmitted affects the nature of the international treaty.

We also confine our attention to equilibria where the message 0 (1) has the intrinsic meaning of endorsing the status quo Q (the proposed treaty a, respectively). In addition, Cameron and Jung (1992) show that these pooling equilibria do not withstand the "neologism proof" refinement. In any equilibrium where the endorser sends message 1 if he or she observed a and 0 if a', there exists a "mirror-image" equilibrium in which the observations and signals are reversed. We are simply excluding these equilibria since they have no meaningful interpretation. We then obtain all the possible pure strategy equilibria that satisfy these conditions.

LEMMA A1.2:   *In any equilibrium* $(\phi^*, \pi^*, \epsilon^*, \gamma^*, \mu^*)$, $\gamma^*(1; 1) \geq \gamma^*(1; 0)$.

PROOF: See Cameron and Jung (1992).

Any endorsement of a proposal does not decrease the probability that the proposed treaty will be ratified. Essentially, if the chooser heeds the endorser's advice, the endorser gives a truthful endorsement (i.e., the endorser truly prefers the proposal to the status quo). This is because the endorser never gets to make the final choice about accepting or rejecting the proposed agreement. We now define three sets of strategies: the endorsement equilibrium, the recalcitrant equilibrium, and the accommodating equilibrium (Matthews 1989), and these exhaust the possible pure strategy equilibria. Define E's preferred-to set as

$$
E = \begin{cases} [q, \underline{e}] & \text{if } e > q \\ [\underline{e}, q] & \text{if } e \leq q \end{cases}
$$

DEFINITION: *The following set of strategies will be called an endorsement equilibrium:*

$$
a^* = \begin{cases} a_T & \text{if } a_T \in E; \\ \min E & \text{if } a_T < \min E; \\ \max E & \text{if } a_T > \max E; \end{cases} \qquad \epsilon^*(1, a) = \begin{cases} 1 & \text{if } a \in E; \\ 0 & \text{otherwise}; \end{cases}
$$

$$
\gamma^*(1; m) = \begin{cases} 1 & \text{if } m = 1; \\ 0 & \text{otherwise}. \end{cases}
$$

In an endorsement equilibrium, the proposers agree to send a_T if it lies between q and $\underline{e}$. If a_T does not, P and F are constrained to offer the closest ratifiable treaty — either q or $\underline{e}$. The endorser signals positively when it observes an offer lying in its set of preferred policies (relative to the status quo), and the chooser C listens to E's instructions and relies on the endorsement for its ratification decision.

DEFINITION: *The following set of strategies will be called a recalcitrant equilibrium*:

$$a^* = a_T; \quad \epsilon^*(1, a) = \begin{cases} 1 & \text{if } a \in E; \\ 0 & \text{otherwise}; \end{cases} \quad \gamma^*(1; m) = 0 \, \forall m \in M.$$

P and F will agree to send their unconstrained proposal a_T , and the endorser will endorse if it lies in its set of preferred policies relative to the status quo. Congress is recalcitrant and does not ratify any offer.

DEFINITION: *The following set of strategies will be called an accommodating equilibrium*:

$$a^* = a_T; \quad \epsilon^*(1, a) = \begin{cases} 1 & \text{if } a \in E; \\ 0 & \text{otherwise}; \end{cases} \quad \gamma^*(1; m) = 1 \, \forall m \in M.$$

P and F again agree to send their unconstrained proposal a_T , anticipating now that it will be accepted. The endorser again responds honestly, and since the chooser's beliefs are optimistic, it accepts all offers.

The following propositions specify the conditions under which each of these equilibria exist and are proved for the cases where $q < \max\{e, c\}$. The results apply for the symmetric case where $q > \max\{e, c\}$ in the conditions specified in the square brackets. For $q \in (e, c)$ or $q \in (c, e)$, Proposition A1.V applies.

PROPOSITION A1.III: *We consider the case $q < e < c$ [or $c < e < q$]. Define θ as the point in T such that*

$$\frac{\int_{-1}^{q} U^C(t)\psi(t)\,dt + \int_{\theta}^{1} U^C(t)\psi(t)\,dt}{\int_{-1}^{q} \psi(t)\,dt + \int_{\theta}^{1} \psi(t)\,dt} = U^C(q).$$

If $q \le \theta \le \underline{e}\,[\underline{e} \le \theta \le q]$ or if θ does not exist, an endorsement equilibrium exists. If $\underline{e} \le \theta \le \underline{c}\,[\underline{c} \le \theta \le \underline{e}]$, both an accommodating and an endorsement equilibrium exist.

PROOF: In all cases, the endorser is easily seen to be optimizing, and P and F are behaving as required — offering the NBS (given the chooser's strategy) for ratification. All we need to check is the behavior of the chooser C.

Consider the accommodating equilibrium first: that is, the case where $q \le \theta \le \underline{e}$. In the case of an endorsement, equilibrium payoff is clearly larger than the defection: $\int_{q}^{e} U^C(t)\mu(t; 1)\,dt > U^C(q)$ since $U^C(t) > U^C(q) \, \forall t \in [q, \underline{e}]$. If no endorsement is forthcoming, and c is large enough, there may be some set of a's (bounded below by θ) such that the expected utility for C weighted by the probability that a lies in this set dominates the status quo equilibrium; that is, $\int_{-1}^{q} U^C(t)\mu(t; 0)\,dt + \int_{\theta}^{1} U^C(t)\mu(t; 0)\,dt = U^C(q)$.

So if $\underline{e} > \theta$, then $\int_{-1}^{q} U^C(t)\mu(t; 0)\,dt + \int_{\underline{e}}^{1} U^C(t)\mu(t; 0)\,dt > U^C(q)$ and the chooser is optimizing. Using Bayes's Law and the interim beliefs, the condition can be rewritten as in the statement of the proposition.

Consider now the endorsement equilibrium: The equilibrium expected utility of the chooser on obtaining an endorsement is $\int_q^{\underline{e}} U^C(t)\mu(t; 1)\,dt +$ $\int_{\underline{e}}^{1} U^C(\underline{e})\mu(t; 1)\,dt > U^C(q)$, the utility obtained from deviation since $U^C(t) \geq$ $U^C(q)$ for all $\underline{e} \geq t \geq q$. If $a < q$, there will be no endorsement and C knows that either p or f has been offered. By rejecting, $U^C(q)$ exceeds either $U^C(p)$ or $U^C(f)$ if either p or f were to be accepted. Can P and F gain by offering something different? The best possible defection for P and F is to offer q yielding the same utility as in equilibrium. By a trembling-hand argument, P and F will offer p or f, and not defect.

PROPOSITION A1.IV: *We consider the case where $q < c < e$ [or $e < c < q$].*
If

$$\frac{\int_Q^{\underline{e}} U^C(t)\psi(t)\,dt + \int_{\underline{e}}^{1} U^C(\underline{e})\psi(t)\,dt}{\int_q^{1} \psi(t)\,dt} \geq U^C(q)$$

$$\left[\frac{\int_{\underline{e}}^{q} U^C(t)\psi(t)\,dt + \int_{-1}^{\underline{e}} U^C(\underline{e})\psi(t)\,dt}{\int_{-1}^{q} \psi(t)\,dt} \geq U^C(q) \right]$$

then an endorsement equilibrium exists. If

$$\frac{\int_q^{\underline{e}} U^C(t)\psi(t)\,dt}{\int_q^{\underline{e}} \psi(t)\,dt} < U^C(q)$$

$$\left[\frac{\int_{\underline{e}}^{q} U^C(t)\psi(t)\,dt}{\int_{\underline{e}}^{q} \psi(t)\,dt} < U^C(q) \right],$$

then a recalcitrant equilibrium exists.

PROOF: The first condition ensures that the chooser will ratify any offer that receives a positive endorsement in the endorsement equilibrium. The rest of the proof is identical to the previous proposition. For the recalcitrant equilibrium, if an endorsement occurs, the chooser must still reject the offer if $\int_q^{\underline{e}} U^C(t)\mu(t; 1)\,dt < U^C(q)$ in order for $\gamma^*(1; m) = 0\,\forall m \in M$. Using Bayes's Law and the interim beliefs generates the second condition. In the case of no endorsement, $U^C(q) > \int_{-1}^{q} U^C(t)\mu(t; 0)\,dt + \int_{\underline{e}}^{1} U^C(t)\mu(t; 0)\,dt$ since $a < q$ or $a > \underline{e}$.

PROPOSITION A1.V: *We consider the case where $e < q < c$ or $c < q < e$. No information is revealed in this case. In equilibrium:*

$$a^* = a_T; \quad \epsilon^*(m, a) = \epsilon^*(m, a') \,\forall\, a, a' \in T;$$

$$\gamma^*(1; m) = \begin{cases} 1 & \text{if } \int_T U^C(t)\psi(t)\,dt > U^C(q) \\ \alpha \in [0, 1] & \text{if } \int_T U^C(t)\psi(t)\,dt = U^C(q) \\ 0 & \text{if } \int_T U^C(t)\psi(t)\,dt < U^C(q) \end{cases}$$

PROOF: This is the no-information case — all decisions are made relative to the interim beliefs.

PROPOSITION I: *For any structure of preferences, the regions of cooperation are larger in the incomplete information game with the endorser than without the endorser.*

PROOF: A cooperative outcome is an outcome where mutual gains have been achieved for P and F (when such gains exist). If no mutual gains exist, the status quo is pareto optimal, and it remains the outcome — no new agreements are possible. Define a "region of cooperation" as a set of initial qs yielding any cooperative outcome. In the incomplete information game with no endorser (Figure 3.4), the region of cooperation is $T^{Cooperative}_{Incomplete, No\ Endorser} = \{q | q \in [-1, f] \cup [c_h, 1]\}$. In the game with the endorser, $T^{Cooperative}_{Incomplete, Endorser} = \{q | q \in [-1, f] \cup [p, 1]\}$ for $e < c$, and $T^{Cooperative}_{Incomplete, Endorser} = \{q | q \in [-1, f] \cup [c, 1]\}$ for $c < e$. In either case, $T^{Cooperative}_{Incomplete, No\ Endorser} \subseteq T^{Cooperative}_{Incomplete, Endorser}$.

PROPOSITION II: *For any structure of preferences, the regions of cooperation are larger in the incomplete information game with the endorser than in the full information domestic game.*

PROOF: In the incomplete information game with domestic politics (as represented in Figure 3.2), $T^{Cooperative}_{Complete} = \{q | q \in [-1, f] \cup [c, 1]\}$. In the incomplete information game, $T^{Cooperative}_{Incomplete, Endorser} = \{q | q \in [-1, f] \cup [p, 1]\}$ for $e < c$ and $T^{Cooperative}_{Incomplete, Endorser} = \{q | q \in [-1, f] \cup [c, 1]\}$ for $c < e$. In either case, $T^{Cooperative}_{Complete} \subseteq T^{Cooperative}_{Incomplete, Endorser}$.

PROPOSITION III: *In any informative equilibrium to the incomplete information game (with the endorser), there is an outcome such that C obtains utility (i) at least as large as in the complete information domestic game, and (ii) at least as large as in the incomplete information game without the endorser.*

PROOF: Consider the utility to C from the complete information domestic game:

$$U^C = \begin{cases} -(c-f) & \text{if } q \le f \\ -(c-q) & \text{if } q \in (f, c] \\ -(q-c) & \text{if } q \in (c, 2c-p) \\ -(c-p) & \text{if } q \ge 2c-p \end{cases}$$

Conduct a similar exercise for the incomplete information game with the endorser when $p < c < e$. Where multiple (informative) equilibria generate multiple outcomes, choose the outcome (and hence the equilibrium) with the highest utility for C (we are concerned with existence, not necessity). The equilibrium that yields the given payoff is specified:

$$U^C = \begin{cases} -(c-f) & \text{if } q \le f \text{ endorsement} \\ -(c-q) & \text{if } q \in (f, c] \text{ endorsement} \\ -(2e-q-c) & \text{if } q \in [e, 2e-c] \text{ endorsement} \\ -(c-2e+q) & \text{if } q \in (2e-c, 2e-p) \text{ endorsement} \\ -(c-p) & \text{if } q \ge 2e-p \text{ endorsement/accommodating} \end{cases} \qquad A1.1$$

Note that the interval $q \in (c, e)$ is not considered since no informative equilibrium exists in this interval. Now the first, second, and fifth intervals of the incomplete information game payoffs correspond to and are identical to those in intervals one, two, and four. For $q \in [e, 2e-c]$, $-(2e-q-c) > -(q-c)$ since $e < q$. For $q \in (2e-c, 2e-p)$, $-(-2e+q+c) > -(q-c)$ since $e > c$. When $p < e < c$, the payoffs are

$$U^C = \begin{cases} -(c-f) & \text{if } q \le f \text{ endorsement/accommodating} \\ -(c-q) & \text{if } q \in (f, e] \text{ endorsement/accommodating} \\ -(q-c) & \text{if } q \in [c, 2e-p] \text{ recalcitrant} \\ -(c-p) & \text{if } q \ge 2e-p \text{ endorsement} \end{cases} \qquad A1.2$$

which is identical to the complete information game. So item (i) is established. Consider now the payoffs to C in the incomplete information game without the endorser and compare them sequentially with the payoffs in A1.1 and A1.2 above:

$$U^C = \begin{cases} -(c-f) & \text{if } q \le f \\ -(c-q) & \text{if } q \in (f, c] \\ -(q-c) & \text{if } q \in (c, c_h) \\ -(c-p) & \text{if } q \ge c_h \end{cases}$$

Case: $p < c < e$

I. $c_h \in (c, e)$. The payoffs when $q \le c$ and $q \ge 2e - p$ are the same. For $q \in (c, e)$ the equilibria are uninformative. For $q \in (e, 2e - p)$ either

$q \in (e, 2e - c)$, in which case $U^C_{No\ Endorser} < U^C_{Endorser}$ since $c > p$; or $q \in (2e - c, 2e - p)$ where $U^C_{No\ Endorser} < U^C_{Endorser}$ since $2e - p > q$.

II. $c_h \in (e, 2e - c)$. The payoffs when $q \leq c$ and $q \geq 2e - p$ are the same. For $q \in (e, 2e - p)$ either $q \in (e, c_h)$, in which case $U^C_{No\ Endorser} < U^C_{Endorser}$ since $q > e$; or $q \in (c_h, 2e - c)$ where $U^C_{No\ Endorser} < U^C_{Endorser}$ since $c > p$; or $q \in (2e - c, 2e - p)$, where $U^C_{No\ Endorser} < U^C_{Endorser}$ since $2e - p > q$.

III. $c_h \in (2e - c, 2e - p)$. The payoffs when $q \leq c$ and $q \geq 2e - p$ are the same. For $q \in (e, 2e - p)$ either $q \in (e, 2e - c)$, in which case $U^C_{No\ Endorser} < U^C_{Endorser}$ since $q > e$; or $q \in (2e - c, c_h)$, where $U^C_{No\ Endorser} < U^C_{Endorser}$ since $c > e$; or $q \in (c_h, 2e - p)$, where $U^C_{No\ Endorser} < U^C_{Endorser}$ since $2e - p > q$.

IV. $c_h \in (2e - p, 1)$. The payoffs when $q \leq c$ and $q \geq c_h$ are the same. For $q \in (e, c_h)$ either $q \in (e, 2e - c)$, in which case $U^C_{No\ Endorser} < U^C_{Endorser}$ since $q > e$; or $q \in (2e - c, 2e - p)$, where $U^C_{No\ Endorser} < U^C_{Endorser}$ since $c > e$; or $q \in (2e - p, c_h)$, where $U^C_{No\ Endorser} < U^C_{Endorser}$ since $2c - p < q$.

Case: $p < e < c$

I. $c_h \in (c, 2e - p)$. The payoffs when $q \leq c_h$ and $q \geq 2e - p$ are the same; for $q \in (c_h, 2e - p)$, $U^C_{No\ Endorser} < U^C_{Endorser}$ since $c > e$.

II. $c_h \in (2e - p, 1)$. The payoffs when $q \leq 2e - p$ and $q \geq c_h$ are the same; for $q \in (2e - p, c_h)$, $U^C_{No\ Endorser} < U^C_{Endorser}$ since $q > 2e - p$.

The Multiple Endorser Environment

Let e_j be the strategies of the two endorsers. The chooser C will take a ratification decision based now on the vector of messages observed $m = (m_L, m_R)$. Let L be L's preferred-to set, and R be R's preferred-to set. After appropriately redefining the players' utilities and the definition of the equilibrium, we can establish the following results.

DEFINITION: *The following sets of strategies will be called a pessimistic endorsement equilibrium:*

$$a^* = \begin{cases} a_T & \text{if } a_T \in L \\ \min L & \text{if } a_T < \min L \\ \max L & \text{if } a_T > \max L \end{cases} \qquad \epsilon_j^*(1, a) = \begin{cases} 1 & \text{if } a \in P_j \\ 0 & \text{otherwise} \end{cases}$$

$$\gamma^*(1; m) = \begin{cases} 1 & \text{if } m_L = 1 \\ 0 & \text{otherwise} \end{cases}$$

where $P_j = L$ for $j = L$ and $P_j = R$ for $j = R$.

DEFINITION: *The following sets of strategies will be called an optimistic endorsement equilibrium:*

$$a^* = \begin{cases} a_T & \text{if } a_T \in R \\ \min R & \text{if } a_T < \min R \\ \max R & \text{if } a_T > \max R \end{cases} \qquad \epsilon_j^*(1, a) = \begin{cases} 1 & \text{if } a \in P_j \\ 0 & \text{otherwise} \end{cases}$$

$$\gamma^*(1; m) = \begin{cases} 1 & \text{if } m = (1, 1) \text{ or } (0, 1) \\ 0 & \text{otherwise} \end{cases}$$

PROPOSITION IV: *(a) If $q < l < c < r$, then a pessimistic endorsement equilibrium to the two endorser game exists. (b) If $q < l < c < r$ and*

$$\frac{\int_l^r U^C(t)\psi(t)\,dt + \int_r^1 U^C(r)\psi(t)\,dt}{\int_l^1 \psi(t)\,dt} \geq U^C(q),$$

then an optimistic endorsement equilibrium to the two endorser game exists.

PROOF: (a) The equilibrium follows from a comparison of expected utilities for P, F, L, R, and C and the assumption that the message 0 has the intrinsic meaning of endorsing the status quo, while 1 has the meaning of endorsing the proposal a. (b) This follows from the appropriate comparison of utilities. The condition follows from observing that in the case of $m = (0, 1)$, $a^* \in [l, r]$. In order for C to accept such an offer, it must be the case that the equilibrium payoff exceeds the utility from defection to the status quo, that is $\int_l^r U^C(t)\mu(t; (0, 1))\,dt + \int_r^1 U^C(r)\mu(t; (0, 1))\,dt \geq U^C(q)$. Using Bayes's Law and the interim beliefs generates the condition as in the statement of the theorem.

In both equilibria, endorsements occur along the equilibrium path and the agreements are ratified whenever $a_T > q$. If $a_T < q$, no endorsement and no ratification occurs. If an offer is made that gets the endorsement of L, then it lies between 0 and l. It will then also get the endorsement of R and $m = (1, 1)$. Between l and r only R endorses, while L does not ($m = (0, 1)$), and in the rest, above r and 1 and below q, neither endorser signals ($m = (0, 0)$).

Bibliography

Achen, Christopher, and Duncan Snidal. 1989. "Rational Deterrence Theory and Comparative Case Studies." *World Politics* 41:143–69.

Alesina, Alberto, and Nouriel Roubini. 1992. "Political Cycles in OECD Economies." *Review of Economic Studies* 59:663–88.

Alesina, Alberto, and Howard Rosenthal. 1995. *Partisan Politics, Divided Government, and the Economy*. New York: Cambridge University Press.

Allison, Graham. 1971. *The Essence of Decision: Explaining the Cuban Missile Crisis*. Boston: Little, Brown.

Alt, James, and Barry Eichengreen. 1989. "Parallel and Overlapping Games." *Economics and Politics* 1:119–44.

Anderson, Irvine. 1981. *ARAMCO, the United States, and Saudi Arabia*. Princeton, N.J.: Princeton University Press.

Andrews, David. 1992. "The Structural Roots of European Monetary Convergence." Manuscript.

Arrow, Kenneth. 1963. *Social Choice and Individual Values*. 2nd ed. New Haven, Conn.: Yale University Press.

Artis, Michael, and Sylvia Ostry. 1986. *International Economic Policy Coordination*, London: Chatham House papers #30, Routledge and Keegan Paul.

Artus, Patrick. 1989. *Macroéconomie*. Paris: Presses Universitaires de France.

Austen-Smith, David. 1991."Rational Consumers and Irrational Voters: A Review Essay on *Black Hole Tariffs and Endogenous Policy Theory*." *Economics and Politics* 3:73–92.

Austen-Smith, David, and John Wright. 1992. "Competitive Lobbying for a Legislator's Vote." *Social Choice and Welfare* 9:229–57.

Bachrach, Peter, and Morton Baratz. 1962. "The Two Faces of Power." *American Political Science Review* 56:947–52.

Baldwin, David. 1985. *Economic Statecraft*. Princeton, N.J.: Princeton University Press.

Baldwin, David. 1989. *Paradoxes of Power*. New York: Basil Blackwell.

Banks, Jeffrey. 1990. "Monopoly Agenda Control with Asymmetric Information." *Quarterly Journal of Economics* 105:445–64.

———. 1991. *Signaling Games in Political Science*. Chur, Switzerland: Harwood Academic Publishers.

———. 1993. "Two-sided Uncertainty in the Monopoly Agenda Setter Model." *Journal of Public Economics* 50:429–44.

Baron, David, and John Ferejohn. 1989a. "Bargaining in Legislatures." *American Political Science Review* 83:1181–1206.

———. 1989b. "The Power to Propose." In Peter Ordeshook, ed., *Models of Strategic Choice in Politics*, pp. 343–66. Ann Arbor: University of Michigan Press.

Bates, Robert. 1981. *Markets and States in Tropical Africa*. Berkeley: University of California Press.

Bates, Robert, and Da-Hsiang Lien. 1985. "A Note on Taxation, Development, and Representative Government." *Politics and Society* 14:53–70.

Baum, William. 1958. *The French Economy and the State*. Princeton, N.J.: Princeton University Press.

Baumgartner, Frank, and Bryan Jones. 1993. *Agendas and Instability in American Politics*. Chicago: University of Chicago Press.

Baumol, William, and W. Oates. 1975. *The Theory of Environmental Policy*. Englewood Cliffs, N.J.: Prentice-Hall.

Baylis, Thomas. 1996. "Presidents versus Prime Ministers: Shaping Executive Authority in Eastern Europe." *World Politics* 48:297–323.

Becker, Josef, and Franz Knipping, eds. 1986. *Power in Europe? Great Britain, France, Italy, and Germany in a Postwar World, 1945–1950*. New York: Walter de Gruyter.

Binmore, Ken. 1992. *Fun and Games*. Lexington, Mass.: Heath.

Blackburn, Keith, and M. Christensen. 1989. "Monetary Policy and Policy Credibility." *Journal of Economic Literature* 27:1–45.

Blair, John. 1976. *The Control of Oil*. New York: Pantheon.

Blank, Stephen. 1978. "Britain: The Politics of Foreign Economic Policy, the Domestic Economy, and the Problem of Pluralistic Stagnation." In Peter Katzenstein, ed., *Between Power and Plenty*, pp. 89–138. Madison: University of Wisconsin Press.

Blau, Peter. 1964. *Exchange and Power in Social Life*. New York: Wiley.

Block, Fred. 1977. *The Origins of International Economic Disorder*. Berkeley: University of California Press.

Brander, James, and Barbara Spencer. 1985. "Export Subsidies and International Market Share Rivalry." *Journal of International Economics* 16:83–100.

Browne, Eric, and Keith Hamm. 1996. "Legislative Politics and the Paradox of Voting: Electoral Reform in Fourth Republic France." *British Journal of Political Science* 26:165–98.

Buchanan, James, and Gordon Tullock. 1962. *The Calculus of Consent*. Ann Arbor: University of Michigan Press.

Budge, Ian, and Hans Keman. 1990. *Parties and Democracy*. New York: Oxford University Press.

Bueno de Mesquita, Bruce, and David Lalman. 1992. *War and Reason*. New Haven, Conn.: Yale University Press.

Butler, David, and Austin Ranney, eds. 1978. *Referendums: A Comparative Study of Practice and Theory*. Washington, D.C.: American Enterprise Institute.

Calvert, Randall. 1985. "The Value of Biased Information." *Journal of Politics* 47:530–55.

Calvijo, Fernando. 1993. "Discussion." In Jaime De Melo and Arvind Panagariya, eds., *New Dimensions in Regional Integration*, pp. 382–84. Cambridge: Cambridge University Press.

Cameron, David. 1993. "British Exit, German Voice, and French Loyalty." Manuscript.

Cameron, Charles, and Joon Pyu Jung. 1992. "Strategic Endorsements." Manuscript.

Campbell, Colin. 1983. *Governments under Stress*. Toronto: University of Toronto Press.

Canzoneri, Matthew, and Dale Henderson. 1991. *Monetary Policy in Interdependent Economies*. Cambridge, Mass.: MIT Press.

Carr, Edward H. 1946. *The Twenty Years' Crisis, 1919–1939*. 2nd ed. New York: Harper and Row.

Caves, Richard. 1976. "Economic Models of Political Choice," *Canadian Journal of Economics* 9:278–300.

Clarida, Richard, and Mark Gertler. 1996. "How the Bundesbank Conducts Monetary Policy." Manuscript.

Clausewitz, Carl von. 1832. *On War*. Various editions.

Cohen, Benjamin. 1993. "Beyond EMU: The Problem of Sustainability." In Barry Eichengreen and Jeffry Frieden, eds., "The Political Economy of European Monetary Unification." *Economics and Politics* 5 (special issue): 187–203.

Cooper, John. 1947. *The Right to Fly*, New York: Holt.

Cooper, Richard. 1985. Economic Interdependence and Coordination of Economic Policies." In R. Jones and P. Kenen, eds., *Handbook of International Economics*. Vol. 2. Amsterdam: Elsevier.

———. 1986. *Economic Policy in an Interdependent World*. Cambridge: MIT Press.

———. 1989. "International Cooperation in Public Health as a Prologue to Macroeconomic Cooperation." In Richard Cooper et al., eds., *Can Nations Agree?*, pp. 178–254. Washington, D.C.: Brookings Institution.

Copeland, Gary, and Samuel Patterson, eds. 1994. *Parliaments in the Modern World*. Ann Arbor: University of Michigan Press.

Cotta, Maurizio. 1994. "The Rise and Fall of 'Centrality' of the Italian Parliament." In Gary Copeland and Samuel Patterson, eds., *Parliaments in the Modern World*, pp. 59–84. Ann Arbor: University of Michigan Press.

Cox, Gary, and Samuel Kernell, eds. 1991. *The Politics of Divided Government*. Boulder, Colo.: Westview.

Crawford, Vincent. 1990. "Bargaining and Price Formation under Incomplete Information: Theories and Experiments." *American Economic Review* 80:213–19.

Cronin, Thomas. 1980. *The State of the Presidency*. 2nd ed. Boston: Little, Brown.

Crossman, Richard. 1972. *The Myth of Cabinet Government*. Cambridge, Mass.: Harvard University Press.

Dahl, Robert. 1984. *Modern Political Analysis*. Englewood Cliffs, N.J.: Prentice-Hall.

De Beaumont, E. 1983. *La Quatrième république*. Paris: Presses Universitaires de France.

Dell, Edmund. 1995. *The Schuman Plan and the British Abdication of Leadership in Europe*. New York: Oxford University Press.

Destler, I. M. 1992. *American Trade Politics*. Washington, D.C.: International Institute for Economics.

Destler, I. M., and Randall Henning. 1989. *Dollar Politics: Exchange Rate Policymaking in the United States*. Washington, D.C.: Institute of International Economics.

DeSwann, Abram. 1973. *Coalition Theories and Cabinet Government*. Amsterdam: Elsevier.

Deutsch, Morton. 1949. "A Theory of Cooperation and Conflict." *Human Relations* 2:129–52.

Diebold, William. 1952. *The End of the ITO*. Princeton, N.J.: International Finance section, Economics Department, Princeton University.

———. 1959. *The Schuman Plan: A Study in Economic Cooperation, 1950–1959*. New York: Praeger.

Dixon, William. 1986. "Reciprocity in U.S.-Soviet Relations: Multiple Symmetry or Issue Linkage?" *American Journal of Political Science* 30:421–45.

Dobson, Alan. 1991. *Peaceful Air Warfare*. Oxford: Oxford University Press.

Doern, G. Bruce, and Brian Tomlin. 1991. *Faith and Fear*. Toronto: Stoddart.

Dornbusch, Rudiger. 1980. *Open-Economy Macroeconomics*. New York: Basic.

Dowding, Keith, and Desmond King. 1995. *Preferences, Institutions, and Rational Choice*. Oxford: Oxford University Press.

Downs, Anthony. 1957. *An Economic Theory of Democracy*. New York: Harper and Row.

Downs, George, and David Rocke. 1995. *Optimal Imperfection: Domestic Uncertainty and Institutions in International Relations*. Princeton, N.J.: Princeton University Press.

Doyle, Michael. 1986. "Liberalism and World Politics." *American Political Science Review* 80:1151–70.

Duverger, Maurice. 1959. *Political Parties*. Translated by R. North and B. North. New York: Wiley.

Duverger, Maurice. 1987. *La Cohabitation française*. Paris: presses Universitaires de France.

Eckes, Alfred. 1975. *A Search for Solvency: Bretton Woods and the International Monetary System, 1941–1971*. Austin: University of Texas Press.

Ehrmann, Henri. 1953. "The French Trade Associations and the Ratification of the Schuman Plan." *World Politics* 6:453–81.

———. 1957. *Organized Business in France*. Princeton, N.J.: Princeton University Press.

Eichengreen, Barry. 1989. "Hegemonic Stability Theories of the International Monetary System." In Richard Cooper et. al., eds., *Can Nations Agree?*, pp. 255–307. Washington, D.C.: Brookings Institution.

Elster, Jon. 1979. *Ulysses and the Sirens*. Cambridge: Cambridge University Press.

———, ed. 1986. *Rational Choice*. New York: New York University Press.

Enelow, James, and Melvin Hinich. 1990. *The Spatial Theory of Voting*. New York: Cambridge University Press.

Epstein, David, and Sharyn O'Halloran. 1993. "Interest Group Oversight, Information, and the Design of Administrative Procedures." Manuscript.

Evangelista, Matthew. 1989. "Issue-Area and Foreign Policy Revisited." *International Organization* 43:147–71.

Evans, Peter, Harold Jacobson, and Robert Putnam, eds. 1993. *Double-Edged Diplomacy*. Berkeley: University of California Press.

Fearon, James. 1994. "Domestic Audiences and the Escalation of International Disputes." *American Political Science Review* 88:577–92.

———. 1995. "Rationalist Explanations for War." *International Organization* 49:379–414.

Featherstone, Kevin. 1988. *Socialist Parties and European Integration*. Manchester: Manchester University Press.

Feldstein, Martin, ed. 1988. *International Economic Cooperation*. Chicago: University of Chicago Press.

Fenno, Richard, Jr. 1973. *Congressmen in Committees*. Boston: Little, Brown.

Ferejohn, John, and Charles Shipan. 1990. "Congressional Influence on Bureaucracy." *Journal of Law, Economics, and Organization* 6:1–20.

Ferguson, Thomas. 1984. "From Normalcy to New Deal." *International Organization* 38:41–94.

Fiorina, Morris. 1992. *Divided Government*, New York: MacMillan.

Fischer, Stanley. 1988. "International Macroeconomic Coordination." In Martin Feldstein, ed., *International Economic Cooperation*, pp. 11–42. Chicago: University of Chicago Press.

Fitzmaurice, John. 1988. "National Parliaments and European Policy-Making: The Case of Denmark." *Parliamentary Affairs*, 281–92.

Frankel, Jeffrey. 1988. "Obstacles to International Macroeconomic Policy Coordination." *Journal of Public Policy* 8:353–74.

Frankel, Jeffrey, and Katherine Rocket. 1988. "International Macroeconomic Policy Coordination When the Policymakers Do Not Agree on the True Model." *American Economic Review* 78:318–40.

Frears, John. 1990. "The French Parliament: Loyal Workhorse, Poor Watchdog." *West European Politics* 13:32–51.

Frenkel, Jacob, and Assaf Razin. 1992. *Fiscal Policies and the World Economy*. 2nd ed. Cambridge, Mass.: MIT Press.

Freud, Sigmund. 1961. *Civilization and Its Discontents*. New York: Norton.

Frieden, Jeffry. 1988. "Sectoral Conflict and American Foreign Economic Policy, 1914–40." *International Organization* 42:59–90.

———. 1990. *Debt, Development, and Democracy*. Princeton, N.J.: Princeton University Press.

———. 1991. "Invested Interests: The Politics of National Economic Policies in a World of Global Finance." *International Organization* 45:425–51.

Frieden, Jeffry, and Ronald Rogowski. 1996. "The Impact of the International Economy on National Policies." In Robert Keohane and Helen Milner, eds., *Internationalization and Domestic Politics*, pp. 25–47. New York: Cambridge University Press.

Friman, H. Richard. 1993. "Sidepayments Versus Security Cards: Domestic Bargaining Tactics in International Economic Negotiations." *International Organization* 47:387–410.

Funabashi, Yoichi. 1989. *Managing the Dollar*. Washington, D.C.: Institute for International Economics.

Furlong, Paul. 1990. "Parliament in Italian Politics." *West European Politics* 13:52–67.

Fursdon, Edward. 1979. *The European Defense Community: A History*. New York: St. Martin's.

Gardner, Lloyd. 1964. *The Economic Aspects of New Deal Diplomacy*, Boston: Beacon Press.

Gardner, Richard. 1980. 2nd ed. *Sterling-Dollar Diplomacy in Current Perspective*. New York: Columbia University Press.

Garrett, Geoffrey. 1993. "The Politics of Maastricht." In Barry Eichengreen, and Jeffry Frieden, eds., "The Political Economy of European Monetary Unification." *Economics and Politics* 5 (special issue): 105–23.

George, Stephen. 1991. *Britain and European Integration since 1945*. Oxford: Basil Blackwell.

Gerbet, Pierre. 1956. "La Genèse du Plan Schuman," *Revue Française de Science Politique* 6:525–53.

Ghosh, Atish, and Paul Masson. 1994. *Economic Cooperation in an Uncertain World*. Cambridge, Mass.: Blackwell.

Giavazzi, Francesco, and Alberto Giovannini, eds. 1989. *Limiting Exchange Rate Flexibility*. Cambridge, Mass.: MIT Press.

Gilligan, Thomas, and Keith Krehbiel, K. 1987. "Collective Decisionmaking and Standing Committees." *Journal of Law, Economics, and Organization* 3:287–35.

Gillingham, John. 1991. *Coal, Steel, and the Rebirth of Europe, 1945–1955*. Cambridge: Cambridge University Press.

Gilpin, Robert. 1987. *The Political Economy of International Relations*. Princeton, N.J.: Princeton University Press.

Giovannini, Alberto. 1993. "Economic and Monetary Union: What Happened?" In Centre for Economic Policy Research (CEPR), ed., *The Monetary Future of Europe*, La Coruña, Portugal: CEPR.

Gjørtler, Peter. 1993. "Denmark: Ratifying the Treaty on European Union." *European Law Review* 18:356–60.

Goldstein, Judith. 1988. "Ideas, Institutions, and American Trade Policy." *International Organization* 42:179–218.

———. 1993. *Ideas, Interests, and American Trade Policy*. Ithaca, N.Y.: Cornell University Press.

Goodman, John, and Louis Pauly. 1993. "The Obsolescence of Capital Controls?" *World Politics* 46:50–82.

Gourevitch, Peter. 1986. *Politics in Hard Times*. Ithaca, N.Y.: Cornell University Press.

Gowa, Joanne. 1993. *Allies, Adversaries, and International Trade*. Princeton, N.J.: Princeton University Press.

Green, Donald, and Ian Shapiro. 1994. *Pathologies of Rational Choice Theory*. New Haven, Conn.: Yale University Press.

Grieco, Joseph. 1990. *Cooperation among Nations*. Ithaca, N.Y.: Cornell University Press.

Gros, Daniel, and Niels Thygesen. 1992. *European Monetary Integration*. New York: St. Martin's.

Grosser, Alfred. 1961. *La Quatrième République et sa Politique Extérieure*. Paris: Armand Colin.

Grossman, Gene, and Elhanan Helpman. 1994. "Protection for Sale." *American Economic Review* 84:833–50.

———. 1995. "The Politics of Free Trade Agreements." *American Economic Review* 85:667–90.

Gunther, Richard. 1980. *Public Policy in a No-Party State*. Berkeley: University of California Press.

Haas, Ernest. 1968. *The Uniting of Europe*. Stanford: Stanford University Press.

Haas, Peter. 1990. *Saving the Mediterranean*. New York: Columbia University Press.

———, ed. 1992. "Knowledge, Power, and International Policy Coordination." *International Organization* 46 (special issue).

Hackford, Robert. 1947. "Our International Aviation Policy." *Harvard Business Review* 25:492–93.

Haggard, Stephen. 1988. "The Institutional Foundations of Hegemony: Explaining the Reciprocal Trade Agreements Act of 1934." *International Organization* 42:91–120.

———. 1990. *Pathways from the Periphery*. Ithaca, N.Y.: Cornell University Press.

Hall, Peter. 1986. *Governing the Economy*. New York: Oxford University Press.

Hancock, Donald, David Conradt, B. Guy Peters, William Safran, and Ralph Zariski. 1993. *Politics in Western Europe*. Chatham, N.J.: Chatham House.

Heath, Anthony. 1976. *Rational Choice and Social Exchange*. Cambridge: Cambridge University Press.

Henning, C. Randall. 1994. *Currencies and Politics in the United States, Germany, and Japan*. Washington, D.C.: Institute for International Economics.

Heredia, Carlos. 1994. "NAFTA and Democratization in Mexico." *Journal of International Affairs* 48:13–38.

Hibbs, Douglas. 1978. "Political Parties and Macroeconomic Policy," *American Political Science Review* 71:1467–87.

Hiden, John, and John Farquharson, eds. 1989. *Explaining Hitler's Germany*. 2nd ed. London: Basford Academic and Educational Ltd.

Hilsman, Roger. 1993. *The Politics of Policy-Making in Defense and Foreign Affairs*. Englewood Cliffs, N.J.: Prentice-Hall.

Hirschman, Albert. 1970. *Exit, Voice, and Loyalty*. Cambridge, Mass.: Harvard University Press.

Homans, George. 1961. *Social Behavior*. New York: Harcourt, Brace, Javonovich.

Huber, John. 1992. "Restrictive Legislative Procedures in France and the U.S." *American Political Science Review* 86:675–87.

———. 1996. "The Vote of Confidence in Parliamentary Democracies." *American Political Science Review* 90:269–82.

Hufbauer, Gary, and Jeffrey Schott. 1993. *NAFTA: An Assessment*. Washington, D.C.: Institute for International Economics.

Hufbauer, Gary, and Kimberly Ann Elliott. 1994. *Measuring the Costs of Protection in the United States*. Washington, D.C.: Institute for International Economics.

Iida, Keisuke. 1991. "Do Negotiations Matter? The Second Image Reversed in Two-Level Games." Manuscript.

———. 1993a. "Analytic Uncertainty and International Cooperation." *International Studies Quarterly* 37:431–57.

———. 1993b. "When and How do Domestic Constraints Matter?" *Journal of Conflict Resolution* 37, no. 3 (September): 403–26.

Ikenberry, G. John. 1992. "A World Economy Restored: Expert Consensus and the Anglo-American Postwar Settlement." In Peter Haas, ed., "Knowledge, Power, and International Policy Coordination." *International Organization* 46 (special issue): 289–322.

———. 1993. "Creating Yesterday's New World Order: Keynesian 'New Thinking' and the Anglo-American Postwar Settlement." In Judith Goldstein and Robert Keohane, eds., *Ideas and Foreign Policy*, 57–86. Ithaca, N.Y.: Cornell University Press.

IMF (International Monetary Fund). Various years. *The World Factbook*. Washington, D.C.: IMF.

———. 1960. *International Financial Statistics*. Washington, D.C.: IMF.

ISQ (*International Studies Quarterly*). 1985. "Theory and Method in IR." Special issue. 29:121–54.

Jervis, Robert. 1970. *The Logic of Images*. Princeton, N.J.: Princeton University Press.

———. 1976. *Perception and Misperception in International Politics*. Princeton, N.J.: Princeton University Press.

Johnson, Chalmers. 1982. *MITI and the Japanese Miracle*. Stanford: Stanford University Press.

Jones, George. 1991. "Presidentialization in a Parliamentary System?" In Colin Campbell and Margaret Wyszomirski, eds. *Executive Leadership in Anglo-American Systems*, pp. 111–37. Pittsburgh: University of Pittsburgh Press.

Jonsson, Christer. 1987. *International Aviation and the Politics of Regime Change*. New York: St. Martin's.

Katzenstein, Peter, ed. 1978. *Between Power and Plenty*. Madison: University of Wisconsin Press.

Keenan, John, and Robert Wilson. 1993. "Bargaining with Private Information." *Journal of Economic Literature* 31:45–104.

Kenen, Peter. 1987. "Exchange Rates and Policy Coordination." *Brookings Discussion Papers in International Economics*, #61. Washington, D.C.: Brookings Institution.

Keohane, Robert. 1984. *After Hegemony*. Princeton, N.J.: Princeton University Press.

———. 1989. *International Institutions and State Power*. Boulder, Colo.: Westview.

———. 1993. "Institutionalist Theory and Realist Challenge after the Cold War." In David Baldwin, ed., *Neorealism and Neoliberalism*. New York: Columbia University Press.

———, ed. 1986. *Neorealism and Its Critics*. New York: Columbia University Press.

Keohane, Robert, and Helen Milner, eds. 1996. *Internationalization and Domestic Politics*. New York: Cambridge University Press.

Kindleberger, Charles. 1973. *The World in Depression, 1929–39*. Berkeley: University of California Press.

King, Anthony. 1976. "Modes of Executive-Legislative Relations: Great Britain, France, and West Germany." *Legislative Studies Quarterly* 1:11–36.

Kingdon, John. 1984. *Agendas, Alternatives, and Public Policies*. New York: Harper-Collins.

Knight, Jack. 1992. *Institutions and Social Conflict*. New York: Cambridge University Press.

Kock, Karin. 1969. *International Trade Policy and the GATT, 1947–1967*, Stockholm: Almqvist and Wiksell.

Kolko, Gabriel. 1968. *The Politics of War*. New York: Random House.

Krasner, Stephen. 1976. "State Power and the Structure of International Trade." *World Politics* 28:317–47.

———. 1978. *Defending the National Interest*. Princeton, N.J.: Princeton University Press.

———. 1991. "Global Communications and National Power: Life on the Pareto Frontier." *World Politics* 43:336–66.

———, ed. 1983. *International Regimes*. Ithaca, N.Y.: Cornell University Press.

Krehbiel, Keith. 1991. *Information and Legislative Organization*. Ann Arbor: University of Michigan Press; Ann Arbor: University of Michigan Press, 1992 (paperback edition).

Kreps, David. 1990. *Game Theory and Economic Modelling*. Oxford: Oxford University Press.

Kreps, David, and Robert Wilson, 1982. "Sequential Equilibria," *Econometrica* 50:863–94.

Krugman, Paul. 1993. "What Do We Need to Know about the International Monetary System?" *Essays in International Finance*, International Finance Section, #190. Princeton, N.J.: Princeton University Department of Economics.

———, ed. 1986. *Strategic Trade Policy and the New International Economics*. Cambridge, Mass.: MIT Press.

Krugman, Paul, and Maurice Obstfeld. 1991. *International Economics*. 2nd ed. New York: HarperCollins.

Kuisel, Richard. 1983. *Capitalism and the State in Modern France*. Cambridge: Cambridge University Press.

Lake, David. 1988. *Power, Protection, and Free Trade*. Ithaca, N.Y.: Cornell University Press.

———. 1993. "Leadership, Hegemony, and the International Economy." *International Studies Quarterly* 37:459–89.

Laver, Michael, and Kenneth Shepsle. 1990. "Coalitions and Cabinet Government." *American Political Science Review* 84:873–90.

———. 1991. "Divided Government: America Is not 'Exceptional.'" *Governance* 4:250–69.

———. 1994. *Cabinet Ministers and Parliamentary Government*. New York: Cambridge University Press.

———. 1995. *Making and Breaking Governments*. New York: Cambridge University Press.

Laver, Michael, and Ben Hunt. 1992. *Policy and Party Competition*, New York: Routledge.

Laver, Michael, and Norman Schofield. 1990. *Multiparty Government*, New York: Oxford.

Lavergne, Real. 1983. *The Political Economy of U.S. Tariffs*. Toronto: Academic Press.

Lenin, Vladimir I. 1917. *Imperialism: The Highest Stage of Capitalism*. New York: International.

Lerner, Daniel, and Raymond Aron. 1957. *France Defeats the EDC*. New York: Praeger.

Lewis-Beck, Michael. 1990. *Economics and Elections*. Ann Arbor: University of Michigan Press.

Lijphart, Arendt. 1984. *Democracies*, New Haven, Conn.: Yale University Press.

———, ed. 1992. *Parliamentary versus Presidential Government*. Oxford: Oxford University Press.

Lindbeck, Assar. 1976. "Stabilization Policies in Open Economies with Endogenous Politicians." *American Economic Review Papers and Proceedings*. May 1–19.

Lindblom, Charles. 1977. *Politics and Markets*. New York: Basic.

Little, Virginia. 1949. "The Control of International Air Transport." *International Organization* 3 (February): 29–40.

Lohmann, Susanne. 1993. "Electoral Cycles and International Policy Cooperation." *European Economic Review* 37:1373–91.

———. 1995. "Federalism and Central Bank Autonomy: The Politics of German

Monetary Policy, 1957–1992." Manuscript.

Lohmann, Susanne, and Sharyn O'Halloran. 1994. "Divided Government and U.S. Trade Policy." *International Organization* 48:595–632.

Loriaux, Michael. 1991. *France after Hegemony*. Ithaca, N.Y.: Cornell University Press.

Lowi, Theodore. 1964. "American Business, Public Policy, Case Studies, and Political Theory." *World Politics* 16:677–715.

Luce, Duncan, and Howard Raiffa. 1957. *Games and Decisions*. New York: Wiley.

Lupia, Arthur. 1992. "Busy Voters, Agenda Control, and the Power of Information." *American Political Science Review* 86:390–403.

Lustig, Nora, Barry Bosworth, and Robert Lawrence. 1992. *Assessing the Impact of North American Free Trade*. Washington, D.C.: Brookings Institution.

Lynch, Frances. 1984. "Resolving the Paradox of the Monnet Plan: National and International Planning in French Reconstruction." *Economic History Review* 37:229–43.

Magee, Stephen, William Brock, and Leslie Young. 1989. *Black Hole Tariffs and Endogenous Policy Theory*. New York: Cambridge University Press.

Mallalieu, William. 1956. *British Reconstruction and American Policy, 1945–1955*. New York: Scarecrow.

Mansfield, Edward. 1996. "Data on the War-Proneness of Autocracies and Democracies from Polity II and Singer and Small." Computer file.

March, James, and Johan Olson. 1989. *Rediscovering Institutions*. New York: Free Press.

Marston, Richard. 1988. "Exchange Rate Policy Reconsidered." In Martin Feldstein, ed., *International Economic Cooperation*, pp. 79–135. Chicago: University of Chicago Press.

Martin, Lisa. 1992. *Coercive Cooperation*. Princeton, N.J.: Princeton University Press.

Marwell, Gerald, and David Schmitt. 1975. *Cooperation*. New York: Academic Press.

Matthews, Steven A. 1989. "Veto Threats: Rhetoric in a Bargaining Game." *Quarterly Journal of Economics* 104:367–69.

Mayer, Frederick. 1992. "Managing Domestic Differences in International Relations." *International Organization* 46:793–818.

Mayer, Wolfgang. 1984. "Endogenous Tariff Formation." *American Economic Review* 74:970–85.

Mayhew, David. 1991. *Divided We Govern*. New Haven, Conn.: Yale University Press.

McCubbins, Matthew, and Thomas Schwartz. 1984. "Congressional Oversight Overlooked: Police Patrols and Fire Alarms." *American Journal of Political Science* 2:165–79.

McGinnis, Michael. 1986. "Issue Linkage and the Evolution of Cooperation." *Journal of Conflict Resolution* 30:141–70.

McKelvey, Richard. 1976. "Intransitivities in Multidimensional Voting Models and Some Implications for Agenda Control." *Journal of Economic Theory* 12:472–82.

———. 1979. "General Conditions for Global Intransitivities in Formal Voting Models." *Econometrica* 47: 1085–111.

McKeown, Timothy. 1983. "Hegemonic Stability Theory and 19th Century Tariff Levels in Europe." *International Organization* 37:73–91.

McNamara, Kathleen. 1994. "Consensus and Constraint: Ideas and Interests in Monetary Cooperation in the EC." Ph.D. diss. Columbia University, New York.

Mearsheimer, John. 1990. "Back to the Future: Instability in Europe after the Cold War." *International Security* 16:5–56.

Miller, Aaron. 1980. *Search for Security*, Chapel Hill: University of North Carolina Press.

Miller, Nicholas. 1977. "Logrolling, Vote Trading, and the Paradox of Voting: A Game Theoretical Overview." *Public Choice* 30:51–76.

Miller, Steven. 1984. "Politics over Promise: Domestic Impediments to Arms Control." *International Security* 8:67–90.

Milner, Helen. 1988. *Resisting Protectionism*. Princeton, N.J.: Princeton University Press.

———. 1991. "The Assumption of Anarchy in International Politics: A Critique." *Review of International Studies* 17:67–85.

———. 1992. "International Theories of Cooperation: Strengths and Weaknesses." *World Politics* 44:466–96.

Milner, Helen, and B. Peter Rosendorff. 1996. "Trade Negotiations, Information, and Domestic Politics." *Economics and Politics* 8:145–89.

———. 1997. "Democratic Politics and International Trade Negotiations." *Journal of Conflict Resolution*. 41:117–46.

Milward, Alan. 1984. *The Reconstruction of Western Europe, 1945–51*. London: Methuen.

Mishan, E. J. 1971. "The Postwar Literature on Externalities: An Interpretative Essay," *Journal of Economic Literature* 9:1–28.

Mo, Jongryn. 1991. "International Bargaining and Domestic Political Competition." Unpublished manuscript.

———. 1994. "Two-Level Games with Endogenous Domestic Coalitions." *Journal of Conflict Resolution* 38:402–22.

———. 1995. "Domestic Institutions and International Bargaining: The Role of Agent Veto in Two-Level Games." *American Political Science Review* 89:914–24.

Moravcsik, Andrew. 1991. "Negotiating the Single European Act." *International Organization* 45:19–56.

———. 1993. "Preferences and Power in the EC." *Journal of Common Market Studies* 31:473–523.

Morgenthau, Hans J. 1958. *Politics among Nations*. 6th ed. Revised by Kenneth W. Thompson. New York: Knopf.

Morrow, James. 1991. "Electoral and Congressional Incentives and Arms Control." *Journal of Conflict Resolution* 35:245–65.

Mundell, Robert. 1963. "Capital Mobility and Stabilization Policy under Fixed and Flexible Exchange Rates." *Canadian Journal of Economics and Political Science* 29:475–85.

———. 1968. *International Economics*. New York: Macmillan.

Mussa, Michael. 1979. "Macroeconomic Interdependence and the Exchange Rate Regime." In Rudiger Dornbusch and Jacob Frenkel, eds., *International Economic Policy*. Baltimore: The Johns Hopkins University Press, 160–204.

Nacif-Hernandez, Benito. 1995. "The Mexican Chamber of Deputies: The Political Significance of Non-Consecutive Terms." Ph.D. diss., Oxford University.

Nash, John F. 1950. "The Bargaining Problem," *Econometrica* 18:155–62.

Nelson, Douglas. 1988. "Endogenous Tariff Theory: A Critical Survey." *American Journal of Political Science* 32:796–837.

North, Douglass. 1990. *Institutions, Institutional Change, and Economic Performance*. New York: Cambridge University Press.

Norton, Philip. 1990a. "Parliament in the United Kingdom." *West European Politics* 13:10–31.

———, ed. 1990b. *Legislatures*. Oxford: Oxford University Press.

O'Connor, William. 1971. *Economic Regulation of the World's Airlines*, New York: Praeger.

Odell, John. 1988. "From London to Bretton Woods." *Journal of Public Policy* 8:287–316.

Odell, John, and Thomas Willett, eds. 1988. "International Monetary Cooperation, Domestic Politics, and Policy Ideas." *Journal of Public Policy* 8 (special issue).

O'Halloran, Sharyn. 1994. *Politics, Process, and American Trade Policy*. Ann Arbor: University of Michigan Press.

Olson, Mancur. 1965. *The Logic of Collective Action*. Cambridge, Mass.: Harvard University Press.

———. 1982. *The Rise and Decline of Nations*. New Haven, Conn.: Yale University Press.

———. 1993. "Dictatorship, Democracy, and Development." *American Political Science Review* 87:567–76.

Oudiz, Gilles, and Jeffrey Sachs. 1984. "Macroeconomic Policy Coordination among the Industrial Countries." *Brookings Papers on Economic Activity* 1:1–64.

Oye, Kenneth. 1992. *Economic Discrimination and Political Exchange*. Princeton, N.J.: Princeton University Press.

———, ed. 1986. *Cooperation under Anarchy*. Princeton, N.J.: Princeton University Press.

Padoa-Schioppa, Tomasso. 1988. "The EMS: A Long-Term View." In Francesco Giavazzi, Stefano Micossi, and Mark Miller, eds., *The European Monetary System*. Cambridge: Cambridge University Press.

Pahre, Robert. 1994. "Who's on First, What's on Second, I Don't Know's on Third: Actors and Institutions in Indeterminate Two-Level Games." University of Michigan Institute of Public Policy, Discussion paper #352.

Paige, Jeffry. 1975. *Agrarian Revolution*. New York: Free Press.

Painter, David. 1986. *Oil and the American Century*, Baltimore: The Johns Hopkins University Press.

Papandreou, Andreas. 1994. *Externality and Institutions*. New York: Oxford University Press.

Parsons, Talcott. 1951. *The Social System*. Glencoe, Ill.: Free Press.

Pastor, Manuel, and Carol Wise. 1994. "The Origins and Sustainability of Mexico's Free Trade Policy." *International Organization* 48:459–89.

Persson, Torsten, and Guido Tabellini. 1990. *Macroeconomic Policy, Credibility, and Politics*. Chur, Switzerland: Harwood Academic Publishers.

Peters, B. Guy. 1991. *European Politics Reconsidered*. New York: Holmes and Meier.

Peterson, Susan. 1996. *Crisis Bargaining and the State*. Ann Arbor: University of Michigan Press.

Pierce, Roy. 1991. "The Executive Divided against Itself: Cohabitation in France, 1986–1988." *Governance* 4:270–94.

Pierce, Roy, Henry Valen, and Ola Listhaug. 1983. "Referendum Voting Behavior: The Norwegian and British Referenda on Membership in the European Community." *American Journal of Political Science* 27:43–63.

Pious, Richard. 1979. *The American Presidency*. New York: Basic.

Plott, Charles. 1967. "A Notion of Equilibrium and Its Possibility under Majority Rule." *American Economic Review* 57:787–806.

Poitras, Guy, and Raymond Robinson. 1994. "The Politics of NAFTA in Mexico." *Journal of InterAmerican Studies and World Affairs* 36:1–35.

Poole, Keith, and Howard Rosenthal. 1991. "Patterns of Congressional Voting." *American Journal of Political Science* 35:228–78.

Popkin, Samuel. 1979. *The Rational Peasant*. Berkeley: University of California Press.

Powell, G. Bingham. 1982. *Contemporary Democracies*. Cambridge: Harvard University Press.

Powell, Robert. 1990. *Nuclear Deterrence Theory*. Cambridge: Cambridge University Press.

Przeworski, Adam, and Henry Teune. 1970. *The Logic of Comparative Social Inquiry*. New York: Wiley.

Putnam, Robert. 1988. "Diplomacy and Domestic Politics." *International Organization* 42:427–60.

Putnam, Robert, and Nicholas Bayne. 1987. *Hanging Together: Conflict and Cooperation in the Seven-Power Summits*. Rev. ed. Cambridge, Mass.: Harvard University Press.

Ra'anan, Gavriel. 1983. *International Policy Formation in the USSR*. Hamden, Conn.: Archon.

Raiffa, Howard. 1982. *The Art and Science of Negotiation*. Cambridge, Mass.: Harvard University Press.

Ramseyer, Mark, and Frances Rosenbluth. 1993. *Japan's Political Marketplace*. Cambridge, Mass.: Harvard University Press.

Riker, William. 1962. *The Theory of Political Coalitions*. Westport, Conn.: Greenwood.

————. 1980. "Implications from the Disequilibrium of Majority Rule for the Study of Institutions." *American Political Science Review* 74:432–46.

————, ed. 1993. *Agenda Formation*. Ann Arbor: University of Michigan Press.

Rioux, Jean-Pierre. 1987. *The Fourth Republic, 1944–1958*. Cambridge: Cambridge University Press.

Rogowski, Ronald. 1987. "Trade and the Variety of Democratic Institutions." *International Organization* 41:203–24.

————. 1989. *Commerce and Coalitions*. Princeton, N.J.: Princeton University Press.

Romer, Thomas, and Howard Rosenthal. 1978. "Political Resource Allocation, Controlled Agendas, and the Status Quo." *Public Choice* 33:27–43.

————. 1979. "Bureaucrats and Voters: On the Political Economy of Resource Allocation by Direct Democracy." *Quarterly Journal of Economics* 93:563–88.

Rosenau, James. 1966. "Pre-Theories and Theories of Foreign Policy." In R. Barry Farrell, ed., *Approaches to Comparative and International Politics*, pp. 27–92. Evanston, Ill.: Northwestern University Press.

————. 1969. "Toward the Study of National-International Linkages." In James Rosenau, ed., *Linkage Politics*, pp. 44–63. New York: Free Press.

Rosenthal, Howard. 1989. "The Setter Model." In James Enelow and Melvin Hinich, eds., *Advances in the Spatial Theory of Voting*, pp. 199–234. New York: Cambridge University Press.

Rubinstein, Ariel. 1982. "Perfect Equilibrium in a Bargaining Model." *Econometrica* 50:97–110.

Rubinstein, Ariel, and Martin J. Osborne. 1990. *Bargaining and Markets*. San Diego, Calif.: Academic Press.

Ruggie, John. 1983. "International Regimes, Transactions, and Change." In Stephen Krasner, ed., *International Regimes*, pp. 196–232. Ithaca, N.Y.: Cornell University Press.

Russett, Bruce. 1993. *Grasping the Democratic Peace*. Princeton, N.J.: Princeton University Press.

Saalfeld, Thomas. 1990. "The West German Bundestag after 40 Years." *West European Politics* 13:68–89.

Sampson, Anthony. 1975. *The Seven Sisters: The Great Oil Companies and the World They Made*. New York: Viking.

Sandholtz, Wayne. 1993. "Choosing Union: Monetary Politics and Maastricht." *International Organization* 47:1–40.

Sandholtz, Wayne, and John Zysman. 1989. "1992: Recasting the European Bargain." *World Politics* 42:95–128.

Sayre, Francis. 1939. *The Way Forward: The American Trade Agreements Program*. New York: Macmillan.

Schattschneider, E. E. 1960. *The Semi-Sovereign People*. New York: Collier.

Schelling, Thomas. 1960. *The Strategy of Conflict*. Cambridge, Mass.: Harvard University Press.

Schlesinger, Arthur. 1992. "Leaving the Constitution Alone." In Arendt Lijphart, ed., *Parliamentary versus Presidential Government*, pp. 90–96. Oxford: Oxford University Press.

Schmitt, Hans. 1962. *The Path to European Union: From the Marshall Plan to the Common Market*. Baton Rouge: Louisiana State University Press.

Schofield, Norman. 1983. "Generic Instability of Majority Rule." *Review of Economic Studies* 50:695–705.

Schonhardt-Bailey, Cheryl. 1991. "Lessons for Lobbying for Free Trade in 19th Century Britain." *American Political Science Review* 85:37–58.

Schott, Jeffrey. 1989. *Free Trade Areas and U.S. Trade Policy*. Washington, D.C.: Institute for International Economics.

Schultze, Charles. 1988. "Comment." In Martin Feldstein, ed., *International Economic Cooperation*, pp. 49–61. Chicago: University of Chicago Press.

Sebenius, James. 1983. "Negotiation Arithmetic." *International Organization* 37:281–316.

Shafer, Michael. 1994. *Winners and Losers*. Ithaca, N.Y.: Cornell University Press.

Shaw, Malcolm. 1990. "Committees in Legislatures." In Philip Norton, ed., *Legislatures*. Oxford: Oxford University Press.

Shepsle, Kenneth. 1979. "Institutional Arrangements and Equilibria in Multidimensional Voting Models." *American Journal of Political Science* 23:27–59.

———. 1992. "Congress Is a 'They,' Not an 'It': Legislative Intent as Oxymoron." *International Review of Law and Economics* 12:239–56.

Shepsle, Kenneth, and Barry Weingast. 1984. "Uncovered Sets and Sophisticated Voting Outcomes with Implications for Agenda Institutions." *American Journal of Political Science* 28:49–74.

Shonfield, Andrew. 1965. *Modern Capitalism: The Changing Balance between Public and Private Power.* Oxford: Oxford University Press.

Shugart, Matthew, and John Carey. 1992. *Presidents and Assemblies.* New York: Cambridge University Press.

Sikkink, Kathryn. 1991. *Ideas and Institutions.* Ithaca, N.Y.: Cornell University Press.

Smith, Dale, and Jurgen Wanke. 1993. "Completing the Single European Act." *American Journal of Political Science* 37:529–54.

Smith, Henry Ladd. 1950. *Airways Abroad.* Madison: University of Wisconsin Press.

Snidal, Duncan. 1985. "The Limits of Hegemonic Stability Theory." *International Organization* 39:579–614.

Snyder, Glen, and Paul Diesing. 1977. *Conflict among Nations.* Princeton, N.J.: Princeton University Press.

Snyder, Richard, H. W. Bruck, and Burton Sapin. 1962. *Foreign Policy Decision-Making.* New York: Free Press.

Stein, Arthur. 1980. "The Politics of Linkage." *World Politics* 32:62–81.

———. 1990. *Why Nations Cooperate.* Ithaca, N.Y.: Cornell University Press.

Stoff, Michael. 1980. *Oil, War, and American Security: The Search for a National Oil Policy, 1941–1947.* New Haven, Conn.: Yale University Press.

Strange, Susan. 1987. "The Persistent Myth of Lost Hegemony."*International Organization* 41:551–74.

Stratmann, Thomas. 1992. "The Effects of Logrolling on Congressional Voting." *American Economic Review* 82:1162–76.

Sundquist, James. 1981. *The Decline and Resurgence of Congress.* Washington, D.C.: Brookings Institution.

Thayer, Frederick. 1965. *Air Transport Policy and National Security.* Chapel Hill: University of North Carolina Press.

Thornton, Robert. 1969. "Governments, International Airlines, and Change." Ph.D. diss. Ann Arbor: University of Michigan Press.

Tilly, Charles. 1990. *Capital and Coercion.* Princeton, N.J.: Princeton University Press.

———, ed. 1975. *The Formation of National States in Western Europe.* Princeton, N.J.: Princeton University Press.

Tint, Herbert. 1972. *French Foreign Policy since the Second World War.* London: Weidenfield and Nicolson.

Tirole, Jean. 1989. *The Theory of Industrial Organization.* Cambridge, Mass.: MIT Press.

Tollison, Robert, and Thomas Willett. 1979. "An Economic Theory of Mutually Advantageous Issue Linkages in International Negotiations." *International Organization* 33:425–50.

Trefler, Daniel. 1993. "Trade Liberalization and the Theory of Endogenous Protection." *Journal of Political Economy* 101:138–60.

Tsebelis, George. 1990. *Nested Games.* Berkeley: University of California Press.

———. 1995. "Decision Making in Political Systems: Veto Players in Presidentialism, Parliamentarianism, Multicameralism, and Multipartyism." *British Journal of Political Science* 25:289–325.

Tsoukalis, Loukas. 1993. *The New European Economy*. 2nd ed. Oxford: Oxford University Press.

Tversky, Amos, and Daniel Kahneman. 1986. "Rational Choice and the Framing of Decisions." *Journal of Business* 59:251–78.

U.S. Congress, House Ways and Means Committee. 1934. *Hearings on the Passage of the Reciprocal Trade Agreements Act*. 73rd Congress, 2nd session. Washington, D.C.: U.S. Government Printing Office.

Van Dormael, Armand. 1978. *Bretton Woods: Birth of a Monetary System*. New York: Holmes and Meier.

Vernon, Raymond, and Deborah Spar. 1989. *Beyond Globalism*. New York: Free Press.

Wade, Robert. 1990. *Governing the Market*. Princeton, N.J.: Princeton University Press.

Wall, Irwin. 1991. *The United States and the Making of Postwar France*. New York: Cambridge University Press.

Walt, Stephen. 1987. *The Origin of Alliances*. Ithaca, N.Y.: Cornell University Press.

Waltz, Kenneth. 1979. *Theory of International Politics*. Reading, Mass.: Addison-Wesley.

Watson, Richard. 1956. "The Tariff Revolution: A Study of Shifting Party Attitudes." *The Journal of Politics* 18:678–701.

Weaver, Kent, and Bert Rockman, eds. 1993. *Do Institutions Matter?* Washington, D.C.: Brookings Institution.

Webb, Michael. 1991. "International Economic Structures, Government Interests, and International Coordination of Macroeconomic Adjustment Policies." *International Organization* 45:309–42.

Weingast, Barry, and Douglass North. 1989. "Constitutions and Commitments: The Evolution of Institutions Governing Public Choice in Seventeenth Century England." *Journal of Economic History* 69:803–32.

Whalley, John. 1993. "Regional Trade Arrangements in North America." In Jaime De Melo and Arvind Panagariya, eds., *New Dimensions in Regional Integration*, pp. 352–87. Cambridge: Cambridge University Press.

Wilcox, Clair. 1949. *A Charter for World Trade*. New York: Macmillan.

Williams, Philip. 1966. *Crisis and Compromise: Politics in the Fourth Republic*. Garden City, N.Y.: Anchor.

Willis, F. Roy. 1968. *France, Germany, and the New Europe*. Rev. ed. Stanford: Stanford University Press.

Winham, Gilbert. 1986. *International Trade and the Tokyo Round Negotiations*. Princeton, N.J.: Princeton University Press.

Wolfers, Arnold. 1962. *Discord and Collaboration*. Baltimore: The Johns Hopkins University Press.

Wooley, John. 1984. *Monetary Politics: The Federal Reserve and the Politics of Monetary Policy*. New York: Cambridge University Press.

Yergin, Daniel. 1991. *The Prize: The Epic Quest for Oil, Money, and Power*. New York: Simon and Schuster.

Young, Oran. 1989. *International Cooperation.* Ithaca, N.Y.: Cornell University Press.

Zimmerman, William. 1973. "Issue-Area and Foreign Policy Process: A Research Note in Search of a General Theory." *American Political Science Review* 67:1204–12.

Zysman, John. 1983. *Governments, Markets, and Growth.* Ithaca, N.Y.: Cornell University Press.

Index